Experimental Methodology
Third Edition

Larry B. Christensen
Texas A & M University

Allyn and Bacon, Inc.
Boston   London   Sydney   Toronto

To my dear wife Barbara and my precious children Tanya and Troy,
who have tolerated my absence and supported me
in the lengthy process of preparing this book

Series Editor: Wendy Ritger
Managing Editor: Bill Barke
Production Service: Lifland et al., Bookmakers

Library of Congress Cataloging in Publication Data

Christensen, Larry B., 1941–
  Experimental methodology.

  Bibliography: p.
  Includes index.
  1. Psychology, Experimental.   2. Psychology—Experiments.
3. Experimental design.   I. Title.
BF181.C48   1985   150'.724   84-14548
ISBN 0-205-08244-0
ISBN (International) 0-205-08321-8

Printed in the United States of America.

10 9 8 7 6 5 4   89 88 87

Contents

Preface

Within the field of psychology, there are at least two courses whose content remains relatively constant over time, one of which is the research methods course. However, subtle changes do occur within its subject matter, and the present revision of this text reflects the latest of these. Some designs have been deleted and others have been added because some of the designs that appeared to be promising (such as the cross-lag panel design) have recently been questioned. Until the controversy surrounding such designs is resolved, the best policy seems to be to delete them. The chapter on evaluation research also has been deleted because most psychologists seem to feel that this material is best suited to another course. Several chapters have been expanded or completely revised. For example, revisions of the code of ethics and of the publication manual have been published since the last edition of this book. Consequently, Chapter 10 and the Appendix reflect the changes that have been incorporated into the ethical principles and the publication policies.

Changes in this edition also have been oriented toward making the text much more understandable to the student. Thus, a number of the chapters have been reorganized to improve the flow and readability of the material. Chapter overviews have been added to give the student a set with which to approach the chapter. Key words have been highlighted for the student in boldface type, and the definitions of these words have been placed in the margin; graphics and exhibits have been added to clarify the subject matter. The sample research report in the Appendix is the type of paper that is submitted to a journal for publication. Students can use this sample report as a guide for preparing their own.

Once again, I am extremely indebted to many people who have assisted in the completion of this edition of the book. Special thanks go to Wendy Ritger for her constant support and excellent selection of reviewers. I also want to thank the following reviewers for their thoughtful suggestions—not only concerning the components of the book that needed to be revised but also about the content of the changes: Roger Black, University of South Carolina; Helen Crawford, University of Wyoming; Lambert Deckers, Ball State University; George Hampton, University of Houston; Peter Hanford, Purdue University; Elvis Jones, Frostburg State College; B. Kent Parker, West Virginia University; and Douglas Ross, Indiana University of Pennsylvania. Their comments and suggestions have definitely enhanced the quality of the book. Finally, I want to express my gratitude to the authors and publishers who granted permission to quote material and to reproduce figures.

1

What Is Science?

Chapter Overview

In your introductory psychology course, you in all probability encountered a definition of psychology as the science of behavior. Most students would read such a definition and assume that they understood it, seldom asking themselves if they really knew its meaning. If you consider this definition for a moment, you should be able to see what I am talking about. All of us know what the word "behavior" means—it refers to the things people say and do. What about the word "science?" Many people use this term in both written and spoken English, but few could state exactly what it means. The scientist is usually conceptualized as a person with a white coat who works in a laboratory, conducting experiments on some complex theory that is far beyond the comprehension of the average individual. The actual process or method by which the scientist uncovers the mysteries of the universe totally eludes most people. It is as if the scientific process were encompassed in a shroud of secrecy and could only be re-vealed to the scientist. Science, however, is not a mysterious phenomenon. It is a very logical and rigorous method for attempting to gather facts.

This chapter is designed to remove the mystery surrounding science and to acquaint you with the scientific process. In this chapter, I will explain not only the meaning of science but also the unique characteristics that distinguish the scientific method from other methods of gathering information. Therefore, it is recommended that you answer the following questions as you read this chapter:

1. What is the scientific method, and how does this method differ from other methods of acquiring information?

2. What are the unique characteristics of the scientific method, and why is each of these characteristics necessary?

3. What use is made of the scientific knowledge that is acquired?

4. What type of person would be most adept at pursuing the scientific enterprise?

Introduction

As we go through our daily lives, we constantly encounter problems and questions relating to the behavior of ourselves and others. For

1

example, one person may have a tremendous fear of taking tests. Another individual may have a problem with marital problems, alcoholism, or drug abuse. People who encounter such problems typically want to eliminate them but frequently do not have the knowledge or ability to handle the problem themselves. Consequently, they seek out professionals, such as psychologists, who will assist them in remediating such difficulties. Other people may enlist the assistance of a professional in understanding the behavior of others. For example, salespeople differ greatly in their ability to sell merchandise. One used car salesperson may be capable of selling twice as many cars as another salesperson. If a sales manager could discover why such differences in ability exist, he or she might be able to develop either better training programs or more effective criteria for the selection of the sales force.

In an attempt to attain information about behavior, people turn to the field of psychology. As you should know by now, a great deal of information about the behavior of organisms has been accumulated. We have knowledge that enables us to treat disorders such as "test anxiety." Similarly, we have identified many of the variables influencing behaviors such as persuasion and aggression. Although we know a great deal about the behavior of humans and infrahumans, there is a great deal yet to be learned. For example, we still have an inadequate understanding of childhood autism and leadership ability. In order to learn more about such behaviors, we must engage in scientific research because this is the only way in which we can fill the gaps in our knowledge. However, the ability to understand and engage in the research process does not come easily; it is definitely not an ability that comes from taking content courses such as introductory psychology or abnormal psychology. These courses give little insight into the way in which psychological facts and data are acquired. They state implicitly or explicitly that such facts and data were acquired from scientific research, but the nature of the scientific research process remains elusive.

In order to learn about the scientific research process, one needs more direct instruction. The course in which you are now enrolled is directed toward providing you with information regarding the way in which the scientific research process is conducted. Some students object to taking such a course on the grounds that it is not necessary for their education because they have no intention of becoming research psychologists. But there are a number of very good reasons for all students to study experimental methodology. First, at some time in the future you may be asked to conduct a study (such as a community survey) on some issue. Second, virtually all the material you are required to learn in your science courses is based on knowledge acquired from the scientific method, so you should be familiar with the method. Third, we are all constantly bombarded by the results of scientific research, and we need experimental tools to determine which research outcomes are conclusive. For example, saccharin has been demonstrated to cause cancer in laboratory animals, yet there are many people who consume saccharin and do not contract cancer. You as a consumer must be able to resolve these discrepancies and decide whether or not you are going to eat foods containing saccharin.

Similarly, we often see television commercials that give the appearance of a scientific test in order to convince us of the benefits or superiority of one product over another. Several years ago, the manufacturers of Schlitz beer were concerned with the decline in the sales of their product. In an effort to reverse this decline, the company conducted a live "challenge" on television in which devotees of another brand were challenged to see if they could distinguish their preferred brand from Schlitz. This live demonstration consistently showed that about 50 percent of these beer drinkers chose Schlitz over their preferred brand as the better tasting beer. On the surface, this challenge seems to reveal that Schlitz is an excellent beer because so many people chose it. If you had some knowledge of research design and statistics, however, you would be able to see that this contest did not say anything about the superiority of Schlitz over other beers because the challenge was conducted on live television, in the midst of a lot of noise and commotion. Such distractions would minimize the ability of a person to distinguish one beer from another. If enough distractions existed so that people could not distinguish one beer from another, they would probably select one beer about the same number of times as the other. This is exactly what happened, since Schlitz and the other brand were *each* picked by about 50 percent of the people. From this example, you can see that an understanding of the scientific research process induces a way of thinking that will enable you to critically evaluate the information with which you are confronted. Given that our society is constantly becoming more complex and we are having to rely more and more on scientific evidence, our ability to intelligently evaluate the evidence becomes increasingly important

Methods of Acquiring Knowledge

The scientific research process is important because it is the process by which we acquire our most objective and factual information. However, it is not the only means by which we learn. In fact, Helmstadter (1970) has revealed that there are at least six different approaches to acquiring knowledge, only one of which is the scientific method. In order to enable you to gain an appreciation of the rigor and accuracy that is achieved by the scientific method, we will begin by taking a look at the five unscientific approaches to acquiring knowledge and then look at the scientific method. You should be able to see that each successive approach represents a more acceptable means of acquiring knowledge.

Tenacity

The first approach can be labeled **tenacity**, defined in the dictionary as "the quality or state of holding fast." This approach to acquiring knowledge seems to boil down to the acquisition and persistence of superstitions, because superstitions represent beliefs that are reacted to as if they were fact. A gambler, for example, may easily acquire such a superstition by observing that he has won a number of times when he has worn a certain hat. He makes the association between winning and wearing the hat and comes to the conclusion that he must wear the hat in order to win. In the future, winning while wearing the hat will only strengthen this association. The gambler has generated the belief that the hat promotes winning and therefore he must wear the hat when gambling. The acquisition of such superstitious behavior has been described by Skinner (1948).

Tenacity
Persistance of a superstition

Intuition

Intuition is the second approach to acquiring knowledge. The dictionary defines intuition as "the act or process of coming to direct knowledge or certainty without reasoning or inferring." Psychics such as Edgar Cayce seem to have derived their knowledge from intuition. The predictions and descriptions of psychics are not based on any known reasoning or inferring process; therefore, such knowledge must be intuitive knowledge. This does not mean that knowledge acquired from psychics is undesirable or inappropriate—only that it is not scientific knowledge. In fact, it has been suggested that intuitive thought resides in the right hemisphere of the brain and logical thinking resides in the left hemisphere. Consequently, instruction in the scientific process may involve exercising and using only the left hemisphere.

Intuition
Knowledge that is not based on reasoning or inferring

Authority

Authority as a method of acquiring knowledge represents an acceptance of information or facts stated by another because that person is a highly respected source. Authority exists within the various religions: A religion typically has a sacred text, tribunal, person, or some combination of these that represents the facts, which are considered indisputable and final. This example is not meant to be critical of religions, but is used only to demonstrate that the authority approach to gaining

Authority
Acceptance of information because it is acquired from a highly respected source

knowledge differs from the scientific approach. Another example comes from the political-social arena. On July 4, 1936, the Central Committee of the Communist Party of the Soviet Union issued a "Decree Against Pedology" (Woodworth and Sheehan, 1964), which, among other things, outlawed the use of standardized tests in schools. Since no one had the right to question such a decree, it had to be accepted as fact.

The authority approach should not be confused with our increasing dependence on experts for information. Experts do transmit scientific knowledge, and they usually base their opinions on scientific knowledge. The distinction between the authority approach and an appeal to an expert is that the authority approach dictates that we accept whatever is decreed whereas the appeal to an expert does not dictate such indiscriminate acceptance. We are free to accept or reject whatever the expert says.

Rationalism

A fourth way of gaining knowledge is the approach of **rationalism.** This approach uses reasoning to arrive at knowledge and assumes that valid knowledge is acquired if the correct reasoning process is used. Consider the following classical syllogism:

Rationalism
Knowledge acquired through reasoning

> All men are mortal.
> Socrates is a man.
> Therefore, Socrates is mortal.

Few people would argue with the conclusion, even though it does depend on the validity of the first two statements. Although the first two statements may be correct and therefore would lead to a valid conclusion, such is not the case with all syllogisms. Consider the following example provided by Helmstadter (1970, p. 11).

> Two weeks ago, Team A beat Team C in football.
> Last week, Team C beat Team B in football.
> Therefore, next week Team A will beat Team B in football.

Is the conclusion valid? Events such as those represented by the first two statements have happened frequently, yet the conclusion depends on the performance of the two teams. Performance is highly variable, and so the conclusion could turn out to be true or false. An upset, which illustrates the variability of performance, is not uncommon in any sport. However, the premises do not take such variability into account, and one may thus arrive at a faulty conclusion. Such assumptions reveal the limitations of the rationalistic approach to gaining knowledge. Does this mean that science does not use the reasoning process? Obviously, the answer to this question is no! Reasoning is essential to the scientific process, but the two are not synonymous. Reasoning is used to arrive at hypotheses. These hypotheses are then tested, using the scientific method, to determine their validity.

Empiricism

The fifth and final unscientific approach to gaining knowledge is through **empiricism.** This approach says, "If I have experienced something, then it is valid and true." Therefore, any facts that concur with experience are accepted and those that do not are rejected. You often here people say, "I won't believe it until I see it." This statement illustrates the empirical approach and indicates that we tend to believe the information acquired through our senses.

Empiricism
Knowledge acquired through experience

What is wrong with this approach? Although this approach is very appealing and has much to recommend it, several dangers exist if it alone is used. Our perceptions are affected by a number of variables. Research has demonstrated that variables such as past experiences and our motivations at the time of the perceiving can drastically alter what we see. Research has also revealed that our memory for events does not remain constant. Not only do we tend to forget things, but at times an actual distortion may take place. Also, we experience only a fraction of the total number of possible situations that could occur. The situations we experience may represent a biased sample, which could lead to an inaccurate conclusion. If, for example, you had contact with only ten females, all of whom were extremely tall, you would probably conclude that all women were extremely tall. The bias in your sample of women would lead you to an inaccurate conclusion. Factors such as these limit the veridicality of the empirical approach.

Again, I am not saying that empiricism is not included in the scientific approach—it is. Empiricism is a vital element in science, but the scientific approach requires more than just one element.

Science

The best method for acquiring knowledge is the scientific method. To understand this approach, we must first take a look at the definition of science. Most philosophers of science define it as a *process* or *method*—a method for generating a body of knowledge. **Science,** therefore, represents a *logic of inquiry*, or a specific method to be followed in solving problems and thus acquiring a body of knowledge. This method can be broken down into a series of five steps, which will be presented here as a prelude to the remainder of the book, the primary focus of which is a detailed discussion of each of these steps.

Science
A method or logic of inquiry

Identifying the Problem and Hypothesis Formation

The beginning point of any scientific inquiry involves identifying a problem, which is actually a simple process. All one has to do is look at the events taking place, and numerous problems that need solutions come readily to mind. Child abuse, cancer, alcoholism, and crime are just a few of the more apparent problems. However, it is not enough to just identify a problem and say that you are going to investigate it. For a problem to be investigated, it must be refined and narrowed so that it is researchable. Once the problem has been stated in researchable terms, hypotheses are formulated that state the expected or predicted relationships between the variables. These hypotheses must in turn be stated in such a way that they are testable and capable of being refuted.

Designing the Experiment

The stage of actually designing the experiment is crucial and demands a tremendous amount of preparation on the part of the experimenter to ensure that the hypotheses stated are actually those tested. Proper controls over extraneous variables have to be established, and the experimental variable as well as the response variable must be specified. These procedures are extremely important, since this stage represents the outline or the scheme to be followed in conducting the experiment. This scheme or outline is one that is constructed to overcome the difficulties that would otherwise distort the results and to help make sure that the data are properly analyzed and interpreted.

Conducting the Experiment

After the experiment has been designed, the researchers must make a number of very important decisions regarding the actual conduct of the experiment. Before any data are collected, they must decide what subjects are to be used, what instructions are necessary, and what equipment and materials are needed. Actually, this involves filling in the outline set forth in the design stage of the experiment. After these decisions have been reached, the experimenters are then ready to collect the data, following precisely the prescribed procedure and recording responses made by the subjects. For some studies, this involves little more than plugging in electronic equipment. Other studies are much more demanding, since the experimenters must interact with the subjects and record the responses made by the subjects. In many experiments, debriefing or postinterviews must be conducted with the subjects to determine their reaction to the experiment and to eliminate any undesirable influence the experiment may have created.

Hypothesis Testing

After the data have been collected, the experimenters must analyze and interpret the data to determine if the stated hypotheses have been supported. With the advent of the computer and its statistical packages, the investigators are spared the task of making the necessary computations (some investigators prefer to use a desk calculator). Even though the computer is a marvelous piece of machinery, it still will do only what it is told to do. The investigators must decide on the appropriate statistical analyses. After the statistical analyses have been conducted, the investigators must interpret the results and specify exactly what they mean.

Communicating the Research Results

After the data have been analyzed, the scientists want to communicate the results to others. Communication most frequently takes place through the professional journals in a field. Consequently the scientists must write a research report that states how the research was conducted and what was found.

Reality and the Scientific Research Process

The five steps just described represent the *logical* analysis of the scientific research process. They suggest that research flows in an orderly process, from the first to the last step. A logical analysis such as this one has didactic value but is not an accurate representation of actual practice.

Selltiz et al. (1959, p. 9) identify two ways in which the actual research process differs from the model presented. First, the neat sequence of activities suggested is almost never followed. There tends to be a tremendous amount of overlap among the various activities outlined. Definition of the problem and statement of the hypotheses in part determine both the design and the conduct of the experiment. The design of the experiment in turn has a great deal to say about the method to be followed in collecting the data and the way the results are analyzed. The point is that there is a tremendous interaction between the various components. One activity cannot be carried out without affecting another. Second, the research process involves many activities not included in published studies or in the model presented. Frequently, equipment breaks down, subjects do not show up at the designated time and place, experimenters have to be trained, cooperation has to be obtained not only from subjects (assuming human subjects are used) but also from administrative personnel. These are only a few of the additional activities that may be required as a study gets underway.

The veteran researcher moves back and forth through the research steps to accomplish the goal of obtaining scientific knowledge. On the other hand, the student, who is a novice at research, may perform better if the logical sequence of steps is followed. As a researcher gains more experience, the need for rigid adherence to these steps declines. Skinner's 1956 talk, "A Case History in Scientific Method," depicts the informal nature of the scientific process as utilized by the seasoned researcher. This informality is depicted in his description of the "unformalized principles of scientific practice." These principles, derived from his own experience, are as follows:

1. When you run onto something interesting, drop everything else and study it.

2. Some ways of doing research are easier than others. (The now famous *Skinner box* resulted from the fact that Skinner, in his early maze studies, saw no reason why he always had to retrieve the rat at the end of the runway or why the rat could not deliver his own reinforcement.

3. Some people are lucky. (Skinner's construction of the cumulative recorder and observation of other aspects of the rate of responding were a result of not discarding an apparently useless appendage of the discarded apparatus from which he built his first food magazine.)

4. Apparatuses sometimes break down. (The jamming of the food magazine resulted in an extinction curve, which he later investigated.)

5. Never underestimate serendipity—the art of finding one thing while looking for another. (This principle led to his investigation of schedules of reinforcement.)

Skinner's principles reveal both the informality of the scientific process and some characteristics of scientists. However, you should not get the impression that Skinner, because he has elaborated on the informality of the scientific process, is lax or fuzzy in his approach to experimentation. Quite the contrary. He advocates *more* careful control and thought about experimentation and *more* rigorous definition of terms and quantification of research findings.

Advantage of the Scientific Method

The scientific method has been contrasted with five other methods of acquiring knowledge, and it has been stated that the scientific method is the preferred method. If you scrutinize closely the six methods of acquiring knowledge, you should be able to see why. Science relies on data obtained through systematic empirical observation. The scientific method specifies that we obtain our observations through a specific and systematic logic of inquiry. This systematic logic of inquiry is established in order to allow us to obtain **objective observations.** In other words, the scientific method enables us to make observations that are independent of opinion, bias, and prejudice. Such is not the case with the other five methods. Empiricism, although based on experience, does not provide a means for eliminating the possibility that our experience is biased in some manner. Similarly, rationalism, intuition, authority, and tenacity do not preclude the existence of prejudice. In order for us to uncover the basic laws of behavior, we must acquire data that are void of such bias, and the only way we can obtain such unbiased data is through the scientific method.

Objective observation Observation that is independent of opinion or bias

The scientific method is also better than the other methods of attaining knowledge because it enables us to establish the superiority of one belief over another. For example, two people may experience different results from taking a vitamin supplement. One person may suddenly become more energetic, while another person may feel no difference. Based on their experience, the two people would hold different beliefs regarding the vitamin supplement. Which belief is correct? Or are they both correct? Only through the systematic logic specified by the scientific method can we ultimately weed out fact from fiction.

Characteristics of the Scientific Approach

Science has been defined as a logic of inquiry, and it has been specified that this method of acquiring information is superior to other methods because it allows us to obtain knowledge that is free of bias and opinion. In order to produce such objective knowledge, the process must possess certain characteristics, which, although necessary to science, are not limited to the realm of science. We will now look at the three most important characteristics of science: control, operational definition, and replication.

Control

Control is perhaps the single most important element in the scientific methodology. Control is important because it enables scientists to identify the causes of their observations. Experiments are conducted in an attempt to answer certain questions, such as why something happens, what causes some event, or under what conditions an event occurs. In order to provide unambiguous answers to such questions, experimenters must use control. Marx and Hillix (1973, p. 8) present an example of how control is necessary in answering a practical question.

> A farmer with both hounds and chickens might find that at least one of his four dogs is sucking eggs. If it were impractical to keep his dogs locked away from the chicken house permanently, he would want to find the culprit so that it could be sold to a friend who has no chickens, or to an enemy who does. The experiment could be run in just two nights by locking up one pair of hounds the first night and observing whether eggs were broken; if so, one additional dog would be locked up the second night, and the results observed. If none were broken, the two dogs originally released would be locked up with one of the others, and the results observed. Whatever the outcome, the guilty dog would be isolated. A careful farmer would, of course, check negative results by giving the guilty party a positive opportunity to demonstrate his presumed skill, and he would check positive results by making sure that only one dog was an egg sucker.[1]

In this example, the farmer, in the final analysis, controlled for the simultaneous influence of all dogs by releasing only one dog at a time to isolate the egg sucker. To answer questions in psychology, we also have to eliminate the simultaneous influence of many variables to isolate the cause of an effect. Controlled inquiry is an absolutely essential process in science because without it the cause of an effect could not be isolated. The observed effect could be due to any one or a combination of the uncontrolled variables. A historical example will serve to illustrate the necessity of control in arriving at causative relationships.

In the thirties, Norman Maier presented a paper at a meeting of the American Association for the Advancement of Science. In this paper (Maier, 1938), he presented a technique for producing abnormal symptoms in rats by presenting them with a discrimination problem that had no solution. Shortly thereafter, other investigators examined the procedure used by Maier and became interested in one of its components. Maier had found that the rats, when confronted with the insoluble problem, normally refused to jump off the testing platform. To induce jumping behavior, a blast of hot air was directed at an animal. Shortly therafter, Morgan and Morgan (1939) duplicated Maier's results by simply exposing rats to the high-pitched tones of the hot air blast that Maier had used to make his rats leave the jumping stand. The significant point made in the Morgan and Morgan study was that conflict and the elaborate discrimination training were not necessary to generate the abnormal symptoms. This led to a controversy regarding the role of frustration in fixation that lasted for a number of years (Maier, 1949).

[1]From *Systems and theories in psychology* by Marx and Hillix. Copyright © 1973 by McGraw-Hill, Inc. Used by permission of McGraw-Hill Co.

The important point for our purposes is that the potential effect of the auditory stimulus was not controlled. Therefore, one could not conclude from Maier's 1938 study that the insoluble discrimination problem produced the abnormal behavior, since the noise also could have been the culprit. Exercise of control over such variables is essential in science.

Operational Definition

The principle of operational definition was originally set forth by Bridgman (1927) and was incorporated into psychology shortly thereafter. **Operationism** means that terms must be defined by the steps or operations used to measure them. Such definition is necessary to eliminate confusion in communication. Consider the statement "Hunger causes one to perceive food-related objects selectively." One might ask, "What is meant by hunger?" Stating that hunger refers to being starved only adds to the confusion. However, stating that hunger refers to eight hours of food deprivation communicates a clear idea. Now others realize what hunger means and can, if they so desire, generate the same degree of hunger. Setting down an operational definition forces one to identify the empirical references, and so ambiguity is minimized.

Operationism
The definition of terms by the operations used to attain them

Consider a more difficult statement. Assume that you just had an encounter with a car salesperson whom you thought was excellent. How would you operationally define an excellent salesperson as opposed to a poor one? First, the empirical referents that correspond to this term must be identified. As Figure 1.1 reveals, these referents

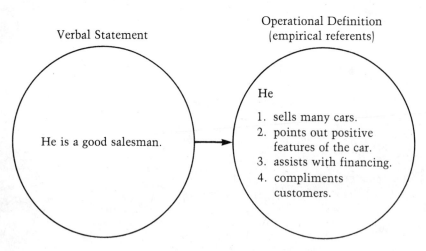

Figure 1.1   *Example of an operational definition of a good car salesperson.*

might consist of selling many cars, pointing out a car's good features, helping the customer to find financing, and complimenting the customer on an excellent choice. Once such behaviors have been identified, meaning can be communicated with minimal ambiguity. This does not mean, as Stevens (1939) has pointed out, that operationism is a panacea. It is merely a statement of one of the requirements of science that must eventually be used if science is to provide communicable knowledge.

One of the early criticisms of operationism was that its demands were too strict. If everything had to be defined operationally, one could never begin the investigation of a problem. Critics were concerned that it would be virtually impossible to formulate a problem concerning the functional relationships between events. Instead of stating a relationship betwen hunger and selective perception, one would have to talk about the relationship between number of hours of food deprivation and inaccurate description of ambiguous stimuli presented tachistoscopically. Operationism, however, does not preclude verbal concepts and higher-level abstraction. Problems and questions are originally formulated in nonoperational terms such as hunger, anxiety, and frustration. Once the problem is formulated, then the terms must be operationally defined. Verbal concepts are, therefore, admissible and useful in the pursuit of science.

Another criticism leveled at operationism was that each operational definition completely specified the meaning of the term. Any change in the set of operations would specify a new concept, which would lead to a multiplicity of concepts. Such a notion suggests that there is no overlap among the operations, that—for example—there is no relationship among three different operational measures (responses to a questionnaire, GSR readings, and amount of urination and defecation by rats in an open-field situation) of a concept such as anxiety or that they are not concerned with the same thing. Stevens addresses this issue and notes that this "process of generalization proceeds on the basis of the notion of classes" (Stevens, 1939, p. 233). Verbal concepts such as anxiety merely represent the name or symbol that has been given to that class of events. Each of the many operational definitions that can be given to a verbal concept merely represents a member of that class; consequently, the various operational definitions of a verbal concept are concerned with the same thing.

More recently, Deese (1972) has criticized operationism as being a hocus-pocus procedure. In conducting research, we must translate abstract concepts such as hunger or intelligence into events or procedures that can be unambiguously understood by others. This is where the problem arises, according to Deese. For example, consider the concept of intelligence. If we were to use this concept in a study, we would want to define it operationally. One way to define it is to identify intelligence as a score on a specific intelligence test. Doing this satisfies the criteria of operationsim. However, Deese states that although we have operationally defined intelligence in terms of a score on a specific test, we still may not know whether we have really measured intelligence or how or why intelligence tests measure intelligence. Although it is appropriate for Deese to question our knowledge and ability to measure intelligence, this does not seem to be related to operationism. Operationism merely refers to defining terms by the operations used to obtain them. In the case of intelligence, this was done. Whether the operational definition is in fact accurate or valid is quite another matter.

Replication

A third requirement of science is that the observations made must be replicable. As a characteristic of science, **replication** refers to the ability to reproduce the results obtained from a study. In other words, the data obtained in an experiment must be reliable—the same results must be found if the study is repeated. The need for science to have such a requirement is quite obvious, since the goal of science is to obtain knowledge about the world in a scientific manner. If observations are not repeatable, our descriptions and explanations are unreliable and therefore useless.

Replication
The ability to reproduce the results of a study

Reproducibility of observations can be investigated by making intergroup, intersubject, or intrasubject observations. Intergroup observations involve attempting to duplicate the results on another group of subjects, intersubject observations involve assessing the reliability of observations on other individual subjects, and intrasubject observations involve attempting to duplicate the results with the same subject on different occasions.

While there is acceptance of replication as a characteristic of science, Campbell and Jackson (1979) have pointed out that an inconsistency exists between the acceptance of this characteristic and the behavioral commitment on the part of researchers to replication research. Few researchers are conducting replication research primarily because it is difficult to publish such studies. Also, it seems as though most researchers believe that well-designed and well-controlled studies can be replicated and, therefore, that replication research is not as important as original research. The one exception is in the field of parapsychology. Numerous replication studies are conducted in this area because it is very difficult to attain replication. Lack of commitment to conducting replication studies does not, however, diminish the role of replication as one of the salient characteristics of science. Only through replication can we place any confidence in the fact that the results of our studies are valid and reliable.

Objectives of Science

Ultimately, the objective of science is to understand the world in which we live. This objective pervades all scientific disciplines, but to say that the objective of science is understanding is rather nebulous. Ordinary people as well as scientists demand understanding. Is there a difference in the level of understanding referred to by the scientist and by the ordinary person? The answer obviously is yes. Understanding on the part of the nonscientist most typically consists of being able to provide some explanation, however crude it may be, for the occurrence of a phenomenon. Most people, for example, do not totally understand the operation of the internal combustion engine. Some individuals are satisfied with knowing that it requires turning a key in the ignition switch and simultaneously depressing the accelerator. Others are not satisfied until they acquire additional information. For the ordinary person, understanding—or knowing the reasons—ceases when curiosity rests.

Science is not satisfied with such a superficial criterion; it demands a detailed examination of a phenomenon. Only when a phenomenon is accurately described and explained—and therefore predictable and in most cases capable of being controlled—will science say that it has understanding. Consequently, scientific understanding requires the four specific objectives of description, explanation, prediction, and control.

Description

The first objective of science, the process of **description,** requires one to portray an accurate picture of the phenomenon, to identify the variables that exist, and then to determine the degree to which they exist. For example, Piaget's theory of child development arose from his detailed observations and descriptions of his own child. Usually, any new area begins with the descriptive process because it identifies the variables that exist. Only after we have some knowledge of which variables exist can we begin to explain why they exist. For example, we would not be able to explain the existence of separation anxiety (the crying and visual searching behavior engaged in by infants when the mother departs) if we had not first identified this behavior. Scientific knowledge typically begins with description.

Description
The portrayal of a situation or phenomenon

Explanation

The second objective is the **explanation** of the phenomenon, and this requires knowledge of why the phenomenon exists or what causes it. Therefore, we must be able to identify the antecedent conditions that

Explanation
Determining the cause of a given phenomenon

result in the occurrence of the phenomenon. Assume that the behavior connoting separation anxiety existed when an infant was handled by few adults other than its parents and that it did not exist when the infant was handled by and left with many adults other than parents. We would conclude that one of the antecedent conditions of this behavior was frequency of handling by adults other than parents. Note that frequency was only *one* of the antecedents. Scientists are cautious and conservative individuals. They recognize that most phenomena are multidetermined and that new evidence may necessitate replacing an old explanation with a better one. As the research process proceeds, we acquire more and more knowledge as to the causes of phenomenon. With this increasing knowledge comes the ability to predict and possibly control the phenomenon.

Prediction

Prediction represents the third objective of science and refers to the ability to anticipate an event prior to its actual occurrence. We can, for example, predict very accurately when an eclipse will occur. Making an accurate prediction such as this requires knowledge of the antecedent conditions that produce such a phenomenon. It requires knowledge of the movement of the moon and the earth and of the fact that the earth, moon, and sun have to be in a particular position before an eclipse can occur. In short, prediction requires knowledge of antecedent conditions. If we knew the combination of variables that resulted in academic success, we could then very accurately predict who would and would not succeed academically. To the extent that we cannot accurately predict a phenomenon, we have a gap in our understanding of it.

Prediction
The ability to anticipate the occurrence of an event

Control

The fourth objective of science is control. **Control** as an objective of science refers to the manipulation of the *conditions that determine a phenomenon* (note the emphasis). Control, in this sense, refers to having knowledge of the causes or antecedent conditions of a phenomenon. When the antecedent conditions are known, they can be manipulated so as to produce the desired phenomenon. Psychologists, therefore, indirectly influence behavior by directly controlling the variables that, in turn, influence behavior.

Frequently, it has been stated that the psychologist is interested in the control of behavior. Books such as *Walden Two* (Skinner, 1948) and *Beyond Freedom and Dignity* (Skinner, 1971) have promoted this kind of statement because readers of these books note that Skinner is explaining or laying out a scheme for making people behave in a certain way. Thus they conclude that psychologists destroy or eliminate people's free will and have the ability to control the behavior of others. The point that most nonscientists miss is that Skinner's concern is with identifying the antecedent variables that generate the behavior in question. Skinner believes that behavior is determined and that the psychological task is to isolate the antecedent conditions.

Psychologists are interested in behavior, but their main interest lies in the conditions that produce behavior. Once these conditions are understood, the behavior can be controlled by allowing or not allowing the conditions to exist. Consider the frustration-aggression hypothesis: Frustration leads to aggression. Assume that this hypothesis is completely correct—that aggression is produced by the condition of frustration. Knowing this, we can control aggressive behavior by allowing or not allowing a person to be frustrated. As can be seen, control refers to the manipulation of conditions that produce a phenomenon such as aggression and not to the phenomenon itself.

At this point, it seems appropriate to provide some additional insight into the concept of control. So far, control has been discussed in two slightly different ways. In the discussion of the characteristics of the scientific approach, control was referred to in terms of holding constant or eliminating the influence of extraneous variables in an experiment. In the present discussion, control refers to the antecedent conditions determining a behavior. Boring (1954) noted that the word "control" has three meanings attached to it. First, control refers to a check or verification in terms of a comparison. Second, control refers to a restraint—keeping conditions constant or eliminating the influence of extraneous conditions from the experiment. Third, control refers to a guidance or directing in the sense of producing an exact change or a specific behavior. The second and third meanings identified by Boring are those used in this book so far. Since all of these meanings will be used at various times, it would be to your advantage to memorize them.

Control
(1) A comparison group; (2) eliminating the influence of extraneous variables; or (3) manipulating antecedent conditions to produce a change in behavior

Basic Assumption Underlying Science

In order for scientists to have confidence in the fact that scientific inquiry can achieve a solution to questions and problems, they must accept one basic axiom about the nature of the objects, events, and things with which scientists work. Scientists, implicitly or explicitly, must believe that there is uniformity in nature, because otherwise there can be no science. Skinner (1953, p. 13), for example, has stated that science is "a search for order, for uniformities, for lawful relations among the events in nature." If there were no uniformity in nature, there could be no understanding, explanation, or knowledge about nature. Without uniformity, we could not develop theories, laws, or facts. Implicit in the assumption of uniformity is the notion of determinism. By **determinism** I mean the belief that there are causes, or determinants, of behavior. In our efforts to uncover the uniform laws of behavior, we attempt to identify the variables that are linked together. We construct experiments that attempt to identify the effects produced by given events; in this way, we try to establish the determinants of events. Once we have determined the events that produce a given behavior or set of behaviors, we have uncovered the uniformity of nature.

Determinism
The belief that behavior is caused by specific events

Method Versus Technique

Up to this point, I have focused attention on the scientific method as a logic of inquiry. This logic of inquiry must be distinguished from technique. **Technique** refers to the specific manner in which the scientific method is implemented. Many people confuse methodology with technique. This confusion leads individuals to believe that psychology uses a scientific method that is somehow different from that used by other sciences. Actually, all sciences are characterized by a common logic of inquiry in their quest for knowledge. Psychology does not use a different scientific method, or logic of inquiry; psychology merely uses different techniques in applying the basic scientific method. The techniques used in applying the scientific method vary in as many ways as there are different types of problems and disciplines. Specifically, technique varies with the nature of the subject matter, the nature of the specific problem, and the stage of inquiry.

Technique
The specific manner in which the scientific method is implemented

Variation in technique as a function of subject matter can be illustrated by contrasting the various fields of inquiry as well as by contrasting the techniques used in the various areas of psychology. Consider, for example, the different observational techniques used by the astronomer, the biologist, and the psychologist doing research on small groups. The astronomer uses a telescope and, more recently, interplanetary probes. The biologist uses the microscope, and the small-group researcher may use a one-way mirror to unobtrusively observe subjects' interactions. The scientists in these various fields are all using the same scientific method, the key aspect being controlled inquiry, but the techniques they must use in implementing this method differ. The techniques used in different fields do not necessarily vary any more than the techniques used in the different areas of psychology. The physiological psychologist might use stimulation electrodes in investigating cortical processes, whereas the learning psychologist uses reinforcement techniques.

Variation in technique as a function of the nature of the problem can be illustrated by contrasting two studies, one conducted by Hayes and Cone (1981) and the other conducted by Yoburn, Cohen, and Campagnoni (1981). Table 1.1 shows that Hayes and Cone (1981) investigated the influence of feedback on electrical consumption, whereas Yoburn et al. (1981) investigated the influence of interrupted access to food on attack behavior. Hayes and Cone used a feedback technique that was administered to residential consumers; Yoborn et al. used a reinforcement technique as well as a specific technique for projecting an image on a screen. These varying techniques were absolutely necessary, because the two studies investigated different problems. But even though the studies used different techniques, Table 1.1 indicates that both studies followed the logic of inquiry inherent in the scientific method. What is perhaps not so apparent is that both studies also employed other characteristics of science, such as control. For ex-

Table 1.1 *Contrasting Techniques Used by Two Studies Employing the Scientific Method*

SCIENTIFIC METHOD OR LOGIC OF INQUIRY	HAYES AND CONE (1981) STUDY	YOBORN, COHEN, AND CAMPAGNONI (1981) STUDY
Identify problem and form hypothesis	Is residential consumption of electricity decreased through monthly feedback of changes in kilowatt-hours and cost over the same month in previous years?	Will interrupted access to food induce attacks in pigeons?
Design experiment	Residential consumers were randomly assigned to feedback and no-feedback groups.	Pigeons were given preliminary training in obtaining food under a specific reinforcement schedule and then tested to see if they would attack an image projected on a screen.
Conduct experiment	Consumers either received or did not receive feedback and information on change in cost and kilowatt-hours used.	Pigeons were given one type of reinforcement; an image was presented on 21st session. The rate of attack on the image was recorded.
Test hypothesis	Changes in electrical consumption for feedback and no-feedback groups were compared, and feedback groups revealed reduction in electrical consumption.	Changes in rate of attack when image was present and absent were compared.
Write research report	Research was published in the *Journal of Applied Behavior Analysis*	Research was published in the *Journal of the Experimental Analysis of Behavior.*

ample, Hayes and Cone controlled for differences that may exist in residential consumers' use of electricity by randomly assigning the consumers to either a feedback or a no-feedback group.

The point that one has reached in the research process also dictates the technique used. If one is at the data collection stage, then questionnaires, verbal responses, bar pressing, or any of numerous other techniques could be used. The technique used is determined by the demands of the study. Likewise, if one is at the data analysis stage, the appropriate statistical technique has to be selected.

The wide variances that exist among different fields (and even among different areas within a field) are, therefore, primarily a function of the diverse techniques used in applying the same scientific method.

Role of the Scientist in Science

One very significant component in the scientific approach is the scientist—the individual who employs the scientific approach and who ultimately makes science possible. Is the scientist just any person, or does he or she possess special characteristics? As might be expected, certain characteristics are necessary. A scientist is any individual who rigorously employs the scientific method in the pursuit of knowledge. However, nature's secrets are revealed reluctantly even when the scientific method is used. The scientist must actively search and probe nature to uncover orderly relationships. As a result, the scientist must, among other things, be curious, patient, objective, and tolerant of change.

Curiosity

The scientist's goal is the pursuit of knowledge, the uncovering of the laws of nature. The scientist attempts to answer questions: What? When? Why? How? Under what conditions? With what restriction? These questions not only represent the starting point of scientific investigation but continue to be asked throughout the investigation. To ask these questions, the scientist must be inquisitive, must exhibit curiosity, and must never think that the ultimate solution has been reached. If questions such as these ever cease, then the scientific process also ceases.

The scientist must maintain an open mind, never becoming rigid in orientation or in method of experimentation. Such rigidity could cause him or her to become blinded and incapable of capitalizing on, or even seeing, unusual events. This relates to Skinner's "fifth unformalized principle of scientific practice . . . serendipity—the art of finding one thing while looking for another" (1972, p. 112). Without being inquisitive and open to new and different phenomena, scientists would never make the accidental discoveries that periodically occur.

Patience

The reluctance of nature to reveal secrets is seen in the slow progress made in scientific inquiry. When individuals read or hear of significant advances in some field of scientific inquiry, they marvel at the scientists' ability and think of the excitement and pleasure that must have surrounded the discovery. Indeed, such excitement and pleasure does exist. However, most people do not realize the many months or years of tedious, painstaking work that went into achieving this advancement in knowledge. Many failures are encountered before success is achieved. As a result, the scientist must be extremely patient and must be satisfied with rewards that are few and far between. Note the many years of effort that have gone into cancer research; although many advances have been made, a cure is still not available.

Objectivity

One of the prerequisites of scientific inquiry is objectivity. The scientific method requires that the scientists' observations not be affected by their own wishes and attitudes. Perfect objectivity probably can never be attained, since scientists are only human. No matter how severe the attempt to eliminate bias, the scientist still has certain desires that may influence the research being conducted. Rosenthal (1966), for example, has repeatedly demonstrated that experimenter expectancies may influence the results of experiments.

Change

Scientific investigation necessitates change. The scientist is always devising new methods and new techniques for investigating phenomena. This process typically results in change. When a particular approach to a problem fails, a new approach must be devised, which also necessitates change. When change no longer exists, the scientific process ceases because we then continue to rely on and accept old facts and methods of doing things. We are no longer asking questions and are basically saying that we have solved all problems. Change does not necessitate abandoning all past facts and methods; it merely means the scientist must be critical of the past and constantly alert to facts or techniques that may represent an improvement.

Summary

There are at least six different approaches to acquiring knowledge. Five of these approaches—tenacity, intuition, authority, rationalism, and empiricism—are considered to be unscientific. Tenacity, or the state of holding fast, represents knowledge acquired through superstition. Intuition refers to knowledge acquired in the absence of any reasoning or inferring. Authority represents knowledge acquired from a highly respected source of information. Rationalism refers to knowledge acquired through correct reasoning. Empiricism represents knowledge acquired from experience.

The sixth and best approach to acquiring knowledge is science, which is a specific logic of inquiry. Therefore, the scientific approach requires that a specific method be followed. The five different activities that can be identified as comprising the scientific method are (1) identifying the problem and formulating the hypotheses, (2) designing the experiment, (3) conducting the experiment, (4) testing the hypotheses, and (5) writing the research report. The advantage of the scientific method is that it enables us to make objective observations and to establish the superiority of one belief over another.

The scientific method as a logic of inquiry has certain rules or characteristics. *Control* is the most important characteristic because it enables the scientist to identify causation—without control, it would be impossible to identify the cause of a given effect. A second characteristic of the scientific method is *operational definition,* which refers to the fact that terms must be defined by the steps or operations used to measure them. Defining terms operationally is necessary to eliminate confusion in meaning and communication. The third characteristic of the scientific method is *replication.* The scientific observations that are made must be able to be repeated. If these characteristics are not satisfied, the results of an investigation are useless because they are not reliable.

Science has certain objectives that it strives to achieve in attempting to reach the ultimate goal of understanding the world in which we live. The first objective is *description,* or portraying an accurate picture of the phenomenon under study. The second objective is *explanation,* or determining why a phenomenon exists or what causes it. The third objective is *prediction,* or the anticipation of an event prior to its occurrence. The fourth and last objective is *control* in the sense of being able to manipulate the antecedent conditions that determine the occurrence of a given phenomenon. The scientist must believe that there is uniformity in nature, for otherwise it would be impossible to pursue these goals.

Science is a logic of inquiry—a method for generating a body of knowledge. As such, science must be distinguished from technique, which represents the specific manner in which one implements the scientific method. The various fields that use the scientific method for generating data make use of a wide variety of techniques. These techniques differ across various fields and across areas within a given field of study, but the logic of inquiry used is identical.

In attempting to gain knowledge through use of the scientific method, the scientist must implement this methodology. Any individual who rigorously employs the scientific method is a scientist. Nature is reluctant to reveal its secrets, however, so the successful scientist must be curious enough to ask questions and patient enough to gain the answers. The scientist must also be objective so as not to bias the data and must accept change in the form of new techniques and facts.

2

Approaches to Using the Scientific Method

Chapter Overview

As you have just seen, the scientific method represents a general logic of inquiry. Science, therefore, is a process by which we acquire knowledge. Within the field of psychology, we attempt to acquire knowledge regarding the behavior of organisms. This means that we want to identify not only what organisms do but also why they do it. In others words, we want not only to describe the behavior of organisms but also to explain the cause of that behavior, and so we use the scientific method. The approach taken in implementing the scientific method differs slightly depending on whether one is attempting to describe or to explain behavior. Therefore, two basic research approaches to using the scientific method can be identified—the descrip-tive and the experimental research approaches. The present chapter is designed to acquaint you with the basic characteristics of each of these methodologies. As you read this chapter, you should answer the following questions:

1. What are the basic characteristics of the descriptive and the experimental research approaches?

2. What are the different types of descriptive research approaches and how do they differ?

3. How does the experimental research approach attempt to identify causal relations, and what are the advantages and disadvantages of this method?

4. What are the different views on causation?

Introduction

The two basic approaches to using the scientific method, the descriptive and the experimental research approaches, differ because they seek to attain different bodies of knowledge. Descriptive research attempts to describe a given situation, whereas experimental research tries to ferret out cause-and-effect relationships. In order to give you an appreciation of the differences in these two research styles, an overview of the basic characteristics of each approach will be presented.

Descriptive Research Approach

The primary characteristic of the **descriptive research approach** is that it represents an attempt to provide an accurate description or picture of a particular situation or phenomenon. This approach does not try to ferret out the so-called cause-and-effect relationships. Instead, it attempts to identify variables that exist in a given situation and, at times, to describe the relationship that exists between these variables. Therefore, the descriptive approach is widely used and is of great importance. We see the results of the descriptive approach whenever the results of Gallup polls or other surveys are reported. Helmstadter (1970, p. 65) has even gone so far as to state that the "descriptive approaches are the most widely used . . . research methods."

When initially investigating a new area, scientists use the descriptive method to identify the factors that exist and to identify relationships that exist among the factors. Such knowledge is used to formulate hypotheses that are subjected to experimental investigation. Also, the descriptive method is frequently used to describe the status of a situation once a solution, suggested by experimental analyses, has been put into effect. Here the descriptive method can provide input regarding the effectiveness of the proposed solution and also can provide hypotheses about how a more effective solution could be reached. Thus the descriptive method is useful in both the initial and the final stages of investigation into a given area.

Descriptive research approach
A technique that provides a description or picture of a particular situation, event, or set of events.

Naturalistic Observation

Naturalistic observation is a technique that enables the investigator to collect data on naturally occurring behavior. Ebbesen and Haney (1973), for example, were interested in determining the relationship between the proportion of drivers who turned in front of an oncoming car and the risk of a collision with that car. The investigators naturally hypothesized that as the risk of a collision increased the proportion of drivers turning would decrease. To obtain data to test the hypothesis, the researchers situated an unobtrusive observer in a parking lot next to the T-shaped intersection that was selected for study. Results of the study supported the hypothesis. However, it was observed that males took significantly greater risks than females and that risk taking increased if drivers had to wait in a line of cars before being allowed to turn, particularly if they had no passengers with them.

A study such as this illustrates the characteristics of naturalistic observation. Perhaps a unique characteristic is the unobtrusiveness of the observer. Rather than taking an active part in the experiment, the observer must remain completely aloof in order to record natural be-

Naturalistic observation
A descriptive research technique for unobtrusively collecting data on naturally occurring behavior

havior. If subjects had known they were being observed, their behavior probably would not have been the same. A second and related characteristic is the lack of artificiality of the situation. The subjects are not behaving in an environment removed from real life. They are left in their natural environment so as to eliminate any artificial influence that may be caused by bringing the organism out of its natural habitat.

For certain types of studies it is necessary that these characteristics exist. If a research project were directed at answering the question of what baboons do during the day, naturalistic observation would be the technique to use. Such research would also generate hypotheses that could be tested with field or laboratory experimentation. If we observe that baboons fight when conditions *a, b, c,* and *d* exist and we want to know *why* they fight, we could conduct an experiment to determine this. Condition *a* would be presented without *b, c,* or *d,* and we would observe whether fighting occurs. Then condition *b* would be presented without *a, c,* or *d,* and so forth, until all conditions and combinations has been presented. We have now moved from observation to experimentation.

Naturalistic observation is of course necessary when one is conducting a study that is not amenable to experimentation. It is not experimentally feasible, for example, to study suicide.

While there are many positive components of naturalistic observation, it also has a number of constraints. Naturalistic observation is great for obtaining an accurate description, but causes of behavior are almost impossible to isolate. Any given behavior could be produced by a number of agents operating independently or in combination, and observation does not provide any means of sorting these out. In no way could the Ebbesen and Haney study have isolated why males take more risks than females. Also, the observational approach is very time consuming. Observers in the Ebbesen and Haney study spent about a month observing drivers at selected time intervals between 10:00 A.M. and 5:00 P.M. to collect data for just one portion of the study. These are just some of the difficulties encountered in such a study.

Field Studies

A second descriptive research approach is that of field study. **Field studies** are similar to naturalistic observation in that both are conducted in the real world. Consequently, both approaches avoid the criticism of artificiality of the environments in which the data are collected. However, the field studies differ from naturalistic observation by virtue of the fact that the investigator intervenes in the data collection. A prerequisite for a study to be classified as naturalistic observation is that the investigator remain unobtrusive. In field studies, the investigator actively interacts with subjects in the course of collec-

Field studies
A group of descriptive research techniques for obtrusively collecting data regarding specific behaviors

tion of data. The approaches that fall under the classification of field studies are the survey, correlational studies, longitudinal and cross-sectional studies, and the field experiment. The field experiment will not be included in the present discussion, since it represents an experimental approach and will be treated with that topic.

The Survey

The **survey** is a widely used descriptive research technique. It is often defined as a method of collecting standardized information by interviewing a representative sample of some population. In other words, the survey represents a probe into a given state of affairs that exists at a given time, Therefore, direct contact has to be made with the individuals whose characteristics, behaviors, or attitudes are relevant to the investigation.

Survey
A field study in which an interview technique is used to gather data on a given state of affairs in a representative sample of the population

Probably the most widely known surveys are those conducted by the Gallup organization. Gallup polls are frequently conducted to survey the voting public's opinions on such issues as the popularity of the president or a given policy, or to determine the percentage of individuals who may be expected to vote for a given candidate at election time. Surveys are initially conducted to supply answers to the questions of "how many" and "how much." But collection of frequency data is only a preliminary phase of the research in many studies. Studies often want to answer the questions of "who" and "why." Who votes for the Republican candidate, and who votes for the Democratic candidate? Why do people buy a certain make of car or brand of a product? Such information helps us to understand why a particular phenomenon took place and increases our ability to predict what will happen.

For example, Table 2.1 illustrates the results of a Gallup poll (1980) concerning the issue of hand guns. One of the questions asked in the survey was "Do you think there should or should not be a law which would forbid the possession of pistols and revolvers except by police and other authorized persons?" The responses to this question reveal that only 31 percent of the individuals polled would favor such a law. However, opinions varied according to the background characteristics of the respondents. A greater percentage of Catholics, Easterners, and individuals living in large cities were for such a law (as opposed to Protestants, Southerners, and those living in rural communities). From the responses to this one question, answers can be obtained to the questions of who and how many are in favor of a law restricting gun ownership.

Although the survey technique is applicable to a wide range of problems, a number of disadvantages are associated with it. The three most obvious disadvantages are sampling error, time required, and constraints in the length of the survey.

Table 2.1   *Response Obtained from a Gallup Poll to the Question "Do you think there should or should not be a law which would forbid the possession of pistols and revolvers except by police and other authorized persons?"*

	YES, SHOULD	NO, SHOULD NOT	NO OPINION
National	31%	65%	4%
Sex			
Male	25	71	4
Female	36	59	5
Race			
White	32	65	3
Non-white	22	67	11
Education			
College	33	64	3
High school	29	66	5
Grade school	32	63	5
Region			
East	46	50	4
Midwest	32	62	6
South	20	77	3
West	23	73	4
Age			
Total under 30	30	65	5
18–24 years	28	66	6
25–29 years	33	65	2
30–49 years	29	67	4
50 & older	33	63	4
Income			
$25,000 & over	32	66	2
$20,000–$24,999	33	66	1
$15,000–$19,999	32	60	8
$10,000–$14,999	27	67	6
$5,000–$9,999	30	65	5
Under $5,000	29	68	3
Politics			
Republican	33	65	2
Democrat	32	64	4
Independent	26	69	5
Religion			
Protestant	24	72	4
Catholic	44	53	3
Occupation			
Professional & business	33	64	3
Clerical & sales	38	59	3
Manual workers	25	70	5
Non–labor force	32	64	4

Table 2.1   (continued)

	YES, SHOULD	NO, SHOULD NOT	NO OPINION
City size			
1,000,000 & over	46	47	7
500,000–999,999	35	58	7
50,000–499,999	37	61	2
2,500–49,999	22	76	2
Under 2,500, rural	18	78	4
Labor union families	28	65	7
Non–labor union families	31	65	4

Source: *Gallup Opinion Index: Political, Social, and Economic Trends*, January, 1980, Report no. 174, p. 29.

1. *Sampling error.* Sampling error arises from the fact that most surveys are not administered to the total population of individuals. **Population** refers to all of the events, things, or individuals to be represented. A **sample** (any number less than the population) of individuals is selected for inclusion in the study, and the results obtained from this sample are considered to be the same as those that would have been obtained if the survey had been administered to the total population. The Gallup polls, for example, do not survey all voting members in the United States. They select perhaps 1500 people to survey and base their predictions on these 1500 responses. Since the survey is based on a sample, it is subject to sampling error. Investigators have devised sampling techniques that have minimized, but not eliminated, the magnitude of sampling bias. Employment of these sampling procedures does increase the time required to conduct a survey, but the benefits accrued far outweigh the time disadvantage. Information attained without the use of appropriate sampling procedures would be virtually worthless.

Population
All of the things, people, or events that are the object of the investigation

Sample
Any number of things, people, or events less than the total population

2. *Time required.* Surveys typically require a considerable investment of time and manpower not only to collect data but also to construct the survey, code the data once they have been obtained, and then analyze the data after they have been coded.

3. *Constraints in the length of the survey.* In any survey, there are numerous significant questions that can be asked. But every data-gathering instrument has an optimal length for the population to which it is being administered. After a certain point, the respondents' interest and cooperation diminish. The survey researcher must, therefore, ensure that the questionnaire is not too long, even though some important questions may have to be sacrificed.

Correlational Studies. In its simplest form, a **correlational study** consists of measuring two variables and then determining the degree of relationship that exists between them. Consequently, a correlational study can be incorporated into any of the descriptive research approaches. A relatively old study that is commonly cited in introductory and developmental texts is the study by Conrad and Jones (1940). They were interested in the relationship between the IQ scores of parents and their offspring. To accomplish the goals of this study, Conrad and Jones measured the IQs of the parents and correlated them with their children's IQs. In this way, a descriptive index was obtained that accurately and quantitatively portrayed the relationship between these two variables. As you can see, correlational studies do not make any attempt to manipulate the variables of concern but measure them in their natural state.

The correlational approach enables us to accomplish the goals of prediction. If a reliable relationship is found between two variables, then we not only have described the relationship between these two variables but also have gained the ability to predict one variable from a knowledge of the other variable. Sears et al. (1953), for example, found that a positive relationship existed between severity of weaning and later psychological adjustment. Knowledge of this relationship enables one to predict a child's psychological adjustment when given knowledge only of the severity with which the child has been weaned.

The weakness of the correlational approach is apparent in the Sears et al. study. Given knowledge of the relationship that they found, some individuals are prone to say that severity of weaning was the agent causing the later psychological maladjustment. Such an inference is not justified. Causation is frequently inferred from correlational studies, but these studies provide no such evidence. If evidence of causation is found between the two correlated variables, it will typically be found by the experimental approach. The later psychological maladjustment found by Sears et al. was probably due to generally inappropriate parent-child relationships, which, among other things, were manifested in severe weaning.

Let us look at a hypothetical example to drive this point home. Assume we find a correlation between the number of inches of rainfall in the Dallas–Fort Worth area each month and the number of babies born each month. Could we then say that the monthly rainfall in the Dallas–Fort Worth area caused a certain number of babies to be born or vice versa? Certainly not! The example does, however, reveal the fallacy of assuming causation from correlation. There are some rather complex correlational procedures that do give evidence of causation. However, the two-variable cases just presented do not.

The fallacy of assuming causation is not inherent in the correlational study but is merely a tendency of users of the results of such a

Correlational study
A study that seeks to describe the degree of relationship that exists between two measured variables

study. If the purpose of an investigation is to describe the degree of relationship which exists between variables, this approach is the appropriate one to use.

Longitudinal and Cross-Sectional Studies.   Longitudinal and cross-sectional studies are of the developmental type, since they investigate developmental changes that take place over time. However, the approaches that these two basic techniques use are somewhat different. The **longitudinal study** involves choosing a single group of subjects and measuring them repeatedly at selected time intervals to note changes that occur over time in the specified characteristics. For example, Brown, Cayden, and Bellugi-Klima (1969) were interested in the language development of children. They systematically recorded the verbalizations and language productions of three children for almost two years. On the other hand, a **cross-sectional study** identifies representative samples of individuals at specific age groups and notes the changes in the selected characteristics of subjects in these different age groups. Liebert et al. (1969) took this approach in their study of language development. They identified three relatively large groups of children at three different age levels and then observed and recorded the differences among these groups.

Longitudinal study
A developmental field study that repeatedly measures the same characteristics in a single sample of individuals at selected time intervals

Cross-sectional study
A developmental field study that measures the same characteristics in representative samples of individuals at different age levels

The longitudinal and cross-sectional descriptive approaches to developmental research have frequently been used in the past, and there has been much discussion about the relative advantages and disadvantages of each technique. One significant point is that these two techniques have not always generated similar results. The classic example of this discrepancy in results is in data obtained regarding the development of intelligence during adulthood. As seen in Figure 2.1, cross-sectional studies have suggested that adult intelligence begins to decline around the age of 30, whereas longitudinal studies show an increase or no change in intellectual performance until the age of 50 or 60 (Baltes, Reese, and Nesselroade, 1977). This difference has been attributed to what is called an age-cohort effect. In other words, longitudinal studies follow just one group or cohort of individuals over time, so all individuals within this cohort are experiencing similar environmental events. However, cross-sectional studies investigate a number of different groups of individuals or different cohorts. Because of changes in environmental events, these cohorts have not been exposed to similar experiences. For example, members of a 40-year-old cohort would not have been exposed to video games or computers when they were 10 years old, but a group of 11-year-old individuals would have. Such differences are confounded with actual age differences in cross-sectional studies.

I have presented longitudinal and cross-sectional studies as descriptive research approaches because most of the studies using either of

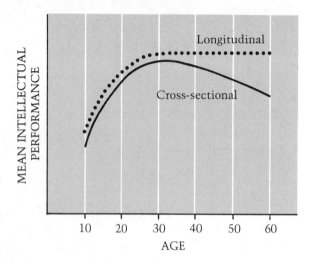

Figure 2.1 *Change in intellectual performance as a function of the longitudinal versus the cross-sectional method.*
(From *Life-Span Developmental Psychology: Introduction to Research*, by
P. B. Baltes, H. W. Reese, and J. R. Nesselroade. Copyright © 1977 by
Wadsworth Publishing Company, Monterey, California.)

these methods are in fact descriptive in nature. However, it is possible to conduct an experimental longitudinal or cross-sectional study. There is currently a great deal of emphasis on prevention research. A number of recent studies have involved instituting a prevention technique and then following the individual on whom the technique is administered to determine, for example, if that person becomes a drug abuser. Such research requires an experimental longitudinal approach.

Ex Post Facto Studies

Ex post facto inquiries are actually field studies, but they are given separate status here for two reasons. First, many of then closely resemble an experiment. Second, some have combined the ex post facto and the experimental approaches into a single study.

An **ex post facto study** is a study in which the variable or variables of interest to the investigator are not subject to direct manipulation but have to be chosen after the fact. The investigator begins with two or more groups of subjects that already differ according to one variable, such as their sex, age, prior experience, or internal state, and then records their behavior to determine if they respond differently in a common situation. These and other characteristics of the ex post facto research are revealed in a study by Atkeson et al. (1982) that inves-

Ex post facto study
A study comparing the effects of two or more variables where the variables being manipulated are not under the experimenter's control

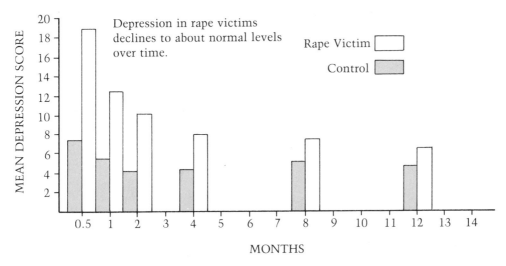

Figure 2.2   *Mean depression scores for rape victims and control subjects.* (Based on data from Atkeson et al., *Journal of Consulting and Clinical Psychology,* 1982, 50, 96–102.)

tigated the incidence, severity, and duration of the depressive symptoms of rape victims. Using several measures of depression, these researchers compared rape victims over time with a group of females who had not been raped. As Figure 2.2 illustrates, the results show that rape victims initially exhibited quite a bit of depression but that their depression declined to an approximately normal level over time.

If you look at Table 2.2, you can see that the Atkeson et al. study has the appearance of a field experiment by virtue of the fact that the experience of being raped was varied and then the consequence of

Table 2.2   *Graphic Illustration of the Design of the Atkeson et al. (1982) Study*

| | | TIME IN MONTHS | | | | |
		.5	1	4	8	12
	RAPE VICTIMS					
Ex post facto variable						
	NON-RAPED FEMALES					

having been raped was assessed across time. Consequently, the investigation compared the degree of depression experienced by rape victims with that of control, or non-raped, females. However, the nature of the manipulation of the experience of rape determines the ex post facto nature of the study. The experimenters did not have control over who was and who was not raped. Instead, the females came to the study with their prior differential experiences and, therefore, *assigned themselves* to one of the two groups. So the variable of interest was out of the experimenter's control, which is the distinguishing characteristic of an ex post facto study. The process of self-selection that determines the ex post facto nature of the research also is responsible for its weakness. Subjects who comprise the different groups because of some self-selected characteristic or experience may also possess other characteristics extraneous to the research problem. It may be one of these other characteristics and not the variable supposedly being manipulated in the study that produced the observed difference. Atkeson et al. recognized this limitation of the study and, instead of concluding that the experience of being raped was the causative factor of the observed differences, discussed the possible contribution of other factors (such as repeated assessment of degree of depression, the subjects' knowledge of the fact that they were in a psychological study, the stress on the poorer victims created by living in an area with a high crime rate, and the age of the research participants). As can be seen from this example, ex post facto studies resemble correlational studies in that the obtained relationships may have been produced by variables other than those investigated in the study.

Experimental Research Approach

The **experimental research approach** is the technique that attempts to ferret out cause-and-effect relationships. This research method enables one to identify causal relationships because it allows one to observe, under controlled conditions, the effects of systematically changing one or more variables. Because of its ability to identify causation, the experimental approach has come to represent the prototype of the scientific method for solving problems. The assumption seems to be that the knowledge acquired in this fashion is somehow better than that acquired by the descriptive method, an assumption promoted by the fact that evidence of causation can be attained from experimentation. We will take a look at the advantages and disadvantages of this approach, and then you can draw your own conclusions.

Experimental research approach
The research approach in which one attempts to identify causal relationships among variables

The Psychological Experiment

Zimney (1961, p. 18) defines a **psychological experiment** as "objective observation of phenomena which are made to occur in a strictly controlled situation in which one *or more* factors are varied and the others are kept constant" (italics mine). This definition seems to be one of the better ones because of the components that it includes, each of which will be examined separately. Analysis of this definition, with one minor alteration, should provide a definition of an experiment, an appreciation of the many facets of experimentation, and a general understanding of how experimentation enables causative relationships to be identified.

Objective Observation.   Impartiality and freedom from bias on the part of the investigator, or **objectivity,** was previously discussed as a characteristic that the scientist must exhibit. In order to be able to identify causation from the results of the experiment, the experimenter must avoid doing anything that may influence the outcome of the experiment. Rosenthal (1966) has demonstrated that the experimenter is probably capable of greater biasing effects that one would expect. In spite of this, and recognizing that complete objectivity is probably impossible to attain, freedom from bias is the goal for which the investigator must strive.

Science requires that we make **empirical observations** in order to arrive at answers to questions that are posed. Observations are necessary because they provide the data base used to attain the answers. To provide correct answers, experimenters must make a concerted effort to avoid mistakes, even though they are only human and therefore are subject to errors in recording and observation. For example, work in impression formation has revealed the biased nature of impressions of others. These biases are so pervasive that Gage and Cronback (1955, p. 420) have stated that social impressions are "dominated far more by what the Judge brings to it than by what he takes in during it." Once scientists realize that they are capable of making mistakes, they can proceed to guard against them. Zimney (1961) presents three rules that investigators should follow to minimize recording and observation errors. The first rule is to accept the possibility that mistakes can occur. This means that we need to understand that we are not perfect, that our perceptions and therefore our responses are influenced by our motives, desires, and other biasing factors. Once we accept this fact, we can then proceed to attempt to identify where the mistakes are likely to occur—the second rule. To identify potential mistakes, we must carefully analyze and test each segment of the entire experiment in order to anticipate the potential sources and causes of the errors. Once the

Psychological experiment
Objective observation of phenomena that are made to occur in a strictly controlled situation in which one or more factors are varied and the others are kept constant

situation has been analyzed, then the third rule can be implemented, which is that the experimenter should take the necessary steps to avoid the errors. Many times this involves constructing a more elaborate scenario or just appropriately designing equipment, procedures, etc. In any event, every effort should be expended in constructing the experiment so that accurate observations are recorded.

Of Phenomena Which Are Made to Occur.   Webster's dictionary defines phenomenon as "an observable fact or event." In psychological experimentation, **phenomenon** refers to any publicly observable behavior, such as actions, appearances, verbal statements, responses to questionnaires, and physiological recordings. Focusing on such obervable behaviors is a must if psychology is to meet the previously discussed characteristics of science. Only by focusing on these phenomena can we satisfy the demands of operational definition and replication of experiments. Defining a phenomenon as publicly observable behavior would seem to exclude the internal or private processes and states of the individual. In the introductory psychology course, processes such as memory, perception, personality, emotion, and intelligence are discussed. Is it possible to retain these processes if we study only *publicly* observable behavior? Certainly these processes have to be retained, since they also play a part in determining an individual's responses. Without getting into intervening variables and hypothetical constructs and the controversy over these (Marx, 1963, pp. 24–31), let me simply state that such processes are studied diligently by many psychologists. In studying these processes, researchers investigate publicly observable behavior and infer from these observations the existence of internal processes. It is the behavioral manifestation of the inferred processes that is observed. For example, intelligence is inferred from responses to an intelligence test; aggression is inferred from verbal or physical attacks on another person. You should also realize that not all psychologists accept this position. Notably, B. F. Skinner considers the inferring of internal states as inappropriate and not the subject matter of psychology. He feels that psychology should study only environmental phenomena and forget anything that cannot be observed or has to be inferred. Psychologists with this opinion believe that we should investigate only those environmental sequences, such as stimuli-response reinforcement, that determine behavior, and they have had a great deal of success with this approach. Pribram (1971, p. 253) makes two cogent points regarding this issue. First, the behaving organism is required to define each of the environmental variables. Only the organism can tell you what is reinforcing. Likewise, the response of the organism defines the stimulus and the stimulus defines the response. Second, it is the *internal* processes of the organism that enable the sequencing of events to take place. In order to determine what makes the sequencing occur, we must return to the organism and to the things taking place inside of that organism.

In the discussion of control as a goal of science, we saw that the psychologist does not have a direct controlling influence on behavior. The psychologist arranges the antecedent conditions that result in the behavior of interest. In an experiment, the experimenter precisely manipulates one or more variables and objectively observes the phenomena *that are made to occur* by this manipulation. This part of the definition of experimentation refers to the fact that the experimenter is manipulating the conditions that cause a certain effect. In this way, experimenters identify the cause-and-effect relationships from experimentation by noting the effect or lack of effect produced by their manipulations.

In a Strictly Controlled Situation.   This part of the definition refers to the need for eliminating the influence of variables other than those manipulated by the experimenter (Boring's second meaning of the word control). As you have seen, control is one of the most pressing problems facing the experimenter and one to which considerable attention is devoted, since without control, causation could not be identified. Because of the magnitude of this issue, it will be given extended coverage in later chapters.

In Which One or More Factors Are Varied and the Others Are Kept Constant.   The ideas expressed in this phase of the definition are epitomized by the *rule of one variable*, which states that all conditions in an experiment must be kept constant except one, which is to be varied along a defined range, and the result of this variation is to be measured on the response variable. The two major ideas expressed in the rule of one variable are constancy and variation. Constancy refers to controlling or eliminating the influence of all variables except the one (or ones) of interest. This requirement is necessary to determine the cause of the variation on the response variable. If the constancy requirement is violated, cause for the variation cannot be determined and the experiment is ruined. A learning experiment can easily illustrate the constancy component of the rule. Assume that you are interested in the effect of the length of a list of words on speed of learning. How does increasing the length influence the speed with which one learns that list of words? The length of the list of words could be systematically varied and related to the number of trials required to learn the list. In such an experiment, a number of factors that could influence learning speed need to be controlled, including the factors of difficulty level of the words, ability level of the subjects, familiarity with the words, and motivation level of the subjects. Only if these factors are held constant (and therefore do not exert an influence) can you say that the difference in speed of learning is a function of the change in the length of the list of words. The idea of variation means that one or more variables must be deliberately and precisely varied by some given amount to determine their effect on behavior. In the learning experiment, the length of the list of words must be changed by an exact predetermined amount. The questions that frequently arise are how and how much is the variable to be varied? The answers to these questions will be discussed at a later point in the book.

Advantages of the Experimental Approach

The first and foremost advantage of the experimental approach is the control that can be exercised. Control, as was stated in Chapter 1, is the most important characteristic of the scientific method, and the experimental approach enables one to effect the greatest degree of control. In an experiment, one is seeking an answer to a specific question. In order to obtain an unambiguous answer to the question, it is necessary to institute control over irrelevant variables by either eliminating their influence or holding their influence constant. Such control can be achieved by bringing the experiment into the laboratory, thereby eliminating noise, the presence of others, and other potentially distracting stimuli. Control is also achieved by use of such techniques as random assignment and matching. Since a whole chapter will be devoted to control techniques, they will not be discussed further at this point. Suffice it to say that the primary advantage of experimentation is the rigor afforded by the ability to utilize excellent control techniques.

A second advantage of the experimental approach is the ability to precisely manipulate one or more variables of the experimenter's choosing. If one were interested in studying the effects of crowding on any of a variety of behaviors, crowding could be manipulated in a very precise and systematic manner by varying the number of people in a constant amount of space. If interest also existed in the effects of sex of the subject and degree of crowding on some subsequent behavior, male and female subjects could be included in both the crowded and noncrowded conditions. In this way, the experimenter can precisely manipulate two variables: sex of subject and degree of crowding. The experimental approach enables one to control precisely the manipulation of variables by specifying the exact conditions of the experiment. The results can then be interpreted unambiguously, since the subjects should be responding primarily to the variables introduced by the experimenter.

A third advantage of the experimental approach is a completely pragmatic one. Use of the experimental approach has produced results that have lasted over time, that have suggested new studies, and, perhaps of most importance, that have suggested solutions to practical problems. This approach has proved to be extremely useful, which makes it important.

Disadvantages of the Experimental Approach

The most frequently cited and probably the most severe criticism leveled against the experimental approach is that laboratory findings are obtained in an artificial and sterile atmosphere that precludes any generalization to a real-life situation. The following statement by Bannister (1966, p. 24) epitomizes this point of view:

> In order to behave like scientists we must construct situations in which subjects are totally controlled, manipulated and measured. We must cut our subjects down to size. We must construct situations in which they can behave as little like human beings as possible and we do this in order to allow ourselves to make statements about the nature of their humanity.

Is such a severe criticism of experimentation justified? It seems to me as though the case is overstated. Underwood (1959) takes a totally different point of view; he does not see artificiality as a problem at all. He states:

> One may view the laboratory as a fast, efficient, convenient way of identifying variables or factors which are likely to be important in real-life situations. Thus, if four or five factors are discovered to influence human learning markedly, and to influence it under a wide range of conditions, it would be reasonable to suspect that these factors would also be important in the classroom. But, one would *not* automatically conclude such; rather, one would make field tests in the classroom situation to deny or confirm the inference concerning the general importance of these variables.[1]

The artificiality issue seems to represent a problem only when an individual makes a generalization from an experimental finding without first determining if the generalization can be made. Competent psychologists rarely blunder in this fashion because they realize that laboratory experiments are contrived situations.

Additional difficulties of the experimental approach include problems in designing the experiment and the fact that the experiment may be extremely time-consuming. It is not unusual for an experimenter to

---

[1]Benton J. Underwood, "Verbal Learning in the Educative Processes," *Harvard Educational Review*, 29, Spring 1959, 107–117. Copyright © by President and Fellows of Harvard College.

have to go to extreme lengths to set the stage for the subject, to motivate the subject, and occasionally to deceive the subject. Then, when the experiment is actually conducted, it is not uncommon for the experimenter and maybe one or two assistants to be required to spend quite some time with each subject.

More recently, a new twist has been added to the list of criticisms levied at the experimental approach; it is that the experimental approach as a method of scientific inquiry into the study of human behavior is inadequate. Gadlin and Ingle (1975) believe that a number of anomalies inherent in the experimental approach make it an inappropriate paradigm for use in the study of human behavior. For example, they state that the experimental approach promotes the view that humans are manipulable mechanistic objects because twentieth-century psychology mirrors the mechanistic method and assumptions of nineteenth-century physics. Gadlin and Ingle recommend the search for an alternative methodology that is not fraught with such inadequacies. However, when such criticisms are given close inspection, they do not hold up. Kruglanski (1976) has refuted each of the criticisms Gadlin and Ingle levied at the experimental approach. For example, the mechanistic manipulable assumption exists only to the extent that the experimenter arranges a set of conditions that may direct the individual's behavior in a given manner. This in no way "suggests that the subject is an empty machine devoid of feelings, thoughts, or a will of his own" (Kruglanski, 1976, p. 656). In the final analysis, it again appears that we must resort to use of the experimental approach to find the answers to our research questions. This does not mean that it is the only approach and that adherence to it will enable us to make great strides in understanding human behavior. However, at the present time it seems to be one of the better approaches available to us.

Illustrative Example

To drive home the advantages and disadvantages of the experimental approach, we will take a detailed look at a laboratory experiment conducted by Wellman, Malpas, and Witkler (1981). The investigators tested the hypothesis that phenylpropanolamine (PPA), the drug used in most over-the-counter diet preparations, causes animals to avoid eating by making them feel bad rather than by suppressing their desire to eat.

To test this hypothesis, researchers initially trained 40 albino rats on six consecutive days to consume their daily water intake during a 30-minute period. On the seventh day, the rats were given a 0.1 percent saccharin solution instead of water and then were randomly assigned to receive an injection of either 0.9 percent saline (the placebo or control condition) or 10, 20, or 40 mg/kg of PPA. During the next five days, the rats were given access to either water or a 0.1 percent saccharin solution, and the consumption of both water and the saccharin solution was recorded.

The advantages of control of extraneous variables and the precise manipulation of the variable of interest can easily be demonstrated. This study required control of a number of extraneous variables, which was possible because it was a laboratory study. The amount of fluid that the rats consumed was controlled by randomly assigning the subjects to the various groups. Additionally, the level of thirst of the animals was controlled by allowing them to drink only at a certain time of the day. Consequently, all rats were deprived of water for equal periods of time. If this variable had not been controlled, the rats' consumption of water or of the saccharin solution might have been caused by the fact that some of the rats had consumed water during the preceding 30 minutes whereas others had not consumed any water for the last two hours.

It was also necessary to precisely manipulate the dosage of PPA. This was rather easily accomplished in this experiment because the animals could be weighed. Once an animal's weight was determined, a dosage corresponding to 10, 20, or 40 mg/kg could be exactly identified and injected into the rat.

The primary disadvantage of the laboratory experiment is also demonstrated in this study. The laboratory experiment has most frequently been criticized for creating an artificial, sterile atmosphere. In this experiment, the rats were individually housed in wire-mesh cages with controlled lighting and temperature and were allowed to drink only during a predetermined 30-minute time period each day. Seldom in real life would organisms confine their fluid consumption to only a 30-minutes period of time each day. Critics of laboratory experiments would also attack the Wellman et al. experiment on the basis of the organism used to test the hypothesis of the study. Wellman and his colleagues used rats to test the adverse effects of PPA. However, the ultimate goal is not to determine how rats respond to PPA, but to generalize the results to humans. Seldom can we automatically generalize from infrahumans to humans. Instead, we must identify effects on organisms such as rats and then verify the existence of such effects using humans as the research participants.

Experimental Research Settings

The experimental approach is used in two different research settings—a laboratory setting and a field setting. Most experimental work has always been conducted in the laboratory. Although the laboratory will probably continue to be the most frequent setting for experimentation, we are hearing pleas for more field experimentation. Field and laboratory experimentation both use the experimental approach, but they have slightly different attributes that deserve mention.

Field Experimentation.   A **field experiment** is an experimental research study that is conducted in a real-life setting. The experimenter actively manipulates variables and carefully controls the influence of as many extraneous variables as the situation will permit. Freedman and Fraser (1966), for example, wanted to find out if people who initially complied with a small request would be more likely to comply with a large request. The basic procedure used was initially to ask one group of housewives if they would answer a number of questions about what household products they used. Three days later, the experimenter again contacted these same housewives and asked if they would allow a group of men to come into their home and spend approximately two hours classifying all of their household products. Another group of housewives was contacted only once, during which time the large request was made. Results revealed that the housewives who initially complied with the small request were significantly more likely to comply with the large request.

This study represents a field study because it was conducted in the natural setting of the housewives' homes while they were engaging in daily activities. It also represents an experimental study because variable manipulation was present (small request followed by large request or just large request) and control was present (the subjects for each group were randomly selected from the telephone directory). Field experiments such as this one are not subject to the artificiality problem that exists with laboratory experiments, and field experiments are, therefore, excellent for studying many problems. Their primary disadvantage is that control of extraneous variables cannot be accomplished as well as with laboratory experiments. In the Freedman and Fraser study, even though subjects were randomly selected from the telephone directory, only those subjects who were actually home could be included in the study. Consequently, a selection bias may have existed. Even though it is more difficult to exercise control in field experiments, such experiments are necessary, and a number of individuals are saying that we need to get out of the laboratory and get more involved with field experimentation.

Tunnell (1977) has carried such a suggestion a step further. He states that we not only must engage in more field experimentation but also should do so in a manner that makes all variables operational in real-world terms. Consider the study conducted by Ellsworth, Carlsmith, and Henson (1972). They had a confederate pedestrian stare at car drivers who were waiting at a red light. In this way, they hoped to assess the influence of staring on the speed with which the

Field experiment
An experimental research study that is conducted in a real-life setting

driver left the intersection. As might be expected, staring increases that speed. In this study, Ellsworth et al. included the three dimensions of naturalness identified by Tunnell: natural behavior, natural setting, and natural treatment. The natural behavior investigated was speed of leaving the intersection when the light turned green. The setting was natural because the individual remained in his or her car as opposed to being brought into an artificial laboratory setting, and the natural treatment was the staring. In reality, the treatment was imposed by a confederate, but it mirrored a behavior that could have naturally occurred. These are the types of behaviors Tunnell says we must strive for when we conduct field experimentation, as opposed to asking subjects for self-reports or to recall their own behavior in some prior situation. Asking for such retrospective data only serves to introduce possible bias in the study.

Laboratory Experimentation.   The **laboratory experiment** is the same type of study as the field experiment except that where the field experiment is strong, the laboratory experiment is weak, and where the laboratory experiment is strong, the field experiment is weak. The laboratory experiment epitomizes the ability to control or eliminate the influence of extraneous variables. This is accomplished by bringing the problem into an environment apart from the subjects' normal routines. In this environment, outside influences (such as the presence of others and noise) can be eliminated. However, the price of this increase in control is the artificiality of the situation created. This issue was covered in detail when I discussed the disadvantages of the experimental approach. Even though precise results can be obtained from the laboratory, applicability of these results to the real world must always be verified.

Laboratory experiment
An experimental research study that is conducted in the controlled environment of a laboratory

The laboratory experiment is a study that is conducted in the laboratory and in which the investigator precisely manipulates one or more variables, and controls the influence of all or nearly all of the extraneous variables. Stronger conclusions are probably yielded from such studies than from any other research technique.

Causation

Causation is one of those terms that people frequently use but often don't really understand. People are continually asking questions such as "What causes cancer?" "What causes a person to murder someone else?" "What causes a man to beat his wife?" What do they really mean? Common sense suggests that causality refers to a condition in

Causation
A term whose meaning is debated by philosophers but in everyday language seems to imply that manipulation of one event produces another event

which one event—the cause—generates another event—the effect. However, causality is much more complex.

When individuals discuss the effect of events, they tend to use the words cause and effect rather casually. Individuals tend to assume that manipulation is implicit in the concept of causation. If we manipulate or do something, we expect something else to happen. If something does happen, the thing or event we manipulate is called the cause and the event that happens is called the effect. For example, if we spank a child for coloring on a wall and then observe that he no longer colors on the wall, we assume that the spanking caused the child to stop the coloring. But this casual interpretation of the word causation does not take into consideration the necessity of ruling out alternative explanations. For example, the child may actually have stopped coloring because he got tired of coloring or because his attention was diverted to other interests. Consequently, there are problems associated with the use of the word causation, and these are problems that philosophers have encountered for years.

John Stuart Mill (1874), a British philosopher, set forth a number of canons that could be used for experimentally identifying causality. These canons seem to be quite important because they form the basis of many of the approaches currently used.

The first canon is the **Method of Agreement,** by which one identifies causality by observing the common elements that exist in several instances of an event. This canon can be illustrated by the frequently cited case of the man who wanted to find out scientifically why he got drunk. He drank rye and water on the first night and became drunk. On the second night, he drank scotch and water and became drunk once again. On the third night, he got drunk on bourbon and water. He therefore decided that the water was the cause of his getting drunk because it was the common element each time. This method, as you can see, is inadequate for unequivocally identifying causation because many significant variables, such as the alcohol in the rye, scotch, and bourbon, may be overlooked.

Method of agreement
The identification of the common element in several instances of an event

The second canon is the **Method of Difference.** In this method, one attempts to identify causality by observing the different effects produced in two situations that are alike in all respects except one. The method of difference is the approach taken in many psychological experiments. In an experiment designed to test the effect of a drug on reaction time, the drug is given to one group of subjects while a placebo is given to another group of matched subjects. If the reaction time of the drug group differs significantly from that of the placebo group, the difference is usually attributed to the drug (the causal agent). This method provides the basis for a great deal of work in psychology aimed at identifying causality.

Method of difference
The identification of the different effects produced by variation in only one event

The third canon set forth by Mill is the **Joint Methods of Agreement and Difference.** This method is exactly what the name implies. The method of agreement is first used to observe common elements, which are then formulated as hypotheses to be tested by the method of difference. In the case of the man who wanted to find out why he got drunk, the common element of water should have been formulated as a hypothesis to be tested by the method of difference. Using the method of difference, researchers would give one group of subjects water and a matched group another liquid (such as straight bourbon). Naturally, the group drinking only water would not get drunk, indicating that the wrong variable had been identified even though it was a common element.

Joint methods of agreement and difference
The combination of the methods of agreement and difference to identify causation

The fourth canon is the **Method of Concomitant Variation.** This method states that a variable is either a cause or an effect or else is connected through some factor of causation if variation in the variable results in a parallel variation in another variable. Plutchik (1974) interprets this canon to be an extension of the method of difference in that, rather than just using two equated groups in an experiment, the researchers use three or more, with each one receiving a different amount of the variable under study. In the previously cited drug example, rather than just a placebo group and a drug group, one placebo and several drug groups could be used, with each drug group receiving a different amount of the drug. Reaction times could then be observed to determine if variation in the drug results in a parallel variation in reaction time. If this parallel variation is found, then the drug is interpreted as being the cause of the variation in reaction time. Others interpret this canon as also including correlation studies. When including correlational studies under this canon, one is on extremely shaky ground in attempting to infer causative relationships, since most correlational studies represent descriptions of degree of relationship. Identification of causation requires direct manipulation of the variables of interest. However, recent work is making strides in enabling causation to be inferred from correlational studies.

Method of concomitant variation
The identification of parallel changes in two variables

When looking at the works of people like Mill, one gets the idea that we have a fairly adequate grasp of what causation is and how to obtain evidence of it. This belief is further confirmed when we see that the way in which experiments to obtain evidence of causation are conducted tends to follow the canons set forth by Mill. However, such philosophizing and experimentation have not completely clarified the meaning of the word "cause."

Exhibit 2.1, which presents Morison's (1960, pp. 193–194) discussion of the history of attempts to find the cause of malaria, illustrates the ambiguity of this word.

Exhibit 2.1   *Morison's discussion of the history of attempts to find the cause of malaria.*

Whatever the reason, medical men have found it congenial to assume that they could find something called *The Cause* of a particular disease. If one looks at the history of any particular disease, one finds that the notion of its cause has varied with the state of the art. In general, the procedure has been to select as *The Cause* that element in the situation which one could do the most about. In many cases it turned out that, if one could take away this element or reduce its influence, the disease simply disappeared or was reduced in severity. This was certainly desirable, and it seemed sensible enough to say that one had got at the cause of the condition. Thus in ancient and medieval times malaria as its name implied was thought to be due to the bad air of the lowlands. As a result, towns were built on the tops of hills, as one notices in much of Italy today. The disease did not disappear, but its incidence and severity were reduced to a level consistent with productive community life.

At this stage it seemed reasonable enough to regard bad air as the cause of malaria, but soon the introduction of quinine to Europe from South America suggested another approach. Apparently quinine acted on some situation within the patient to relieve and often to cure him completely. Toward the end of the last century the malaria parasite was discovered in the blood of patients suffering from the disease. The effectiveness of quinine was explained by its ability to eliminate this parasite from the blood. The parasite now became *The Cause,* and those who could afford the cost of quinine and were reasonably regular in their habits were enabled to escape the most serious ravages of the disease. It did not disappear as a public health problem, however; and further study was given to the chain of causality. These studies were shortly rewarded by the discovery that the parasite was transmitted by certain species of mosquitoes. For practical purposes *The Cause* of epidemic malaria became the Mosquito, and attention was directed to control of its activities.

Entertainingly enough, however, malaria has disappeared from large parts of the world without anyone doing much about it at all. The fens of Boston and other northern cities still produce mosquitoes capable of transmitting the parasite, and people carrying the organism still come to these areas from time to time; but it has been many decades since the last case of the disease occurred locally. Observations such as this point to the probability that epidemic malaria is the result of a nicely balanced set of social and economic, as well as biological, factors, each one of which has to be present at the appropriate level. We are still completely unable to describe these sufficient conditions with any degree of accuracy, but we know what to do in an epidemic area because we have focused attention on three or four of the most necessary ones.

(From Morison, R. S. "Gradualness, gradualness, gradualness" (I. P. Pavlov). *American Psychologist,* 1960, *15,* 187–198.)

This example of the problems encountered in naming the cause of malaria should illustrate the difficulty involved in using techniques such as Mill's canons to identify causation. Essentially, the method of agreement was used first to hypothesize that the bad air in the lowlands caused malaria because the common element that seemed to exist for individuals living on top of the hills was better air. However, subsequent investigation using the method of difference revealed that only individuals with the malaria parasite in their blood suffered from the disease. The problem with this explanation is that it did not explain how the parasite came to exist in the bloodstream, until it was found that the mosquito transmitted it. As you can see, the various canons set forth by Mill enable us to identify the relationships that exist among a set of variables. However, they do not help us to name the *one* factor that causes an effect just as they did not enable scientists to identify the one factor that caused malaria. This is because the identification of causation should exist when *no* alternative interpretations for an effect exist other than the one specified. When we have reached this stage, we have essentially identified both the necessary and the sufficient conditions for the occurrence of an event. A **necessary condition** refers to a condition that must be present in order for the effect to occur. To become an alcoholic, you must consume alcohol. A **sufficient condition** refers to a condition that will always produce the effect. Destroying the auditory nerve always results in a loss of hearing.

Necessary condition
A condition that must exist for an effect to result

Sufficient condition
A condition that will always produce the effect under study

A condition must be both necessary and sufficient to qualify as a cause, because under such a situation the effect would never occur unless the condition were present and whenever the condition was present the effect would occur. If a condition were only *sufficient,* then the effect could occur in other ways. There are several ways one can lose one's hearing in addition to destruction of the auditory nerve. In like manner, a necessary condition does not mean that the effect will necessarily occur. All people who consume alcohol do not become alcoholics; however, one must have consumed alcohol to become an alcoholic.

To state that we have found the cause for an event means that both the *necessary* and the *sufficient* conditions have been found. It means that a complete explanation of the occurrence of the event has been isolated and that *no change* in the explanation, unlike that noted with the malaria example, *will ever occur.*

It is, however, rather presumptuous to assume that we will ever find the conditions necessary and sufficient for the occurrence of an event, since the behavior of organisms is extremely complex. Seldom do we encounter situations or behaviors that cannot be explained in several different ways. Popper (1968) has perhaps been most explicit in his insistence on the necessity of ruling out alternative explanations. According to inductive logic, science must be capable of deciding between the truth and falsity of hypotheses and theories. In other words, if we conduct a scientific experiment testing the hypothesis that depression can be treated with psychotherapy, we should be able to decide if this hypothesis is true or false. Popper rejects the notion of such inductive logic. He maintains that we cannot use the results of one or even several scientific experiments to infer that a given hypothesis or theory is true, or proven. Even if five experiments reveal the success of treating depressives with psychotherapy, one does not have proof that psychotherapy can successfully treat depressives. The attained relationship could be due to flaws in the experiment or to unknown variables operating simultaneously with the psychotherapy. To Popper, a confirmation of an experiment only states that the hypothesis or theory that has been tested has survived the test. On the other hand, if the experiment fails to confirm a prediction or a theory, the prediction or theory being tested is falsified. Therefore, Popper focuses attention on a **position of falsification** rather than a position of confirmation. For him, a theory or prediction can only achieve the status of "not yet disconfirmed"; it can never be proven. In other words, if an experiment supports the prediction that psychotherapy is beneficial in treating depressives, Popper would state that this prediction has maintained the status of not yet disconfirmed instead of stating that the prediction has been confirmed. However, this status of not yet disconfirmed is very precious in science because it means that the theory or prediction passed the test of rigorous experimentation and thus only states one of the possible true explanations.

Position of falsification
The belief that the best position a theory or prediction can attain is one of "not yet falsified"

Deese (1972) provides yet another view of causation. He views causation as a large network of cause-and-effect relations. Any given cause-and-effect relation that is isolated in a study is only one such relation embedded in a matrix of others. Consider the case of Morison's discussion of malaria, in which he illustrates the covariation between a number of events and malaria, which would be considered a specific cause-and-effect relationship. The bad air of the lowlands was found to covary with the incidence of malaria. Later it was found that the presence of a parasite covaried with the appearance of malaria, and even later it was found that a certain species of mosquito caused malaria because it carried the malaria parasite. Note that a number of specific cause-and-effect relationships, in terms of covariation of events, were involved in the history of trying to identify the cause of malaria. However, it is also apparent that none of these specific relationships could be labeled as the cause of malaria, since many of the so-called causative events (such as the mosquitoes) still exist and yet the presumed effect of malaria no longer occurs. Such a state of affairs suggests, as Morison pointed out, that a nicely balanced system of interrelated conditions must exist for a given effect to occur. For malaria to occur, the mosquitoes and parasites must exist in a system of other specific social economic conditions. Any one condition by itself is not sufficient to produce the effect. Proponents of this view of causation advocate study of the relationship among the levels or amounts of the variables operating within a system rather than focusing on the covariation between one variable, which can be labeled the cause, and another, which can be labeled the effect. Such a viewpoint sees any given study as representing only a small part of the overall system, and the relationship found in a given study exists only if certain relationships exist among the remainder of the elements of the system.

It is clear that causation is subject to quite a bit of debate. [Brand (1976) provides a detailed discussion of this debate.] Where does this leave the psychologist who is attempting to identify causal relations? The behavior of organisms is extremely complex and multidetermined. Consequently, behavior rarely—if ever—is caused by one event. Therefore, not only is it impossible in most instances to name "the" cause of an event, but in reality a single cause for a behavior seldom exists. Given this state of affairs, we must conduct our scientific investigations in a manner that will enable us to identify most of the interacting causes rather than attempting to find the single cause of an event or given behavior.

Summary

The descriptive approach to gaining scientific knowledge differs from the experimental approach in that the practitioner attempts to paint a picture of a particular phenomenon. There are three basic research approaches used in attaining this objective. In naturalistic observation one tries to fulfill this objective by unobtrusively observing and recording naturally occurring behavior. In field studies, one generates a description by collecting data through use of the survey, by conducting a correlational study, or by conducting a longitudinal or cross-sectional study. Ex post facto studies accomplish the same goal by describing the relationship that exists between a given behavior and a variable on which groups of subjects naturally differ, such as skin color. Although ex post facto studies resemble experimental studies, they are not the same because the experimenter does not have control over the manipulated variable. However, it is not uncommon to find a study that includes both an ex post facto component and an experimental component.

The experimental approach is the research method in which one attempts to identify cause-and-effect relationships by conducting an experiment. The psychological experiment achieves the goal of the experimental approach by allowing one to observe, under controlled conditions, the effects of systematically varying one or more variables. The experimental approach has the primary advantage of providing for control of extraneous variables. Other advantages are that it permits one to manipulate precisely one or more variables, produces lasting results, suggests new studies, and suggests solutions to practical problems. Although the experimental approach has these excellent features, it also has the disadvantages of creating an artificial environment and frequently being difficult to design and time consuming.

The experimental approach is used in both field and laboratory settings. Using a field setting, the experimenter conducts an experiment in a real-life situation and therefore avoids the criticism of having created an artificial environment. However, one typically does not have as much control over extraneous variables. In a laboratory setting, the experimenter brings the subjects into the laboratory, where there is maximum control over extraneous variables. However, this usually means that an artificial environment has been created.

Causation is a concept that is little understood, and yet it is causative relationships that the experimental method attempts to identify. John Stuart Mill set forth four canons—the methods of agreement, difference, and concomitant variation and the joint methods of agreement and difference—which he said could be used in identifying causation. However, in order for one to be able to state that *the* cause of a given effect has been found, this condition must qualify as being both necessary and sufficient. Since behavior is multidetermined, it is highly unlikely that we can overrule all possible alternative explanations for behaviors. This is why Popper rejects the confirmationists' position and takes the position of falsification, stating that the best status a theory can attain is one of "not yet disconfirmed." Deese believes that causal relations are embedded in a matrix of other causal relations. A given relationship between a cause and effect will continue to exist only if all the other variables within the matrix or system remain constant.

3

Problem Identification and Hypothesis Formation

Chapter Overview

The first stage in conducting an experimental research study is the identification of a problem in need of a solution. It does not take an astute observer to realize that many such problems exist; every day we encounter a variety of them, particularly through the news media. We hear of toxic waste contaminating the soil or drinking water of communities, of cancer afflicting thousands of individuals, and even of new disorders, such as Acquired Immune Deficiency Syndrome (AIDS), suddenly arising. It is not as though people are not aware of problems that need to be solved. However, some individuals have trouble singling out a problem that they are capable of investigating.

This chapter will attempt to minimize such difficulties by informing you of the origin of researchable problems and how to begin to convert the problem you have identified into one that can be investigated by the experimental research approach. As you read this chapter, you should answer the following questions:

1. Where can I find researchable problems?

2. How can I find out what is currently known about the research problem I have identified?

3. How should I specify my research problem?

4. Should I formulate a hypothesis relating to my research problem?

Introduction

Up to this point in the text, I have discussed the general characteristics of the scientific method and the two basic approaches to using this method of inquiry. However, use of either of these two approaches requires that we first have a problem in need of a solution. Within the field of psychology, identification of a research idea should be relatively simple because psychology is the scientific study of behavior—including human behavior. Our behavior represents the focus of attention of a great deal of psychological investigation. To convert our observations of our own behavior and that of others into legitimate research questions, we must be inquisitive and ask ourselves why we see certain types of behavior occur. For example, assume that you hear a person express an extremely resentful, hostile, and prejudiced attitude toward Russians. The next day you see this person interacting with a Russian and note that they are both being very polite and courteous. You have seen a contradiction between the attitude expressed by this individual and her behavior. Two well-founded research questions would be "Why is there a lack of correspondence between attitude and behavior?" and "Under what circumstance do attitudes *not* predict behavior?"

Everyday life issues do not represent the only sources of research questions; let us now take a look at the major sources that can be used to generate such questions.

Sources of Research Ideas

Where do ideas or problems originate? Where should we look for a researchable problem? In all fields, there are a number of common sources of problems, such as existing theories and past research. We are even more fortunate in psychology; we have our own personal experience and everyday events to draw on. The things we see, read about, or hear about can serve as ideas to be turned into a research topic. However, the identification of these ideas as research topics requires an alert and curious scientist. Rather than just passively observing behavior or reading material relating to psychology, we must actively question the reasons for the occurrence of an event or of a certain behavior. If you ask the question "Why?" you will find many researchable topics. A brief glance at the *Psychological Abstract Index* provides an indication of the many areas within psychology that have unsolved problems. The four sources from which problems typically originate are theory, everyday life, practical issues, and past research.

Theory

A **theory,** defined as "a group of logically organized (deductively related) laws" (Marx, 1963, p. 9), is supposed to serve a number of distinct functions. Marx states that theory is both a tool and a goal. The goal function is evidenced by the proposition that laws are ordered and integrated by theories; theories summarize and integrate existing knowledge. The tool function is evidenced by the proposition that theories guide research. This is the function of interest to us. A good theory goes beyond the goal function to suggest new relationships and

Theory
A group of logically organized and deductively related laws

to make new predictions. Thus, it serves as a source of researchable ideas.

Leon Festinger's (1957) theory of cognitive dissonance is an example of a theory that stimulated an extraordinary amount of research in the decade that followed its publication. From this theory, Festinger and Carlsmith (1959) hypothesized and validated the nonobvious prediction that, after completing a boring task, subjects who were given $1 to tell a "stooge" that the boring task was interesting and fun actually stated that they enjoyed the task more than did the subjects who were given $20 to do the same thing.

Everyday Life

As we proceed through the daily routine dictated by our current point in life, we come into contact with many phenomena that pose questions in need of solution; parents want to know how to handle their children, students want to know how to learn material faster. When we interact with others or see others react, we note many individual differences. When one is observing children on a playground, these differences are readily apparent. One child may be very aggressive, while another is much more reserved, waiting for others to encourage interaction. The responses of a particular person also vary according to the situation. A child who is very aggressive in one situation may be very passive in another. Why do these differences exist not only among children but also within the same child? What produces these varying responses? Why are some people leaders and others followers? Why do we like some people and not others? There are many such researchable questions that can be identified from the interactions and personal experiences that everyone has.

In the late 1960s, Darley and Latané (1968) began a series of investigations that epitomize the use of life's experiences and the events taking place around us as a source of research problems. They were concerned about the fact that bystanders frequently do not lend assistance in emergency situations. A case in point is the often-cited incident involving Kitty Genovese, who was stabbed to death in New York City. There were 38 witnesses to the longer than half-hour attack, and no one even called the police. Many other similar and more recent cases can be recounted. For example, a woman was raped by four men on a bar-room pool table while onlookers cheered her attackers on. In St. Louis, a 13-year-old girl was raped by two youths as several adults stood around and watched. It took a 13-year-old boy to finally summon the police. Darley and Latané asked why. They began a series of experimental studies to investigate the conditions that facilitate or inhibit bystander intervention in emergency situations.

Practical Issues

Many experimental problems arise from practical issues that require solution. Private industry faces problems such as employee morale, absenteeism, turnover, selection, and placement, to name only a few. Work is, has been, and will continue to be conducted in these areas. Clinical psychology is in need of a great deal of research to identify more efficient modes of dealing with mental disturbances. Units of the federal and state governments also support experimentation designed to solve practical problems. The government is spending large sums of money to find a cure for cancer. Large expenditures are also being directed toward finding better ways to conduct the educational process.

Law enforcement agencies are concerned not only with obtaining accurate eyewitness testimony but also with extracting leads or clues from eyewitnesses. To that end, these agencies are now using hypnosis, under the assumption that hypnosis can extract accurate evidence that otherwise would not be available. However, the validity of such an assumption was not tested until recently. Sanders and Simmons (1983) asked eyewitnesses, some of whom were hypnotized and some of whom were not hypnotized, to identify a thief from a lineup. As Figure 3.1 reveals, hypnotized subjects, contrary to expectations, identified the thief *fewer* times than did the subjects who were not hypnotized. Such evidence suggests that hypnosis is not an effective technique for extracting accurate evidence.

Past Research

Previously conducted experiments are an excellent source of research ideas. This may sound like a contradiction, since research is designed to answer questions, but one of the interesting features about research is that it tends to generate more questions than it asks. Although each well-designed study does provide additional knowledge, phenomena are multidetermined. In any experiment, only a limited number of variables can be studied. Investigation of certain variables may lead to hypotheses about the effects of other variables. The multidimensional nature of phenomena is also frequently the cause of lack of agreement between experimental results. An unidentified variable may be the source of conflict between various studies on a given problem, and experiments must be conducted to uncover this variable and thereby eliminate the apparent contradiction.

To illustrate what has just been said, consider the study conducted by Mellgren, Seybert, and Dyck (1978). They investigated the influence of presenting different orders of schedules of continuous reinforcement, nonreinforcement, and partial reinforcement on resistance to extinction. Prior research had revealed conflicting results when resistance to extinction of subjects who had received continuous reward and

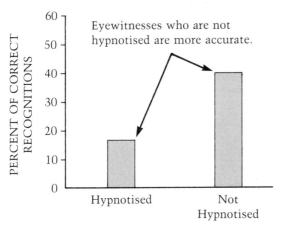

Figure 3.1 *Accuracy of eyewitness identification as a function of being hypnotized.*

Eyewitnesses who are not hypnotised are more accurate.

PERCENT OF CORRECT RECOGNITIONS

60 —
50 —
40 —
30 —
20 —
10 —
0 —

Hypnotised   Not Hypnotised

STATE OF THE EYEWITNESS

(Based on data from Sanders and Simmons, *Journal of Applied Psychology*, 1983, 68, 70–77.)

then partial reward was compared to that of subjects given only partial reward schedules. Some studies indicated that resistance to extinction decreased, others indicated that it increased, and still others showed that the existence of an increase or a decrease in resistance to extinction depended on the stage of extinction. Mellgren et al. attempted to resolve this inconsistency. Results of their study revealed that greatest resistance to extinction occurred when a large number of nonreinforced trials preceded a partial reinforcement schedule. Therefore, this study showed which schedule produced the greatest resistance to extinction. But it left other questions unanswered. The study, for example, did not provide an explanation as to why resistance to extinction was increased if a large number of nonreinforced trials preceded partial reinforcement. This led to another study which attempted to answer this new question. As you can see, each study leads to a subsequent study, and so people have spent their whole lives investigating a particular area. Research is an ongoing process.

Review of the Literature

After a topic of research has been obtained from one of the sources just mentioned, the next step in the research process is to become familiar with the information available on the topic. Practically all psychological problems have had some prior work conducted on them.

At this point you might be asking yourself, "Why should I review the literature on my selected topic? Why not just proceed to the laboratory and find an answer to the problem?" There are several good reasons to do one's homework in the form of a literature review prior to conducting any experimentation. The general purpose of the library search is to gain an understanding of the current state of knowledge about the selected topic. Specifically, a review of the literature will tell you if the problem you have identified has already been researched. If it has, you should either revise the problem in light of the experimental results or look for another problem. If the topic you have identified has not been investigated, related studies may indicate how you should proceed in attempting to reach an answer to the problem. A literature review should also point out methodological problems specific to the area of study. Are special control groups or special pieces of equipment needed to conduct the research? If so, the literature can give clues as to where to attain the equipment or how to identify the particular groups of subjects needed. These are just a few of the more salient reasons for conducting a review of the literature.

Assuming that you are convinced of the necessity of a literature review, you are now probably asking, "Where do I look? What sources should be investigated?" There are two primary sources that should be investigated when reviewing the literature: books dealing with the topic of interest and psychological journals. Although these are the two standard sources of information, additional sources are also available. Helmstadter (1970, Chapter 5) presents an extremely thorough review of the sources available for conducting the literature review.

Books

Books have been written about most, if not all, of the areas in psychology. These texts should be examined for material relating to the research topic. The pertinent material may consist of actual information or may point to where information can be obtained. One book that is frequently very useful is the *Annual Review of Psychology*. Published yearly since 1950, this book presents an in-depth discussion by an expert of the principal work done during the preceding year on a variety of topics. One of the topics may relate to your own, so it is worthwhile to check this source.

Psychological Journals

Most of the pertinent information about a research topic is usually found in the psychological journals. Frequently, a review that has started with books leads to the journals. Since books are generally the outgrowth of work cited in journals, this progression from books back to journals is a natural one.

How should one proceed in reviewing the work cited in the journals? A survey of the number of psychological journals reveals that it

Exhibit 3.1   *Procedure for Use of* Psychological Abstracts

Each monthly issue of *Psychological Abstracts* contains summaries listed under 16 major classification categories. These abstracts are indexed according to subject and author. Each separate issue is indexed, and an expanded and integrated *volume index* is published every six months. Use of this volume index will enable you to use your time most efficiently.

The following procedure is recommended for conducting a literature search on a specific topic:

A. Obtain a copy of the *Thesaurus of Psychological Index Terms* from the library, and identify the terms that relate to your research topic. This reference is excellent as a beginning point because the subject index terms used in *Psychological Abstracts* are taken from it.

B. In the subject index section of the volume index of *Psychological Abstracts*, find each term that you identified in the *Thesaurus of Psychological Index Terms*, and read the entries below that term. Each entry will consist of a concise statement of an article's contents, as in the following example:

Subject index
Ability Level

Concise statement of the article

uncertainty about ability as related to academic performance in 4th- and 8th-grade females, 55731

Number of the abstract

The number following the description of the article refers to the number of the abstract.

C. From the description of each article, identify those that may be related to your research topic, and record the numbers corresponding to the abstracts.

D. Find the abstract of the article corresponding to each number you recorded. This is accomplished by finding the number you have recorded in the body of *Psychological Abstracts*, since this number identifies the abstract you selected:

Abstract number

55731. Doe, John B. The influence of uncertainty on academic performance. *Journal of Educational Excellence*, 1983, 19, 476–483. Investigated 4th- and 8th-grade female students' academic performance as a function of their own perceptions of academic ability. Results revealed no difference in 4th-grade students as a function of perceived academic ability. However, 8th-grade students who were unsure of their academic abilities did not perform as well as did 8th-grade students who gave their academic abilities a high evaluation. (15 ref.)— *Journal Abstract.*

From this hypothetical entry, you can see that the abstract not only gives you a brief synopsis of the article but also tells you where you can locate the article and who authored the article. Such information should be sufficient to enable you to decide if the article might be of value to you.

E. Record the references of the articles that are related to your research topic so you can find the journals in which the articles were published.

would be an impossible task to go through each and every journal looking for relevant information. This is where *Psychological Abstracts* comes in. **Psychological Abstracts** is a journal consisting of brief abstracts (summaries) of published articles, books, and so forth from sources throughout the world but predominently within the United States. This journal contains abstracts of over 950 journal and technical reports, monographs, and other scientific documents. Exhibit 3.1 pro-

Psychological Abstracts
A journal that contains abstracts of books, journal and technical reports, monographs, and other scientific documents

vides a brief outline of the way in which one should proceed when using *Psychological Abstracts*. By following the steps specified in Exhibit 3.1, you should be able to obtain a workable list of articles pertaining to your study.

Information Retrieval Systems

Books and journals have been identified as the basic sources of information regarding a topic. However, the tradition of each individual investigator's going to the library and manually performing a comprehensive literature search is becoming less and less practical. The impracticality of this approach is due to the so-called information explosion. Helmstadter states that the number of published research articles doubles about every ten years. The validity of such a statement can be seen just by looking at the increase in size of *Psychological Abstracts*. The volumes have more than doubled in size in the past ten years. Such an explosion of knowledge has drastically increased the amount of time and energy necessary to identify and record the results of relevant studies.

In an effort to overcome such problems, a number of attempts have been made to provide a comprehensive information storage and retrieval system. The one of importance for the psychologist is **PASAR,** *Psychological Abstracts* Search and Retrieval. PASAR, a nonprofit organization operated by the American Psychological Association, had a data base of 417,806 records as of 1983, and this data base has been growing at a rate of over 2400 records per month. For a fee ranging from about $40 to $60, PASAR will search its records and provide you with a list of relevant publications. A search of material earlier than 1967 still has to be conducted by the individual investigator. PASAR forms are located in the back of *Psychological Abstracts*. The investigator desiring to use this service can make a copy of this form, fill it in, and send it to the address given on the form.

PASAR
The comprehensive information storage and retrieval system operated by the American Psychological Association

There are additional information centers and exchanges in existence, such as ERIC (Educational Resources Information Center). However, these additional sources are more specific in purpose. Because of its general orientation, PASAR seems to be the primary source for the student. For a description of these other sources, see Helmstadter (1970).

Additional Information Sources

The regional and national psychological association meetings are an excellent source of *current* information. I emphasize *current* because of the publication lag that exists in journals and books. A research study that appears in these sources may be several years old. Studies presented at professional meetings are typically much more recent. An additional advantage of securing information at professional meetings is that you can frequently interact with the investigator. Exchanging ideas with this individual will frequently generate added enthusiasm and many more research ideas.

Many times, the beginning researcher also returns from meetings with renewed confidence in his or her developing research skills. The novice frequently feels that researchers at other institutions are more skilled or more adept at research. Attending professional meetings can illustrate that others use the same techniques and skills that he or she has acquired.

Information can also be gained from direct communication with colleagues. It is not unusual for one researcher to call or write another to inquire about current studies or methodological techniques.

Formulation of the Research Problem

You should now be prepared to make a clear and exact statement of the specific problem to be investigated. The literature review has revealed not only what is currently known about the problem but also the ways in which the problem has been attacked in the past. Such information is a tremendous aid in formulating the problem and in indicating how and by what methods the data should be collected. Unfortunately, novices sometimes jump from the selection of a research topic to the data collection stage, leaving the problem unspecified until after data collection. They thus run the risk of not obtaining information on the problem of interest. An exact definition of the problem is very important because it guides the research process.

Definition of a Research Problem

What is a **research problem?** Kerlinger (1973, p. 17) defines a problem as "an interrogative sentence or statement that asks: 'What relation exists between two or more variables?' " For example, Milgram (1964) asked the question "Can a group induce a person to deliver punishment of increasing severity to a protesting individual?" This statement conforms to the definition of a problem, since it contains two variables—group pressure and severity of punishment delivered—and asks a question regarding the relation between these variables.

Research problem
An interrogative sentence that states the relationship between two variables

Are all problems that conform to the definition good research problems? Assume that you posed the problem "How do we know that God influences our behavior?" This question meets the definition of a problem, but it obviously cannot be tested. Kerlinger (1973) presents three criteria that good problems must meet. First, the variables in the problem should express a relation. This criterion, as you can see, was contained in the definition of a problem. The second criterion is that the problem should be stated in question form. The statement of the problem should begin with "What is the effect of," "Under what conditions do," "Does the effect of," or some similar form. Sometimes only the purpose of a study is stated, which does not necessarily communicate the problem to be investigated. The purpose of the Milgram study was to investigate the effect of group pressure on a person's behavior. Asking a question has the benefit of presenting the problem directly, and in this way interpretation and distortion are minimized. The third criterion, and the one that most frequently distinguishes a researchable from a nonresearchable problem, states that "The problem statement should be such as to imply possibilities of empirical testing" (p. 18). Many interesting and important questions fail to meet this criterion and therefore are not amenable to scientific inquiry. Quite a few philosophical and theological questions fall into this category. Milgram's problem meets all of these criteria. A relation was expressed between the variables, the problem was stated in question form, and it was possible to empirically test the problem. Severity of punishment was measured by the amount of electricity supposedly delivered to the protesting individual, and group pressure was applied by having two confederates suggest increasingly higher shock levels.

Specificity of the Question

In formulating a problem, **specificity of the research question** is an important consideration. Think of the difficulties facing the experimenter asking the following question: "What effect does the environment have on learning ability?" This question meets all the criteria of a problem, and yet it is stated in such a vague way that the investigator could not pinpoint what was to be investigated. The concepts of environment and learning ability are vague (what environmental characteristics? learning of what?). The experimenter must specify what is meant by environment and by learning ability to be able to conduct the experiment. Contrast this question which the following: "What effect does the amount of exposure to words have on the speed with which they are learned?" This question specifies exactly what the problem is.

The two examples of questions presented in the preceding paragraph demonstrate the advantages of formulating a specific problem. A specific statement helps to ensure that the experimenters understand the problem. If the problem is vaguely stated, the experimenters probably do not know exactly what they want to study and therefore may design a study that will not provide a solution to the problem. A specific problem statement also assists in the decisions that must be

Specificity of the research question
The preciseness with which the research question is stated

made about such factors as subjects, apparatus, instruments, and measures. A vague problem statement helps very little with such decisions. To drive this point home, go back and reread the questions given in the preceding paragraph and ask yourself, "What subjects should I use? What measures should I use? What apparatus or instruments should I use?"

How specific should one be in formulating a question? The primary purposes of formulating the problem in question form are to ensure that the researcher has a good grasp of the variables to be investigated and to aid the experimenter in designing and carrying out the experiment. If the formulation of the question is pointed enough to serve these purposes, then additional specificity is not needed. To the extent that these purposes are not met, additional specifity and narrowing of the research problem are required. Therefore, the degree of specificity required is dependent on the purpose of the problem statement.

Formulating Hypotheses

After the literature review has been completed and the problem has been stated in question form, you should begin formulating your **hypothesis.** For example, if you were investigating the influence of the number of bystanders on the speed of intervention in emergency situations, you might hypothesize that as the number of bystanders increases, the speed of intervention will decrease. From this sample, you can see that hypotheses represent predictions of the relation that exists among the variables, or tentative solutions to the problem. Formulation of the hypothesis logically follows the statement of the problem, since one could not state a hypothesis without having a problem. This does not mean that the problem is always explicitly stated. In fact, if you survey articles published in journals, you will find that most of the authors do not present a statement of their specific problem. It seems that experienced researchers in a given field have such familiarity with the field that they consider the problems to be self-evident. Their predicted solutions to these problems are not apparent, however, and so these are stated.

The hypothesis to be tested is often a function of the literature review. However, this is not the only source of hypotheses; they are also frequently formulated from theory. As stated earlier, theories guide research, and one of the ways in which they do so is by making predictions of possible relationships among variables. Hypotheses also (but less frequently) come from reasoning based on casual observation of events. There are some situations in which it seems to be fruitless even to attempt to formulate hypotheses. When one is engaged in explor-

Hypothesis
The best prediction or a tentative solution to a problem

atory work in a relatively new area where the important variables and their relationships are not known, hypotheses serve little purpose.

More than one hypothesis can almost always be formulated as the probable solution to the problem. Here again the literature review can be an aid, because a review of prior research can suggest the most probable relationships that may exist among the variables.

Regardless of the source of the hypothesis, it *must* meet one criterion: a hypothesis must be stated so that it is capable of being either refuted or confirmed. In an experiment, it is the hypothesis that is being tested and not the problem. One does not test a question such as the one Milgram posed; rather, one tests one or more of the hypotheses that could be derived from this question, such as "group pressure increases the severity of punishment that subjects will administer." A hypothesis that fails to meet the criterion of testability, or is nontestable, removes the problem from the realm of science. Any conclusions reached regarding a nontestable hypothesis do not represent scientific knowledge.

A distinction must be made between the scientific hypothesis and the null hypothesis. The **scientific hypothesis** represents the predicted relationship among the variables being investigated. The **null hypothesis** represents a statement of no relationships among the variables being investigated. For example, Hashtroudi et al. (1983) wanted to explore the nature of the memory deficits that occur through the influence of alcohol. One of the research questions asked by these investigators was whether the memory deficit induced by alcohol is decreased when intoxicated individuals are forced to generate a meaningful context for the word that is to be recalled. Although not specifically stated, these investigators' scientific hypothesis was that the generation of a meaningful context would reduce the memory deficit produced by the alcohol. The null hypothesis predicted that no difference in recall would be found between intoxicated subjects who generated the meaningful context and those who did not.

Scientific hypothesis
The predicted relationship among the variables being investigated

Null hypothesis
A statement of no relationship among the variables being investigated

Although an experimental study would seem to be directed toward testing the scientific hypothesis, such is not the case. In any study, it is the null hypothesis that is always tested, because the scientific hypothesis does not specify the exact amount or type of influence that is expected. To obtain support for the scientific hypothesis, you must collect evidence that enables you to reject the null hypothesis (in the Hashtroudi et al. study, to reject the notion that no difference is found in the recall scores of those intoxicated subjects who did and those who did not use a meaningful context). Consequently, support for the scientific hypothesis is always obtained indirectly by rejecting the null hypothesis. The exact reason for testing the null hypothesis as opposed to the scientific hypothesis is based on statistical hypothesis testing theory, which is beyond the scope of the present text, but basically the point is that it is necessary to test the null hypothesis so as to obtain evidence that will allow you to reject it in order to indirectly get evidence supportive of the scientific hypothesis.

At times individuals wonder why hypotheses should be set up in the first place. Why not just proceed to attempt to answer the question and forget about hypotheses? Hypotheses serve a valuable function. Remember that hypotheses are derived from knowledge obtained from the literature review of other experiments, theories, and so forth. Such prior knowledge serves as the basis for the hypothesis. If the experiment confirms the hypothesis, then, in addition to providing an answer to the question asked, it gives additional support to the literature that suggested the hypothesis. But what if the hypothesis is not confirmed by the experiment? Does this invalidate the prior literature? If the hypothesis is not confirmed, then either the hypothesis is false or some error exists in the conception of the hypothesis. If there is an error in conceptualization, it could be in any of a number of categories. Some of the information obtained from prior experiments may be false, or some relevant information may have been overlooked in the literature review. It is also possible that the experimenter misinterpreted some of the literature. These are a few of the more salient errors that could have taken place. In any event, failure to support a hypothesis may indicate that something is wrong, and it is up to the experimenter to discover what it is. Once the experimenter uncovers what he or she thinks is wrong, a new hypothesis is made to be tested experimentally. The experimenter now has another study to conduct. Such is the continuous process of science. Even if the hypothesis is false, knowledge has been advanced, for now we know an incorrect hypothesis that can be ruled out. We must formulate another hypothesis to test in order to reach a solution to the problem.

Summary

In order to conduct research, it is first necessary to identify a problem that is in need of a solution. Psychological problems arise from the rather traditional sources of theories, practical issues, and past research. Additionally, in psychology we have our own personal experience to draw on for researchable problems, since psychological research is concerned with behavior. Once a researchable problem has been identified, one needs to review the literature relevant to this problem. A literature review will give you an understanding of the current state of knowledge about your selected topic. It will indicate ways of investigating the problem as well as point out related methodological problems. The literature review should probably begin with books written on the topic and progress from there to the actual research as reported in journals. In surveying the past research conducted on a topic, one can make use of one of the many information retrieval systems now in existence, one of which is operated by the American Psychological Association. In addition to using these sources of information, one can also obtain related information by attending conventions or by actually calling or writing other individuals conducting research on the given topic.

Once the literature review has been completed, the experimenter must make a clear and exact statement of the problem to be investigated. This means that the experimenter must formulate an interrogative sentence asking about the relationship between two or more variables. This interrogative sentence must express a relation and be capable of being tested empirically. The question must also be specific enough to assist the experimenter in making decisions regarding such factors as subjects, apparatus, and general design of the study.

Once the question has been stated, the experimenter needs to set down hypotheses. These must be formalized, because they represent the predicted relation that exists among the variables under study. Hypotheses frequently are a function of past research, and if they are confirmed, the results not only answer the question asked but provide additional support to the literature that suggested the hypotheses. There is one criterion that any hypothesis must meet: it must be stated so that it is capable of being either refuted or confirmed. Always remember that it is actually the null hypothesis and not the scientific hypothesis that is being tested in a study.

4

Variables Used in Experimentation

Chapter Overview

Once the research problem has been specified and the hypothesis has been formulated, you are ready to design the experiment. In other words, you now decide on the plan, outline, or strategy to be used in obtaining a solution to the research problem. Designing an experiment requires you to make a variety of decisions. You must choose the variables that are to be investigated in the experiment, the variables that may introduce a confounding influence, and the techniques that must be employed in order to eliminate such a confounding influence. Only when such decisions have been made can you describe the final design of the experiment. This chapter will focus attention on the specification

and formulation of the independent variable and the dependent variable, since these are the two variables that must be included in any experiment. As you read this chapter, you should attempt to answer the following questions:

1. What are independent and dependent variables?

2. How do I formulate an independent and a dependent variable?

3. How many independent and dependent variables should I use in a study?

4. What factors should be considered when specifying the independent and the dependent variables?

Introduction

One of the first decisions that must be made after the research problem and the hypothesis have been specified is which variable or variables are to serve as the independent variable and which variable or variables are to serve as the dependent variable. By **variable** I mean any characteristic of an organism, environment, or experimental situation that can vary from one organism to another, from one environment to another, or from one experimental situation to another. Therefore, independent and dependent variables can be any of the numerous characteristics or phenomena that can take on different values, such as I.Q., speed of response, number of trials required to learn something,

Variable
Any characteristic or phenomenon that can vary across organisms, situations, or environments

or amount of a particular drug consumed. The researcher's task is to select one or more of these variables as the independent variable and another of these variables as the dependent variable. The **independent variable** is the variable that the experimenter changes within a defined range and is the variable in whose effect the experimenter is interested. The **dependent variable,** on the other hand, is the variable that measures the influence of the independent variable. For example, if you were studying the effectiveness of several teaching techniques, the task of the dependent variable would be to assess effectiveness. Consequently, the dependent variable is linked to the independent variable.

There are many possible independent and dependent variables that could be used in a given study. How do we identify the ones that are to be included? The independent and dependent variables for a study are specified by the research problem. You will recall from Chapter 3 that the research problem asks a question about the probable relationship between two variables. For example, one of the research questions Flaherty and Checke (1982) asked was whether the concentration of a solution of sugar and water was important in determining the extent to which rats would decrease their consumption of a solution of saccharin and water. Such a research question specifies which variable must be independent and which dependent. Because Flaherty and Checke varied the sugar-water concentration consumed, it had to be the independent variable. The influence of the sugar-water concentration was assessed by observing the degree to which it reduced the consumption of the saccharin-water solution. The magnitude of this decrease represented the response of the organisms (albino rats, in this instance) and measured the influence of the sugar-water concentration. Therefore, the suppression measure represented the dependent variable.

Although the research problem may specify both the independent and the dependent variables, it is not always a simple task to design an experiment that uses these independent and dependent variables. For example, assume that a research problem involves the investigation of aggression in rats. If aggression is specified to be the independent variable, you have to identify ways to vary aggression. If it is specified to be the dependent variable, you have to identify ways of measuring aggression. As you can see, many decisions and a great deal of thought may be involved in the development of these variables. This chapter will discuss the factors that must be considered when constructing the independent and the dependent variables for an experiment.

Independent variable
One of the antecedent conditions manipulated by the experimenter

Dependent variable
The response of the organism; the variable that measures the influence of the independent variable

The Independent Variable

The independent variable has been defined as the variable manipulated by the experimenter. It is of interest to the investigator because it is the variable hypothesized to be one of the causes of the presumed effect. To obtain evidence of this predicted causal relationship, the investigator manipulates this variable independently of the others. In the Flaherty and Checke (1982) experiment, sucrose concentration was the independent variable manipulated by the experimenter. Marks-Kaufman and Lipeles (1982) investigated the influence of chronic self-administration of morphine on the food rats ate. In this study, rats either were allowed or were not allowed to administer the morphine to themselves, so the ability to self-administer morphine represented the independent variable. In an experiment that examines the influence of rate of presentation of words on speed of learning, the independent variable is speed of presentation. Variation in the rate of presentation from one to three seconds provides an independent manipulation that, with the control of other factors such as ability, enables one to identify the effect of rate of presentation on learning speed.

These examples demonstrate the ease with which one can pick out the independent variable from a study. They also illustrate the requirements necessary for a variable to qualify as an independent variable. In all of the above examples, the independent variable involved variation—variation in rate of presentation of words, sucrose concentration, or self-administration of morphine. This variation was not random but was under the direct control of the experimenter. In all cases, the experimenter created the conditions that provided the type of variation desired. Here we have the two requirements necessary for a variable to qualify as an independent variable: variation and control of the variation. We shall look at each separately and also discuss other issues related to the independent variable.

Variation

To qualify as an independent variable, a variable must be manipulable. The variable must be presented in at least two forms. There are several ways in which the desired variation in the independent variable can be achieved. We will take a look at each of these.

Presence versus Absence. The presence-versus-absence technique for achieving variation is exactly what the name implies: one group of subjects receives the treatment condition and the other group does not. The two groups are then compared to see if the group that received the treatment condition differed from the group that did not. A drug study such as that which appears in Figure 4.1 illustrates this type of variation. One group of subjects is given a drug, and a second group is given a placebo. The two groups of subjects are then compared on some measure such as reaction time to determine if the drug group had significantly different reaction times than did the placebo group. If they did, then the difference is attributed to the drug.

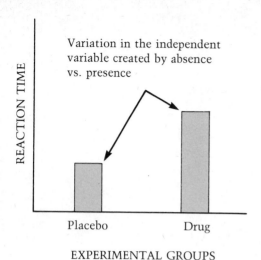

REACTION TIME

Variation in the independent
variable created by absence
vs. presence

Placebo   Drug

EXPERIMENTAL GROUPS

Figure 4.1 *Illustration of presence-versus-absence varia-tion in the independent variable.*

Amount of a Variable.   A second basic technique for achieving varia-tion in the independent variable is to administer different amounts of the variable to each of several groups. For example, Ryan and Isaacson (1983) varied the amount of the drug ACTH administered to rats to determine the minimal dose of ACTH required to induce excessive grooming. Rats were injected with either 0, 20, 50, 80, or 1000 nano-grams of ACTH in the area of the brain known as the nucleus accum-bens. One to two minutes following injection of ACTH, the rats' grooming behavior was recorded. As can be seen from Figure 4.2, the results revealed that even a dose of ACTH as low as 20 nanograms induced excessive grooming.

This study shows not only variation in the amount of a variable but also presence-absence variation, since the first condition consisted of injecting zero nanograms of ACTH, or an absence of ACTH. Actually, one microliter of a saline solution was injected in order to create a placebo condition. The technique of varying the amount of a variable can be combined with the presence-absence technique. This combina-tion of techniques is frequently necessary so that the experimenter can tell not only if the independent variable has an effect but also what influence varying amounts of the independent variable may have. Using a combination of the amount and the presence-versus-absence techniques, Ryan and Isaacson could tell not only that ACTH induced grooming but also that grooming behavior was affected by different amounts of ACTH. However, you should not assume that all studies varying the amount of the independent variable also use a presence-absence technique—in some studies this is not possible. For example, if

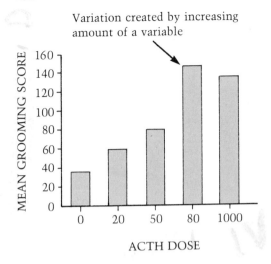

Variation created by increasing
amount of a variable

Figure 4.2 *Illustration of variation of the independent variable by amount of a variable.*

(Based on data from Ryan and Isaacson, *Physiological Psychology*, 1983, *11*, 54–58.)

you were investigating the influence of exposure durations on recognition of different types of words, all subjects would have to be exposed to the words for some period of time. It would not make sense to ask people to identify a word they had never been exposed to. Consequently, you would only vary the amount of time of exposure to the various words and would not include an absence condition.

One question that comes up with regard to establishing variation concerns the number of levels of variation to induce. An exact answer cannot be given other than that there must be at least two levels of variation and that these two must differ from one another. The research problem, past research, and the experience of the investigator should provide some indication as to the number of levels of variation that need to be incorporated in a given experiment.

Also, the type of inference that is to be drawn from the results of the study will suggest the number of levels of variation that should be included. If, for example, the objective of a given drug study is to determine if a drug produces a given effect, you would probably use only two levels of variation. One group of subjects would receive a large dosage of the drug, and another group would receive the placebo. However, if you were concerned with identifying the specific drug dosage that produced a given effect, you would probably have many levels of variation, ranging in small increments from none to a massive dose.

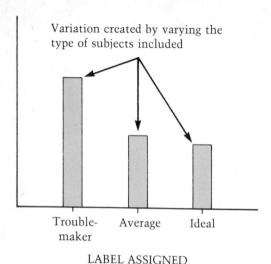

Variation created by varying the type of subjects included

Trouble-   Average   Ideal
maker

LABEL ASSIGNED

Figure 4.3 *Illustration of variation in the independent variable created by type of a variable.*

Type of a Variable.   A third means of generating variation in the independent variable is to vary the type of variable under investigation. Assume that you were interested in determining whether or not a person's reactions to others were affected by the label these others were given. Such a study could be conducted by having a school psychologist and a teacher discuss the teacher's pupils at the beginning of a school year. In this discussion, the school psychologist could apprise the teacher of the type of student he or she would be facing. As illustrated in Figure 4.3, some of the students would be labeled as trouble makers, some would be portrayed as average, run-of-the-mill students who may occasionally create a disturbance, and a third group would be labeled ideal students who never give any trouble. In actuality, a matched group of students would have been randomly assigned to the three groups. Some time after the school term had begun, the teacher would be required to assess the students in terms of problem behavior. The teacher might be asked to rate each of the students in terms of the degree to which they were considered to be problem children, or the teacher could be asked to rank the students in order from those who never gave any trouble to those who were constantly a problem. If the assessments initially provided by the school psychologist were confirmed by the teacher's ratings or rank ordering, then support would be given to the hypothesis that giving a child a certain type of label tends to generate that type of behavior. In this hypothetical example, variation was generated in the type of behavioral label given to each child.

Establishing Variation in the Independent Variable

You have just seen that there are three basic techniques for creating variation in the independent variable. These techniques seem straightforward and relatively simple. However, remember that the variation that is created must be under the control of the experimenter. It is much easier to establish this controlled variation for some variables than it is for others. In drug studies, it is usually quite easy to establish controlled variation, since different doses of a drug can be measured quite accurately. If a presence-versus-absence form of variation were to be used, we could administer a placebo to one group and a specific amount of the drug to the other group. In this way, exact control would be maintained over the independent variable—the amount of the drug administered. It is not always so easy to establish controlled variation, though. Assume that you want to investigate the influence of anxiety or fear on the desire of individuals to be together. You have decided to use the presence-versus-absence technique for varying the level of anxiety or fear. How do you create a controlled variation of this independent variable? Do you try to create anxiety or fear by telling the subjects that you are going to hurt them and hope that this anticipation will create anxiety or fear? Or do you try to create anxiety or fear in some other manner? Clearly, it seldom suffices to state that you are going to achieve variation by a certain technique. You must identify exactly how you plan to establish the variation—by presence or absence, amount, or type.

Next, we will take a look at two concrete ways in which variation can be achieved and the difficulties each technique produces.

Experimental Manipulation.   The term **experimental manipulation** of an independent variable refers to a situation in which the experimenter administers one specific controlled amount of a variable to one group of individuals and a different specific controlled amount of the same variable to a second group of individuals. For example, one of the research questions Shuell (1981) wanted to investigate was the influence of type of practice on long-term retention. To accomplish this, Shuell identified two types of practice—distributed and massed. Shuell operationally defined massed practice as six learning trials administered on the same day and distributed practice as six learning trials distributed over three days. He had one group of subjects learn a list of words under massed practice and another group learn a list of words under distributed practice. The experimenter not only operationally defined the independent variable of massed or distributed practice but also had

Experimental manipulation
The controlled adjustment of the independent variable

total control over the administration of the practice schedule. Thus the researcher, in a controlled manner, experimentally manipulated the independent variable.

The two basic ways of experimentally manipulating the independent variable are instructional manipulation and event manipulation.

Manipulation of Instructions.   One of the techniques available for creating variation in the independent variable is by **instructional manipulation.** One group of subjects receives one set of instructions, and another group receives another set of instructions. Barlow, Sakheim, and Beck (1983), for example, investigated the hypothesis that increases in anxiety level would increase sexual arousal. In order to create a variation in anxiety, experimenters told one group of subjects that there was a 60 percent chance they would receive an electric shock when a light came on. Each subject in a second group was told that there was a 60 percent chance he would receive an electric shock if his level of arousal was less than the average of all of the research subjects. The last group was the control group, and they were told that the light had no meaning. In actuality, no subject received an electric shock. The instructional set was administered only to generate the anticipation of possibly receiving shock. Since shock is unpleasant and anxiety provoking to most individuals, it is probably safe to assume that this instructional manipulation generated anxiety in those who were told they had a 60 percent chance of getting shocked. Those subjects who were not given such instructions would not become anxious in anticipation of shock. Thus instructional manipulation can enable the researcher to establish experimental manipulation.

Instructional manipulation Varying the independent variable by giving different sets of instructions to the subjects

Manipulation of variables through instruction is not without dangers. Two can readily be identified. First, one runs the risk of some subjects' being inattentive when the instructions are given. These subjects will miss part or all of the instructions and therefore will not be operating according to the appropriate manipulation, thereby introducing error into the results. The second danger is the possibility that subject-to-subject variation exists in the interpretation of the instructions. Some subjects may interpret the instructions to mean one thing, while others interpret them in a different way. In this case, an unintentional variation is introduced that represents error or, actually, an uncontrolled variable. The danger of misinterpretation can be minimized if instructions are kept simple, given emphatically, and related to the activity at hand. Probably no more than one variable should be manipulated through instructions. Manipulation of more than one variable will often result in too much complexity and length, rendering the manipulations ineffective by virtue of increasing inattentiveness, misinterpretation, and forgetting.

Manipulation of Events.   A second means of establishing variation in the independent variable is through **event manipulation.** Drug research varies events such as drug dosages, and learning experiments vary events such as meaningfulness of the material presented to subjects. Most human experiments and almost all animal experiments use this method of achieving variation. Communication skills have been developed in chimpanzees (Fouts, 1973), enabling researchers to use instruction with these infrahumans. When a choice exists between using instructions and events to create the variation, the best choice in most cases is to use events. The reason for this is that events are more realistic and thus have more impact on the subject.

Consider the experiment conducted by Aronson and Linder (1965). They wanted to determine if liking for another is partially determined by the behavior exhibited by that other. To investigate this problem, they designed an experiment where a confederate and a subject interacted on seven different occasions. After each of the seven sessions, the subject overheard the confederate's evaluation of her. These evaluations were either all positive, all negative, initially negative and then positive, or initially positive and then negative. After overhearing all evaluations, subjects recorded their impressions of the confederate. In this experiment, the event manipulated was the overhearing of an evaluation of the subject's performance. This manipulation could also have taken place through instructions; the experimenter could have told the subjects how they performed. However, the event manipulation was more meaningful and realistic to the subjects. The advantage of this increased meaningfulness in experimentation is that the problems of inattentiveness and misinterpretation are minimized. Additionally, the response emitted by the subject in a realistic situation is probably a better representation of how he or she would respond outside the experimental environment because the realism probably removes much of the artificiality created by the experiment.

In animal research, the issue of realism seldom exists for two reasons. First, events are used to manipulate the independent variable. Second, the conditions that are used to motivate the animal to respond seem to create the realism. Researchers motivate animals to respond by depriving them of food or water or by administering electric shock. Such conditions seem to be real and meaningful to these subjects, even though this is something about which an animal researcher rarely speculates.

That is not to say that all manipulations of events get the person involved or are as meaningful as real life. In fact, many experiments have little impact on the individual and therefore tend to have little realism. Many person-perception experiments have, for example, manipulated exposure by requiring judges to predict responses of others after viewing different amounts of a filmed interview of them. The filmed interview removes the realism from the experiment. Requiring the judge and the others to spend either ten minutes or a half hour

Event manipulation
Affecting the independent variable by altering the events that subjects experience

together before the judge made any predictions would have increased the realism. Why was this situation not employed? The answer is related to the problem of control. Filming allows control over variables that would not be controlled in the free interaction situation. In the free interaction situation, many differences would exist between the judges and the others, such as what the judge and the other talked about and how each responded. Consequently, judges would have different information upon which to base their judgments and thus many uncontrolled variables would exist. In the filmed interview, each judge receives the same information, so there is control over both the type and the amount of information received.

As realism and meaningfulness of social experiences are increased in an attempt to increase impact, control is decreased. As control over variables is increased, the impact of the experiment is decreased. This is a real dilemma for the scientist trying to experimentally investigate social interaction. On the one hand, the scientist wants control over variables. On the other hand, he or she wants to eliminate the sterile atmosphere of the experiment because such an atmosphere may fail to involve the subject and therefore may not have any significant influence on behavior. There is no simple solution to this problem of maximizing realism and control. However, the first concern of the researcher should be to make sure that the desired experimental effect actually occurs, for if this effect does not occur, it makes no sense to worry about other aspects of the experiment.

Measured Manipulation.   The term **measured manipulation** refers to the situation in which the independent variable is varied by selecting subjects that differ in terms of some measured internal state (e.g., self-esteem or anxiety level). The assumption underlying such a manipulation is that each individual possesses a certain amount of a variety of variables commonly labeled "personality variables." One efficient means of achieving a manipulation would be to select subjects having different levels of a given variable (such as anxiety) and then look for effects of the difference. As illustrated in Figure 4.4, the procedure typically followed is to administer to a large sample of people an instrument measuring the internal state of interest. From the test results, two smaller groups of subjects are selected: one group that has scored high on the variable of interest and one group that has scored low. These two groups are required to perform a task, and then the two groups are compared to determine if a difference exists in the task performance. If a difference does exist, it is typically attributed to the differences in the measured internal states. Ritchie and Phares (1969) were interested in the relationship among internal-external control, communicator status, and attitude change. To examine this relationship, researchers

Measured manipulation
Varying the independent variable by selecting subjects that differ in the amount or type of a measured internal state

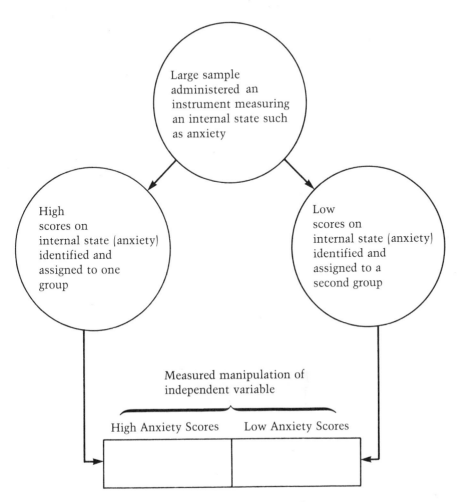

Figure 4.4 *Variation created by the measured manipulation technique.*

first had to classify subjects as internals or externals. To accomplish this task, they administered the Locus of Control Scale to 152 female subjects from whom 42 internals and 42 externals were chosen. The degree of attitude change of these two groups of subjects was compared for different levels of communicator status. Results indicated that a high-prestige communicator produces more change in externals than in internals. This result was attributed to the externals' higher expectancy of reinforcement.

What is wrong with such an experiment? It seems to be appropriately designed and statistically analyzable. The difficulty lies in the fact that the states—internal and external control—were *measured* and not experimentally manipulated.. Subjects were not randomly assigned to conditions but were nonrandomly assigned, or selected, on the basis of their test scores. Thus it is possible that another variable, correlated with the internal and external states, produced the differences in performance. If, in a learning experiment, motivation was highly correlated with tested anxiety, then it would be impossible to determine if the difference in performance of a high- and a low-anxiety group was due to the anxiety factor or to motivation. In the Ritchie and Phares study, if some other variable was highly correlated with the subjects' locus of control, then, in the same manner, one could not determine if the observed effect was due to one's perceived locus of control (internal or external) or to the other correlated variable. An experiment that tries to manipulate variables in this way is therefore an ex post facto type of study, even though it may be conducted in a laboratory with control over other variables. In fairness to Ritchie and Phares, it must be stated that they did manipulate the communicator status variable, so the study they conducted actually included an ex post facto component and an experimental component. I should also add that such measured manipulations are not inherently undesirable. A great deal of good research has been generated through the use of such manipulations. However, you should remain aware of their limitations when using them.

Constructing the Independent Variable

In addition to deciding how variation in the independent variable is to be achieved, the researcher must also decide how the independent variable is to be constructed or operationally defined. In an experiment, we are trying to determine if the independent variable actually produces the hypothesized effect. In order to test the hypothesis and achieve the necessary variation, we must translate the independent variable into concrete operational terms; in other words, we must specify the exact empirical operations that define the independent variable. If the independent variable represents different learning techniques, then we must operationally define each one of the learning techniques. The ease with which the independent variable is translated into operational terms varies greatly among research problems. For example, if the independent variable consists of a drug, then there is no difficulty in operationally defining the independent variable because a specific empirical referent exists in the form of the drug. All that is needed is to obtain the drug and then to administer different dosages to different groups of subjects. Similarly, if the independent variable consists of either the length of time various words are exposed to subjects or the area of a rat's brain that is destroyed, it is simple to translate the independent variables into concrete operations. The only decision that must be made is the length of time the words should be exposed to the subjects or the area of the brain that must be destroyed.

Difficulty in translating the independent variable into concrete operational terms arises when the independent variable consists of some higher-order construct such as attitude, frustration, anxiety, learning, or emotional disturbance. The problem stems from the fact that there is not one single definition or empirical referent for such constructs. For example, learning in albino rats could be operationally defined as speed of acquisition, number of trials to extinction, or latency of response. Aggression in some instances may be defined as including "intent to harm," whereas in other instances "intent to harm" may be irrelevant. The scientist's task is to identify the specific empirical referents that correspond to the meaning denoted by the way the construct is used as the independent variable in the research question. For example, if we were investigating the aggressiveness with which women pursue their jobs, the component of "intent to harm" would probably not be included in the operational definition of aggressiveness. However, if we were investigating the influence of children's aggressive responses on their popularity, then the empirical referent of "intent to harm" probably would be included.

For some types of research, operationally defining a conceptual variable that does not have specific empirical referents does not seem to be a major problem, because standard agreed-upon techniques exist. A study of the effect of schedules of reinforcement on strength of a response requires the construction of the different reinforcement patterns. The schedules of reinforcement identified by Skinner are standard and accepted in the field [the interested student is referred to Ferster and Skinner, (1957)]. These could immediately be incorporated into the study.

In other areas of research, such as in social psychology, difficulty is frequently encountered in constructing conditions that represent a realization of the independent variable specified in the problem. The reason for this is that relatively few standard techniques exist for manipulating the conceptual variable in such areas. Few of the manipulations of such variables as conformity, commitment, and aggression are identical. Aronson and Carlsmith (1968, p. 40) state that this lack of development of specific techniques is a function of the fact that the variables with which the social psychologist works must be adapted to the particular population with which he or she is working. A standard technique would not work with all populations. Therefore, the researchers must use ingenuity in accomplishing the task, capitalizing on previous work by borrowing ideas and innovations and incorporating them. The problem is that many researchers simply use prior ideas and innovations without creating a better translation of the abstract concept. They "cling to settings and techniques that have been used before" (Ellsworth, 1977). Every translation has had its own quirks and characteristic sources of error, and, as Stevens (1939) has pointed out, each operational definition or translation of an abstract concept represents merely a partial representation of that abstract concept. Therefore, one should not automatically assume that prior translations are the best or even the most appropriate translations. In fact, in any translation the investigator has to compromise and sacrifice some methodological advantages for others. Given the problem of translating abstract concepts into operational terms, you should first determine how the topic or phenomenon has been studied in the past. Once that has been determined, you should then decide whether or not any of these translations are appropriate for your study. In making this decision, consider the overall research that has been conducted on the topic. It may be that most prior studies have focused only on a narrow but typical translation of an abstract concept. If this is the case, then it would be appropriate to identify another translation that would help approximate a more complete representation of the concept. For example, fear has typically been studied in the laboratory. However, the range of fear that can be generated in this setting is restricted because of the ethical restrictions on imposing stimuli that may create extreme fear. Given this situation, it may be more appropriate to search for a naturalistic setting where extreme fear is naturally created.

In other areas of research, the problem is not so much one of how the conceptual variable will be translated into specific experimental operations but which of the many available techniques will be used. Plutchik (1974) lists eight different techniques (including approach-avoidance conflict and physiological measures) that Miller (1957) identified for either producing or studying fear in animals. If you were to study the conceptual variable of fear in animals, which one should you use? What specific operations will be used to represent this conceptual variable of fear? To answer this question, you have to determine which techniques most adequately represent the variable. This issue will be discussed later in the chapter.

Why do several different techniques exist for constructing a single variable such as learning, emotion, or fear? Variables such as fear refer to a general state or condition of the body. Therefore, there is probably no single index that is *the* way to produce such a concept. Some ways are probably better than others, but no one index can provide complete understanding. To obtain a better understanding of the concept, you should investigate several indexes, even though they may initially seem to give contradictory results. As our knowledge of the idea increases, the initial results that appear to be contradictory will probably be integrated.

Construct Validity of the Independent Variable

After deciding on the experimental operations that you are going to use as your manifestation of the conceptual variable and the manner in which this variable will be varied, it is a good idea to look back at these operations and ask the following questions: Do the experimental operations represent the conceptual variable that I had in mind? Will the different levels of variation of the independent variable make subjects behave differently? In what ways should they behave differently? These questions are asked in an attempt to ensure that construct validity (Cook and Campbell, 1979) has been attained. By **construct validity,** I mean the extent to which the higher-order construct or conceptual variable of interest can be inferred from the operational definition of that construct. For example, Davis and Memmott (1983) used the rate with which rats pressed a lever to infer that rats can indeed count. Essentially, Davis and Memmott believed that rats could count (the higher-order construct) if their speed of lever pressing changed when three shocks had been administered (the empirical operation indicative of counting). If the change in response following the third shock does indeed indicate counting ability, then construct validity has been attained; but if it does not indicate counting ability, construct validity has not been attained. The problem of construct validity exists because sometimes we must deal with imperfect translations of our higher-order construct and it is possible that the experimental operations do not represent the construct of interest to the experimenter.

Construct validity
The extent to which the higher-order construct can be inferred from the operational definition of that construct

Figure 4.5 illustrates the circularity involved in construct validity as well as the possible imperfect translations that can exist by means of the procedure used by Schachter and Singer (1962) in their study of euphoria. In order to create euphoria in subjects, Schachter and Singer had a confederate waltz around the room shooting rubber bands, play with a hula hoop, and practice hook shots into a wastebasket with wadded paper. The question that these researchers then had to answer was whether these imperfect operations actually created euphoria in their subjects. Unfortunately, whether such empirical operations have construct validity is often a matter of judgment on the part of the experimenter.

Cook and Campbell (1979) provide several suggestions for achieving construct validity, however. According to them, the first step in achieving construct validity is to provide a clear definition of the higher-order construct. Such pre-experimental explication of the construct seems to be a logical first step, since the empirical operations used to represent this construct must arise from its definition. Only by providing a clear definition of euphoria could Schachter and Singer proceed to specify the empirical operations that would generate euphoria.

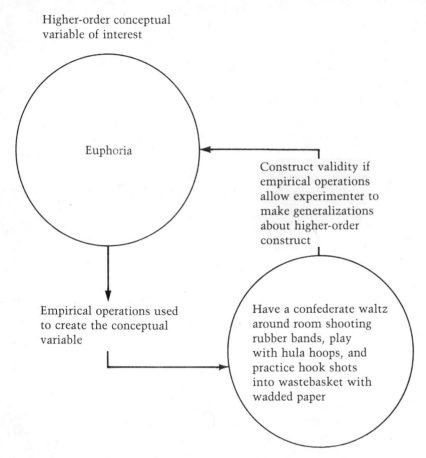

Higher-order conceptual
variable of interest

Euphoria

Construct validity if
empirical operations
allow experimenter to
make generalizations
about higher-order
construct

Empirical operations used
to create the conceptual
variable

Have a confederate waltz
around room shooting
rubber bands, play
with hula hoops, and
practice hook shots
into wastebasket with
wadded paper

Figure 4.5   *Illustration of the requirements for construct validity.*

After the higher-order construct has been defined and translated into specific experimental operations, several types of data can be collected to ensure that construct validity has been attained. First, data can be collected to demonstrate that the empirical representation of the independent variable produces the outcomes expected. If a rat were hungry, we would expect it to engage in such behavior as consuming more food, tolerating more quinine in the food, increasing its rate of bar pressing to obtain food, and producing more stomach contractions. Miller (1957) actually conducted such a study. While these four measures did not produce identical results, depriving the rats of food did result in the expected behavior, giving additional evidence that food deprivation appropriately represents hunger.

Second, data can be obtained to show that the empirical representation of the independent variable does not vary with measures of related but different conceptual variables. For example, an operational definition of "communicator expertise" should be related to the level of knowledge possessed by the communicator but not to the communicator's power, attractiveness, position, or trustworthiness. Therefore, evidence for construct validity can be obtained by collecting both convergent (the expected outcomes are produced) and divergent (outcomes are unrelated to the conceptual variables) data.

Unfortunately, the procedures just suggested are seldom used in psychological experimentation. Most of the time, an experimenter operationally defines the independent variable, and it is up to the reader to judge whether or not an empirical realization of the conceptual variable was actually produced. All too often, no data are given to provide validating evidence that an adequate translation of the conceptual variable was actually attained.

There seem to be at least two reasons why the techniques discussed above are rarely used. First, the techniques are time consuming. It is much easier to select the operational definition and then proceed to investigate the problem area. Second, the techniques are often difficult to carry out. In order to satisfy the divergence criteria, it is necessary not only to identify the related-but-different variables but also to operationally define these variables. For example, to obtain divergent evidence regarding communicator expertise, one would first have to identify the related-but-different variables, such as communicator trustworthiness. Then one would have to operationally define both conceptual variables—trustworthiness and expertise—and collect data on both variables. Therefore, obtaining such evidence typically involves conducting another experiment.

The procedure just discussed for providing assurance of construct validity can be used with both human and infrahuman subjects. When dealing with human subjects, one can use several additional techniques to provide some evidence of whether the conceptual variable is generating the observed results. These additional techniques generally fall under the heading of "manipulation checks" because they represent checks on the manipulation of the independent variable.

The first approach is to conduct interviews with the subject after the independent variable has been introduced to determine if the desired construct was actually attained. Asch (1956), in a study on conformity, wanted to create pressure on each subject to say something that was obviously not correct in order to conform. In such an experiment, one needs to determine whether that pressure is indeed created. One means of doing so is to generate group pressure on several subjects and then to interview them to find out if the pressure was actually created. Naturally, there are difficulties in conducting these interviews. Subjects often identify the response that is wanted and then intention-

ally provide this response. However, if the postinterviews are conducted correctly, this error is minimized. The appropriate means of
conducting debriefing sessions or postinterviews will be discussed in a
later chapter in the book. The benefits that can accrue from this interview are several, the greatest of which is that the interview can point
out possible weaknesses in the operational definition of the independent variable and indicate what needs to be done to eliminate these
weaknesses. It is important that these interviews follow immediately
after the administration of the treatment conditions rather than after
the response data are collected, for the response may influence the
subjects' introspective reports. Research on scapegoating supports this
statement; it has shown that a variable such as aroused hostility may be
diminished by giving the subjects an opportunity to displace it. Since
these interviews follow the administration of the treatment conditions,
they must, as you might suspect, be conducted on subjects comprising a
pilot study conducted for the purpose of investigating the influence of
the experimental operations. Otherwise, the interview may affect the
response data.

A more difficult, but superior, technique involves getting a behavioral indicator that the experimental operations are arousing the desired effect. If you want to arouse anxiety in subjects, get some indication, like a galvanic skin response (GSR), that anxiety is actually being
aroused. Zimbardo et al. (1966) measured subjects' GSR to monitor
anxiety through the course of their experiments. Aronson and
Carlsmith (1963) attempted to create mild and severe threat conditions
in children. Intuitively, they seem to have manipulated threat. They
could have verified the manipulation of the threat conditions by pretesting the children with toys of varying degrees of attractiveness and
various threat conditions until they had a condition where more children disregarded the mild threat than the severe threat in order to play
with the forbidden toy. In this way, they would have had a behavioral
indication that threat was actually varied.

Pretesting can also give some indication of the level of intensity of
the manipulation. If the problem one is investigating has a hypothesis
about three levels of intensity of threat, then three levels of threat have
to be created. How does one know that three levels are created and
how intense they are? Either of the above methods could give some
indication. A verbal report or response to a questionnaire may indicate
level of intensity. In a study that attempted to generate three levels of
threat, level of intensity of the severity of threat could be determined
behaviorally by noting the percentage of children that disregarded the
threat. If in one condition 10 percent of the children disregarded the
threat, in the second condition 50 percent of the children disregarded
the threat, and in the third condition 80 percent of the children disre-

garded the threat, one would have some evidence of the intensity of each of the threat conditions.

The Number of Independent Variables

How many independent variables should be used in an experiment? In looking through the literature in any area of psychology, you will find some studies that used only one independent variable and others that used two or more. What criterion dictated the number used in each study? Unfortunately, there is no rule that can be stated to answer such a question. We do know that behavior is multidetermined, and inclusion of more than one independent variable is often desirable because of the added information that it will give in the form of an interaction. *Interaction* refers to the differential effect that one independent variable has for each level of one or more additional independent variables. For example, Mellgren, Nation, and Wrather (1975) investigated the relationship between magnitude of negative reinforcement and schedule of reinforcement for producing resistance to extinction. As predicted, they found that the effect of magnitude of reinforcement was dependent on the schedule of reinforcement used. The subjects (albino rats) that were performing under a partial reinforcement schedule revealed greater resistance to extinction when administered a large negative reinforcement; rats performing under a continuous schedule of reinforcement displayed greater resistance to extinction when administered a small negative reinforcement. In other words, the effect of reinforcement magnitude is dependent on the schedule of reinforcement. If the second variable of reinforcement schedule had not been included, the study would probably have revealed, as demonstrated by other studies, that no difference existed between magnitudes of negative reinforcement in terms of the ability to affect resistance to extinction. Inclusion of this variable showed that magnitude of negative reinforcement did affect resistance to extinction, but its effect depended on the schedule of reinforcement. Experiments such as the one conducted by Mellgren et al. reveal the advantage and even the necessity of varying more than one independent variable.

Theoretically and statistically, there is no limit to the number of variables that can be varied. Realistically there is a limit. From the subject's point of view, as the number of variables increases, there are more things to be done, such as participate in more events or take more tests. The subject is apt to become bored, irritated, or resentful and thereby introduce a confounding variable into the experiment. From the experimenter's point of view, as the number of variables increases, the difficulty in making sense out of the data increases as well as the difficulty in setting up the experiment. Aronson and Carlsmith (1968,

p. 51) give a rule of thumb that may be followed. They say that the experiment "should only be as complex as is necessary for the important relationships to emerge in a clear manner."[2] In other words, do not use the "why not" approach, in which a variable is included in the experiment because there is no real reason not to include it. Only include in an experiment those variables that seem to be necessary to reveal the important relationships.

The Dependent Variable

The dependent variable has been defined as the behavioral variable designed to measure the effect of the variation of the independent variable. This definition, like the definition of the independent variable, seems straightforward and simple enough. Also, like the independent variable, the dependent variable is relatively easy to identify in a given study. Aronson and Mills wanted to investigate the influence of severity of initiation on liking for a group. Liking for a group represented the dependent variable. Ritchie and Phares (1969) investigated attitude change as a function of communicator status and locus of control. Attitude change represented their dependent variable. However, many decisions have to be made to secure the most appropriate measure of the effect of the variation in the independent variable.

A psychological experiment is conducted to answer a question (What is the effect of . . . ?) and to test the corresponding hypothesis (A certain change in x will result in a certain change in y). In order to answer the question and test the hypothesis, a variable—the independent variable—is varied in order to determine if it produces the desired or hypothesized effect. The issue of concern for the experimenter is to make sure that he or she actually obtains an indication of the effect produced by the variation in the independent variable. To accomplish this task, the experimenter has to select a dependent variable that will be sensitive to, or be able to pick up, the influence exerted by the independent variable. Quite often, researchers believe that an effect was produced because they think they saw behavioral change exhibited, yet their study indicates that the independent variable produces no effect. Such a case may indicate distorted perception, or it may mean that the dependent variable was not sensitive to the effects produced by the independent variable.

[2]Reprinted by special permission from Aronson and Carlsmith, "Experimentation in Social Psychology," *The handbook of social psychology*, Second Edition, Volume Two, 1968, edited by Lindzey and Aronson, Addison-Wesley, Reading, Mass., p. 51.

It is the task of the dependent variable to determine whether the independent variable did or did not produce an effect. If an effect was produced, the dependent variable must indicate if the effect was a facilitating one or an inhibiting one and must reveal the magnitude of this effect. If the dependent variable can accomplish these tasks, the experimenter has identified and used a good sensitive dependent variable. The first decision for the experimenter, then, is what specific measure to use to assess the effect of the independent variable. Once a decision has been made on this issue, the experimenter still has several problems to confront. The experimenter must somehow ensure that the subject is taking the measurement seriously and is doing his or her best. The experimenter must also make sure that the subject is responding in a truthful manner rather than "cooperating" with the experimenter and responding in a manner that he or she feels will be most helpful to the experimenter. The last two problems are most crucial in human experiments.

The Response to Be Used as the Dependent Variable

What response should be selected as the dependent variable? We just saw that the foremost criterion for the dependent variable is sensitivity to the effect of the independent variable. There is not to my knowledge any specific rule or statement that will tell you how to select a dependent variable. Psychologists use as dependent variables a wide variety of responses ranging from questionnaire responses to verbal reports, overt behavior, and physiological responses. The task is to select the response that is the most sensitive to the effect produced by the independent variable. In most experiments, there are several different measures that could be used, and one must choose among them. For example, attitudes can be measured by a response to a questionnaire, by a physiological response, or by observation of a response made by the subject.

The difficulty in identifying the most appropriate dependent variable seems to stem from the fact that psychologists study processes, attributes, or outcomes of the human and infrahuman organism. When an independent variable is introduced, our task is to determine the effect of the independent variable on phenomena such as learning, attitudes, or intelligence. Are these processes, attributes, or outcomes facilitated, inhibited, or affected in some other way? The problem is that the processes, attributes, or outcomes are not directly observable. Since direct observation is not possible, some result of the construct under study that can be observed must be selected for observation to allow inference back to the construct. Consider learning as an example. It is impossible to study the learning process directly. But if a student sits down and studies certain material for an hour and then can answer questions he or she previously could not, we say that learning has taken place. In this case, learning is inferred from an increase in performance. In such a way, we can acquire information about a phenomenon. The decision that the scientist is faced with is selecting the aspect or the type of response that will provide the best representation of change in the construct as a result of the variation in the independent variable. Previous experimentation can help one to make such a decision. Prior research has been conducted on most phenomena, and many dependent variables have been used in these studies. Results of these studies should provide clues as to which responses would be most sensitive.

Aronson and Carlsmith (1968, p. 54) address the problem of selecting the dependent variable with research conducted on humans. They discuss some of the advantages and disadvantages of various techniques that can be used to measure the dependent variable in social psychological research. One very significant point they make is that the more commitment demanded of the subject by the dependent variable, the greater the degree of confidence we can have in the results of our experiment. Why is this so? First, making a commitment to a course of action reduces the probability of faking on the part of the subject because it helps to ensure that subjects take the dependent variable measure seriously. If we wanted to find out which person in a group is most liked by a particular individual, we could have that individual rate each of the group members on a liking rating scale. Or we could have him or her choose a member of the group as a roommate for the next year, with the contingency that the person picked will in fact be the roommate. In this case, if the request were credible, the subject would be motivated to respond truthfully because he or she would have to live with the decision. The second advantage of requiring the subject to make a commitment is that it often increases one's confidence that the dependent variable of interest is really being measured. Recording the frequency with which fights are initiated is a better index of aggression than having a subject verbally state that he or she is angry or evaluate the degree of anger on a rating scale.

Behavior that involves a commitment is probably the best type of dependent variable to use. Sometimes it is not feasible because of cost, time, or some other constraint to use such a dependent variable, and a questionnaire or a verbal report must be used. Questionnaires and verbal reports yield a great deal of useful data. The difficulty with these measures is that there is an increased likelihood of error because the subjects either may not take the measure seriously or may "cooperate" with the experimenter, thereby producing the results they think the experimenter desires.

Reliability and Validity of the Dependent Variable

In deciding on the dependent variable to use as an index of the influence of the independent variable, one must consider the issues of reliability and validity. **Reliability** refers to consistency or stability; **validity** refers to whether you are measuring what you want to measure. Ideally, the dependent variable will be both reliable and valid. However, this is matter in which experimental psychologists have been extremely lax and those involved in the field of test construction have been justifiably rigorous. In constructing a test, first one should establish the reliability of that test and then proceed to attempt to get evidence of its validity. Psychologists conducting experiments seem to assume that reliability and validity exist intrinsically if the dependent variable has been operationally defined. Such an assumption should not be made, because if the dependent variable is not reliable and valid, the experiment is worthless.

Reliability
The extent to which the same results are obtained when responses are measured at different times

Validity
The extent to which you are measuring what you want to measure

Reliability.   Reliability of the dependent variable can, in most experiments, be established by determining the consistency with which responses are made to the dependent variable. If organisms consistently respond in the same way to the dependent variable, then that variable is reliable. However, most experiments are conducted as single-occasion events, which means that the dependent variable is observed only once. In other words, the subject comes to the experiment one time, and the dependent variable is only measured once. Consequently, the reliability of the dependent variable cannot be assessed. According to Epstein (1981), if reliability could be measured, low reliability (usually less than 0.30) would exist for a variety of measures including self-ratings, other ratings, behavioral responses (such as number of minutes late to class), personality test results, and physiological responses. However, as shown in Figure 4.6, Epstein (1979) found that the stability of each of these responses increased as they were averaged over several days. In other words, the reliability of the dependent variable responses increased as the responses were aggregated over time. The lowest reliability existed when reliability was assessed by correlating the responses obtained on one day with those obtained on the second day. When reliability was assessed by correlating the average response obtained over one 12-day period with the average response obtained over another 12-day period, excellent reliability was found to exist.

Such evidence strongly suggests that most dependent variables used in the traditional single-occasion experiment are unreliable. This in turn means that the results obtained from our single-session studies do

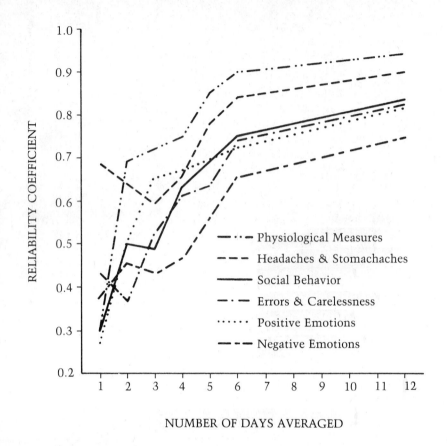

NUMBER OF DAYS AVERAGED

Figure 4.6   *Reliability coefficients as a function of the number of days.*
(From Epstein, S. The stability of behavior: 1. On predicting most of the
people much of the time. *Journal of Personality and Social Psychology*, 1979, 37,
1097–1126. Copyright 1979 by the American Psychological Association.
Reprinted by permission of the author.)

not produce stable findings and are therefore suspect. Where does this
leave us? The results of Epstein's study indicate that we must repeat
each experiment a number of times and then use the average response
as our dependent variable for our findings to be reliable. However,
many studies cannot be repeated on the same group of subjects because
the repetition would alter the subjects' responses. So in many instances
we are locked into the single-occasion experiment. Although Epstein's
study strongly suggests that a single study, by itself, should not be given
much credence, replication of the results of single-occasion studies
provides a good measure of the reliability of dependent measures be-

cause replication of an effect cannot be attained if the dependent variable measure is unreliable. Thus the results from any one study should not be considered seriously except as those results contribute to a population of studies; it is the results from such a population of studies that give us reliable information.

Validity.   Establishing the validity of the dependent variable involves obtaining evidence to support the hypothesis that the dependent variable actually measures the construct we want it to measure. For example, does latency of response really represent degree of learning? Does selection of a person as a roommate for the next year really represent the degree to which the subject likes the person? As you can see, establishing the validity of the dependent variable is the more difficult task. The individuals concerned with test construction have wrestled with this problem and have devised a number of techniques for obtaining evidence of validity. Experimenters quite often do not even consider the validity question because, I believe, it has been obscured by operationism. For example, intelligence could be, and has been, operationally defined as what intelligence tests measure. No one can argue with this operational definition. What you can argue with is whether intelligence tests do really measure intelligence. Operational definitions are necessary for scientific communication, but such definitions in no way say anything about validity. Yet many researchers seem to write off the validity question once they have satisfied the criterion of operational definition.

How do we obtain an index of validity of our operationally defined dependent variable? Again, there is no simple solution. The discussion of commitment alluded to the validity question. As the commitment required of the dependent variable increases, we can increase our faith in the results of the experiment because commitment reduces faking and seems to indicate a more valid representation of the dependent variable that we wanted to measure. Fighting seems to be a more valid index of aggression than a rating of anger. Commitment, therefore, seems to be related to validity. To get additional indicators of validity we must resort to the *construct* validity techniques used by test constructors. One could, for example, correlate the scores obtained on the selected dependent variable with scores obtained by the same subject on another measure that is known to be valid. If the correlation is high, the measure is assumed to be valid. If the correlation is low or nonsignificant, the measure is not valid. The problem that arises in such a case is that many of the constructs that we want to measure are multidimensional and the different dimensions may not be highly correlated. Strength of conditioning has, for example, been inferred from amplitude, latency, and resistance to extinction, and investigators have sometimes used these measures interchangeably. However, Hall and Kobrick (1952) have shown that the correlations between some of these measures are very low. As you can see, the validity question is a very difficult one, but it must be considered in every experiment.

Reducing Subject Error

Once a decision has been made as to what the dependent variable will be, the experimenter using human subjects must make sure that the subject is taking the measure seriously and not trying to fake the responses. The difficulty of this task increases as the degree of commitment decreases. For example, in filling out a questionnaire, some subjects will undoubtedly race through it, reading questions in a haphazard manner and checking answers without putting much thought into them. One way of decreasing such errors is to disguise the measure of the dependent variable. In addition to increasing the likelihood that the subject takes the measure seriously, the disguise also helps guard against the possibility that the subject will cooperate with the experimenter. Aronson and Carlsmith (1968, p. 58) present a number of techniques useful for disguising the dependent variable.

One technique is to assess the dependent variable outside of the context of the experiment. Carlsmith, Collins, and Helmreich (1966) solicited the aid of a consumer research analyst to assess the dependent variable after the subject had supposedly completed the experiment and had left the room. Another technique is to assess behavior of significance to the subject, such as selection of a roommate. A third technique is to construct the experiment in such a way that the subject does not realize that the dependent variable is being observed. Lefkowitz, Blake, and Mouton (1955) observed the frequency with which people jaywalked or disobeyed signs upon introduction of various levels of an independent variable. A fourth technique that is often used in attitude-change experiments is to imbed key items in a larger questionnaire in the hope that the key items will not be recognized and falsely reported on. A similar technique is to disguise the reason for interest in a particular dependent variable. Aronson (1961) was interested in finding out whether the attractiveness of several colors varied as the effort expended in getting them varied. For this study, he needed a measure of attractiveness. When he asked the subjects to rate the attractiveness of colors, he told them that he was investigating a relationship between color preference and a person's performance. Using unsuspicious subjects such as young children is also a very good method for reducing or eliminating cooperation. Young children are very straightforward and are not motivated by more devious means. A sixth technique is to use what Aronson and Carlsmith call the family of "whoops" procedures. The typical procedure is to collect pretest data and then claim that something happened to them so that posttest data can be collected. Christensen (1968) used this method in collecting test-retest reliability data on ratings of a series of concepts. A seventh procedure is to have a confederate collect the data. Karhan (1973) had the learner, a member of the experiment who had supposedly received electric shock for errors made, make a request of the subject. The dependent variable was the subject's response to the confederate's request. A last technique is to use a physiological measure that is presumably not under the subject's conscious control. However, a number of individuals have presented data indicating that these measures may be consciously influenced by the subject.

The Number of Dependent Variables

Should more than one dependent variable be used in a psychological experiment? This is a very reasonable question, particularly when more than one dependent variable could be used to measure the effect of variation of a given independent variable. In a learning experiment using rats, the dependent variable could be the frequency, amplitude, or latency of response. Likewise, in an attitude experiment, the dependent variable could be measured by a questionnaire, by observing behavior, or by a physiological measure. When more than one dependent variable can be used, the scientist usually selects only one and proceeds with the experiment. If the scientist elects to use more than one dependent variable, certain problems arise. Assuming the scientist knows how to measure each of the dependent variables, he or she must be concerned with the relationship among them. If the various dependent variable measures are very highly correlated (e.g., 0.95 or above), there is reasonable assurance that they are identical measures, and all but one can be dropped. If they are not so highly correlated, the experimenter must ask why not. The lack of correspondence could be due to unreliability of the measures or to the fact that they are not measuring the same aspect of the construct under study. Two different measures of learning may be evaluating different aspects of the learning process. These difficulties must be resolved. However, the scientist all too often does not have the data available to solve all of these problems. As a field advances, more and more of the aspects of a phenomenon are unraveled and problems such as these are resolved. Such cases support the notion that multiple dependent variables should be used in some experiments because they contribute to the understanding of a phenomenon, which is what science is trying to accomplish.

The fact that the constructs we are attempting to measure, such as learning or anxiety, can be measured by several different techniques indicates that they are multidimensional. In order to get a good grasp of the effect that our independent variable has on our multidimensional dependent variable, we must use several different measures. Multidimensional statistical procedures have been developed to handle the simultaneous use of several dependent variables in the same study.

When several independent variables and several dependent variables are manipulated in one experiment, a more elaborate statistical technique called multivariate analysis of variance must be used to analyze the results. This approach allows us to take the correlation between the dependent variables into account (Kerlinger and Pedhazur, 1973). Analyzing each dependent variable separately would violate one of the underlying assumptions of the statistical test if a correlation did exist between the different dependent variable measures. Using several dependent variables in a study and appropriately analyzing them can, therefore, increase our knowledge of the complex relationship that exists between antecedent conditions and behavior.

Summary

In seeking an answer to a research question, one must develop a design that will provide the necessary information. Two primary ingredients in a research design are the independent and the dependent variables. Before the research design can be finalized, it is necessary to make a number of decisions regarding these two variables.

For the independent variable, the investigator must first specify not only the number of independent variables to be used but also the exact concrete operations that are going to represent the conceptual variable or variables. For some independent variables, this is easy because specific empirical referents exist; others are not so easily translated. In either case, the conceptual independent variable must be operationally defined. In addition to translating the independent variable, the investigator must also specify how variation is to be established in the independent variable. Generally, variation is created by a presence-versus-absence technique or by varying the amount or type of the independent variable. The investigator must determine, within the framework of one of these techniques, the exact mode for creating the variation. Will the variation be created by manipulating instructions or events or by measuring the internal states of the organism? After these decisions have been made, it is advisable to reexamine the operational definition of the independent variable to determine if the operations really represent the specified construct. There are a number of ways in which concrete information can be attained regarding this issue. If several ways of defining the independent variable all produce the same experimental results, there is added assurance that the conceptual variable was appropriately translated. Also, if several empirical representations of the independent variable produce the expected outcomes, then we are more confident that the correct translation was made. Additional techniques that can be used with human subjects are to conduct long probing interviews and to obtain a behavioral indication that the appropriate translation was made.

Control in Experimentation

Chapter Overview

Once the independent and dependent variables have been identified, it is necessary to identify the extraneous variables that must be controlled. This is one of the most crucial tasks facing the experimenter because without control of these extraneous variables it would be impossible to identify the effect of the independent variable. This chapter discusses some of the major extraneous variables that may creep into an experiment. As you read through the chapter, you should answer the following questions:

1. What does control in experimentation mean?

2. What is an extraneous variable?

3. What types of extraneous variables must be controlled in experimentation?

4. How does each of the extraneous variables bias the results of an experiment?

Introduction

In any experiment, the goal of the researcher is to attain internal validity (Campbell and Stanley, 1963). **Internal validity** refers to the extent to which we can accurately state that the independent variable produced the observed effect. When conducting an experiment, the scientist wants to identify the effect produced by the independent variable. If the observed effect, as measured by the dependent variable, is due only to the variation in the independent variable, then internal validity has been achieved. The difficulty that arises is one of determining whether the observed effect is caused *only* by the independent variable, since the dependent variable could be influenced by variables other than the independent variable. For example, if we were investigating the influence of tutoring (independent variable) on grades (dependent variable), we would like to conclude that any improvement in the grades of the students who received the tutoring over that of

Internal validity
The extent to which the observed effect is caused only by the experimental treatment condition

those who did not was in fact a result of the tutoring. However, if the tutored students were brighter than those who were not tutored, the improvement in grades could be due to the fact that the tutored students were brighter. In such an instance, intelligence would represent an **extraneous variable,** which has the effect of confounding the results of the experiment. Once an extraneous variable creeps into an experiment, we can no longer draw any conclusion regarding the causal relationship that exists between the independent and the dependent variable. Therefore, it is necessary to control for the influence of such outside variables in order to attain internal validity. Since achieving control over the variation produced by extraneous variables is a prime component in the research process, I will discuss it at some length.

Extraneous variable
Any variable other than the independent variable that influences the dependent variable

Control of Extraneous Variables

The neophyte may think that controlling for the effect of extraneous variables means completely eliminating the influence of these variables from the experiment. It is possible to totally eliminate the influence of some variables. The effect of visual stimulation could, for example, be eliminated by conducting the experiment in a lightproof, blacked-out room, since such variables would be held constant at a magnitude of zero. However, most of the variables that could influence a psychological experiment—such as intelligence, past experience, and history of reinforcement—are not of a type that can be eliminated. Although such variables cannot be eliminated and thus it is not possible to eliminate their influence from the experiment, it *is* possible to eliminate any *differential* influence that these variables may have across the various levels of the independent variable. In other words, it is possible to keep the influence of these variables **constant** across the various levels of the independent variable; therefore, any differential influence noted on the dependent variable can be attributed to the levels of variation in the independent variable. Consider the study conducted by Wade and Blier (1974). They investigated the differential effect that two methods of learning had on the retention of lists of words (they actually used consonant-vowel-consonant trigrams). In this study, they had to control for the associations that subjects had with these words, since it has been shown that association value influences rate of learning. Therefore, they chose words that had previously been shown to have an average association value of 48.4 percent for subjects. In this manner, they held the association value of the words constant across the two groups of subjects and eliminated any differential influence that this variable might have had.

Constancy
Stability, or absence of change, in the influence exerted by the extraneous variable in all treatment conditions

Ideally, the scientist would like to keep the amount or type of each extraneous factor identical throughout the experiment. This means that the same amount and type of the factor must be present for all subjects. Variables that are noncontinuous (do not vary as a function of the independent variable or progress through the experiment) can meet the criterion of ideal constancy. Ideal constancy can be obtained for variables such as sex of the subject or rate of presentation of words but not for factors such as interest or learning ability.

Variables such as learning ability cannot be held completely constant for two reasons. First, constancy requires an exact measure, and our measuring devices are too crude to give more than an approximation of the amount of a characteristic such as interest, which is distributed along a continuum ranging from some very low point to some extremely high point. Second, some variables present in an experiment may change as the experiment progresses. Fatigue, motivation, interest, attention, and many other variables fall into this category. If these factors do vary, constancy dictates that the magnitude of these changes has to be the same for all individuals. Degree of fatigue would have to increase and decrease for all subjects simultaneously. Even if it were possible to arrange this (which it is probably not), it is still possible that the waxing and waning of these factors would influence the behavior measured by the dependent variable. Increased fatigue frequently does affect performance. If the waxing and waning of a variable such as fatigue, even though it occurs simultaneously and in the same amount for all subjects, affects the dependent variable of performance, constancy is not achieved. It would then be impossible to determine what caused the variation in the dependent variable of performance. The variation could be due entirely to the independent variable, entirely to the waxing and waning of fatigue, or to a combination of these two. As you can readily see, a situation such as this would not allow you to unambiguously identify the cause of the variation noted in the dependent variable. Constancy requires an equal amount and/or type of a factor in all subjects throughout the course of the experiment.

Although the ideal type of constancy is not always achievable, in most cases it is possible to eliminate the differential effects of these variables on the dependent variable, thereby allowing the scientist to relate unambiguously the variation in the independent variable to the dependent variable. How is constancy achieved; that is, how do we arrange factors in such a way as to have no differential influence on the result of the experiment? The only way is through control. Control means exerting a constant influence. If one wanted to hold constant the trait of dominance, one would attempt to make sure that this trait had an equal influence on all groups of subjects.

Control, or achieving constancy of potential extraneous variables, is often relatively easy to accomplish once the extraneous variables have been identified. The difficulty frequently lies in identifying these variables. Before determining techniques for controlling extraneous variables, one must identify the variables that need to be controlled. The variables identified in this chapter do not run the gamut of extraneous variables, but they do represent the more salient ones.

Extraneous Variables to Be Controlled

In experimentation, the condition the scientist strives for is constancy of all variables except the one or more that are deliberately being manipulated. Campbell and Stanley (1963) state that experiments are internally valid when the obtained effect can be unambiguously attributed to the manipulation of the independent variable. In other words, if the effects obtained in the experiment are due only to the experimental conditions manipulated by the scientist and not to any other variables, the experiment has internal validity. To the extent that other variables may possibly have contributed to the observed effects, the experiment is internally valid.

In any experiment there are always some variables other than the independent variable that could influence the observed effects. These potentially confounding variables have to be identified and then dealt with or held constant. Cook and Campbell (1979) list a number of classes of variables that need to be controlled for internal validity to be attained.

History

The **history variable** operates in an experiment that is designed in such a way as to have both a pre- and a postmeasurement of the dependent variable. History refers to the specific events, other than the independent variable, that occur between the first and second measurement of the dependent variable, as illustrated in Figure 5.1. These events, in addition to the independent variable, could have influenced the postmeasurement; therefore, these events become plausible rival hypoth-

History variable
An extraneous variable occurring between the pre- and the postmeasurement of the dependent variable

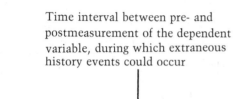

Time interval between pre- and postmeasurement of the dependent variable, during which extraneous history events could occur

Figure 5.1   *Illustration of extraneous history events.*

eses as to the change that occurred between the pre- and the postmeasurement. Consider an attitude-change experiment. One of the typical procedures followed is to pretest subjects to identify their current attitudes. An experimental condition is then introduced in an attempt to change the subjects' attitudes, and a postattitude measurement is given to all subjects. The difference between the pre- and postattitude scores is typically taken as a measurement of the effect of the experimental variable on the attitude. The difficulty with making this automatic assumption is that a certain amount of time elapses between the pre- and the postmeasure. It is possible that the subjects experienced events during this time that had an effect on their attitude—an effect that was reflected in the postmeasurement. If such a condition actually took place, the history variable, in addition to the experimental variable, may have influenced the observed effects, creating *internal invalidity*, since the history events would be plausible rival hypotheses.

A study by Watts (1967) can be used to illustrate history events. He investigated relative persistence of attitude change induced by actively writing an argument or reading an argument for one of three selected issues. Immediately after the active (writing) or passive (reading) participation, subjects took the pretest opinionnaire to measure the change induced by these two techniques. No difference existed in the initial opinion change generated by these two techniques. Actually, Watts modified the passive messages to attempt to ensure that this initial attitude change would be identical in both conditions. He then waited six weeks and posttested the subjects to determine which of the two techniques induced most persistence. Results revealed that subjects in the active participation condition not only maintained the change initially induced by that treatment condition but displayed increased opinion change. The subjects in the passive participation group regressed back toward the opinion they had possessed prior to participation in the passive condition. From such results, it is tempting to conclude that active participation produces greater persistence. However, six weeks intervened between pre- and posttesting, and many events could have taken place during this time. Watts also realized this and took a look at the activities of the subjects during this period. He found that subjects in the active participation group tended to discuss and read about the attitude topic more than subjects in the passive condition. Thus, it seems as though the active participation condition may lead to other events that influence persistence. It is these other events, the history events, that must be identified by the sensitive and alert investigator.

Generally speaking, the longer the time lapse between the pre- and the posttest, the greater the possibility of history becoming a rival explanation. However, it must be recognized that short time lapses can also generate the history effect. If group data are collected and an irrelevant, unique event such as an obstreperous joke or comment occurs between the pre- and the posttest, this event can have an influence on the posttest, making it a rival hypothesis.

Maturation

Maturation refers to changes in the internal conditions of the individual that occur as a function of the passage of time. The changes involve both biological and psychological processes, such as age, learning, fatigue, boredom, and hunger, that are not related to specific external events but reside within the individual. To the extent that such changes affect the response made to the experimental treatment, internal invalidity exists. Consider a study that attempts to evaluate the benefits achieved from a Head Start program. Assume that the investigator gave the subjects a preachievement measure at the beginning of the school year and a postachievement measure at the end of the school year. In comparing the pre- and postachievement measures, she found that significant increases in achievement existed and concluded that Head Start programs are very beneficial. Such a study is internally invalid because there was no control for the maturational influence. The increased achievement could have been due to the changes that occurred with the passage of time. A group of children who did not participate in Head Start may have progressed an equal amount. In order to determine the effect of a program such as Head Start, a control group that did not receive the treatment would also have to be included to control for the potential rival influence of maturation.

Liddle and Long (1958) conducted a study that did not seem to control for the maturational variable. They identified a group of "slow learners," culturally deprived children who had been unsuccessful in the first grade, and set up an experimental room in an attempt to motivate these children and to increase the amount that they learned. The investigators gave the children an initial intelligence test and assigned them a reading-grade placement score. Toward the end of the second year in the experimental room, the Metropolitan Achievement Tests were administered and showed "an improvement of about 1.75 years in less than two school years" (p. 145). Based on such evidence, the authors suggested that an experimental room such as the one they had developed enhances the learning of slow learners. One of the problems with this study is that maturational influences were not ruled out. These slow learners were two years older at the end of the study and therefore were probably more mature. I suspect that some learning would have taken place outside this experimental room. The investigators did not isolate the effect due *just* to the experimental room but allowed many other variables to enter in, one of which could have been maturation.

Maturation
The change in biological and psychological conditions that occurs with the passage of time

Instrumentation

Instrumentation refers to changes that occur over time in the measurement of the dependent variable. This class of variables does not refer to subject changes but to changes that occur during the process of measurement. Unfortunately, many of the techniques that we use to measure our dependent variable are subject to change during the course of the study. The measurement situation that is most subject to the instrumentation source of error is one that requires the use of human observers. Physical measurements show minor changes, but human observers are subject to influences such as fatigue, boredom, and learning processes. In administering intelligence tests, the tester typically gains facility and skill over time, and many collect more reliable and valid data as additional tests are given. Observers and interviewers are often used to assess the effects of various experimental treatments. As the observers and interviewers assess increasingly more individuals, they gain skill. The interviewers may, for example, gain additional skill with the interview schedule or with observing a particular type of behavior, producing shifts in the response measure that cannot be attributed to either the subject or the treatment conditions. This is why studies that use human observers to measure the behavioral characteristics of interest typically use more than one observer and have each of the observers go through a training program. In this way, some of the biases inherent in making observations can be minimized, and the various observers can serve as checks on one another to ensure that accurate data are being collected. Typically, the data collected by the various observers have to coincide before they are considered valid.

Instrumentation
Changes in the assessment of the dependent variable

Statistical Regression

Many psychological experiments (such as the attitude change experiment outlined under the history factor) require pre- and posttesting on the same dependent variable measure or some other equivalent form for the purpose of measuring change. Additionally, these studies sometimes select only the two groups of subjects who have the extreme scores, such as high and low attitude scores. The two extreme scoring groups are then given an experimental treatment condition, and a posttest score is obtained. A variable that could cause the pre- and posttest scores of the extreme groups to change is **statistical regression.** This "refers to the fact that the extreme scores in a particular distribution will tend to move—that is, regress—toward the mean of the distribution as a function of repeated testing" (Neale and Liebert, 1973, p. 38). The scores of the high groups may become lower, not because of any treatment condition introduced, but because of the statistical regression phenomenon. Low scorers could show increases upon retesting because of statistical regression and not because of any experimental

Statistical regression
The lowering of extremely high scores or the raising of extremely low scores during posttesting

Table 5.1　*Illustration of the Statistical Regression Effect*

Subject	PRETEST SCORE	SELECTED SUBJECT	PRESTEST SCORE	SELECTED SUBJECT	POSTTEST SCORE
S_1	110 ⟶ S_1		110 ⟶ S_1		103
S_2	46	S_3	123 ⟶ S_3		116
S_3	123	S_8	105 ⟶ S_8		98
S_4	92				
S_5	59				
S_6	73				
S_7	99				
S_8	105				
S_9	67	S_2	46 ⟶ S_2		57
S_{10}	84	S_5	59 ⟶ S_5		63
S_{11}	61	S_9	67 ⟶ S_9		70
S_{12}	96	S_{11}	61 ⟶ S_{11}		65

treatment effect. This regression phenomenon exists because the first and second measurements are not perfectly correlated. In other words, there is some degree of unreliability in the measuring device.

The regression toward the mean is illustrated in Table 5.1. A total of 12 subjects were pretested, and the scores of these subjects ranged from 46 to 123. A group of three extremely high scorers and four extremely low scorers was selected from the original 12 subjects. These high- and low-scoring subjects were then posttested. The scores of subjects with high pretest scores declined upon posttesting, whereas those of subjects with low pretest scores increased upon posttesting. In this example, an experimental treatment condition was not administered to the subjects to cause a change in their scores. Rather, the decline in the scores of the high-scoring group and the increase in the scores of the low-scoring group were caused entirely by statistical regression resulting from unreliability of the measuring device.

Regression effects are different from those of maturation or history. They constitute a real source of possible internal invalidity, which must be controlled if any conclusive statement is to be drawn regarding the cause of the observed effects.

Selection

The **selection** bias exists when a differential selection procedure is used for placing subjects in the various comparison groups. Ideally, a sample of subjects is randomly chosen from a population, and then these sub-

Selection
Choosing subjects for the various treatment groups on the basis of different criteria

jects are randomly assigned to the various treatment groups. When this procedure cannot be followed and assignment to groups is based on some differential procedure, possible rival hypotheses are introduced. Assume that you wanted to investigate the relative efficacy of a given type of therapy on various types of psychotic behaviors. For your subjects, you selected two groups of psychotic patients. After two months of therapy, progress in therapy was evaluated and you found that the subjects exhibiting one type of psychotic reaction improved significantly more than those with the other classification. With these results, one is tempted to say that the therapy technique used is the agent that produced the difference in improvement between the two groups of psychotic patients. But there may be other differences between the two groups that would provide a better explanation of the observed difference. The psychotic patients who improved most may possess characteristics that predispose them toward more rapid improvement with almost any type of therapy. If this is the case, then it is these characteristics and not the type of therapy that caused the more rapid improvement. Such difficulties are encountered when subjects are differentially selected based on a criterion such as type of psychosis, because the independent variable manipulation represents a measured manipulation. Therefore, a study with a selection bias boils down to an ex post facto study, with all of its inherent difficulties.

Selection can also interact with maturation, history, or instrumentation to produce effects that appear to be results of treatment. Consider the selection by maturation interaction which occurs when the experimental groups selected are maturing at different rates. Kusche and Greenberg (1983) discovered that deaf children's understanding of the concepts of good and bad develops more slowly than that of normal-hearing children, as depicted in Figure 5.2. If these maturational differences were not known, a study that attempted to teach the concepts of good and bad to deaf and to normal-hearing children might conclude that the instructional program was more effective for the normal-hearing children. However, the difference in response would be strictly a result of selection by maturation interaction and not a result of the instructional program. Similar treatment effects can occur if a selection by history or a selection by instrumentation interaction exists. For example, if a history effect influenced one of two treatment groups, a difference may exist between the two groups not because of the treatment effect but because of the impact of history on only one of the groups.

Mortality

Mortality refers to the differential subject loss from the various comparison groups in an experiment. Most psychological experiments, both human and infrahuman, have to contend with this potential source of

Mortality
A differential loss of subjects from the various experimental groups

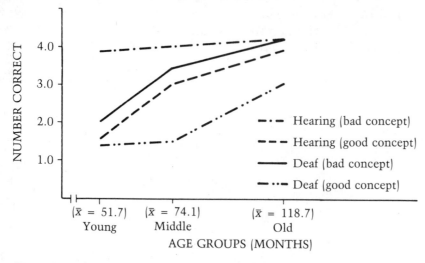

Figure 5.2   *The evaluation of good and bad concepts as a function of age and hearing status.*
(From Kusche, C. A., and Greenberg, M. T. Evaluative understanding and role taking ability: A comparison of deaf and hearing children. *Child Development,* 1983, *54,* 141–147.)

bias at some time. Physiological experiments involving electrode implantation sometimes experience subject loss due to the complications that may arise from the surgical procedures. Human experiments must contend with subjects' not showing up for the experiment at the designated time and place or not participating in all the conditions required by the study. The difficulty arises not just because subjects are lost but because the subjects that are lost may produce differences in the groups that cannot be attributed to the experimental treatment. Consider the following example. Assume that you want to test the effect of a certain treatment condition on conformity. You know that past research has demonstrated that females conform to a greater degree than males do, so you control for this factor by assigning an equal number of males and females to two groups. However, when you actually run the experiment, half of the females assigned to the group that does not receive the treatment condition do not show up, and half of the males assigned to the other group (the one receiving the treatment condition) do not show up. Statistical analysis reveals that the group receiving the treatment condition conforms significantly more than the group not receiving any treatment does. Can you conclude that this significantly greater degree of conformity is caused by the independent variable administered? Such an inference would be incorrect because more females were in the group receiving the experimental treatment and past research indicates that they exhibit greater degrees of conformity. This variable, and not the independent variable, may have produced the observed significant difference.

---

2. Subject-Experimenter Effects to Be Controlled

Any human experiment involves an interaction between an experimenter and a subject. In this situation, two roles can be identified: that of the experimenter and that of the subject. Each role has specific behavioral requirements, and mutual expectations are held by the two role members. These expectations should define the behavior that is appropriate for each member. When agreeing to take part in an experiment, a person is making an implicit contract to play the role of the subject. Theoretically, this means that the subject will listen to the instructions and perform the tasks requested to the best of his or her ability and as truthfully as possible. In reality, such an idealistic situation does not always exist because the subject has certain perceptions of the experiment that may alter behavior. The subject may want to comply and participate in the experiment but, because of certain perceptions and motives, may respond in several different ways. That is to say, there is an interaction between the way a person responds in an experiment and his or her motives and perception of the experiment.

a) Subject Effect

In an experiment, the researcher would like to have ideal subjects. Such subjects would bring no preconceived notions to the laboratory. Once in the laboratory, they would accept instructions and be motivated to respond in as truthful a manner as possible. While such a situation would be wonderful, it exists only in the experimenter's mind. When subjects enter the experiment, they are generally naive regarding its purpose or the task required of them. However, once they appear for the experiment, they receive information from the way the experimenter greets them, from the instructions given regarding the experiment, from the task required of them, from the laboratory setting (including the available equipment), and from any rumors they hear regarding the experiment. This information, also called the **demand characteristics** of the experiment (Orne, 1962), defines the experiment from the subjects' point of view. It provides the subjects with the information from which they create their perceptions of the purpose of the experiment and the task required. Once the subjects identify this task, they are motivated to perform it. It is in the performance of the

Demand characteristics
Any of the cues available in the experiment, such as the instructions, the experimenter, rumors, or the experimental setting

So far:
1. extraneous variables to be controlled
   a) history
   b) maturation
   c) stat regression
   d) instrumentation
   e) selection
   f) mortality

experimental task that the subjects' perceptions can influence the outcome of the experiment.

In the past, it was thought that subjects assumed a specific role (Orne, 1962; Rosenberg, 1969; Fillenbaum, 1966; Masling, 1966) and attempted to portray this role when performing the experimental task. Increasingly, this view is being rejected (e.g., Carlston and Cohen, 1980; Carlopia et al., 1983). In its place is the notion that subjects respond to the experimental task as it is perceived to be. If the experiment involves a learning task, the subject will attempt to learn the material presented. However, subjects do not take an uninvolved, neutral approach, because often their performance implies something about them. For example, a learning task indirectly says something about the subjects' intelligence. If they learn the material rapidly, this suggests that they are intelligent. Most individuals have a desire to appear intelligent, so they will try to learn as rapidly as possible. Similarly, if the task suggests something about emotional stability, subjects will respond in such a way as to appear most emotionally stable (Rosenberg, 1969). Consequently, although subjects seem to approach an experiment with the motivation to perform the task requested, superimposed on this desire is also the wish to make a **positive self-presentation** (Christensen, 1981). This means that subjects use their perceptions of the experiment to determine how to respond to the experimental task in such a way that they appear most positive.

Positive self-presentation Subjects' motivation to respond in such a way as to present themselves in the most positive manner

Consider the experiment conducted by Christensen (1977). In this experiment, an attempt was made to verbally condition, or increase, the subjects' use of certain pronouns such as *we* and *they* by saying "good" whenever the subjects used one of them. Some subjects interpreted the experimenter's reaction of saying "good" as an attempt to manipulate their behavior. These subjects resisted any behavioral manifestation of conditioning. This resistance was caused by their viewing manipulation as negative. If they did not demonstrate any conditioning, then they would show that they could not be manipulated and in this way present themselves most positively. Similarly, Bradley (1978) has revealed that individuals take credit for desirable acts but deny blame for undesirable ones to enhance themselves.

Conditions Producing a Positive Self-Presentation Motive

In order to control the interactive effects that exist between the subjects' behavior and their role in an experiment, it would be advantageous to know the conditions that alter subjects' behavior in their attempt to attain favorable self-presentations. Only when such conditions are identified can one construct conditions that control for the confounding effect that may be produced.

Tedeschi, Schlenker, and Bonoma (1971) provide some insight into the general conditions that may determine whether or not the self-presentation motive will exist within an experiment. They state that this motive arises only when the behavior in which the subject engages is indicative of the subject's true intentions, beliefs, or feelings. If subjects believe that others view their behavior as being determined by some external source not under their control, then the positive self-presentation motive is not aroused. However, our experiments are seldom constructed so that the subjects believe that others think their behavior is externally determined. Therefore, it seems that the positive self-presentation motive would exist in most research studies.

Implication for Research

The implication of the positive self-presentation motive is that experimenters must take into consideration the influence of the subjects' perceptions of the experiment. No longer can we assume that the responses obtained from subjects are a function only of the physical or psychological stimuli representative of the independent variable. Consider the studies conducted by Carlston and Cohen (1980) and Carlopia et al. (1983). Carlston and Cohen contrasted the responses to subjects instructed to portray a good, faithful, negative, or apprehensive role with those of control subjects who were not given a role to portray. These investigators found that the responses of the role-play subjects differed from those of the control subjects. Based on these data, Carlston and Cohen concluded that subject roles probably do not produce experimental bias. This conclusion was objected to both by Christensen (1982) and by Carlopia et al. (1983). Carlopia et al. hypothesized that Carlston and Cohen's conclusion was based on the differential perceptions that subjects had of the experimental hypothesis. These investigators then proceeded to replicate Carlston and Cohen's study. In doing so, they showed that subjects could be divided into those who perceived the experimental hypothesis to be true and those who perceived the experimental hypothesis to be false. Those who did not believe the experimental hypothesis supported Carlston and Cohen's conclusion, whereas those who did believe the experimental hypothesis did *not* support that conclusion. Consequently, the responses produced by the subjects and the conclusions drawn by the experimenters were a function of how the subjects perceived the experiment and not a function of just the independent variable manipulation.

These studies indicate the necessity of trying to ensure that constant subject perceptions exist throughout all phases of the experiment. When such constancy is not maintained, artifactual confounding can be expected to occur from the interaction of the motive of positive self-presentation with the experimental treatment condition. There appear to be two types of interaction that can exist (Christensen, 1981), an intertreatment and an intratreatment interaction. An **intertreatment interaction** exists when subjects' perceptions of the different experimental treatment conditions suggest to them different ways of presenting themselves in a positive manner. For example, Sigall, Aronson, and Van Hoose (1970) found that in one treatment condition subjects increased their performance when told that they were responding to a dull, boring task under decreased illumination levels. However, in another treatment condition subjects decreased their performance when told that rapid performance on the task indicated obsessive, compulsive performance. In the first experimental task, subjects apparently perceived that they could appear most positive by overcoming the obstacles of low illumination and a dull, boring task by performing rapidly. In the other treatment condition, subjects believed that they would appear most positive by performing slowly in order not to seem obsessive-compulsive.

An **intratreatment interaction** exists when different subjects in the same treatment condition perceive different ways of presenting themselves in the most positive light. For example, Turner and Soloman (1962) found that some subjects participating in an avoidance conditioning paradigm failed to learn to move a lever to avoid shock. Investigation of the perceptions of these subjects disclosed that they perceived the purpose of the study to be one of determining who could tolerate the shock. Consequently, these subjects apparently believed that they would appear most positive if they could demonstrate their capacity to endure the shock. When the instructions were changed to eliminate this perception, all subjects demonstrated avoidance conditioning.

Experimenter Effect

We have just seen that the subjects who are used in psychological research are usually not apathetic or willing to passively accept and follow the experimenter's instructions. Rather, they have motives that can have an effect on the experimental results. In like manner, the experimenter is not just a passive, noninteractive observer but an active agent who can influence the outcome of the experiment. Friedman (1967, pp. 3–4) has appropriately stated that in the past psychology has

> implicitly subscribed to the democratic notion that all *experimenters* are created equal; that they have been endowed by their graduate training with certain interchangeable properties; that among these properties are the anonymity and impersonality which allow them to elicit from the same subject identical data which they then identically observe and record. Just as inches were once supposed to adhere in tables regardless of the identity of the measuring instrument, so needs, motives, traits, IQs, anxieties, and attitudes were supposed to

Intertreatment interaction
When subjects in different treatment groups perceive that they can fulfill the positive self-presentation motive by responding in different ways

different instructions

Intratreatment interaction
When subjects in the same treatment condition perceive that they can fulfill the positive self-presentation motive by responding in different ways

different perception

adhere to patients and subjects and to emerge uncontaminated by the identity and attitude of the examiner or experimenter.

Such a conception of the experimenter is highly inappropriate, because research, as we shall see, has demonstrated biasing effects that are directly attributable to the experimenter. Take a look at the motives that the experimenter brings with him or her. First, the experimenter has a specific motive for conducting the experiment. The experimenter is a scientist attempting to uncover the laws of nature through experimentation. In performing this task, he or she develops certain perceptions of the experiment and the subject. Lyons (1964, p. 105) states that the experimenter wants subjects to be perfect servants—intelligent individuals who will cooperate and maintain their position without becoming hostile or negative. It is easy to see why such a desire exists. The scientist seeks to understand, control, and predict behavior. To attain this goal, the scientist must eliminate bias, such as that discussed under the subject effect, and so he or she dreams of the ideal subject who does not have such bias. Also, the experimenter has expectations regarding the outcome of the experiment. He or she has made certain hypotheses and would, therefore, like to see these confirmed. While this aspect of science is legitimate and sanctioned, it can, as we shall see, lead to certain difficulties. Additionally, journals have a bias toward publishing primarily positive results, which essentially means that studies that support hypotheses have a greater chance of being accepted for publication. Knowing this, the experimenter has an even greater desire to see the hypotheses confirmed. Can this desire or expectancy bias the results of the experiment so as to increase the probability of attaining the desired outcome? Consider the fascinating story of Clever Hans. Clever Hans was a remarkable horse that could apparently solve many types of arithmetic problems. Von Osten, the master of Clever Hans, would give Hans a problem, and then Hans would give the correct answer by tapping with his hoof. Pfungst (1911) observed and studied this incredible behavior. Careful scrutiny revealed that von Osten would, as Hans approached the correct answer, look up at Hans. This response of looking up represented a cue for Hans to stop tapping his foot. The cue was unintentional and not noticed by observers who attributed mathematical skills to him.

Observations such as that made by Pfungst of Clever Hans would seem to indicate that one's desires and expectancies can somehow be communicated to the subject and that the subject will respond to them. The research has suggested that subjects are motivated to present themselves in the most positive manner. If this is true, then the subtle cues presented by the experimenter in the experimental session may very well be picked up by the subjects and influence their performance in the direction desired by the experimenter. Consequently, the experimenter may represent a demand characteristic.

a cue to help define the experiment to the Ss.

The experimenter, zealous to confirm his or her hypothesis, may also unintentionally influence the recording of data to support the prediction. Kennedy and Uphoff (1939) investigated the frequency of misrecording of responses as a function of subjects' orientation. Subjects, classified on the basis of their belief or disbelief in ESP, were requested to record the guesses made by the "receiver." The receiver was supposedly trying to receive messages sent by a transmitter. Kennedy and Uphoff found that 63 percent of the errors that were in the direction of increasing the telepathic scores were made by believers in ESP, whereas 67 percent of the errors that were in the direction of lowering the telepathic scores were made by disbelievers. Such data indicate that biased recording, unintentional as it may be, exists in some experiments.

Additionally, the experimenter is an active participant in the social interaction that occurs with the subject. As stated earlier, the experiment may be considered a social situation in which two roles exist—that of the experimenter and that of the subject. The role behavior of the subject can vary slightly as a function of the experimenter's attributes. McGuigan (1963), for example, found that the results of a learning experiment varied as a function of the experimenter. Some of the nine researchers used to test the effectiveness of the same four methods of learning found significant differences, whereas the others did not. Such research reveals that certain attributes, behavior, or characteristics of the experimenter may influence the subjects' responses in a particular manner.

The several ways in which the experimenter can potentially bias the results of an experiment can be dichotomized into two types: bias arising from the attributes of the experimenter and bias resulting from the expectancy of the experimenter.

Experimenter Attributes.   The term **experimenter attributes** refers to the physical and psychological characteristics of experimenters, which may interact with the independent variable to cause differential performance in subjects. There currently exists a rather large body of data revealing the differential influence produced by various aspects of experimenters. Rosenthal (1966) has summarized a great deal of this research and has proposed that at least three categories of attributes exist. The first is *biosocial attributes.* Biosocial attributes include factors such as the experimenter's age, sex, race, and religion. The second category proposed is *psychosocial attributes.* These attributes include the experimenter's psychometrically determined characteristics of anxiety level, need for social approval, hostility, authoritarianism, intelligence, and dominance, and social behavior of relative status and warmth. The third category proposed by Rosenthal represents *situational factors,* including whether or not the experimenter and subject

Experimenter attributes
The physical and psychological characteristics of experimenters that may create differential responses in subjects

have had prior contact, whether the experimenter is a naive or experienced researcher, and whether the subject is friendly or hostile. Additionally, the characteristics or physical appearance of the laboratory may influence the outcome of the research study.

A great many biasing factors have been identified. Does this mean that experimenter attributes will always affect the experiment and lead to artifactual results? McGuigan (1963) says that there are three possibilities.

1. *The attributes of the experimenters have absolutely no effect on the outcome of the experiment.* Ideally, this is the type of situation to strive for.

2. *The experimenter attributes affect the dependent variable, but the influence is identical for all subjects.* Such a case would be of no concern, because all subjects would be uniformly affected and therefore all experimenters would attain the same experimental results.

3. *The experimenter attributes differentially affect subjects.* Here, the results of the experiment would be partially a function of the experimenter who conducted it. If, for example, a black experimenter found that subjects in an attitude change experiment responded in a significantly less prejudiced manner whereas a significant change was not found by a white experimenter, one would have to conclude that the biosocial attribute of race differentially affected subjects' responses.

Psychologists are working on the problem of the influence of the experimenter's characteristics. From this research, one should ultimately be able to identify what attributes will influence one's experiments and when. Jung (1971, p. 49) has stated that "the extent to which the variable can affect results may vary with the type of experiment, being stronger in social and personality experiments and weaker with psychophysical, perceptual, and sensory experiments." Psychologists need to work toward the goal of being able to identify where, under what conditions, and in what type of experiments researcher attributes are confounding variables, for these variables (as well as others) may well account for some of the controversies that arise from failure to replicate previously published studies.

About the only experimenter attribute that has been investigated in sufficient depth to allow us to begin to answer these questions is the attribute of experimenter ~~gender~~ sex. Rumenik, Capasso, and Hendrick (1977) reviewed the literature relating to this attribute and found that "despite the sloppy methodological state of most research . . ." (p. 874), the data suggest that young children perform better for female experimenters on a variety of tasks. For adults, male experimenters seem to elicit better performance. Within a client-counselor relation, the studies suggest that male counselors elicit more information-seeking responses, whereas female counselors elicit more self-disclosure and emotional expression.

Before anything definitive can be stated regarding the influence of experimenter attributes on specific types of research, it is necessary that researchers conduct studies that are methodologically sound. Specifically, they must attempt to overcome three deficiencies identified by Johnson (1976). First, they must control for the confounding influence of attributes other than the ones being studied. If gender of the experimenter is being studied, researchers must control for other attributes such as age, race, warmth, and need for social approval. Second, it is necessary to take into account and study the interactive influence of subject and experimenter attributes. For example, it may be that male and female experimenters of one ethnic group obtain different responses from male and female subjects of another ethnic group. Third, it is necessary for researchers to sample a variety of types of tasks. A given experimenter attribute may have an influence on one task but not on another task. Until such methodological refinements are made, about the only thing that can be said about experimenter attributes is that they "may at times affect how subjects perform in the experiment, but we can rarely predict beforehand what experimenter attributes will exert what kind of effects on subjects' performance on what kinds of tasks" (Barber, 1976).

Experimenter Expectancies.   The term **experimenter expectancies** refers to the biasing effects that can be attributed to the expectancies the experimenter has regarding the outcome of the experiment. As noted earlier, experimenters are motivated by several forces to see their hypotheses validated. Therefore, they have expectancies regarding the outcome of the experiment. These expectancies can lead the experimenter to behave unintentionally in ways that will bias the results of the experiment in the desired direction. These unintentional influences can operate on the experimenter to alter his or her behavior and on the subjects to alter their behavior.

Effect on the Experimenter.   It has been well documented that the expectancies we have can color our perceptions of our physical and social world. Research in social perception has repeatedly demonstrated the biased nature of our perceptions of others. With knowledge of such research, it would be rather naive to assume that the expectancies of the experimenter did not have a potential influence on his or her behavior. In fact, there are several documented ways in which these expectancies have actually influenced the outcome of experiments. The expectancies of the experimenter can lead him or her to record responses inaccurately in the direction that supports the expectancies, as was noted in the ESP experiment conducted by Kennedy and Uphoff (1939), discussed earlier. Rosenthal (1978) summarized the results of

Experimenter expectancies
The influence of the experimenter's expectations regarding the outcome of an experiment

21 studies relating to the expectancy issue. These studies showed that, on the average, 60 percent of the recording biases favored experimenter expectancies. In one study, 91 percent of the recording biases supported the experimenters' expectancies. Impressive as these percentages are, it is important to understand that these recording errors, both biased and unbiased, represent only a small portion of the overall number of observations made. Generally speaking, only about 1 percent of all observations are misrecorded, and of this about two-thirds support the experimenters' expectancies (Rosenthal, 1978). Such a rate of misrecordings, even if the majority of them support the expectancies of the experimenters, is so small as to affect only infrequently the conclusions reached in a given study. But just because recording errors occur infrequently does not mean that experimenters can relax regarding this issue, because when we relax we run the risk of increasing such errors. Reviews such as the one conducted by Rosenthal reveal that when we attempt to avoid recording errors we are relatively successful—at least successful enough to avoid reaching an unfounded conclusion that can be directly traced to recording errors.

A second type of bias falling under the category of "effect on the experimenter" involves the effects of expectancies on interpretation of the data collected. Once the data have been collected, the experimenter attempts to explain them. Practically any set of data can be interpreted in different ways, depending on the orientation of the person doing the interpreting. Robinson and Cohen (1954), for example, report finding differences in the psychological reports written for 30 patients by three examiners. Barber and Silver (1968) do not agree with the conclusion Rosenthal reaches regarding experimenter bias. This disagreement does not revolve around the validity of the data collected but around the interpretation of these data. However, the interpreter effects, though real, are not considered to be a serious methodological problem, because the interpretations of the recorded data are assumed to be a function of the experimenter and his or her specific orientation. This is supported by the fact that the debates that occur in the literature seldom involve another's observations but often involve the interpretations that are placed on the observed data.

Effect on the Subject.   It is relatively easy to see and to accept that the experimenters' expectancies may cause them to behave in ways that support their expectancies. It is not so easy to see how these same expectancies can influence the subject to behave in a way that would support them, yet there is a body of research that demonstrates just this influence. Remember that subjects seem to be motivated toward positive self-presentation. How do they know what response will maximize the possibility of achieving such a positive self-presentation? Somehow they make use of the demand characteristics surrounding the experiment, one of which seems to be the experimenter. The researcher has certain expectancies that lead him or her unintentionally to behave in ways that convey these expectancies. Subjects pick up these subtle cues and respond accordingly. Von Osten, for example, conveyed to Clever Hans when he should stop tapping his foot. Rosenthal and his associates have devoted a great deal of attention to this source of bias. They have conducted many studies in which they demonstrate that experimenters definitely can influence the results of the study in the direction of their hypotheses. To put it another way, the experimenter can influence the subjects' responses in such a way that they will support the experimenter's hypothesis. For example, Rosenthal and Fode (1963a) found that researchers who expected to get high success ratings on photographs previously judged neutral actually got significantly higher ratings than researchers who were led to expect that they would get low success ratings.

Do these biasing effects exist in different types of experiments in psychology? One might initially think that the biasing effects of the expectancies of the experimenter on the subjects' responses would be limited to human types of experimentation and more specifically to human experiments in such areas as social and personality psychology. However, when Rosenthal and Rubin (1978) summarized the studies conducted on expectancy, they found, as shown in Table 5.2, that the expectancy effect had been demonstrated in eight different research areas. Perhaps the most revealing bit of information contained in Table 5.2 is that the expectancy effect is not confined to human experiments. Not only has it been demonstrated in animal experiments, but a greater proportion of animal studies display the expectancy effect.

Table 5.2 *Number of Experimenter Expectancy Studies Conducted in Eight Different Research Areas*

RESEARCH AREA	NUMBER OF STUDIES CONDUCTED	PROPORTION DEMONSTRATING EXPECTANCY
Reaction time	9	0.22
Inkblot tests	9	0.44
Animal learning	15	0.73
Laboratory interviews	29	0.38
Psychophysical judgments	23	0.43
Learning and ability	34	0.29
Person perception	119	0.27
Everyday situations	112	0.40

Based on Table 1 in Rosenthal, R., and Rubin, D. B. Interpersonal expectancy effects: The first 345 studies. *The Behavioral and Brain Sciences*, 1978, 3, 377–415.

Mediation of Expectancy

The evidence presented by Rosenthal and others is consistent in indicating that the problem of the biasing effects of the experimenter is serious and needs to be dealt with. To deal most effectively with such biases, we must know what is causing them. In other words, just how is the experimenter transmitting expectancies? In addressing this question, Rosenthal considers the possibility of recording errors, particularly those biased in the direction of the expectancy. This would seem to be an important issue, since several studies (e.g., Johnson and Ryan, 1976) have indicated that recording biases can account for much of the so-called expectancy effects. Rosenthal (1976) directly confronted this issue and found that although recording errors can account for some of the expectancy effect in some studies, they cannot account for all of it. To further support the fact that the experimenter expectancy bias cannot be reduced to a recording bias, Rosenthal (1976) reviewed 36 studies that employed special techniques for the control of recording errors and deliberate cheating. He found that these studies were *more* rather than less likely to demonstrate the experimenter expectancy effect. Exactly why such studies should be more susceptible to an experimenter expectancy effect is not known. It may be that the investigators not only provided safeguards against cheating and recording errors but also reduced the influence of other errors, thereby creating a more powerful and precise test of the expectancy effect.

If recording errors and intentional biases are insufficient to explain expectancy effects, then how can they be explained? Lack of an explanation of expectancy effects represents the primary shortcoming of this research area (Adair, 1978). In all probability, these effects do not work in a unitary fashion, since they have been demonstrated to exist in both animal and human research. In animal studies, differences in animal handling seem to be important (Rosenthal and Fode, 1963a). In human studies, nonverbal cues (Rosenthal, 1980) such as facial or postural signals (Barber, 1976), intonation such as emphasizing different key sections of the instructions (Adair, 1973), or a nod, smile, or glance (Rosenthal, 1969) seems to be important. However, as Rosenberg (1980) stated and I emphasized earlier, we must also consider the subject when discussing the mediating influence of expectancy effects, since it is the subjects' responses that ultimately demonstrate these effects. The subjects are motivated to present themselves in the most positive manner. In doing so, they use the demand characteristics of the experimental situation—including the behavior of the experimenter—to define the most appropriate way of responding to induce a positive self-presentation. Consequently, subjects apparently make use of many nonverbal cues transmitted by the experimenter to define the responses that will maximize the probability that they will present themselves in the most positive manner.

Since there is no conceptual integration or theoretical statement to explain the phenomenon, we do not know when expectancy effects might occur or what may mediate them; the evidence merely tells us that these effects are real possible sources of bias. However, it is precisely because we do not know when expectancy effects are likely to occur that we must always protect ourselves against them as a potential source of bias (Ellsworth, 1978).

Magnitude of the Expectancy Effects

The influence of experimenter expectancies has been demonstrated repeatedly in a wide variety of contexts. Table 5.2 illustrates that about one-third of the studies conducted showed a significant expectancy effect. This rate is about seven times greater than would have been expected if the effect did not exist (Rosenthal, 1976). However, if the effect of experimenter expectancies were extremely small (though real), it might not pose a significant threat to internal validity, which would mean that researchers need not concern themselves with this potential bias. Rosenthal (1978) reviewed five studies that directly addressed this issue. These studies compared the effect produced by the experimental treatment condition with the effect produced by expectancy. In three of these five studies, the expectancy effect was greater than the treatment condition. For example, Burnham (cited in Rosenthal and Rubin, 1978) compared lesioned rats with nonlesioned (sham surgery) rats on a discrimination learning task. Half of the lesioned and half of the nonlesioned rats were assigned to experimenters who were told that they had received lesioned rats. The remainder were assigned to researchers who were told that they had received nonlesioned rats. Figure 5.3 shows that all of the rats tested by experimenters who were told that the rats were nonlesioned performed better than did the rats tested by experimenters who were told that the rats were lesioned. This evidence indicates that expectancy effects can be quite large and that precautions should be taken against them.

---

3. Sequencing Effect to Be Controlled

In an experiment, variation in the independent variable may be established by presence versus absence or by varying the amount or type of a variable. In addition to making a decision as to the manner in which the independent variable will be varied, the investigator must make a decision regarding how the subjects are to be used in the experiment. There are two choices here: the investigator can randomly assign sub-

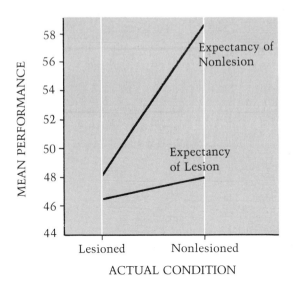

Figure 5.3 *Discrimination learning of lesioned and non-lesioned rats as a function of experimenter expectancy.*

(Based on data from Rosenthal, R., and Rubin, D. B. Interpersonal expectancy effects: The first 345 studies. *The Behavioral and Brain Sciences*, 1978, 3, 377–415.)

jects to the various treatment groups, or he or she can administer the various levels of variation of the independent variable to the same subjects. In a drug experiment having both a placebo and a drug condition, the experimenter could either randomly assign subjects to the placebo and drug conditions or have all subjects respond under both the placebo and drug conditions. While there is a definite advantage (which will be discussed at a later time) to having the same subjects respond in both treatment conditions, there is also a definite disadvantage that involves a sequencing effect.

The sequencing effect occurs when participation in one condition affects the response that the subject will make in a subsequent treatment condition. If subjects first participate in the drug condition and then in the placebo condition, their responses in the placebo condition may be partially a function of carry-over effects of the drug. If so, then a sequencing effect has taken place. Sequencing effects occur any time a subject's response in one treatment condition is partially determined by participation in a prior treatment condition. Carry-over effects may be the result of such factors as practice received or fatigue incurred.

4. Additional Extraneous Variables to Be Held Constant

In addition to the variables already discussed, there are many others that could have an influence on a given experiment, including the subjects' motivation and ability and physical variables such as noise level and lighting. For example, a number of investigations (Page, 1968, 1969; Page and Kahle, 1976; and Page and Scheidt, 1971) have disclosed that **subject sophistication** can have a confounding influence on the results produced in psychological experiments. By subject sophistication I mean subjects' "familiarity with or sophistication in the subject matter, and methods of experimental psychology" (Page, 1968, p. 60). Investigators have revealed that a number of the effects that had previously been identified could not be replicated unless sophisticated subjects were used. Use of novice subjects resulted in a failure to find the effect. For example, Schafer and Murphy (1943) found that subjects reported a pair of ambiguous human profiles that had previously been associated with winning money more frequently than a pair that had been associated with losing money. However, Page (1968) found this difference to exist only for the sophisticated group. Such findings suggest that in some of our experiments we must control for the influence of subject sophistication to eliminate the possibility that our results are due to this extraneous variable. When we gain better understanding of the reason why subject sophistication alters the results of our experiments, we will be in a better position to state which experiments should control for this extraneous variable and which ones can disregard it. At the present time, which experiments are subject to this effect is an empirical question.

Subject sophistication
The biasing influence that can arise from a subject's knowledge of or familiarity with psychology and psychological experiments

The materials and apparatus used should also be constant for all subjects. If an apparatus breaks down, the experimenter should fix it rather than using a nonequivalent piece.

It would be impossible to list all of the variables that could possibly affect an experiment. A number of the more salient ones have been discussed. Beyond this, the experimenter must use his or her own knowledge and foresight to anticipate potential sources of error and build in controls for them.

Summary

One of the most important tasks confronting the researcher is to ensure that the experiment is internally valid. To attain internal validity, the experimenter must control for the influence of extraneous variables that could serve as rival hypotheses for explaining the effects produced by the independent variable. Ideally, attaining the desired control involves completely eliminating the influence of all extraneous variables. However, this is impossible in most cases. Therefore, control most frequently refers to holding the influence of the extraneous variables constant across the various levels of the independent variable. The task of maintaining constancy is difficult for some variables, since they may vary as the subject progresses through the experiment.

Providing the desired control involves first identifying the variables that need to be controlled. Some of the more salient variables that could influence the experiment and serve as rival hypotheses are as follows:

History. Any of the many events other than the independent variable that occur between a pre- and a postmeasurement of the dependent variable.

Maturation. Any of the many conditions internal to the individual that change as a function of the passage of time.

Instrumentation. Any changes that occur as a function of measuring the dependent variable.

Statistical regression. Any change that can be attributed to the tendency of extremely high or low scores to regress toward the mean.

Selection. Any change due to the differential selection procedure used in placing subjects in various groups.

Mortality. Any change due to the loss of a differential subject from the various comparison groups.

Subject effect. Any change in performance that can be attributed to a subject's motives or attitude.

Experimenter effect. Any change in a subject's performance that can be ← *also experimente effect in recording and/or interpretation.* attributed to the experimenter.

Sequencing. Any change in a subject's performance that can be attributed to the fact that the subject participated in more than one treatment condition.

Subject sophistication. Any change in a subject's performance as a function of sophistication or familiarity with the experimental procedures or subject matter of psychology.

6

Techniques for Achieving Constancy

Chapter Overview

In order to attain internal validity, it is necessary not only to identify those extraneous variables that can produce a confounding influence on the results of an experiment but also to use those techniques that will enable you to maintain the necessary control. Consequently, researchers have been just as diligent about identifying control techniques as they have about identifying variables that need to be controlled. Once a decision has been reached regarding the variable or variables that need to be controlled, the experimenter must specify those techniques that will enable him or her to achieve the necessary control. This chapter presents the control techniques most frequently used by researchers. As you read through this chapter, you should attempt to answer the following questions:

1. What are the various control techniques used by researchers?

2. How does each of the control techniques operate to produce the necessary control?

3. What type of variable is controlled by each of the techniques discussed?

Introduction

In order to conduct an internally valid experiment, it is necessary to control for the influence of extraneous variables such as those presented in Chapter 5. This means that some procedure must be incorporated into the study that will eliminate any differential influence that these variables may have on the dependent variable. There are three general techniques that can be used to achieve the desired level of control. First, control can be attained through appropriate design of the experiment. One of the purposes of experimental design is to eliminate the differential influence of extraneous variables. (The control function of appropriate designs will become evident in Chapter 7.) A second means of attaining control involves making statistical adjustments through use of techniques such as analysis of covariance. However, these techniques are beyond the scope of the present text and therefore will not be discussed. A third means of acquiring the desired control is to incorporate one or more of the available control techniques into the design of the experiment. This control technique is intimately related to control through appropriate design of the experiment, since any control technique must be incorporated into the design of the experiment. However, control techniques are discussed separately in the present chapter to allow more effective illustration of the variables that they control and how they control these unwanted sources of variation.

All of the following techniques cannot and should not be incorporated into one study. Indeed, it would be impossible to do so. By the same token, it is often possible and advisable to use more than one of the techniques. The researcher must decide which of the possible extraneous variables could influence the experiment and, given this knowledge, select from the available techniques those that will allow the desired control. Failure to do so will create internal invalidity.

Randomization

Randomization, the most important and basic of all the control methods, is a control technique that has the purpose of providing assurance that extraneous variables, known or unknown, will not systematically bias the results of the study. It is the only technique for controlling unknown sources of variation. As Cochran and Cox (1957) have stated, "Randomization is somewhat analogous to insurance, in that it is a precaution against disturbances that may or may not occur and that may or may not be serious if they do occur. It is generally advisable to take the trouble to randomize even when it is not expected that there will be any serious bias from failure to randomize. The experimenter is thus protected against unusual events that upset his expectations" (p. 8).

How does randomization eliminate systematic bias in the experiment? Randomization refers to use of some clearly stated procedures such as tossing coins, drawing cards from a well-shuffled deck, or using a table of random numbers. To provide for maximum control of extraneous variables, one *ideally* should randomly select subjects from a population. These subjects should then be randomly assigned to the same number of groups as there are experimental treatment conditions, as illustrated in Figure 6.1. The experimental treatment conditions should then be assigned to the experimental treatment groups. While this is the ideal arrangement, one can seldom select subjects randomly from a population. Random selection from a population is not, how-

Randomization
A control technique that equates groups of subjects by ensuring every member an equal chance of being assigned to any group

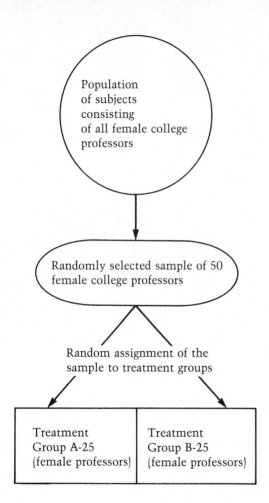

ever, the crucial element for providing control, whereas random assignment of the subjects to treatment conditons is essential. Random selection of subjects provides assurance that your sample is *representative* of the population from which it was drawn. It therefore has implications for generalization of the results of the experiment back to the population. Random assignment provides assurance that the extraneous variables are controlled.

The key word in this whole process of selecting and assigning subjects is *random.* The term *random* "may be used in a theoretical sense to refer to an assumption about the equiprobability of events. Thus a random sample is one such that every member of the population has an equal probability of being included in it" (Ferguson, 1966, p. 133). In a random selection of a sample of 100 subjects from a population of, say, college freshmen, every freshman has an equal chance of being included in the sample of 100. In like manner, random assignment of subjects to the experimental groups assures that each sample subject has an equal opportunity of being assigned to each group.

In order to provide equiprobability of events, it is necessary to use a randomization procedure, such as the one presented in Exhibit 6.1. When such a procedure is used, maximum assurance is provided that any systematic bias will be eliminated from the experimental results. This is because the random selection of subjects and the random assignment of subjects to treatment conditions are assumed to result in random distribution of all extraneous variables. The distribution and influence of the extraneous variables consequently should be about the same in all experiment groups.

Consider the following example using only random assignment of subjects. Professor X was conducting a study on learning. Intelligence naturally is correlated with learning ability, so this factor must be controlled for, or held constant. Let us consider two possibilities—one that provides for the needed control through the use of random assignment and one that does not. Assume first that no random assignment of subjects existed (no control) but that the first ten subjects who showed up for the experiment were assigned to treatment Group A and the second ten subjects were assigned to treatment Group B. Assume further that the results of the experiment revealed that treatment Group B learned significantly faster than treatment Group A. Is this difference caused by the different experimental treatment conditions that were administered to the two groups or by the fact that the subjects in Group B *may* have been more intelligent than those in Group A? Suppose that the investigator also considers the intelligence factor to be a possible confounding variable and therefore gives all subjects an intelligence test. The left-hand side of Table 6.1 depicts the hypothetical distribution of IQ scores of these 20 subjects. From this table, you can see that the mean IQ score of the people in Group B is 10.6 points higher than that of those in Group A. Intelligence is, therefore, a potentially confounding variable and serves as a rival hypothesis for explaining the observed performance difference in the two groups. To state that the treatment conditions produced the observed effect, researchers have to control for potentially confounding variables such as the IQ difference.

One means of eliminating such a bias would have been to randomly assign the 20 subjects to the two treatment groups as they showed up for the experiment. The right-hand side of Table 6.1 depicts the random distribution of the 20 subjects and their corresponding hypothetical IQ scores. Now note that the mean IQ scores for the two groups are very similar. There is only a 0.2 point IQ difference as opposed to the prior 10.6 point difference. For the mean IQ scores to be so similar, both groups of subjects had to have a similar distribution of IQ scores, the effect of which is to control for the potential biasing

Exhibit 6.1 *Procedure for Randomly Assigning Subjects to Experimental Treatment Groups*

The most popular procedure for randomly assigning subjects to experimental treatment conditions is to use a list of random numbers, such as the following list of 200 numbers. (Larger lists are contained in the appendixes of most statistics books.)

	1	2	3	4	5	6	7	8	9	10
1	8	1	4	5	5	6	9	8	7	3
2	2	7	9	6	5	4	6	4	8	3
3	0	0	0	5	5	8	9	7	6	9
4	7	8	3	4	7	0	7	7	5	2
5	8	5	8	6	3	5	4	2	2	2
6	7	3	5	3	6	8	0	7	3	3
7	1	8	6	0	1	0	7	4	4	7
8	7	9	5	3	0	1	5	5	5	1
9	5	6	6	7	8	5	8	1	1	9
10	3	0	3	3	9	1	9	9	1	9
11	9	7	4	7	8	4	7	1	0	9
12	5	6	4	5	1	4	5	4	1	1
13	5	7	4	0	4	2	5	9	6	7
14	8	6	0	5	6	9	4	4	3	2
15	6	7	6	7	3	3	7	1	8	9
16	2	6	0	6	7	3	3	0	6	9
17	6	7	5	5	1	4	7	4	1	2
18	6	3	0	9	9	9	5	3	8	0
19	0	3	7	3	0	3	0	6	8	6
20	7	1	6	8	2	0	5	3	2	1

This list consists of a series of 20 rows and 10 columns. The number in each position is random because each of the numbers from 0 to 9 had an equal chance of occupying that position and the selection of one number for a given position had no influence in the selection of another number for another position. Therefore, since each individual number is random, any combination of the numbers must be random.

Assume that you have 15 subjects and you want to randomly assign them to three experimental treatment groups. First, you would give each subject a number from 0 to 14. You would then block the list of random numbers into columns of two, to provide five pairs of columns, since two columns are necessary to represent the total sample of subjects.

Now you are ready to randomly assign the 5 subjects to each of the three treatment groups. The procedure that is usually followed is to randomly select the first 5 subjects from the group of 15 and assign them to one treatment group. Then randomly select a second group of 5 subjects from the group of 15 and assign them to another treatment group. Once these 10 subjects have been randomly selected and assigned, only 5 subjects remain; these 5 subjects are assigned to the third treatment group.

To randomly select the first subject for the first group, read down the first two columns until you encounter a number less than 15. From the above list, we find that the first such number is 00. Consequently, the first randomly selected subject is the subject with the number 0. Proceed down the columns until you encounter the second number less than 15, which is 03. Subject number 3 represents the second randomly selected subject. Once you have reached the bottom of the first two columns, start at the top of the next two columns. With this procedure, the subject numbers 05, 06, and 09 are selected, which represent the remaining three of the first 5 randomly selected subjects. Note that if you encounter a number that has already been selected (as we did with the number 05), you must disregard it.

To randomly select the second group of 5 subjects, proceed down the columns and identify numbers less than 15 that have not already been chosen. Using this procedure, we find the numbers 10, 01, 14, 07, and 11. These numbers correspond to the second group of randomly selected subjects. The third group represents the remaining subjects.

We now have the following three randomly selected groups of subjects.

00	01	02
03	07	04
05	10	08
06	11	12
09	14	13

Once each of the three groups has been randomly selected, it must be randomly assigned to one of the three experimental treatment conditions. This is accomplished by using only one column of the table of random numbers, since there are only three groups of subjects. The three groups are numbered from 0 to 2. Then, proceed down the first column until you reach the first of these three numbers. In looking at column 1, you can see that the first number is 2. Consequently, group 2 (the third group of subjects) is assigned to the first treatment condition. The second number encountered is 0, so group 0 (the first group of subjects) is assigned to the second treatment condition. This means that group 1 (the second group of subjects) is assigned to the third treatment condition. Now we have randomly selected three groups of subjects and randomly assigned them to three treatment conditions.

TREATMENT CONDITION

A_1	A_2	A_3
Group 2	Group 0	Group 1

Table 6.1 *Hypothetical Distribution of 20 Subjects' IQ Scores*

GROUP ASSIGNMENT BASED ON ARRIVAL SEQUENCE				RANDOM ASSIGNMENT OF SUBJECTS TO GROUPS			
GROUP A		GROUP B		GROUP A		GROUP B	
SUBJECTS	IQ SCORES	SUBJECTS	IQ SCORES	SUBJECTS	IQ SCORES	SUBJECTS	IQ SCORES
1	97	11	100	1	97	3	100
2	97	12	108	2	97	4	103
3	100	13	110	11	100	6	108
4	103	14	113	5	105	12	108
5	105	15	117	13	110	7	109
6	108	16	119	9	113	8	111
7	109	17	120	15	117	14	113
8	111	18	122	10	118	16	119
9	113	19	128	19	128	17	120
10	118	20	130	20	130	18	122
Mean IQ Score	106.1		116.7		111.5		111.3

Mean difference between the two groups: 10.6   Mean difference between the two groups: 0.2

effect of IQ. The IQ scores in Table 6.1 have been rank ordered to show this similar distribution.

Random assignment produces control by virtue of the fact that the variables to be controlled are distributed in approximately the same manner in all groups (ideally the distribution would be exactly the same). When the distribution is approximately equal the influence of the extraneous variables is held constant, because they cannot exert any differential influence on the dependent variable. Does this mean that randomization will *always* result in equal distribution of the variables to be controlled? The control function of randomization stems from the fact that random selection and assignment of subjects also results in the random selection and assignment of most extraneous variables. Since every subject, and therefore the extraneous variables present, had an equal chance of being selected and then assigned to a particular group, the extraneous variables to be controlled are distributed randomly. But because chance determines the distribution of the extraneous variables, it is also possible that, by chance, these variables are not equally distributed among the various groups of subjects. What I am saying is that bias can still exist when one uses the randomization procedure. The smaller the number of subjects with which one deals, the greater the risk that this will happen. However, randomization still decreases the probability of creating a biased distribution even if one has access only to a small group of subjects. Since the probability of the groups being equal is so much greater when one uses randomization, it is an extremely powerful method for controlling extraneous variables. And since it is really the *only* method for control of unknown variables, it is necessary to randomize whenever and wherever possible, even when one is using any of the other control techniques.

There are, however, several extraneous variables that are not controlled for by randomization, including the subject effect and the experimenter effect. The potential influences of the subjects' motive of positive self-presentation and the experimenter's expectancies or attributes are not randomly distributed. Instead, these potential biasing effects are a function of how subjects perceive the experiment or the expectations researchers have regarding the outcome of the experiment. Consequently, these extraneous variables must be controlled by the use of techniques other than randomization.

Matching

While randomization does provide the best guard against interpreting differences in the dependent variable as being the result of variables other than the independent variable, it is not the best technique for increasing the sensitivity of the experiment. In any study, it is desirable to demonstrate the influence of the independent variable regardless of how small its effect may be. Suppose that we want to isolate the potential effect of televised aggression on children's behavior. Assume that the effect is one of increasing aggressive behavior in children (this has been found in a number of studies) but the amount of increase is small. In order to isolate and detect this small effect, we need to construct an experiment that will be as sensitive as possible. The sensitivity of an experiment can be increased by **matching** the subjects in the various experimental treatment groups. An explanation as to how matching accomplishes this requires a discussion of the way in which statistical techniques operate, which is beyond the scope of the text. For our purposes, you need only remember that one of the benefits of matching is that the sensitivity of the experiment is increased. A second benefit of matching is that the variables on which subjects are matched are controlled in the sense that constancy of influence is attained. If subjects in all treatment conditions are matched on intelligence, then the intelligence level of the subjects is held constant and therefore controlled for all groups.

Matching
The use of any of a variety of techniques for equating subjects on one or more variables

Here we have two definite benefits that can accrue from matching. However, it is important to remember that matching is no substitute for randomization. Randomization should still be incorporated whenever possible, because one cannot attain an exact match on most variables and it is impossible to identify and match on all variables that could affect the results of the experiment.

The sections that follow present a number of ways in which matching can be accomplished.

Matching by Holding Variables Constant

One technique that can be used to increase the sensitivity of the experiment and control an extraneous variable is to hold the extraneous variable constant for all experimental groups. This means that all subjects in each experimental group will have the same degree or type of extraneous variable. If we are studying conformity then sex of subjects needs to be controlled, because conformity has been shown to vary with the sex of the subject. As illustrated in Figure 6.2, the sex variable can be controlled simply by using only male subjects in the experiment. This has the effect of matching all subjects in terms of the sex variable, and so the sensitivity of the experiment is increased. Hauri and Ohmstead (1983) used only insomniacs in their investigation of estimates of the length of time required to fall asleep. This matching procedure creates a more homogeneous subject sample, since only subjects with a

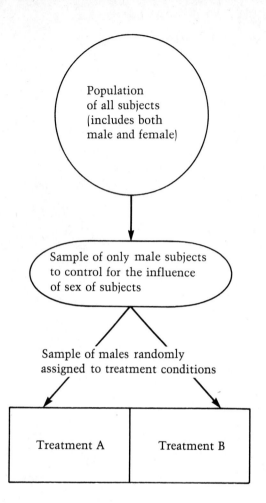

Figure 6.2   *Illustration of matching by holding variables constant.*

certain amount or type of the extraneous variable are included in the subject pool.

Although widely used, the technique of holding variables constant is not without its disadvantages. Two can readily be identified. The first disadvantage is that the technique restricts the size of the subject population. Consequently, it may, in some cases, be difficult to find enough subjects to participate in the study. Consider a study that was conducted to investigate the influence of assistance given to single parents (assistance with child care or with household chores) on their attitudes and perceived interactions with their child or children. The study was limited to single parents, and we had to find volunteers. After two weeks of advertising, 18 single parents had volunteered to participate in the study. If the study had not been limited to single parents, the subject pool from which we could have drawn would have been much larger, with the probable effect of more individuals volunteering their help.

The second disadvantage is more serious. The results of the study can be generalized only to the type of subject that participated in the study. The results obtained from the single-parent study can be generalized only to other single parents. If someone wanted to know whether complete families (both parents present) would derive the same benefit from receiving the same type of assistance, one would have to conduct a similar study using complete families to provide an answer to this question. Results from such a study might indeed provide the same conclusions as those obtained from single parents, but this is an empirical question and not one that can be answered through study of only single persons. The only way we can find out if the results of one study can be generalized to individuals of another population is to conduct an identical study using the second population as subjects.

Matching by Building the Extraneous Variable into the Research Design

A second means of increasing the sensitivity of an experiment is to build the extraneous variable into the research design. Assume that we were conducting a learning experiment and wanted to control for the effects of intelligence. Also assume that we had considered the previous technique of holding the variable constant by selecting only individuals with IQs of 110 to 120, but thought it unwise and inexpedient to do so. In this case, we could select several IQ levels (e.g., 90 to 99, 100 to 109, and 110 to 120), as illustrated in Figure 6.3, and treat them as we would an independent variable. This would allow us to identify and extract the influence due to the intelligence variable. Intelligence, therefore, would not represent a source of random fluctuation, and the sensitivity of the experiment would be increased.

To provide further insight into this control technique, I will cite a study conducted by Kendler, Kendler, and Learnard (1962) that investigated the influence of the subjects' age on their use of internal mediating responses. Prior research conducted on this topic indicated that rats do not use mediational processes whereas college students do and that three- and four-year old children do not use the mediational process whereas nearly half of the children between ages five and seven do. Such data suggested that a developmental process was involved in the use of internal mediating responses, which must be controlled for in order to avoid attaining contradictory results from various studies. Realizing this, Kendler, Kendler, and Learnard controlled for age by building it into the design of their study. Children at five chronological age levels—three, four, six, eight, and ten years of age—were required to engage in a task that would elicit mediational responses. Conse-

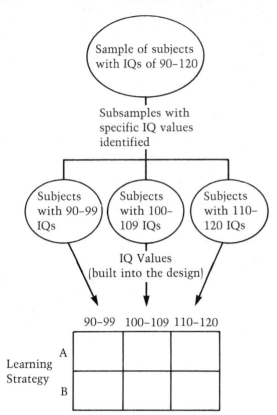

Figure 6.3   *Illustration of matching by building the extraneous variable into the research design.*

quently, they controlled for the age factor by matching the five different age groups, and then used these age groupings as an independent variable. In this way, the age variable was controlled and its influence upon mediational responses was displayed.

Building the extraneous variable into the research design seems like an excellent technique for achieving control and increasing sensitivity. But the technique is recommended only if one is interested in the differences produced by the various levels of the extraneous variable or in the interaction between the levels of the extraneous variable and other independent variables. In the hypothetical learning experiment, one might be interested in the differences produced by the three levels of intelligence and how these levels interact with the learning strategies. The primary reason Kendler, Kendler, and Learnard conducted their study was to investigate the differences produced by subjects of different ages. If they had not been interested in such conditions, then another control technique would probably have been more efficient. When such conditions *are* of interest the technique is excellent, because it isolates the variation caused by the extraneous variable. This control technique takes a factor that can operate as an extraneous variable, biasing the experiment, and makes it focal in the experiment as an independent variable.

Matching by Yoked Control

The **yoked control** matching technique controls for the possible influence of the temporal relationship between an event and a response. Consider the widely quoted study conducted by Brady (1958) in which he investigated the relationship between emotional stress and development of ulcers. Brady trained monkeys to press a lever at least once during every 20-second time interval to avoid receiving electric shock. The monkeys learned this task quite rapidly, and only occasionally would they miss a 20-second time interval and receive a shock. In order to determine whether the monkeys developed ulcers from the psychological stress rather than the physical stress resulting from the cumulative effect of the shocks, Brady had to include a control monkey that would receive an equal number of shocks. This was easily accomplished, but there was still one additional variable that needed to be controlled—the temporal sequence of administering the shocks. It may be that one temporal sequence produces ulcers whereas another does not. If the experimental and the control monkeys received a different temporal sequence of shocks this difference and not the stress variable could be the cause of the ulcers. Consequently, both monkeys had to receive the same temporal sequence to control this variable. Brady placed the experimental and the control monkeys in yoked chain, whereby both monkeys would receive shock when the experimental monkey failed to press the lever during the 20-second time interval. However, the control animal could not influence the situation and essentially had to sit back and accept the fact that sometimes the shock was going to occur. The only apparent difference between these animals was the ability to influence the occurrence of the shock. If only the experimental monkey got ulcers, as was the case in this experiment, the ulcers could be attributed to the psychological stress.

The yoked control technique appears to an excellent way to control the biasing effects of the temporal distribution of events, but there is some controversy over its effectiveness. Church (1964) believes that this control technique may introduce a source of bias in the results of a study; however, Kimmel and Terrant (1968) believe that Church bases his arguments on unwarranted assumptions. Apparently most investigators place more credence in Kimmel and Terrant's arguments, since the yoked control technique continues to be used.

Matching by Equating Subjects

A third technique that can be used to control extraneous variables and also increase the sensitivity of the experiment is to equate subjects on

Yoked control
A matching technique that matches subjects on the temporal sequence of administering an event

the variable or variables to be controlled. If intelligence needs to be controlled, then you need to make sure that the subjects in each of the treatment groups are of the same intelligence level.

Matching by equating subjects is very similar to matching by building the extraneous variable into the study design, as both techniques attempt to eliminate the influence of the extraneous variable by creating equivalent groups of subjects. The difference lies in the procedure for creating the equivalent groups. The previously discussed method creates equivalent groups by establishing categories of the extraneous variable into which subjects are placed, thereby creating another independent variable. The present method does not build the extraneous variable into the design of the study but matches subjects on the variable to be controlled, where the number of subjects is always some multiple of the number of levels of the independent variable. There are two techniques that are commonly used to accomplish this matching, which Selltiz et al. (1959) labeled the precision control technique and the frequency control technique.

Precision Control. The technique of **precision control** requires the investigator to match subjects in the various treatment groups on a case-by-case basis for each of the selected extraneous variables. Scholtz (1973) investigated the defense styles used by individuals who attempted suicide versus those used by individuals who did not attempt suicide. All subjects were neuropsychiatric patients. The suicide subjects were identified as those individuals who, among other things, had attempted suicide during the past year. The other subjects had evidenced "no history of a suicide attempt nor marked suicidal ideation" (p. 71). For a non–suicide attempter to be included in the study, the subject had to be of the same age, sex, race, marital status, diagnosis, and education as a suicide attempter. Matching on these variables on a case-by-case basis resulted in 35 pairs of subjects.

The Scholtz study illustrates the various advantages and disadvantages of the precision control matching technique. Before discussing them I should point out that the Scholtz study was an ex post facto study, since the subjects assigned themselves to the various groups; they could not be randomly assigned after being paired. In a truly experimental study, subjects would be matched and then randomly assigned to the different groups, as illustrated in Figure 6.4. As stated before, matching is never a substitute for random assignment.

The principal advantage of the precision control technique is that it increases the sensitivity of the study by ensuring that the subjects in the various groups are equal on at least the paired variables. For increased sensitivity to exist, the variables on which subjects are matched must, as discussed earlier in this chapter, be correlated with the dependent variable. How much of a correlation should exist? Kerlinger (1973) states that matching is a waste of time unless the variables on

Precision control
A matching technique in which each subject is matched with another subject on selected variables

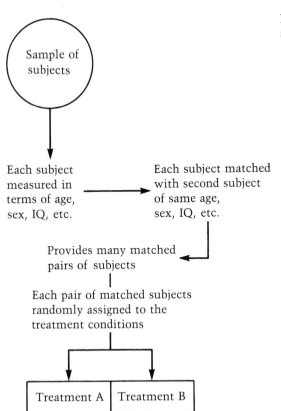

Figure 6.4 *Illustration of matching by the precision control technique.*

which subjects are matched correlate greater than 0.5 or 0.6 with the dependent variable (this criteria holds only for linearly related variables). This corresponds to the data Billewicz (1965) obtained from his simulation experiments.

The precision control technique has three major disadvantages. First, it is difficult to know which are the most important variables to match. In most instances, there are many potentially relevant variables. Scholtz, in his study, selected age, sex, race, marital status, diagnosis, and education, but many other variables *could* have been selected. Variables selected should be those that show the lowest intercorrelation but the highest correlation with the dependent variable.

A second problem encountered in precision control matching is that the difficulty in finding matched subjects increases disproportionately as the number of variables increases. Scholtz matched on six variables, which must have been very difficult. His task would have been much easier if matching had been attempted on only two variables, such as sex and age. In order to match individuals on many variables, one must have a large pool of subjects available in order to obtain a few who are matched on the relevant variables. Fortunately, the relevant variables are generally intercorrelated, so the number that can be used successfully to increase precision is limited. Matching also limits the generality of the results of the study. Assume that you are matching on age and education and that your final sample of matched subjects is between the ages of 20 and 30 and has only a high school education. Since this is the type of subject included in the study, you can generalize the results only to other individuals having the same characteristics.

A third disadvantage is that some variables are very difficult to match. If having received psychotherapy was considered a relevant variable, an individual who had received psychotherapy would have to be matched with another person who had also received psychotherapy. A related difficulty is the inability to obtain adequate measures of the variables to be matched. If we wanted to equate individuals on the basis of the effect of psychotherapy, we would have to measure such an effect. Matching can only be as accurate as available measurement.

Frequency Distribution Control.   The precision control technique of matching is excellent for increasing sensitivity, but many subjects are lost because they cannot be matched. **Frequency distribution control** attempts to overcome this disadvantage while retaining some of the advantages of matching. This technique, as the name implies, matches groups of subjects in terms of overall distribution of the selected variable or variables rather than on a case-by-case basis. If IQ were to be matched in this fashion, the two or more groups of subjects would have to have the same average IQ, as well as the same standard deviation and skewness of IQ scores, as illustrated in Figure 6.5. This means that, generally speaking, the investigator would select the first group of subjects and determine the mean, standard deviation, etc., of their IQ scores. Then another group having the same statistical measures would be selected. If more than one variable was considered to be a relevant variable on which to match subjects, the groups of subjects would have to have the same statistical measures on both of these variables. The number of subjects lost using this technique would not be as great as the number lost using the precision control method, because each additional subject would merely have to contribute to producing the appropriate statistical indices rather than be identical to another subject on the relevant variables. Consequently this technique is more flexible in terms of being able to use a particular subject.

The major disadvantage of matching by the frequency distribution control method is that the combinations of variables may be mismatched in the various groups. If age and IQ were to be matched, one group might include old subjects with high IQs and young subjects with low IQs, whereas the other group might comprise the opposite combi-

Frequency distribution control
A matching technique that matches groups of subjects by equating the overall distribution of the chosen variable

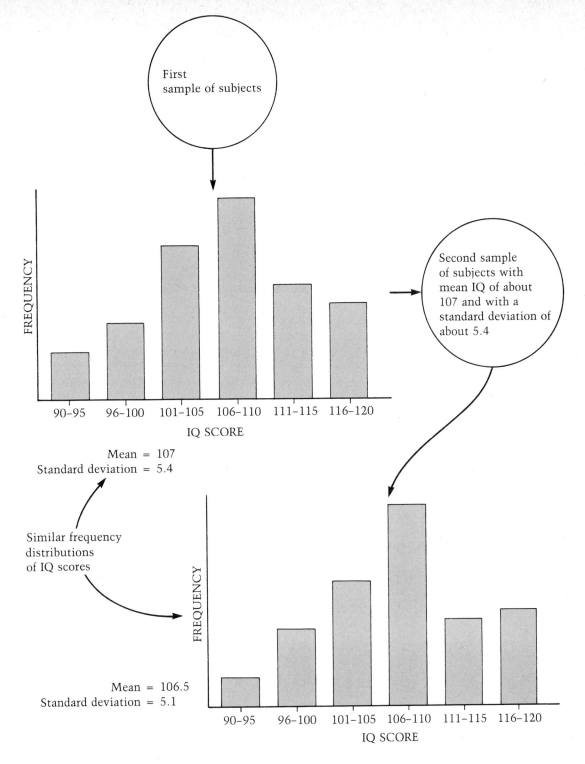

Figure 6.5 *Illustration of the frequency distribution control technique.*

nation. In this case, the mean and distribution of the two variables would be equivalent but the subjects in each group would be completely different. This disadvantage obviously exists only if matching is conducted on more than one variable.

Counterbalancing

Counterbalancing is the technique used to control for sequencing effects. Sequencing effects can occur when the investigator elects to construct an experiment in which all subjects serve in each of several experimental conditions. (See Figure 6.6.) Under these conditions, there are two types of effects that can occur. The first is an **order effect,** which arises from the *order* in which the treatment conditions are administered to the subjects. Suppose that you are conducting a verbal learning experiment in which the independent variable is rate of presentation of nonsense syllables. Nonsense syllables with a 50 percent level of meaningfulness are randomly assigned to three lists. The subject has to sequentially learn list S (the slow list, in which the syllables are presented at 6-second intervals), then list M (the moderate list, in which the syllables are presented at 4-second intervals), and finally list F (the fast list, in which the syllables are presented at 2-second intervals). In such an experiment, there is the possibility that practice with the equipment, learning the nonsense syllables, or just general familiarity with the surroundings of the experimental environment may enhance performance. Let us assume that one or more of these variables does enhance performance and that the increment due to the order effect is four units of performance for subjects progressing from list S to

Counterbalancing
A technique used to control sequencing effects

Order effect
A sequencing effect arising from the order in which the treatment conditions are administered to subjects

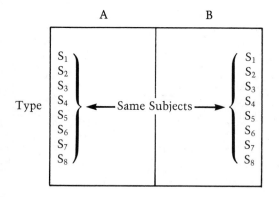

Treatment Conditions

Figure 6.6   *Illustration of the type of design that may include sequencing effects.*

Table 6.2   *Hypothetical Order Effects*

	LIST LEARNED			REVERSED ORDER OF LIST		
	S	M	F	F	M	S
Increment in performance	0	4	2	0	4	2

M and two units of performance for subjects progressing from list M to list F. The left half of Table 6.2 depicts these order effects. As can be seen, order effects could affect the conclusions reached, because performance increments occurred in the learning of these two lists that were entirely the result of order effects. You should also be aware that when the increment in performance is caused by order effects, the particular sequence of the list is irrelevant. We could reverse the order of the lists and the increments in performance would still occur in the same ordinal position, as is shown in the right half of Table 6.2. Increments due to order effects are strictly the result of subjects' increased familiarity and practice with the whole experimental environment. Other experimental factors, such as the time of testing (morning, noon, or night), may produce the order effect. Such effects must be controlled to avoid reaching false conclusions.

The second type of sequencing effect that can occur is a **carry-over effect.** Carry-over effects occur when performance in one treatment condition is partially dependent on the conditions that precede it. D'Amato (1970) provides an excellent example of carry-over effects in his simulated experiment designed to investigate the influence of monetary reward (5, 10, or 15 cents) on performance. In this type of study, it is possible that when subjects serve in all three conditions, performance in a particular treatment condition may be partially a function of the conditions that precede it (a dime may be more rewarding when it is preceded by five cents than when it is preceded by fifteen cents). "Let us simplify the analysis by assuming that the carry-over effects from one condition to another will be directly proportional to the difference in the monetary rewards of the two conditions. We will assume that going from A (5 cents) to B (10 cents) or from B to C (15 cents) results in a positive carry-over (increment in performance) of two units, whereas traveling in the reverse direction results in the same amount of carry-over effect but negative in sign, i.e., leads to a decrement in performance of two units. Transitions from A to C and from C to A both result in four units of carry-over effects, positive and negative, respectively" (p. 53). Table 6.3 illustrates that the carry-over effects for any one treatment condition are a function of the preceding

Carryover effect
A sequencing effect that occurs when performance in one treatment condition affects performance in another treatment condition

Table 6.3 *Calculation of Assumed Carry-Over Effects in Six Sequences*

	VALUE OF THE INDEPENDENT VARIABLE		
SEQUENCE	A (5 cents)	B (10 cents)	C (15 cents)
ABC	0	2	2
ACB	0	−2	4
BAC	−2	0	4
BCA	−4	0	2
CAB	−4	2	0
CBA	−2	−2	0
Total	−12	0	12

From *Experimental psychology methodology: Psychophysics and learning* by M. R. D'Amato. Copyright 1970, McGraw-Hill. Used with permission of McGraw-Hill Book Co.

treatment conditions. Such effects need to be controlled to identify unambiguously the effects due to the independent variable.

The order effects and the carry-over effects are potential sources of bias in any studies in which the subject partakes of several treatment conditions. In such cases, the sequencing effects need to be controlled, and researchers often resort to counterbalancing. Counterbalancing techniques have disadvantages associated with statistical analysis; students having a good statistical background are referred to Gaito (1958, 1961) for a discussion of these dangers.

Intrasubject Counterbalancing: The ABBA Technique

Intrasubject counterbalancing controls for sequencing effects by having each subject take the treatment effect first in one order and then in the reverse order. In an experiment that employed two treatment conditions A and B, subjects would first respond under order AB and then under the reversed order BA, providing an ABBA sequence. In other words, each subject would respond under each treatment condition twice. The results for the two A conditions and the results for the two B conditions are then combined for each subject, returning the study to a two-treatment-condition experiment. Results obtained for each treatment condition can then be compared to determine if the responses are the same. Any observed difference would not be attributable to carry-over or order effects, because they would have been equalized or held constant across groups.

As an example, let us assume that each subject increments his or her performance by one unit for each treatment condition in which he

Intrasubject counterbalancing
Administering the treatment conditions to each individual subject in more than one order

Table 6.4   *Sequencing Effects for the ABBA Technique*

	TREATMENT CONDITION			
	A	B	B	A
Linear sequencing effect				
Sequence effect	0	1	2	3
A sequence effect $0 + 3 = 3$				
B sequence effect $1 + 2 = 3$				
Nonlinear sequencing effect				
Sequence effect	0	4	6	8
A sequence effect $0 + 8 = 8$				
B sequence effect $4 + 6 = 10$				

or she participates solely because of sequencing effects. If the ABBA technique is employed, these sequencing effects will be constant across treatment conditions and will therefore be controlled. This constant influence is illustrated in the top half of Table 6.4.

For both the A and B treatment conditions, performance was increased by a constant amount of three units. Therefore, sequencing was controlled. Note, however, that the sequencing effect was linear in the sense that a constant increment was added to performance in each successive position in the sequence. Would the ABBA technique control for carry-over and order effects if they were not linear? The answer is no. The ABBA method is based on the assumption that the sequencing effects are linear or constant for each successive position in the sequence. (This assumption also exists for the complete and incomplete counterbalancing methods to be discussed later.) If a constant effect is not attained, the sequencing effect will differentially affect the results, as is also shown in Table 6.4. In this case, the sequencing effects are not controlled because ten units of performance increment occurred in condition B and only eight units occurred in condition A. This is because the sequence effect was twice as powerful for progression from the first A condition to the first B condition as for progression through the remainder of the conditions. Can such differential sequence effects be controlled? The answer depends on whether you are considering carry-over effects or order effects.

Differential order effects can be held constant by having each treatment condition appear in every possible position in the sequence. This means that in addition to an ABBA sequence a BAAB sequence must be included to control nonlinear order effects. Half of the subjects can then be assigned to each sequence. Let us assume that each subject increments two units in performance after participating in the first

Table 6.5   *Control for Order Effects Using Intrasubject Counterbalancing*

	SEQUENCE I				SEQUENCE II		
	A	B	B	A	B	A	A	B
Order effect	0	2	3	4	0	2	3	4

Total A order effect $0 + 4 + 2 + 3 = 9$
Total B order effect $2 + 3 + 0 + 4 = 9$

treatment condition and one unit in performance after participating in each subsequent treatment condition just because of order effects. If both the ABBA and the BAAB sequences are employed, the results appearing in Table 6.5 will occur. The total order effects for both treatment conditions are equal, which means that the effect is held constant. This actually represents a combining of intrasubject with intragroup counterbalancing.

It is not as easy to control for differential carry-over effects, which frequently defy control. This is because the carry-over may vary as a function of the treatment conditions that precede it. Such a condition was illustrated earlier in the example of a simulated experiment designed to test the influence of monetary reward on performance. Table 6.3 shows the assumed carry-over effects. Note that the carry-over effect for any one treatment condition varies as a function of the particular treatment conditions that precede it. Also note that the total carry-over effects for the treatment conditions are not identical. Here, then, is a case where carry-over effects are not controlled. When carry-over effects are linear, they can be controlled by the ABBA sequence, but in nonlinear cases such as this, they cannot. The investigator who suspects such a situation should consider using some other technique, such as precision control; otherwise, the carry-over effects serve as a rival hypothesis.

Intragroup Counterbalancing

A primary disadvantage of using the intrasubject counterbalancing techinque is that each treatment condition has to be presented to each subject more than once. As the number of treatment conditions increases, the length of the sequence of conditions each subject must take also increases. For example, with the three treatment conditions A, B, and C, each subject must take a sequence of six treatment conditions— ABCCBA. Intragroup counterbalancing allows the experimenter to avoid this time-consuming process. **Intragroup counterbalancing** differs from intrasubject counterbalancing in that groups of subjects rather than individuals are counterbalanced. In that the intragroup technique attempts to control sequencing effects over groups, it represents a more

Intragroup counterbalancing
Administering the treatment conditions to various members of each group of subjects in more than one order

efficient technique, particularly when more than two treatment conditions exist. The two approaches to intragroup counterbalancing will be discussed separately.

Complete Counterbalancing. The technique of **complete counterbalancing** is distinguishable by virtue of the two requirements that it must meet. First, every possible sequence of the various treatment conditions must be enumerated. Second, every sequence that is enumerated must be used. Assume that we are conducting an experiment in which we have three treatment conditions—A, B, and C. To meet the first requirement, we have to enumerate all six possible sequences of these three values: ABC, ACB, BAC, BCA, CAB, and CBA. If a different group of subjects then takes each sequence of treatment conditions, the second requirement will be met.

Although the complete counterbalancing technique is excellent for controlling linear sequencing effects, it is seldom used because the number of sequences increases factorially as the number of treatment conditions increases arithmetically. With four treatment conditions, 24 ($4 \times 3 \times 2 \times 1$) sequences are enumerated; with five treatment conditions, 120 ($5 \times 4 \times 3 \times 2 \times 1$) sequences are enumerated. As the number of enumerated sequences increases, so does the number of subjects needed. This is because the number of subjects needed is always some multiple of the number of enumerated sequences. In a three-treatment-condition experiment, 6 sequences are enumerated, which means that the number of subjects employed must be some multiple of 6: e.g., 6, 12, 18, 24. As an alternative to using the complete counterbalancing technique, most individuals use the incomplete counterbalancing technique.

Incomplete Counterbalancing. The technique of **incomplete counterbalancing** derives its name from the fact that all possible sequences of treatment conditions are not enumerated. The first criterion that incomplete counterbalancing must meet is that, for the sequences enumerated, each treatment condition must appear an equal number of times in each ordinal position. Also, each treatment condition must precede and be followed by every other condition an equal number of times.

Let us assume that we have four experimental conditions (A, B, C, and D) and we want to counterbalance the order in which they are administered to subjects. Whenever the number of treatment conditions is even, as is the case with four experimental conditions, then the number of counterbalanced sequences equals the number of treatment conditions. The sequences are established in the following way. The first sequence takes the form 1, 2, n, 3, $(n - 1)$, 4, $(n - 2)$, 5, and so forth, until we have accounted for the total number of treatment conditions. In our example using four treatment conditions, the first se-

Complete counterbalancing
Enumerating every possible sequence of treatment conditions and requiring a different group of subjects to take each of the enumerated sequences

Incomplete counterbalancing
Enumerating less than all possible sequences, and requiring different groups of subjects to take each of the enumerated sequences

quence would be ABDC, or 1, 2, 4, 3. If an experiment consisted of six treatment conditions, the first sequence would be ABFCED, or 1, 2, 6, 3, 5, 4. The remaining sequences of the incomplete counterbalancing technique are then established by incrementing each value in the preceding sequence by 1. For example, in the four-treatment-condition example, the first sequence was ABDC. For the second sequence, you would increment each value by 1, with the resulting sequence being BCAD. Naturally, for the last treatment condition, D, you do not proceed to E but go back to A. Such a procedure results in the following set of sequences for the four-treatment-condition example:

SUBJECT		SEQUENCE		
1	A	B	D	C
2	B	C	A	D
3	C	D	B	A
4	D	A	C	B

If the number of treatment conditions is odd, as with five treatment conditions, the criterion that each value precede and follow every other value an equal number of times is not fulfilled if the above precedure is followed. For example, the above procedure would give the following set of sequences:

		SEQUENCE		
A	B	E	C	D
B	C	A	D	E
C	D	B	E	A
D	E	C	A	B
E	A	D	B	C

In this case, each treatment condition appears in every possible position, but, for example, D is immediately preceded by A twice but never by B. To remedy this situation, we must enumerate five additional sequences that are exactly the reverse of the first five sequences. In the five-treatment-condition example, the additional five sequences would appear as follows:

		SEQUENCE		
D	C	E	B	A
E	D	A	C	B
A	E	B	D	C
B	A	C	E	D
C	B	D	A	E

When these ten sequences are combined, the criteria of incomplete counterbalancing are met. Consequently, the incomplete counterbalancing technique provides for control of order effects. Also, an economy in number of subjects is obtained because of the smaller total number of sequences. In the four-treatment-condition situation, the total number of subjects required is some multiple of 4 rather than 24, as would be the case with the complete counterbalancing technique.

How well does the incomplete counterbalancing technique control for sequencing effects? The influence of order effects is controlled, as every treatment condition occurs at each possible position in the sequence. In other words, every condition (A, B, C, and D) precedes and follows every other condition an equal number of times. However, carry-over effects are controlled only if they are linear for all sequences. If they are not, then incomplete counterbalancing is inadequate.

Randomized Counterbalancing

Randomized counterbalancing differs from the previous two techniques in terms of the procedure used to generate the sequence of experimental conditions taken by the subject. The randomized counterbalancing technique, as the name implies, randomly selects the sequence for each subject. If four experimental conditions exist in the experiment, the sequence given to each subject is determined by chance. If 20 subjects are used in the experiment, then 20 sequences are randomly selected and randomly assigned to each subject. This method assumes that the order and carry-over effects are controlled by random distribution. Confidence in such an assumption is increased as the number of subjects is increased. This is why Zimney (1961) states that at least 60 subjects should be included in an experiment in which the randomized counterbalancing method is used.

Randomized counterbalancing Randomly selecting a sequence of treatment conditions for each subject

Now that I have discussed counterbalancing techniques at some length, I want to correct a possible misperception—that is, that these counterbalancing techniques are widely used. The trend actually seems to be away from their use. The biggest contributor to this state of affairs seems to be the increased use of analysis-of-variance designs. One of these, the Latin Square Design, represents the counterbalancing technique and, therefore, effects maximum control over sequencing effects. However, I believe that a discussion of counterbalancing illustrates more clearly what sequencing effects are and how they need to be controlled.

Control of Subject Effects

We have seen that subjects' behavior in the experimental situation can be influenced by the perceptions and motives they bring with them. It seems as though subjects are motivated to present themselves in the best possible light. If the demand characteristics suggest that a particular type of response will allow subjects to fulfill this motive, the subjects' responses will be a function of this motive in addition to the experimental treatment conditions. Such a situation will produce internal invalidity if the demand characteristics that operate in the experiment suggest to the subjects that the self-presentation motive can be fulfilled in different ways. For internal validity to be created, there must be constancy in the subjects' perceptions of the way in which the positive self-presentation motive can be fulfilled. Only then can we state with certainty that the independent variable has caused the variation in the subjects' responses to the dependent variable.

The experimenter can use a number of control techniques to try to ensure identical perceptions in all subjects. The following techniques cannot be used in all types of experiments; they are presented so that the experimenter can choose the most appropriate one for the particular study being conducted.

Double Blind Placebo Model

One of the best techniques for controlling demand characteristics is the **double blind placebo model.** This model requires that one "devise manipulations that appear essentially identical to subjects in all conditions"[1] and that the experimenter not know which group received the placebo condition or the experimental manipulation.

Double blind placebo model
A model in which neither the experimenter nor the subject is aware of the treatment condition administered to the subject

If you were conducting an experiment designed to test the effects of a given drug on reaction time, one group of subjects would receive the drug and the other group of subjects would receive a placebo. Since both groups of subjects would think they had received the drug, expectations would be constant. The experimenter must not know whether a given subject received the drug or placebo in order to avoid communicating the expectancy of a given response; that is, the experimenter must be "blind." For some time, drug research has recognized the influence of patients' expectations on their experiences subsequent to taking a drug. Thus drug research consistently uses this model to eliminate subject bias.

Using this technique Beecher (1966) found no difference in pain alleviation between a placebo group that was administered a weak saline solution and a drug group that was administered a large dose of morphine. Such results ran counter to a large body of previous research. However, Beecher communicated with another experienced drug re-

---

[1] Reprinted by special permission from Aronson and Carlsmith, "Experimentation in Social Psychology," *The handbook of social psychology*, Second Edition, Volume Two, 1968, edited by Lindzey and Aronson, Addison-Wesley, Reading, Mass., p. 62.

searcher, who revealed that demand characteristics probably existed in the prior studies. This researcher said that he "found that as long as he knew what the subject had received, he could reproduce fine dose-effect curves; but when he was kept in ignorance, he was no more able than we were to distinguish between a large dose of morphine and an inert substance such as saline" (p. 841). In the former cases, the subject knew the correct response and acted accordingly.

Use of the double blind placebo model is a way to eliminate the development of differential subject perceptions, because all subjects are told that they are given (and appear to be given) the same experimental treatment. And since the researcher does not know which subjects have received the experimental treatments, he or she cannot communicate this information to the subjects. Therefore, the demand characteristics surrounding the administration of the treatment conditions are controlled by the double blind placebo model.

Unfortunately, many types of experiments cannot use such a technique because all conditions cannot be made to appear identical in all respects. In such cases, other techniques must be employed.

Deception

One of the more common methods used to solve the problem of subject perceptions is the use of deception in the experiment. **Deception** involves providing all subjects with a hypothesis that is unrelated to or orthogonal to the real hypothesis. Almost all experiments contain some form of deception, ranging from minor deceit (an omission or a slight alteration of the truth) to elaborate schemes. Gagné and Baker (1950), in their investigation of transfer of training, refrained from telling the subjects anything about the purpose of the study. The instructions given to subjects pertained directly to the task at hand. Subjects knew that the experiment was concerned with learning, but they did not know that it was concerned with transfer of training. At the other end of the continuum, there are experiments in which subjects are given unrelated or bogus hypotheses to ensure that they do not discover the real hypothesis.

Aronson and Mills (1959) repeatedly used deception in their study; at just about every stage of the experiment, some type of cover for the real purpose was given. For example, rather than telling the subjects that the experiment was investigating the effect of severity of initiation, the researchers said that the study was investigating the "dynamics of the group discussion process." Is it better to use such deception or to simply refrain from giving any rationale for the tasks to be completed in the experiment? It seems as though providing subjects with a false, but plausible, hypothesis is the preferred procedure, because the subjects may have their curiosity satisfied and not try to devise their own

Deception
Giving the subject a bogus reason for conducting the experiment

hypotheses. If the subjects perceive the study to be investigating different hypotheses, their responses may create a source of bias.

The rationale underlying the deception approach is "to provide a cognitive analogy to the placebo."[2] In a placebo experiment, all subjects think they have received the same independent variable. In the deception experiment, all subjects receive the same false information about what is being done, which should produce relatively constant subject perceptions of the purpose of the experiment. Therefore, deception seems to be an excellent technique for controlling the potential biasing influence that can arise from the differential perceptions subjects can have regarding the hypothesis of the experiment. The one problem is that it is frequently objected to on ethical grounds (see Chapter 10).

Disguised Experiment

The **disguised experiment** is conducted in a context that does not communicate to the subjects that they are in an experiment. This means that a procedure has to be established so that the independent variable as well as the dependent variable can be administered without telling the subjects that they are in an experiment. Abelson and Miller (1967) conducted such a study in their investigation of the influence of a personal insult on persuasion. The experimenter, disguised as a roving reporter, approached a subject seated on a park bench. The experimenter explained to the subject that he was conducting a survey on a particular issue. The individual was asked to give an opinion regarding the issue, and then the person seated next to him or her—an experimental confederate—was asked for his or her views on the same topic. In one treatment condition, the confederate derogated the subject before expressing an opposite point of view. The experimenter then obtained a second measure of the subject's opinion to assess the influence of the confederate's insult. This whole experiment was disguised in the sense that the subjects had no way of knowing that they were participants, so demand characteristics were minimal.

Use of the disguised experiment has much to recommend it and is an excellent way of controlling experimental demand characteristics. But this method is not without its limitations. First, many studies cannot be disguised in this way. Second, disguised experiments generally have to be field studies, and associated with field studies is the difficulty of controlling extraneous variables. The third area of difficulty is an ethical one: subjects are not informed that they are participating in an experiment and therefore are not given the option of declining.

Disguised experiment
A study that is conducted without communicating to the subject that he or she is in the experiment

---

[2]Reprinted by special permission from Aronson and Carlsmith, "Experimentation in Social Psychology," *The handbook of social psychology*, Second Edition, Volume Two, 1968, edited by Lindzey and Aronson, Addison-Wesley, Reading, Mass., p. 63.

Independent Measurement of the Dependent Variable

In **independent measurement of the dependent variable,** the experimenter measures the dependent variable in a context that is completely removed from the manipulation of the independent variable. One way to accomplish this is by manipulating the independent variable within the context of one experiment and measuring the dependent variable at some later time within the context of an unrelated experiment. Carlsmith, Collins, and Helmreich (1966) conducted a study that illustrates this procedure. They were investigating the influence of one's attitude toward a task when one was paid various amounts of money to state that the boring task performed was actually interesting. All subjects performed the tasks required of them and thought that they had completed the experiment when they were asked to participate in another study conducted by a different group of individuals. This second study was actually a bogus one set up especially to measure the subjects' attitudes toward the boring task they had completed in the first experiment. Such a situation minimizes subject bias, because the subjects think they are participating in another study (assuming there is nothing about the procedure that arouses the subjects' suspicions) and form hypotheses relative to this new study. Consequently, any biasing effects should not systematically influence one group over another.

This technique is good when it can be used—in cases in which the dependent variable can be independently measured. In many studies, this cannot be accomplished because the variables are interdependent. There is also an ethical issue involved here, since subjects are not told the true purpose of the experiment.

Independent measurement of the dependent variable
Assessment of the dependent variable in a situation that is removed from the experiment

Procedural Control, or Control of Subject Interpretation

The four techniques just discussed are excellent for controlling some of the demand characteristics of the experiment. "However, these control techniques seem to be limited to ensuring that subjects have a unified perception of the treatment condition they are in, whether or not they receive a given treatment, and the purpose of the experiment" (Christensen, 1981, p. 567). Little recognition is given to the fact that the subjects' perceptions are also affected by the many demand characteristics that surround the whole procedure. For example, it has been demonstrated that subjects respond differently to a verbal conditioning task depending on how they interpret the verbal reinforcer (Christensen, 1977). To provide adequate control of subject perceptions and the positive self-presentation motive, we need to know the types of situations and instructions that will alter subjects' perceptions of how to create the most positive image. However, the literature on this issue is in its infancy. At the present time, therefore, it is necessary to consider each experiment separately and try to determine if subjects' perceptions of the experiment might lead them to respond differentially to the levels of variation in the independent variable.

A variety of techniques that can be used to gain insight into subjects' perceptions of the experiment are summarized in Christensen (1981) and Adair and Spinner (1981). These methods can be grouped into the two categories of retrospective verbal reports and concurrent verbal reports. A **retrospective verbal report** consists of a technique such as the **postexperimental inquiry,** which is exactly what it says it is—questioning the subject regarding the essential aspects of the experiment after completion of the study. What did the subject think the experiment was about? What did he or she think the experimenter expected to find? What type of response did the subject attempt to give and why? How does the subject think others will respond in this situation? Such information will help to expose the factors underlying the subject's perception of his or her response.

Retrospective verbal report
An oral report in which the subject retrospectively recalls aspects of the experiment

Postexperimental inquiry
An interview of the subject after the experiment is over

Concurrent verbal reports include such techniques as Solomon's "sacrifice" group (Orne, 1973), concurrent probing, and the "think-aloud" technique (Ericsson and Simon, 1980). In Solomon's **sacrifice groups,** each group of subjects is "sacrificed" by being stopped at different points in the experiment and probed regarding the subjects' perceptions of the experiment. **Concurrent probing** requires subjects to report, at the end of each trial, the perceptions they have regarding the experiment. The **think-aloud technique** requires subjects to verbalize any thoughts or perceptions they have regarding the experiment as they are performing the experimental task. Ericsson and Simon (1980) consider this the most effective technique, since it does not require the subject to recall information and hence eliminates distortions in reporting due to failure to remember or due to the biasing influence that may result from the experimenter's probing.

Concurrent verbal report
A subject's oral report of the experiment that is obtained as the experiment is being performed

Sacrifice groups
Groups of subjects that are stopped and interviewed at different stages of the experiment

Concurrent probing
Obtaining a subject's perceptions of the experiment after completion of each trial

Think-aloud technique
A method that requires subjects to verbalize their thoughts as they are performing the experiment

None of these techniques is foolproof or without disadvantages. However, use of these methods will provide some evidence regarding subjects' perceptions of the experiment and will enable you to design an experiment in such a way as to minimize the differential influence of the subjects' motive of positive self-presentation.

Control of Experimenter Effects

Experimenter effects have been defined as the unintentional biasing effects that the experimenter can have on the results of the experiment. The experimenter is not a passive noninfluential agent in an experi-

Experimenter effects
The biasing influence that can be exerted by the experimenter

ment but an active potential source of bias. This potential bias seems to exist in most types of experiments, although it may not be quite as powerful as Rosenthal purports it is.

Page and Yates (1973) have shown that 90 percent of the respondents they surveyed felt the implications of experimenter bias for psychology were serious. Additionally, 81 percent of the respondents felt that the presence of experimenter-related controls should be a major criterion for publishability of studies. Such data suggest that psychologists in general consider the experimenter bias effect to be of importance in psychological research and see the need to incorporate techniques to control for such potential effects. According to Wyer, Dion, and Ellsworth (1978), problems such as experimenter bias are widely understood in social psychology, and it is assumed "that most persons who submit papers to JESP avoid these problems as a matter of course" (p. 143). However, Silverman (1974) concluded from his survey that "despite all of the rhetoric and data on experimenter effects, it appears that psychologists show little more concern for their experimenters as sources of variance than they might for the light fixtures in their laboratories" (p. 276). Such data indicate that it is quite important to present and emphasize the utilization of controls for experimenter bias.

Control of Recording Errors

Errors resulting from the misrecording of data can be minimized if the person recording the data remains aware of the necessity of making careful observations to ensure the accuracy of data transcription. An even better approach would be to use multiple observers or data recorders. If, for example, three individuals independently recorded the data, discrepancies could be noted and resolved to generate more accurate data. Naturally, all data recorders could err in the same direction, which would mask the error, but the probability of this occurring is remote. This procedure could be improved even further if the data recorders were kept blind regarding the experimental conditions in which the subject was responding (Rosenthal, 1978).

The best means for controlling recording errors, although not possible in all studies, is to eliminate the human data recorder and have responses recorded by some mechanical or electronic device. In some research laboratories, the subjects' responses are automatically fed into a computer.

Control of Experimenter Attribute Errors

At first glance, there seems to be a simple and logical solution to the problem created by experimenter attributes. Throughout much of this

Table 6.6 *Hypothetical Data Illustrating the Mean Difference in Learning Obtained from a Warm and a Cold Experimenter*

EXPERIMENTERS	EXPERIMENTAL GROUPS		MEAN DIFFERENCE
	A	B	
Experimenter attributes controlled			
Warm	10	20	10
Cold	7	17	10
Experimenter attributes not controlled			
Warm	8	21	13
Cold	17	17	0

text, I have referred to control in terms of constancy. Most extraneous variables cannot be eliminated, so they are held constant, and in this way a differential influence is not exerted on the subjects' responses in the various treatment groups. In like manner, the influence of experimenter attributes could be held constant across all treatment conditions. Some experimenters, because of their attributes, may obtain more of an effect than other experimenters. But this increased effect should be constant across all treatment groups. Therefore, the influence of the experimenter attributes should not significantly affect the *mean differences* among treatment groups. Assume that a cold and a warm experimenter independently conduct the same learning study and that the warm experimenter obtains an average of 3 more units of learning from subjects in each of the two treatment groups than does the cold experimenter (as shown in the top half of Table 6.6). Note that the mean difference between Groups A and B is identical for both experimenters, indicating that they would have reached the same conclusions even though each obtained different absolute amounts of learning. In such a situation, the effects of the experimenter attributes would not have had any influence on the final conclusion reached.

Control through the technique of constancy does imply that the variable being held constant—experimenter attributes, in this case—produces an equal effect on all treatment groups. If this assumption is not accurate or if the experimenter's attributes interact with the various treatment effects, control has not been achieved. If, in the above example, a warm experimenter obtained an average of 8 units of performance from subjects in Group A and 21 units of performance from subjects in Group B, whereas the cold experimenter obtained identical performance from subjects in both treatment groups (as shown in the bottom half of Table 6.6), we would not have controlled for the influence of experimenter attributes. In this case, the two experimenters would have produced conflicting results. Unfortunately, we not know which attributes interact with numerous independent variables that exist within psychology. Since we do not know how much difference is exerted by various experimenters, a number of individuals (e.g., McGuigan, 1963; Rosenthal, 1966) have suggested that several experimenters be employed in a given study. (The ideal but impractical recommendation is that a random sample of experimenters be selected to conduct the experiment.)

If more than one experimenter were employed, evidence could be acquired as to whether or not there was an interaction between the treatment conditions and an experimenter's attributes. If identical results were produced by all experimenters, one would have increased assurance that the independent variable and the experimenter attributes did not interact. However, if the experimenters produced different results, we would know that an interaction existed and we might be able to identify the probable cause of the interaction.

Since such interaction effects do occur in some studies, several individuals (e.g., McGuigan, 1963) have recommended that the experimenter be studied as an independent variable. Lyons (1964), however, feels this merely complicates the issue, since an experimenter with given attributes still has to study the influence of other experimenters' attributes and certain investigators may find an influence of certain attributes whereas others may not. How far back can we push the problem? The solution that Lyons proposes is to automate the experiment and thus get rid of the experimenter. But even if this solution is employed, some human contact is still necessary in the form of recruiting subjects and greeting them before turning them over to the automated section. Also, automation is not always feasible and is often expensive.

Aronson and Carlsmith (1968) believe that the presence of an experimenter, as well as potentially producing bias, is frequently necessary in an experiment to eliminate bias. They argue that the experimenter can help standardize the extent to which all subjects understand the instructions. Jung (1971) also states that the experimenter may be necessary to detect the occurrence of unanticipated phenomena that could affect the outcome of the experiment and to identify ways of improving the experiment. In the final analysis, the possible gains of having a live experimenter must be weighed against the possible bias that he or she may produce.

As you can see, we do not yet have a good means for controlling the potential artifactual influence of the experimenter, in cases where automation cannot be used. To obtain knowledge about the influence of experimenter attributes, we must conduct experiments that systematically vary experimenter attributes and types of psychological tasks as well as subject attributes. It may be that subject and experimenter attributes interact in some fashion to produce artifactual results (Johnson, 1976). But stating that additional research is needed to identify the situations that require control of experimenter attributes provides little direction or assistance to the investigator who must use live experimenters. Johnson (1976), based on his review of the literature, has found that the experimenter attributes effect can be minimized if one controls for "those experimenter attributes which correspond with the psychological task" (p. 75). In other words, if the experimenter attribute is correlated with the dependent variable, then it should be controlled. On hostility-related tasks, it is necessary to hold the experimenters' hostility level constant. In a weight reduction experiment, the weight of the therapist may be correlated with the success of the program. Therefore, to identify the relative effectiveness of different weight reduction techniques, it would be necessary, at the very least, to make sure the therapists were of approximately the same weight. Such an attribute consideration may not, however, have an artifactual influence in a verbal learning study. At the present time, it is necessary for the investigator to use his or her judgment as well as any available research to ascertain whether the given attributes of the experimenters may have a confounding influence on the study.

Control of Experimenter Expectancy Error

Rosenthal and his associates have presented a rather strong argument for the existence of experimenter expectancy effects in most types of psychological research. In spite of the fact that certain individuals, notably Barber and Silver (1968), have presented counterarguments against Rosenthal, it seems important to devise techniques for eliminating bias of this type. There are a number of techniques that can be used for eliminating or at least minimizing expectancy effects. Generally, they involve automating the experiment or keeping the experimenter ignorant of the condition the subject is in so that appropriate cues cannot be transmitted. Rosenthal (1966) discusses such techniques, several of which will now be presented.

The Blind Technique.   The **blind technique** actually corresponds to the experimenter's half of the double blind placebo model. In the blind technique, the experimenter knows the hypothesis but is blind as to which treatment condition the subject is in. Consequently, the experimenter cannot unintentionally treat groups differently.

Blind technique
A method in which the experimenter is kept blind regarding the treatment condition subjects are in

Rosenthal (1966) has suggested that we need a professional experimenter—a trained data collector analogous to the laboratory technician. This person's interest and emotional investment would be in collecting the most accurate data possible and not in attaining support of the hypothesis. The scientist would not attempt to keep the hypothesis from this individual, since it would be very difficult to do so

(Rosenthal et al., 1963) and in any case the experimenter would probably just develop his or her own. However, since this person's primary interest would be in collecting accurate data, he or she would have less incentive to bias the results and therefore would probably not be as much of a biasing agent. As Rosenthal pointed out, this idea has already been implemented with survey research and may have merit for experimental psychology. However, Page and Yates (1973) have indicated that most psychologists are not favorably disposed toward this alternative.

At the present time, the blind technique is probably the best procedure for controlling experimenter expectancies. There are many studies in which it is impossible to remain ignorant of the condition the subject is in, though, and in those cases the next best technique should be employed—the partial blind technique.

The Partial Blind Technique.   In cases where the blind technique cannot be employed, it is still sometimes possible to keep the experimenter ignorant of the condition the subject is in for a portion of the study. The experimenter could remain blind while initial contact was made with the subject and during all conditions prior to the actual presentation of the independent variable. When the treatment condition was to be administered to the subject, the experimenter could use some technique (such as pulling a number out of a pocket) that would designate which condition the subject was in. Therefore, all instructions and conditions preliminary to the manipulations would be standardized and expectancy minimized. Aronson and Cope (1968) used this procedure in investigating the attraction between two people who share a common enemy. The experimenter explained the purpose of the study and instructed each subject in the performance of a task. After the task had been completed, the subject was randomly assigned to one of two experimental conditions. This was accomplished by having the experimenter unfold a slip of paper—given to him or her just prior to running the subject—that stated the subject's experimental condition. Only at this point did the experimenter receive any knowledge of the subject's experimental condition.

While this procedure is only a partial solution, it is better than having knowledge of the subject's condition throughout the experiment. If the experimenter could leave the room immediately following administration of the independent variable and allow another person (who was ignorant of the experimental manipulations administered to the subject) to measure the dependent variable, the solution would come closer to approaching completeness. Again, in many experiments this is not possible because the independent and dependent variables cannot be temporally separated.

Partial blind technique
A method in which the experimenter is kept blind regarding the condition subjects are in through as many stages of the experiment as possible

Automation. A third possibility for eliminating expectancy bias in animal and human research is total **automation** of the experiment. Indeed, numerous animal researchers currently use automated data collection procedures. Many human studies could also be completely automated by having instructions written, tape recorded, filmed, or televised, and by recording responses via timers, counters, pen recorders, or similar devices. These procedures are easily justified to the subject on the basis of control and standardization, and they minimize the subject-experimenter interaction. Johnson and Adair (1972) have provided some evidence that automation can reduce expectancy effects for male experimenters. Videbeck and Bates (1966) have demonstrated that the computer can be used to totally replace the experimenter.

Automation
The technique of totally automating the experimental procedures so that no experimenter-subject interaction is required

Psychological experiments are becoming increasingly automated. With each passing year, we find increasing numbers of electronic devices manufactured for use in our experiments. However, at the present time few of them totally remove the researcher from the experimental environment. Complete automation, via such approaches as the computer, is restricted by such practical considerations as cost of equipment and programming. In most animal research, the experimenter has to transport the animals to and from the home cages as well as feed and care for them; seldom is this operation totally automated. With human research, Aronson and Carlsmith (1968) make the point that the experimenter sometimes eliminates bias rather than acting as a biasing agent. Rosenthal (1966) states that when the experimenter's participation is considered vital, his or her behavior should be as constant as possible and experimenter-subject contact and interaction should be minimal.

Likelihood of Achieving Control

So far we have looked at a number of categories of extraneous variables that need to be controlled and a number of techniques for controlling them. Do these methods allow us to achieve the control that is desired? Are they effective? The answer to these questions seems to be both yes and no. The control techniques are effective, but not 100 percent effective. Actually, we do not know exactly how effective they are. If we are controlling by equating subjects on some phenomenon, then the effectiveness of the control is dependent on such factors as the ability of the measure (e.g., the ability of an intelligence test to measure intelligence). Likewise, the effectiveness of control through randomization depends on the extent to which the random procedure equated the groups. Since subjects were randomly assigned to groups, it is also possible that the factors that affect the experiments were unequally distributed among the groups, which would result in internal invalidity.

The point is that we can never be certain that complete control has been effected in the experiment. All we can do is increase the probability that we have attained the desired control of the extraneous variables that would represent sources of rival hypotheses.

Summary

In conducting an experiment that attempts to identify a causal relationship, an important task that must be accomplished by the experimenter is to control for the influence of extraneous variables. This is usually accomplished by using an available control technique. The technique of randomization is extremely valuable because it provides control for unknown as well as known sources of variation by distributing them equally across all experimental conditions so that the extraneous variables exert a constant influence.

Matching is a control technique that is less powerful in terms of ability to equate groups of subjects on all extraneous variables. The prime advantage of the matching technique is that it increases the sensitivity of the experiment while providing control on those extraneous variables that are matched. There are four basic matching techniques. One technique, matching by holding variables constant, produces control by including in the study only subjects with a given amount or type of an extraneous variable. Certain extraneous variables are therefore excluded from the study, which means they cannot influence the results. A second matching technique involves building the extraneous variable into the design of the experiment. In this case, the extraneous variable actually represents another independent variable, so its effect on the results is noted and isolated from the effects of other independent variables. The yoked control matching technique is very restrictive in that it controls only for the temporal relationship between an event and a response. It accomplishes this by having a yoked control subject receive the stimulus conditions at exactly the same time as does the experimental subject. The last matching technique involves equating subjects in each of the experimental groups on either a case-by-case basis (precision control) or by matching the distribution of extraneous variables in each experimental group. Regardless of which approach is used, the matching technique represents an attempt to generate groups of subjects that are equated on the extraneous variables considered to be of greatest importance.

The counterbalancing technique attempts to control for both order and carry-over sequencing effects. Order effects exist where a change in performance arises from the order in which the treatment conditions are administered, whereas carry-over effects refer to the influence that one treatment condition has on performance under another treatment condition. Three counterbalancing techniques can provide some control over sequencing effects. Intrasubject counterbalancing involves counterbalancing subjects, whereas intragroup counterbalancing refers to counterbalancing groups of subjects. These two techniques are effective in controlling for all sequencing effects except nonlinear carry-over effects. The randomized counterbalancing technique involves randomly assigning a sequence of experimental conditions to each subject. Sequencing effects are supposedly controlled because they are randomly distributed, but many subjects are needed for this procedure to be trustworthy.

Subjects and experimenters have also been shown to be a potential source of bias in psychological experiments. The biasing influence of subjects is the result of their differential perceptions regarding the most effective mode for presenting themselves in the most positive manner. Use of the double blind placebo model, deception, disguising the experiment, and obtaining an independent measurement of the dependent variable are all effective ways of creating constant perceptions of the experimental hypothesis, the purpose of the experiment, and knowledge of being in the experiment. However, differential subject perceptions can be caused by other procedural aspects of the experiment. To determine if these other procedures create differential perceptions, it is necessary to use a technique such as the retrospective or concurrent verbal report. Experimenter effects can be minimized by using some technique that either conceals from the experimenter the treatment condition that the subject is in or else eliminates experimenter-subject interaction. Such techniques include automation, the blind technique, and the partial blind technique.

After all of these control techniques have been considered for a given study and the appropriate ones have been used, one still cannot be completely sure that all extraneous variables have been controlled. The only sure thing that can be said is that more control exists with use of these techniques than would exist without their use.

7

Experimental Research Design

Chapter Overview

Up to this point in the text, we have been concerned with factors that must be considered before the final research design can be formulated. We have examined the various issues involved in identifying the independent and dependent variables, the variables that need to be controlled in order to attain internal validity, and the techniques that control the influence of these extraneous variables. The next step is designing a study that incorporates not only the independent and dependent variables but also the control techniques. At this stage of the scientific method, we specify the overall plan or strategy to be used in the collection of the data that will provide an answer to the research question. This chapter will present the basic research designs used in most experimental research. As you read through this chapter, you should answer the following questions:

1. What are the basic requirements of a good research design?

2. In what ways do true research designs differ from faulty ones?

3. What are the true experimental research designs, and how do they vary?

4. What is the difference between a "between-subjects" research design and a "within-subjects" research design?

Introduction

Research design refers to the outline, plan, or strategy specifying the procedure to be used in seeking an answer to the research question. It specifies such things as how to collect and analyze the data. Design also has as its purpose the control of unwanted variation, which is accomplished by incorporating one or more of the control techniques discussed in Chapter 6 or by incorporating a control group. The significance of the control group will be discussed in detail later in the chapter, and the manner in which it assists in achieving control will be discussed in conjunction with the various research designs.

Research design
The outline, plan, or strategy used to investigate the research problem

To illustrate the purposes of research design, let us evaluate the study conducted by Ossip-Klein et al. (1983) in which they attempted to determine if switching to low tar/nicotine/carbon monoxide cigarettes actually decreases a smoker's level of carbon monoxide. Forty adult smokers were recruited through advertising in newspapers, television, radio, and posters. The subjects were randomly assigned to two groups: control and experimental. Members of the control group were told to continue smoking their usual brand of cigarettes, whereas those in the experimental group were instructed to smoke a low tar/nicotine/ carbon monoxide cigarette. The results of this study revealed that the level of carbon monoxide in the body was not altered by switching to a low tar/nicotine/carbon monoxide cigarette.

The procedure specified in the design selected by Ossip-Klein et al., depicted in Figure 7.1, is quite simple. First, the 40 subjects were to be randomly assigned to the two groups, and then each group was to smoke a different brand of cigarettes. All subjects were to be tested for carbon monoxide levels before and after smoking their designated brand. The design also suggests which statistical test to use in analyzing the data. Since there were to be two groups and these two groups were to be assessed twice, a two-factor repeated measures analysis of variance was called for. Note the intimate connection that exists between research design and statistics.

Researchers sometimes design an experiment and collect data according to the specifications of the design without attempting to determine if the design will permit statistical analysis. To their dismay, these individuals frequently find either that their data cannot be analyzed (so the research problem cannot be tested) or that analysis would not be worthwhile. This difficulty can be traced to the fact that the studies were not appropriately designed. As a general rule of thumb, never conduct an experiment until you have determined if your research design permits analysis that will answer your research questions.

	PRERESPONSE MEASURE	TREATMENT CONDITION	POSTRESPONSE MEASURE
EXPERIMENTAL GROUP	Carbon monoxide measure	Smokes low tar/nicotine cigarettes	Carbon monoxide measure
CONTROL GROUP	Carbon monoxide measure	Smokes typical brand of cigarettes	Carbon monoxide measure

Figure 7.1 *Design of the Ossip-Klein et al. study.*

The design of the experiment also suggests the conclusions that can be drawn. With the design illustrated in Figure 7.1, a statistical test could be computed to determine if differences existed between the two groups of subjects, if the pre- and postmeasurements of the carbon monoxide level varied, and if the differences between the pre- and postmeasurements depended on the group being considered (an interaction effect that will be discussed in more detail later).

The design also shows how the controls for extraneous variables are incorporated. In the Ossip-Klein et al. experiment, the randomization control technique was incorporated by randomly assigning subjects to the two groups. Prior to being assigned, subjects were matched on several variables, such as number of cigarettes smoked per day.

Because the design suggests the observations that will be made and how these observations will be analyzed, it determines whether or not valid, objective, and accurate answers to research questions will be obtained. Whether designs are good or bad depends on whether they enable one to attain the answers sought. It is usually much easier to design an experiment inappropriately, because careful thought and planning are not required. However, to the extent that the design is faulty, the results of the experiment will be faulty. How does one go about conceiving a good research design that will provide answers to the questions asked? It is no simple task, and there is no set way of instructing others in how to do it. Designing a piece of research requires thought—thought about the components to include and pitfalls to avoid. We will look first at some faulty research designs and then at some appropriate research designs.

Faulty Research Design

In seeking solutions to questions, the scientist conducts experiments, conceiving a certain strategy to be followed. Unfortunately, research is and has been conducted using designs that are inappropriate. The purpose in presenting some examples of defective designs is to demonstrate the types of extraneous variables that produce internal invalidity.

One-Group After-Only Design

In the **one-group after-only design,** a single group of subjects is measured on a dependent variable after having undergone an experimental treatment (see Figure 7.2). Consider a hypothetical situation in which an institution starts a training program X (the treatment condition). The institution wants to evaluate the effectiveness of the program, so on completion of the program they assess behaviors, the Y measure

One-group after-only design
A faulty research design in which the influence of a treatment condition on only one group of individuals is investigated

TREATMENT   RESPONSE MEASURE   **Figure 7.2**   *One-group after-only design.*
   X   Y

(Adapted from Campbell, D. T., and Stanley, J. C. *Experimental and quasi-experimental designs for research.* Chicago: Rand McNally and Co., 1963. Copyright 1963, American Educational Research Association, Washington, D.C.)

(e.g., the opinions, attitudes, and perhaps performance of the individuals who went through the program). If the Y measures are positive and if the individuals' performances are good, then the validity of the program is thought to be established.

For yielding scientific data, the design in Figure 7.2 is, as Campbell and Stanley (1963) state, of almost no value, because it is impossible to determine if a change in performance occurred as a result of the experimental treatment without some sort of comparison. At a minimum, one needs to pretest the subjects to determine if the subjects changed their responses after receiving the experimental treatment. Also, an equated comparison group that did not receive the treatment condition must be included. Without an equated comparison group or multiple pretests, it is impossible to determine if change resulted from the experimental treatment or from some extraneous variable, such as a history, maturation, or statistical regression effect.

One-Group Before-After (Pretest-Posttest) Design

Most researchers recognize the deficiencies in the one-group after-only design and attempt to improve on it by including a pretest. In evaluation of a curriculum or training program, some measure of improvement is necessary. However, it seems as though some individuals assume that they need only include a pretest that can be compared with a test taken after administration of some treatment condition. Figure 7.3 depicts such a plan, which corresponds to the **one-group before-after design.**

A group of subjects is measured on the dependent variable, Y, prior to administration of the treatment condition. The independent variable, X, is then administered, and Y is again measured. The difference between the pre- and posttest scores is taken as an indication of the effectiveness of the treatment condition. In evaluation of a new curriculum, an attitude scale and an achievement test might be given at the beginning of the school year (pretest Y). The new curriculum—X—is then introduced to the students. At the end of the school year, the attitude scale and the achievement test (posttest Y) are again administered. The pre- and posttest scores on the attitude scale and the

One-group before-after design
A faulty research design in which a treatment condition is interjected between a pre- and posttest of the dependent variable

PRERESPONSE MEASURE   TREATMENT   POSTRESPONSE MEASURE

Figure 7.3   *One-group before-after design.*
(Adapted from Campbell, D. T., and Stanley, J. C. *Experimental and quasi-experimental designs for research.* Chicago: Rand McNally and Co., 1963. Copyright 1963, American Educational Research Association, Washington, D.C.)

achievement test are examined for change. A significant change between these two scores is attributed to the new curriculum.

The Liddle and Long (1958) study represents an example of the use of this design. Liddle and Long selected 18 slow learners, who were administered an intelligence test and assigned a reading grade placement score (pre Y) prior to being placed in the experimental classroom. After students had spent approximately two years in the experimental classroom, the Metropolitan Achievement Tests were administered (post Y) and these scores were compared with the previously assigned placement scores. This comparison indicated "an improvement of about 1.75 years in less than two school years" (p. 145). Such a study has intuitive appeal and at first seems to represent a good way to accomplish the research purpose—a change in performance can be seen and documented. In actuality, this design represents only a small improvement over the one-group after-only study because of the many uncontrolled rival hypotheses that could also explain the obtained results.

In the Liddle and Long study, almost two years elapsed between the pre- and posttests. Consequently, the uncontrolled rival hypotheses of history and maturation could have crept in and produced some, if not all, of the observed change in performance. In order to determine conclusively that the observed change was caused by the treatment effect (the experimental classroom) and not by these rival hypotheses, researchers should have included an equated group of slow learners who were not placed in the experimental room. This equated group's performance could have been compared with the performance of the children who received the experimental treatment. If a significant difference had been found between the scores of these two groups, it could have been attributed to the influence of the experimental classroom, because both groups would have experienced any history and maturation effects that had occurred and, therefore, these variables would have been controlled. The design of the study was inadequate, not so much because the sources of rival hypotheses *can* affect the results, but because we do not know *if* they did.

Although the one-group before-after design does not allow us to control or to test for the potential influence of these effects, it is not totally worthless. In situations in which it is impossible to obtain an equated comparison group, the design can be used to provide some information. However, one should remain constantly aware of the possible confounding extraneous variables that can jeopardize internal validity.

Nonequivalent Posttest-Only Design

The primary disadvantage of the previous two designs is the lack of a comparison group and the consequent impossibility of drawing any unambiguous conclusions as to the influence of the treatment condition. The **nonequivalent posttest-only design** makes an inadequate attempt to remedy this deficiency by including a comparison group. In this design, one group of subjects receives the treatment condition (X) and is then compared on the dependent variable (Y) with a group that did not receive this treatment condition. Figure 7.4 depicts the design.

Nonequivalent posttest-only design A faulty research design in which the performance of an experimental group is compared with that of a nonequivalent control group

Brown et al. (1971) conducted a study that illustrates the use of this scheme. They wanted to evaluate the influence of a student-to-student counseling program on potential college freshman dropouts. One group of potential dropouts received the student-to-student counseling, and another matched group—the comparison group—did not. Following the series of counseling sessions, all students were administered several tests designed to evaluate the effects of the program. First-semester grade point averages were also obtained. Results revealed that, on all dependent variable measures, the group receiving the counseling performed in a superior manner.

The design of this study seems to be adequate. A comparison group was included to evaluate the influence of the treatment condition, and subjects in both groups were matched. Why, then, is this design included as an example of one that is faulty? The reason is that the two

TREATMENT   RESPONSE MEASURE

Figure 7.4   *Nonequivalent posttest-only design.*

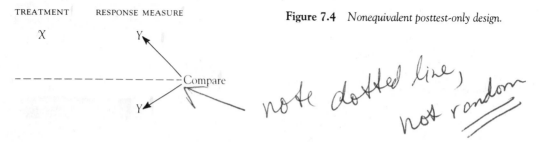

(Adapted from Campbell, D. T., and Stanley, J. C. *Experimental and quasi-experimental designs for research.* Chicago: Rand McNally and Co., 1963. Copyright 1963, American Educational Research Association, Washington, D.C.)

groups are *assumed* to be equated on variables other than the independent variable. Granted, Brown et al. did match on a number of variables such as age, sex, and ACT composite scores. However, matching is no assurance of having attained equated groups. As Campbell and Stanley (1973, p. 12) have stated, "Matching on background characteristics other than 0 [, *the dependent variable,*] is usually ineffective and misleading. . . ." The only way one can have any assurance that the groups are equated is to assign subjects randomly to the two groups. As indicated by the dashed lines in Figure 7.4, random assignment is not included in the nonequivalent posttest-only design. In studies where it is not possible to assign subjects randomly, the next best technique is to match on relevant variables. However, matching is no substitute for random assignment because it does not control for other variables such as motivation.

Requirements of True Research Designs

The designs just presented are considered faulty because, in general, they do not represent a means for isolating the effect of the treatment condition; rival hypotheses are not excluded. What then is a true research design? Kerlinger (1973) discusses three criteria that need to be met in a research design. The first criterion is whether the design answers the research questions, or adequately tests the hypothesis. Periodically, one encounters a situation in which an investigator designs a study and collects and analyzes the data, only to realize when he or she attempts to interpret the data that there is no answer to the research question. Such instances could have been avoided if, after the study was designed, the researcher had asked the following question: "What conclusion or conclusions can I draw from this experiment?" Remember that the design of the study suggests the statistical tests that can be performed on the data, which in turn determine the conclusions that can be drawn. If the design allows one to conduct statistical tests that will provide an answer to the research question, the first criterion has been met.

The second measure of a true research design is whether extraneous variables have been controlled. This criterion relates to the concept of internal validity. If the observed effects can be attributed to the independent variable, the experiment is internally valid. In order to achieve internal validity, one must eliminate potential rival hypotheses. This can be accomplished by two means—control techniques or a control group.

Of the control techniques discussed in Chapter 6, the most important is randomization. The importance of this technique cannot be overemphasized; it is the only means by which unknown variables can be controlled. Also, statistical reasoning is dependent upon the randomization procedure, so I emphasize again, *randomize whenever and wherever possible*.

The second means for effecting control is inclusion of a control group. A **control group** is a group of subjects that does not receive the independent variable, receives zero amount of it, or receives a value that is in some sense a *standard* value, such as a typical treatment condition. An **experimental group** is a group of subjects that receives some amount of the independent variable. In the study conducted by Aronson and Mills on severity of initiation, the group that did not have to take the embarrassment test represented the control group, whereas the other two groups, which had to read either embarrassing or not very embarrassing material, represented the two experimental groups. In a drug study, the subjects receiving a placebo would represent the control group and the subjects receiving the drug would represent the experimental group.

A control group serves two functions. First, it serves as a source of comparison. The one-group after-only and the one-group before-after designs were considered faulty primarily because there was no way to tell if the treatment condition, X, caused the observed behavior, Y. To arrive at such a conclusion, one must have a comparison group or a control group that did not receive the treatment effect. Only by including a control group—assuming all other variables are controlled—can you get any concrete indication of whether or not the treatment condition produced results different from those that would have been attained in the absence of the treatment. Consider a hypothetical case of a father whose daughter always cries for candy when they go into a store. The parent does not like the behavior so, in order to get rid of it, he decides to spank the child whenever she cries for candy in the store and also to refuse to let her have any candy. After two weeks, the child has stopped the crying behavior, and the parent concludes that the spanking was effective. Is he correct? Note that the child also did not receive any candy during the two weeks, so a rival hypothesis is that crying was extinguished. To determine whether it was the spanking or extinction that stopped the behavior, we would also have to include a control child who did not receive the spanking. If both stopped crying in two weeks, then we would know that the spanking was not the variable causing the elimination of the crying behavior.

This hypothetical example also demonstrates the second function of a control group—that is, to serve as a control for rival hypotheses. All variables operating on the control and experimental groups must be identical, except for the one being manipulated by the experimenter. In this way, the influence of extraneous variables is held constant. The

Control group
The group of subjects that serves as a standard of comparison for determining if the treatment condition produced any effect

Experimental group
The group of subjects that receives the treatment condition

extinction variable was held constant across the child who did receive the spanking and the child who did not, and therefore did not confound the results. In the one-group before-after design, extraneous variables such as history and maturation can serve as rival hypotheses unless a control group is included. If a control group is included, these variables will affect the performance of both the control subjects and the experimental subjects, effectively holding their influence constant. It is in this way that a control group also serves a control function.

Before we leave the topic of the control group, one additional point needs to be made. A necessary requirement of the control group is that the subjects in the group be similar to those in the experimental group. If this condition does not exist, the control group cannot act as a baseline for evaluating the influence of the independent variable. The responses of the control group must stand for the responses that members of the experimental group would have given if they had not received the treatment condition. The subjects in the two groups must be as similar as possible so that theoretically they would yield identical scores in the absence of the introduction of the independent variable.

The third criterion of a true research design is generalizability, or external validity, as presented by Campbell and Stanley (1963). Generalizability asks the question "Can the results of this experiment be applied to individuals other than those who participated in the study?" If the answer is yes, then we need to follow with the question "To whom do the results apply?" Can we say that the results should apply to everyone, only to females, or just to females who are attending college? In all cases, we would like to be able to generalize beyond the confines of the actual study. Whether or not we can generalize and how far we can generalize our results, though, is never completely known.

The above three criteria represent the ideal. Naturally, the first criterion must be met by all studies. However, the degrees to which the second and third are met will vary from one study to another. Basic research focuses primarily on the criterion of internal validity because its foremost concern is the examination of the relations among variables. Applied research, on the other hand, places equal emphasis on external and internal validity, since the central interest of such research is to apply the results to people and to situations.

Pretesting Subjects

One means for obtaining information regarding the pretreatment condition of the organism is to pretest subjects, such as was done in the one-group before-after design. The experimenter can then directly observe change in the subjects' behavior as a result of the treatment effect. But one may legitimately question the need to pretest. Is it not sufficient and appropriate to assign subjects randomly to experimental and control groups and forget about pretesting? One can then assume comparability of the subjects in the two groups, and those in the control group provide the comparison data. Hence a pretest is unnecessary. However, there are several reasons (Selltiz et al., 1959; Lana, 1969) for including a pretest in the experimental design. These are as follows:

1. *Increased sensitivity.* One can increase the sensitivity of the experiment by matching subjects on relevant variables. Such matching requires pretesting. (See Chapter 6.)

2. *Ceiling effect.* Another reason for pretesting is to determine if there is room for the treatment condition to have an effect. Suppose you were investigating the efficiency of a particular persuasive communication for positively increasing attitudes toward ecology. If, by chance, all subjects in the experiment already had extremely positive attitudes toward ecology, there would be no room for the treatment condition to have an effect. Such a case could exist if, on a 10-point rating scale (with 10 being the positive end), all subjects were evaluated as being 8, 9, or 10. In such a situation, the effect of the persuasive communication cannot be assessed. Pretesting enables the investigator to identify the existence of a possible ceiling effect and take it into consideration when evaluating the effects of the independent variable.

3. *Initial position.* Many psychological studies are conducted in which it is necessary to know a person's initial position on the dependent variable because it may interact with the experimental condition. A treatment condition that tries to induce hostility toward a minority group may find that the effectiveness of this treatment condition is a function of the subjects' initial level of hostility. The treatment may be very successful with individuals having little hostility but unsuccessful with extremely hostile individuals. With such conditions, it is very helpful to pretest subjects. LeUnes, Christensen, and Wilkerson (1975), for example, pretested subjects on their attitudes toward various components of mental retardation. Subjects were then separated into a positive and a negative group in order to identify whether subjects' initial attitudes affected whether or not an institutional tour provoked a change in attitude toward the various components of mental retardation. These investigators found that the subjects' initial attitudes were a significant factor.

4. *Initial comparability.* Another reason for pretesting is to assure that subjects are initially comparable on relevant variables. Ideally, subjects are randomly assigned to conditions. While random assignment provides the greatest assurance possible of comparability of subjects, it is not infallible. Should there be a failure of randomization to

provide comparability, comparison of the subgroup's pretest mean scores would tell us so.

In field research, we cannot always assign subjects randomly; rather, they have to be taken as intact groups. Educational experiments, for example, are sometimes restricted to using one intact class for one group of subjects and another class for another group of subjects. In such instances, it is advisable to make sure that subjects do not differ initially on the independent variable. This kind of compromise occasionally has to be made. We must also recognize that the results of the experiment could be caused by group differences on characteristics other than the pretested variables. The pretest does, however, give some indication that the observed differences result from the treatment condition.

5. *Evidence of change.* Perhaps the most common reason for pretesting is to gain an empirical demonstration of whether or not the treatment condition succeeded in producing a change in the organisms. The most direct way of gaining such evidence is to measure the difference obtained before and after a treatment is introduced.

As you can see, there are a number of legitimate reasons for including a pretest in the study design. Unfortunately, there are also some difficulties that accompany pretesting (Oliver and Berger, 1980). First, pretesting may increase the amount of time or money required to complete the investigation. A more serious problem is that it may sensitize subjects to the experimental treatment condition. For example, pretesting subjects' opinions may alert them to the fact that they are participating in an attitude experiment, and this knowledge could heighten their sensitivity to the independent variable. Pretested subjects may therefore produce results that are not representative of those that would be obtained from an unpretested population. This potential error is considered by Campbell and Stanley (1963) to be a factor jeopardizing external validity.

Lana (1969), however, has summarized the research that seeks to document this potential source of bias and reached some interesting conclusions. When the pretest involves a learning process such as requiring subjects to recall previously learned material, the posttest score may very well be affected. "Ordinarily, if the task of the recall demanded by the pretest procedure is properly understood by the subject, the effect on the posttest should be facilitative" (p. 132). However, the conclusion regarding attitude research is somewhat different. "In attitude research pretest measures, if they have any impact at all, depress the effect being measured; any differences which can be attributed to the experimental treatment probably represent strong treatment effects" (p. 139).

Thus, although pretesting may influence the subjects' responses to the experimental treatment, the nature of this influence appears to depend on the type of study being conducted.

True Research Designs

In this section we will consider some "true" experimental research designs. To be a **true experimental design,** a research design must enable the researcher to maintain control over the situation in terms of assignment of subjects to groups, in terms of who gets the treatment condition, and in terms of the amount of the treatment condition that subjects receive. In other words, the researcher must have a controlled experiment in order to have confidence in the relations discovered between the independent variables and the dependent variable. There are two basic types of true research designs: the after-only design and the before-after design.

True experimental design An experimental design in which the influence of extraneous variables is controlled for while the influence of the independent variable is tested

After-Only Research Design

The **after-only research design** contains the basic components of most research plans used in the field of psychology. Its name is derived from the fact that the dependent variable is measured only once and this measurement occurs after the experimental treatment condition has been administered to the experimental group, as depicted in Figure 7.5. From this figure, you can see that the responses obtained from an experimental condition are compared with the responses obtained from a control condition after the treatment has been administered. However, the format illustrated here represents only the basic structure of the after-only design. The exact structure of the final design is dependent on several factors, such as the number of independent variables included in the investigation, the number of levels of variation of each independent variable, and whether the same or different subjects are to

After-only research design A true experimental design in which the experimental and the control groups' posttest scores are compared to assess the influence of the treatment condition

	TREATMENT	RESPONSE MEASURE
EXPERIMENTAL CONDITION	X	Y
		> Compare
CONTROL CONDITION		Y

no dotted line, so random assignment of the 2 groups

Figure 7.5 *After-only design.*
(Adapted from Campbell, D. T., and Stanley, J. C. *Experimental and quasi-experimental designs for research.* Chicago: Rand McNally and Co., 1963. Copyright 1963, American Educational Research Association, Washington, D.C.)

be used in each treatment condition. After-only research designs are usually dichotomized in terms of this last factor. If different subjects are used in each experimental treatment condition, then the after-only design is typically labeled a between-subjects design. If the same subjects are used in each experimental condition, then the after-only design is labeled a within-subjects design.

Between-Subjects After-Only Research Design. The **between-subjects after-only research design** is one in which the subjects are randomly assigned to as many groups as there are experimental treatment conditions. For example, if a study was investigating only one independent variable and the presence-versus-absence form of variation was being used with this independent variable, subjects would be randomly assigned to two treatment groups, as illustrated in Figure 7.6. This design is similar in appearance to the nonequivalent posttest-only design. However, there is one basic and important difference. Remember that the nonequivalent posttest-only design was criticized primarily from the standpoint of not providing any assurance of equality among the various groups. This between-subjects after-only design provides the necessary equivalence by randomly assigning subjects to the two groups. If enough subjects are included to allow randomization to work, then, theoretically, all possible extraneous variables are controlled (excluding those such as experimenter expectancies).

Two difficulties can be identified in the design just presented. First, randomization is used to produce equivalence between the two groups. Although this is the best control technique available for achieving equivalence, it does not provide complete assurance that the necessary equivalence has been attained. (This is particularly true when the group of subjects being randomized is small.) If there is any doubt, it is advisable to combine matching with the randomization technique. Second, it is not the most sensitive design for detecting an effect due to the independent variable. As discussed earlier, matching is the most effective technique for increasing the sensitivity of the experiment, and so these difficulties with the after-only design can be eliminated by matching subjects prior to randomly assigning them to the experimen-

Between-subjects after-only research design
A type of after-only research design in which subjects are randomly assigned to the experimental and control groups

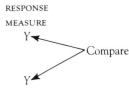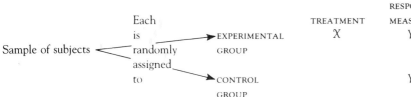

Figure 7.6   *Two-group between-subjects after-only research design.*

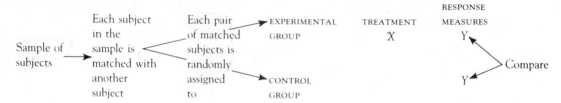

Figure 7.7   *Matched between-subjects after-only research design.*

tal treatment groups. However, the benefits of matching should always be weighted against the accompanying disadvantages, such as limitation of the available subject pool.

When, in the opinion of the investigator, the advantages of matching outweigh the disadvantages, a matched between-subjects after-only design should be used. As illustrated in Figure 7.7, this design requires that each member of the sample of subjects be matched with another subject on the variable or variables that are correlated with the dependent variable. The matched subjects are then randomly assigned to the experimental groups. Note that matching has taken place in addition to randomization; randomization was not replaced with matching. When the two techniques are used, one increases both the probability that the groups are equivalent on the extraneous variables that must be controlled and the sensitivity of the experiment.

The two-group between-subjects after-only design just discussed illustrates the basic conceptual structure of the between-subjects design. However, seldom are experiments confined to two levels of variation of one independent variable. Instead, most studies use several levels of variation of one or more independent variables, and their schemes are extentions of the between-subjects after-only design. The two primary extentions are represented by the simple randomized subjects design and the factorial design.

Simple Randomized Subjects Design.   The **simple randomized subjects design** is a between-subjects after-only type of design that has been extended to include more than one level of the independent variable. There are many situations in which it is desirable to give varying amounts or degrees of an independent variable to different groups of subjects. In drug research, the investigator may want to administer different amounts of a drug to see if they produce differential reactions to the dependent variable. In such a case, subjects would be randomly assigned to the various treatment groups. If there were three experimental groups and one control group, subjects would be randomly assigned to the four groups, as shown in Figure 7.8. A statistical test would then be used to determine if a significant difference existed in the average responses of the four groups of subjects to the dependent variable.

Simple randomized subjects design A between-subjects design in which the influence of several levels of variation on the independent variable is investigated

Figure 7.8 *Simple randomized subjects design with four levels of variation of the independent variable. R indicates that the two groups of subjects were randomly selected.*

Sigall, Aronson, and Van Hoose (1970) used the simple randomized subjects design in attempting to determine if subjects are motivated to look good or if they are motivated to cooperate with the experimenter to produce the results that he or she wants. To investigate these motives, they had a control group and three experimental groups. In one experimental group, the subjects were led to believe that they should increase performance; in another group, they were led to believe that they should decrease performance; and in a third group, evaluative apprehension was generated by telling subjects that increased performance was indicative of obsessive-compulsive behavior. Consequently, the design of this experiment was identical to that depicted in Figure 7.8.

Analysis by Sigall et al. of their data revealed significant differences among the various groups. Additional statistical tests showed that the three experimental groups differed significantly from the control group and that the evaluative apprehension group differed significantly from the other two experimental groups. From this they concluded that a subject's primary motive is to look good rather than to cooperate with the experimenter. They arrived at this conclusion because the obsessive-compulsive group performed more slowly than any other group, whereas the other two experimental groups performed better than either the control or the obsessive-compulsive experimental group.

The simple randomized subjects design considers only one independent variable. In psychological research, as in other types of research, one is frequently interested in the effect of several independent variables acting in concert. In research on instructional effectiveness, interest lies in methods of instruction (e.g., tutorial, discussion, lecture) as well as in other factors such as instructor attitude or experience. The simple randomized subjects design does not enable one to simultaneously investigate several independent variables, but a factorial design does.

Factorial Designs.   A **factorial design** is one in which two or more independent variables are simultaneously studied to determine their independent and interactive effects on the dependent variable. Let us look at a hypothetical example that considers the effect of two independent variables, A and B. Assume that variable A has three levels of

Factorial design
A between-subjects design that enables one to investigate the independent and interactive influences of more than one independent variable

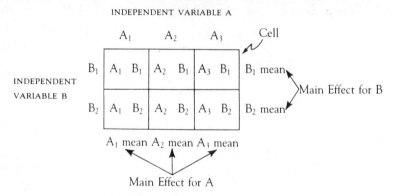

Figure 7.9 *Factorial design with two independent variables.*

variation (A_1, A_2, and A_3) and that variable B has two levels of variation (B_1 and B_2). Figure 7.9 depicts this design, in which there are six possible combinations of the two independent variables—A_1B_1, A_1B_2, A_2B_1, A_2B_2, A_3B_1, and A_3B_2. Each one of these treatment combinations is referred to as a **cell.** There are six cells within this design to which the subjects would be randomly assigned. The subjects randomly assigned to A_1B_1 would receive the A_1 level of the first independent variable and the B_1 level of the second independent variable. In like manner, the subjects randomly assigned to the other cells would receive the designated combination of the two independent variables.

In an experiment that uses the design shown in Figure 7.9, two types of effects need to be analyzed—main effects and interaction effects. A **main effect** refers to the influence of one independent variable. The term *main effect* did not arise in the simple randomized experiment or in the two-group between-subjects after-only experiment because only one main effect or one independent variable existed. However, more than one independent variable exists in a factorial design, and the separate effects of each independent variable must be identified. To make a distinction between the influence of the different independent variables, we refer to each one as a separate main effect. In Figure 7.9, the two independent variables A and B each have a main effect. The main effect for A simply tells us if A produced a significant influence on behavior or if there was a significant difference in the three A mean scores. Similarly, the main effect for B tells us if B had a significant impact on behavior or if there was a significant difference between the two B mean scores.

An **interaction effect** refers to the influence that one independent variable has on another. The concept of interaction is rather difficult for most students to grasp, so we will digress in order to clarify this idea. First, I will present a number of possible outcomes that could accrue from an experiment having the design shown in Figure 7.9. Some of

Cell
A specific treatment combination in a factorial design

Main effect
The influence of one independent variable in a factorial design

Interaction effect
When the influence of one independent variable depends on the level of the second independent variable being considered

the outcomes will represent interactions and others will not, so that you can see the difference in the two situations. I will set up a progression from a situation in which one main effect is significant to a situation in which both main effects and the interaction are significant. The letter A will always represent one independent variable, and the letter B will always represent a second independent variable. Table 7.1 and Figure 7.10 depict these various cases. For the sake of clarity, the hypothetical scores in the cells will represent the mean score for the subjects in each cell.

Illustrations (a), (b), and (d) represent situations in which one or both of the main effects were significant. In each case, the mean scores for the level of variation of at least one of the main effects differ. This can readily be seen from both the numerical examples presented in Table 7.1 and the graphs in Figure 7.10. Note also from Figure 7.10 that the lines for levels B_1 and B_2 are parallel in each of these three cases. In such a situation an interaction cannot exist, because an interaction means that the effect of one variable, such as B_1, depends on

Table 7.1 *Tabular Presentation of Hypothetical Data Illustrating Different Kinds of Main and Interaction Effects*

	A_1	A_2	A_3	MEAN		A_1	A_2	A_3	MEAN
B_1	10	20	30	20	B_1	20	20	20	20
B_2	10	20	30	20	B_2	30	30	30	30
MEAN	10	20	30		MEAN	25	25	25	

(a) A is significant; B and the interaction are not significant

(b) B is significant; A and the interaction are not significant

	A_1	A_2	A_3	MEAN		A_1	A_2	A_3	MEAN
B_1	30	40	50	40	B_1	10	20	30	20
B_2	50	40	30	40	B_2	40	50	60	50
MEAN	40	40	40		MEAN	25	35	45	

(c) Interaction is significant; A and B are not significant

(d) A and B are significant; interaction is not significant

	A_1	A_2	A_3	MEAN		A_1	A_2	A_3	MEAN
B_1	20	30	40	30	B_1	10	20	30	20
B_2	30	30	30	30	B_2	50	40	30	40
MEAN	25	30	35		MEAN	30	30	30	

(e) A and the interaction are significant; B is not significant

(f) B and the interaction are significant; A is not significant

	A_1	A_2	A_3	MEAN
B_1	30	50	70	50
B_2	20	30	40	30
MEAN	25	40	55	

(g) A, B, and the interaction are significant

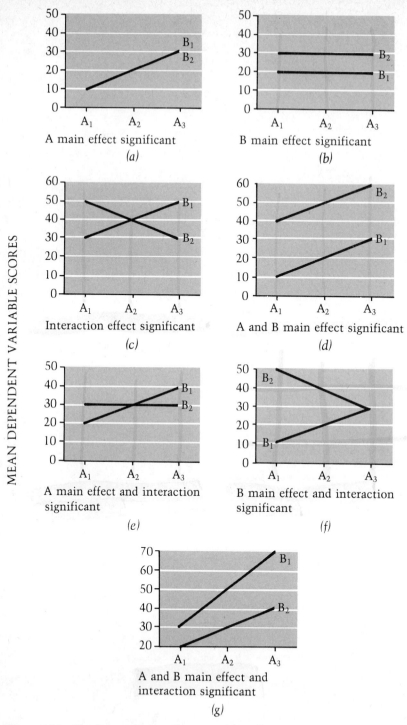

Figure 7.10 *Graphic presentation of hypothetical data illustrating different kinds of main and interaction effects.*

the level of the other variable being considered, such as A_1, A_2, or A_3. In each of these cases, the B effect is the same at all levels of A.

Illustration (c) depicts the classical example of an interaction. Neither main effect is significant, as noted by the fact that the three-column means are identical and the two-row means are identical and reveal no variation. However, if the A treatment effect is considered only for level B_1, we note that the scores systematically increase from level A_1 to level A_3. In like manner, if only level B_2 is considered, then a systematic decrement exists from level A_1 to A_3. In other words, A is effective but in opposite directions for levels B_1 and B_2, or the effect of A depends on which level of B one is considering. This is the definition of interaction. From my experience, I have found graphs to be more helpful than tables in depicting the interaction and aiding in its interpretation. However, you should use whichever mode better conveys the information.

Illustrations (e) and (f) show examples of situations in which a main effect and an interaction are significant; illustration (g) represents a case in which both main effects and the interaction are significant These illustrations exhaust the possibilities that exist in a factorial design having two independent variables. The exact nature of the main effects or the interaction may change, but one of these types of conditions will exist. Before we leave this section, one additional point needs to be made regarding the interpretation of significant main and interaction effects. Where either a main or an interaction effect *alone* is significant, you naturally have to interpret this effect. However, when *both* main and interaction effects are significant, and the main effect is contained in the interaction effect, only the interaction effect is interpreted, because the significant interaction effect qualifies the meaning that would arise from the main effect alone.

The design under discussion was used by Baron (1973) to investigate the influence of threatened retaliation on inhibiting aggression. Specifically, he hypothesized that aggression would be inhibited by threatened retaliation only if the victim had not previously angered the person. The victim who had previously angered the person would act aggressively even if the victim could retaliate. In investigating this hypothesis, Baron used two independent variables: probability of retaliation and prior anger arousal. The first independent variable had three levels of variation of probability of retaliation: high, moderate, and low. The second independent variable had two levels of prior anger arousal: anger and nonanger. This gives us a 2×3 (two levels of one independent variable times three levels of the other) factorial design, with six cells, as seen in Figure 7.11.

Analysis of the data yielded significant main effects and interaction effect, showing that "threatened retaliation from the victim was more effective in inhibiting subsequent aggression under conditions where

PROBABILITY OF RETALIATION

		Low (A$_1$)	Moderate (A$_2$)	High (A$_3$)
PRIOR				
ANGER	Nonangry (B$_1$)	A$_1$B$_1$	A$_2$B$_1$	A$_3$B$_1$
AROUSAL	Angry (B$_2$)	A$_1$B$_2$	A$_2$B$_2$	A$_3$B$_2$

Figure 7.11   *Design of Baron's study (1973).*

subjects had not previously been exposed to anger arousal, than under conditions where they had previously experienced strong provocation" (Baron, 1973, p. 110).

So far, the discussion of factorial designs has been limited to those with two independent variables. There are times when it would be advantageous to include three or more independent variables in a study. Factorial designs enable one to include as many independent variables as one considers important. Mathematically or statistically, there is just about no limit to the number of independent variables that can be included in a study, but practically speaking there are a number of difficulties associated with such increases. First, there is an associated increase in the number of subjects required. In an experiment with two independent variables, each of which has two levels of variation, a 2 × 2 arrangement is generated, yielding 4 cells. If 10 subjects are required for each cell, the experiment requires a total of 40 subjects. In a three-variable design, with two levels of variation per independent variable, a 2 × 2 × 2 arrangement exists, yielding 8 cells, and 80 subjects are required in order to have 10 subjects per cell. Extending to four variables, 16 cells and 160 subjects are required. As you can see, the required number of subjects rapidly increases with an increase in the number of independent variables. However, this difficulty does not seem to be unsurmountable; many studies are conducted with large numbers of subjects.

A second difficulty of factorial designs incorporating more than two variables is that the difficulty of simultaneously manipulating the combinations of independent variables increases. In an attitude study, it is harder to simultaneously manipulate credibility of the communicator, type of message, sex of the communicator, prior attitudes of the audience, and intelligence of the audience (a five-variable problem) than it is to just manipulate credibility of the communicator and prior attitudes of the audience.

A third complication arises when higher-order interactions are significant. In a design with three independent variables, it is possible to have a significant interaction among the three variables A, B, and C. Consider a study that includes the variables of age, sex, and intelligence. A three-variable interaction means that the effect on the dependent variable is a joint function of the subjects' ages, sex, and intelligence levels. The investigator has to look at this triple interaction and interpret its meaning, deciphering what combinations produce what effect and why. Triple interactions can be quite difficult to interpret, and interactions of an even higher order tend to become unwieldy. Therefore, it is advisable to restrict the design to no more than three variables.

In spite of these problems, factorial designs are very popular because of their overriding advantages when appropriately used. The following four advantages of factorial designs were adapted from Kerlinger (1973, p. 257).

The first advantage is that more than one independent variable can be manipulated in an experiment and therefore more than one hypothesis can be tested. In a one-variable experiment, only one hypothesis can be tested—i.e., did the treatment condition produce the desired effect? In an experiment with three independent variables, seven hypotheses can be tested: one regarding each of the three main effects—A, B, and C—and one regarding each of the four interactions—A × B, A × C, B × C, and A × B × C.

A second positive feature is that one can control a potentially confounding variable by building it into the design. This, as noted in Chapter 5, is a mechanism for eliminating the influence of an extraneous variable. Naturally, the decision as to whether to include the extraneous variable (such as sex) in the design will partially be a function of how many independent variables are already included. If three or four are already included, it may be wise to effect control in another manner (perhaps by including only females). If only one or two independent variables exist, then the decision in most cases should be to include the extraneous variable in the design. Including the extraneous variable not only controls it but may also provide valuable information about its effect on the dependent variable.

The third advantage of the factorial design is that it provides greater precision than an experiment with only one variable. The reasoning underlying this statement was discussed earlier and will not be reiterated.

The final benefit of the factorial design is that it enables one to study the interactive effects of the independent variables on the dependent variable. This advantage is probably the most important, since it enables one to hypothesize and test interactive effects. Testing main effects does not require a factorial design, but testing interactions does. It is this testing of interactions that lets us investigate the complexity of behavior and see that behavior is caused by the interaction of many independent variables. Lana (1959), for example, specifically set out to test an interactive hypothesis put forth by Solomon (1949) and Campbell (1957). They stated that pretests have a potentially sensitizing

TREATMENT CONDITIONS

Figure 7.12 *Within-subjects after-only research design.*

A	B	C
S_1	S_1	S_1
S_2	S_2	S_2
S_3	S_3	S_3
.	.	.
.	.	.
.	.	.
S_n	S_n	S_n

Same subjects in
all treatment
conditions

effect on attitudes. Lana used the four-group design to test this interactive hypothesis and found no significant interaction. Pretesting apparently did not have the hypothesized sensitizing effect on attitudes.

Within-Subjects After-Only Research Design

In the **within-subjects after-only research design,** the same subjects participate in all experimental treatment conditions (see Figure 7.12). Actually, this is a repeated measures design, since all subjects are repeatedly measured under each treatment condition. Haslerud and Meyers (1958) used this scheme in their investigation of the transfer value of individually derived principles. All subjects were first trained on problems in which rules were given and on problems in which the subjects had to derive their own rules. After this training, *all* subjects solved problems using both the rules they had been given and the rules they had derived. In other words, subjects served under both conditions.

Within-subjects after-only research design
A type of after-only research design in which the same subjects are repeatedly assessed on the dependent variable after participating in all experimental treatment conditions

Among the benefits of using the within-subjects after-only design is the fact that the investigator need not worry about creating equivalence in the participating subjects, because the same subjects are involved in each treatment condition. In other words, subjects serve as their own control, and variables such as age, sex, and prior experience remain constant over the entire experiment. Since the subjects serve as their own control, the subjects in the various treatment conditions are perfectly matched, which increases the sensitivity of the experiment. Therefore, the within-subjects design is maximally sensitive to the effects of the independent variable.

Also, the within-subjects design does not require as many subjects as does the between-subjects design. In the former, with all subjects participating in all treatment conditions, the number of subjects needed for an entire experiment is equal to the number of subjects needed in one experimental treatment condition. In the between-subjects design, the number of subjects needed equals the number of subjects required for one treatment condition times the number of treatment conditions. If 10 subjects are needed in each treatment condition and there are three treatment conditions, then 10 subjects would be needed in a within-subjects design, whereas 30 subjects would be needed in a between-subjects design.

With all of these advantages, one might think that the within-subjects design would be used more than the between-subjects design. Actually, the reverse is true because of the disadvantages that also accompany the within-subjects design. The most serious handicap of this design is the confounding influence of a sequencing effect. Remember that a sequencing effect can occur when subjects participate in more than one treatment condition. Since the primary characteristic of a within-subjects design is that all subjects participate in all experimental treatment conditions, a sequencing rival hypothesis is a real possibility. In order to overcome the sequencing effect, investigators frequently use one of the counterbalancing techniques discussed earlier. However, counterbalancing controls only linear sequencing effects; if the sequencing effects are nonlinear, then a confounding sequencing influence exists even if counterbalancing is used. Even if the sequencing effect can be overcome by counterbalancing, in a within-subjects design there is no way to identify any impact of the extraneous variables of history, maturation, and statistical regression.

As you can see, there are some rather serious problems associated with the within-subjects design, and they are generally more difficult to control than they are in the between-subjects design. As a result, it is not the most commonly used design.

Combining Between- and Within-Subjects Designs

In conducting psychological research, there are many times when one is interested in several variables, of which one or more would fit into a between-subjects design and the others would fit into a within-subjects design. Does this mean that two separate studies have to be conducted, or can they be combined? As you probably suspected, they can be incorporated into one design, called a **factorial design based on a mixed model.** The simplest form of such a design involves a situation in which two independent variables have to be varied in two different ways. One independent variable requires a different group of subjects for each level of variation. The other independent variable is con-

Factorial design based on a mixed model
A factorial design that represents a combination of the within-subjects and the between-subjects designs

		WITHIN-SUBJECTS INDEPENDENT VARIABLE		
		A_1	A_2	A_3
	B_1	S_1 S_2 S_3 S_4 S_5	S_1 S_2 S_3 S_4 S_5	S_1 S_2 S_3 S_4 S_5
BETWEEN-SUBJECTS INDEPENDENT VARIABLE	B_2	S_6 S_7 S_8 S_9 S_{10}	S_6 S_7 S_8 S_9 S_{10}	S_6 S_7 S_8 S_9 S_{10}

Figure 7.13   *Factorial design based on a mixed model with two independent variables.*

structed in such a way that all subjects have to take each level of variation. Consequently, the first independent variable requires a between-subjects design, and the second independent variable requires a within-subjects design. When these two independent variables are included in the same scheme, it becomes a factorial design based on a mixed model, as illustrated in Figure 7.13.

In this design, subjects are randomly assigned to the different levels of variation of the between-subjects independent variable. All subjects then take each level of variation of the within-subjects independent variable. Therefore, we have the advantage of being able to test for the effects produced by each of the two independent variables as well as for the interaction between the two independent variables. Additionally, we have the advantage of needing fewer subjects, since all subjects take all levels of variation of one of the independent variables. Therefore, the number of subjects required is only some multiple of the number of levels of the between-subjects independent variable.

The discussion of the factorial design based on a mixed model has been limited to consideration of only two independent variables. This in no way is meant to imply that the design cannot be extended to include more than two independent variables. As with the factorial designs, one can include as many independent variables as are considered necessary. We could include any combination of the between-subjects type of independent variable with the within-subjects type of independent variable. If we were conducting a study with three independent variables, two of which required all subjects to take each level of variation of both the independent variables, our design would include two independent variables of the within-subjects variety and one of the between-subjects variety.

	PRERESPONSE MEASURE	TREATMENT	POSTRESPONSE MEASURE	DIFFERENCE
EXPERIMENTAL GROUP	Y	X	Y	Pre-Y — Post-Y
CONTROL GROUP	Y		Y	Pre-Y — Post-Y

R

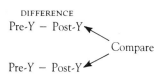

Compare

Figure 7.14 *Before-after design.*
(Adapted from Campbell, D. T., and Stanley, J. C. *Experimental and quasi-experimental designs for research.* Chicago: Rand McNally and Co., 1963. Copyright 1963, American Educational Research Association, Washington, D.C.)

Before-After Research Design

The before-after design is in some ways similar to the one-group before-after design. However, there are important basic differences between the two: the existence or nonexistence of a control group and randomization. In a **before-after research design,** subjects are randomly assigned to groups and then pretested on the dependent variable, Y. The independent variable, X, is administered to the experimental group, and the experimental and control groups are posttested on the dependent variable, Y. The differences between the pre- and postscores for the experimental and control groups are then tested statistically to assess the effect of the independent variable. Figure 7.14 depicts this design.

The before-after design is also a good experimental design and does an excellent job of controlling for rival hypotheses such as history and maturation. The similar but faulty one-group before-after design was said to have been contaminated by extraneous variables, including history and maturation. The before-after plan neatly controls for many of these rival hypotheses. The history and maturation variables are clearly controlled, since any history events that may have produced a difference in the experimental group would also have produced a difference in the control group. Note, however, that an intragroup history effect could exist in this or any design that includes more than one group of subjects. If all the subjects in the experimental group were treated in one session and all the subjects in the control group were treated in another session, it is possible that events took place in one group that did not take place in the other group. If a differential event did take place (e.g., laughter, a joke, or a comment about the experimental procedure), there would be no way of eliminating its influence, and it may have produced an effect that would be picked up by the dependent variable. Such an event would have to be considered a possible cause for any significant difference noted between the groups.

The intragroup history effect can be controlled by individually testing subjects who are randomly assigned to the treatment groups and

Before-after research design
A true experimental design in which the treatment effect is assessed by comparing the difference between the experimental and control groups' pre- and posttest scores

by randomly determining when a control and an experimental treatment will be administered. If group administration of each level of variation of the independent variable is essential, then each separate group potentially has a different intrasession history. In this case, it would be necessary to statistically test the various groups to determine if differences exist as a function of intrasession history. In other words, groups would have to be included as another independent variable.

Maturation and instrumentation are also controlled in this design because they should be equally manifested in both the experimental group and the control group. Equal manifestation of the testing effect in experiments that use observers or interviewers to collect the dependent variable data does, however, assume that the observers are randomly assigned to individual observation sessions. This ensures that the instrumentation effect is randomly distributed across groups. When this assumption cannot be met, a double-blind model should be used, with each available observer used in both experimental and control sessions.

Regression and selection variables are controlled by virtue of the fact that subjects are randomly assigned to both the experimental and the control groups. Randomization assures initial equality of groups as well as equality in the extent to which each group regresses toward the mean. Since subjects are randomly assigned, each group should have the same percentage of extreme scores and, therefore, demonstrate the same degree of regression toward the mean. Selection is naturally ruled out, since random assignment has assured equality of the experimental and control groups at the time of randomization. As stated earlier, randomization does not provide 100 percent assurance, and one will occasionally be wrong. However, it is our *best* protection against the selection rival hypothesis.

In the past (Cronbach and Furby, 1970; Kerlinger, 1973), it has been stated that a statistical analysis computed on the differences between pretest and posttest scores was inappropriate because such gain scores may have low reliability. However, Nicewander and Price (1978) ascertained that the reliability of our dependent variable measures do not have any general relationship to the power of the statistical test. This means that one cannot conclude that the experiment is faulty if the difference score has low reliability. Therefore, it seems appropriate to statistically analyze differences in the gain scores achieved by the experimental and control groups to determine if the experimental groups' gains were significantly greater than those achieved by the control group.

Choice of a Research Design

It is your task to choose which of the several types of research designs discussed in this chapter is most appropriate for a particular research study. There are some rather straightforward factors to consider in making the design selections. The choice requires a thorough knowledge of your problem, of the extraneous variables you must control in your study, and of the advantages and disadvantages inherent in the alternative designs available.

Research Question

First and foremost, you must select a design that will give you an answer to your problem. There are times when investigators try to force a problem into a specific research design. This is an example of the tail wagging the dog and seldom allows you to arrive at an appropriate answer. Therefore, the primary criterion for selection of a design is whether or not it will enable you to arrive at an answer to the research question.

Control

The second factor to consider in the selection of a research design is whether or not you can incorporate control techniques that will allow you to unambiguously arrive at a conclusion. If you have the choice of several designs that could enable you to answer your research question, then you should select the design that will provide maximum control over variables that could also explain the results obtained from the experiment. Control, therefore, appears to be the second most important criterion.

Between- Versus Within-Subjects
Research Design

The third factor to consider is the nature of the research design. In some cases, the problem dictates the type of design. For example, if you are engaged in a learning study, you must give subjects a number of trials to enable them to learn the material. Where trials have to be incorporated into the design, a within-subjects design is necessary. Where this is not the case, the investigator has the choice of manipulating the independent variable or variables with either a between-subjects or a within-subjects design.

When one has a choice of a between- or within-subjects design, the decision is usually made in favor of the latter. This is because, as I have previously pointed out, the within-subjects design provides a more sensitive test of the independent variable.

Summary

The design of a research study is the basic outline of the experiment, specifying how one will collect and analyze the data as well as how unwanted variation will be controlled. The design determines to a great extent whether or not one will attain an answer to the research question. Studies based on inappropriate designs such as the one-group after-only design, the one-group before-after design, and the nonequivalent posttest-only design do not provide the desired answers because they do not control for the influence of the many extraneous variables that can have an effect on the results of an experiment.

A true research design satisfies three criteria. First, the design must test the hypotheses advanced. Second, extraneous variables must be controlled so that the experimenter can attribute the observed effects to the independent variable. The third criterion is that it must be possible to generalize the results. These three criteria are the ideal; seldom will a study satisfy them all.

In designing a study that attempts to meet the conditions just stated, many investigators use a pretest. There are a number of good reasons for administering a pretest. It can be used to match subjects and thereby increase the sensitivity of the experiment. It can also be used to determine if a ceiling effect exists or to test a subject's initial position on a variable to see if the variable interacts with the independent variable. Other reasons include testing for initial comparability of subjects and establishing that subjects actually changed as a result of the independent variable.

The after-only and the before-after designs are true, or good, general research designs because they have the ability to eliminate the influence of extraneous variables that serve as sources of rival hypotheses for explaining the observed results. These designs can control for unwanted variation, for they include a comparison control group and subjects are randomly assigned to the experimental and control groups. The after-only design represents the prototype of most research designs. While the basic after-only design is not commonly used, its variants—the between-subjects after-only design and the within-subjects after-only design—are very popular. The between-subjects type is used when subjects must be randomly assigned to the various experimental treatment groups. The within-subjects type is used when subjects must participate in all treatment groups. When different subjects must participate in some experimental treatment conditions and all subjects must participate in other experimental treatment conditions, a combination of the between- and the within-subjects designs is called for.

Quasi-Experimental Designs

Chapter Overview

Up to this point, the emphasis has been on the need for conducting true experimental studies because they provide the most unambiguous answers to questions asked and have the greatest capacity for reducing alternative explanations that may arise from the influence of extraneous variables. However, use of true experimental designs requires the use of control techniques such as randomization. As one moves out of the laboratory setting, it becomes more difficult to use such control techniques, so it is harder to control for the influence of extraneous variables. There are many events taking place in the natural setting of the real world that should be experimentally investigated, in spite of the fact that it is not possible for the experimenter to have manipulative control over some of the variables involved. For example, we need to conduct research on the causes of child abuse; however, it would not be ethical or even feasible to randomly assign parents and their children to conditions that may cause them to abuse their children. This is where quasi-experimental designs are useful; they enable one to investigate problems that preclude the use of procedures required by a true experimental design.

This chapter will present a variety of quasi-experimental designs and will discuss the manner in which the influence of rival hypotheses must be considered when these designs are used. As you read this chapter, you should answer the following questions:

1. How do quasi-experimental designs differ from true experimental designs?

2. What are the basic characteristics of each of the quasi-experimental designs?

3. How are rival hypotheses ruled out in each of the quasi-experimental designs discussed?

Introduction

A **quasi-experimental design** is a design that applies "an experimental mode of analysis and interpretation to bodies of data not meeting the full requirements of experimental control" (Campbell, 1968, p. 259). There are many situations outside of the laboratory that preclude the

Quasi-experimental design
A research design in which an experimental procedure is applied but all extraneous variables are not controlled

use of control techniques. For example, there is currently a great deal of attention focused on the relationship between nutrition and juvenile delinquency. Some advocates believe that the food that young people eat is to a great extent the cause of their delinquent behavior. However, there is little evidence to support such a postulated relationship, and it would be very difficult to conduct a true experimental study within the area of juvenile delinquency. Several other researchers and I were recently approached by the head of the probation department in a large metropolitan area and asked to design a study to investigate the validity of the hypothesized nutrition-behavior relationship. This administrator said that we could use the juveniles who had been committed to one of the detention facilities as our subject pool. Since these youngsters were required to spend all of their time at this detention facility and the food available to them was prepared there, this was an ideal setting in which to test the nutrition-behavior hypothesis. Once we started designing the experiment, however, we encountered some of the constraints that investigators may find when moving out of the laboratory and into the real world. First, we were told that we could not randomly assign the juveniles into experimental and control groups; they all had to be treated in the same manner. Consequently, we realized at the outset that a true experiment was impossible and that we had to settle for a quasi-experiment.

You may question whether it is possible to draw causal inferences from studies based on a quasi-experimental design. Many causal inferences are made without use of the experimental framework; they are made by rendering other rival interpretations implausible. If a friend of yours unknowingly stepped in front of an oncoming car and was pronounced dead after being hit by the car, you would probably attribute her death to the moving vehicle. Your friend might have died as a result of numerous other causes (a heart attack, for example), but such alternative explanations are not accepted because they are not plausible. In like manner, the causal interpretations arrived at from quasi-experimental analysis are those that are consistent with the data in situations where rival interpretations have been shown to be implausible. Of course, the identification of what is and is not plausible is not always as apparent as this illustration suggests. If it were, we would not need to conduct the experiment. I am simply demonstrating the type of procedure that must be used within the framework of quasi-experimental designs.

Before-After Quasi-Research Designs

There are two quasi-research designs that fall into the category of before-after designs, so categorized because a measurement of the dependent variable is made both before and after the experimental treatment condition is imposed. These two designs are the nonequivalent control group design and the simulated before-after design.

Nonequivalent Control Group Design

A number of designs have been identified by Cook and Campbell (1979) as being **nonequivalent control group designs.** These designs include both an experimental and a control group, but subjects are not randomly assigned. The fact that subjects in the control and experimental groups are not equivalent on all variables may affect the dependent variable. These uncontrolled variables operate as rival hypotheses to explain the outcome of the experiment, making these designs quasi-experimental designs. But where a better design cannot be used, some form of a nonequivalent control group design is frequently recommended. The basic scheme, depicted in Figure 8.1, consists of giving an experimental group and a control group first a pretest and then a posttest (after the treatment condition is administered to the experimental group). The pre- to posttest difference scores of the two groups are then compared to determine if significant differences exist. The design appears identical to the before-after experimental design. However, there is one basic difference that makes one a *true* experimental design and the other a *quasi*-experimental design. In the before-after design subjects are randomly assigned to the experimental and control groups, whereas in the nonequivalent control group design they are not. This is the component that makes this design a quasi-experimental design.

Consider the study conducted by Becker, Rabinowitz, and Seligman (1980), which was concerned with the impact of the billing procedure on energy consumption. Because of the large energy bills resulting from increased energy costs, a number of utility companies have given their customers the option of using an "equal monthly payment plan." This scheme requires the utility company to bill the resident for one-twelfth of the yearly utility cost each month as opposed to billing for

Nonequivalent control group design
A quasi-experimental design in which the results obtained from nonequivalent experimental and control groups are compared

	PRERESPONSE MEASURE	TREATMENT	POSTRESPONSE MEASURE	DIFFERENCE	
EXPERIMENTAL GROUP	Y_1	X	Y_2	$Y_1 - Y_2$	Compare
CONTROL GROUP	Y_1		Y_2	$Y_1 - Y_2$	

Figure 8.1 *Nonequivalent control group design.*
(Adapted from Campbell, D. T., and Stanley, J. C. *Experimental and quasi-experimental designs for research.* Chicago: Rand McNally and Co., 1963. Copyright 1963, American Educational Research Association, Washington, D.C.)

	PRETEST RESPONSE	TREATMENT CONDITIONS	POSTTEST RESPONSE
EXPERIMENTAL GROUP	Magnitude of electricity consumed	Equal monthly payment plan	Magnitude of electricity consumed
CONTROL GROUP	Magnitude of electricity consumed	Conventional payment plan	Magnitude of electricity consumed

Figure 8.2   *The design of the Becker, Rabinowitz and Seligman study.*

the actual amount consumed. While such a plan apparently produces a great deal of customer satisfaction, it runs the risk of increasing energy use, since there is not a direct connection beween energy used and the magnitude of the monthy bill. The study conducted by Becker et al. was designed to determine if the equal monthly payment plan actually led to an increased use of energy.

In conducting such a study, one would ideally assign subjects randomly to either the equal monthly payment plan or the conventional payment plan (in which energy is paid for as it is consumed). However, the utility companies contacted would not allow such random assignment for a variety of reasons, so the investigators had to formulate two groups in the absence of randomization. This meant that a quasi-experimental design had to be used, and Becker et al. selected the nonequivalent control group type. Figure 8.2 shows that the design of the Becker et al. study consisted of pretesting both groups on consumption of electricity prior to the implementation of the equal payment plan. Following this pretesting (which occurred during the summer months), the treatment plan was implemented for the experimental group, and consumption of electricity was measured for both groups during the following summer.

In formulating the experimental and control groups, Becker et al. did not have the opportunity to randomly assign subjects, although they were aware of the necessity of having equated groups. Consequently, they devised a system that seemed to match the subjects on the variables that would influence electrical consumption. One of the companies whose customers were used in the study maintained records in such a way that it was possible to identify next-door neighbors. The investigators reasoned that next-door neighbors would be more likely to have similar-sized homes and be more similar on other variables that may affect electrical consumption than would a random sample of individuals not on the equal monthly payment plan. Therefore, the control group consisted of next-door neighbors of those individuals who were on the equal monthly payment plan.

The results of this study for one company are depicted in Figure 8.3. Figure 8.3 shows that a difference in electrical consumption ex-

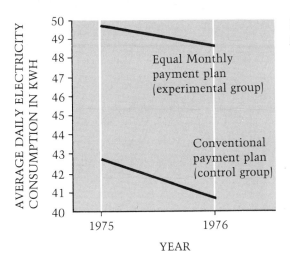

Figure 8.3 *Average daily electricity consumption for two payment plans.*

(Based on data from Becker, Rabinowitz, and Seligman. Evaluating the impact of utility company billing plans on residential energy consumption. *Evaluation and Program Planning,* 1980, 3, 159–164.)

isted between the two groups at pretesting time. However, the change in consumption between pretesting and posttesting was about the same for both groups. The question now becomes one of interpreting these results. The difference in pretest scores suggests that the two groups were not equivalent at the beginning of the experiment, in which case variables other than the experimental condition may have produced the obtained results. For example, those selecting the equal monthly payment plan used more electricity at the outset and, therefore, may have differed from the control group in a variety of ways.

Cook and Campbell (1979) have pointed out that the rival hypotheses in such a situation tend to be directly related to the results obtained from the experiment. Cook and Campbell identified several different experimental outcomes that could occur from the use of a nonequivalent control group design. They then pointed out the rival hypotheses that could also explain the obtained results. We will first take a look at these outcomes and the rival hypotheses that threaten them and then attempt to relate them to the Becker et al. study.

Outcomes with Rival Hypotheses

Increasing Treatment Effect I.   In the **increasing treatment effect I outcome,** illustrated in Figure 8.4, the control group scores reveal no change from pretest to posttest but the experimental group starts at a higher level and shows a significant positive change. Such an outcome appears to suggest that the experimental treatment was effective. However, this outcome could also have occurred as a result of a selection-maturation effect or a local history effect.

Increasing treatment effect I outcome
An outcome in which the experimental and the control groups differ at pretesting and only the experimental group's scores change from pre- to posttesting

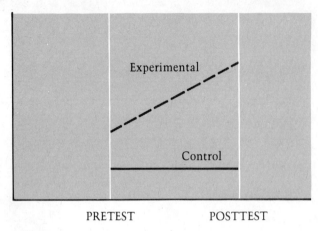

PRETEST   POSTTEST

Figure 8.4   *Increasing treatment effect I.*
(From Cook, T. D., and Campbell, D. T., "The design and conduct of quasi-experiments and true experiments in field settings," in *Handbook of industrial and organizational psychology* edited by M. D. Dunnette. Copyright © Rand McNally College Publishing Company, 1976.)

A **selection-maturation effect** refers to the fact that one of the two groups of subjects was selected in such a way that the subjects were growing or developing faster than the subjects in the other group. One group may progress faster because it members are more intelligent or capable than those in the other group. In the Becker et al. study, an increasing treatment effect I outcome would have been indicated if the experimental group had consumed more electricity during pretesting and had continued to increase consumption between pre- and posttesting, while control-group consumption remained stable. Such an increase could have been caused by the type of payment plan used by the experimental group; however, it could also have been caused by the fact that the salary level of this group was increasing and so these subjects were less concerned with electrical costs. If this were the case, then the posttest increase could be accounted for by the fact that the selection procedure happened to place in the experimental group individuals whose salary levels were increasing more rapidly.

In an attempt to eliminate the potential biasing of this type of selection-maturation effect, many investigators try to match subjects. This procedure is supposed to equate subjects on the matched variables not only at the time of matching but also during the remainder of the study. If matching is conducted during the pretest, then experimental and control subjects should not differ on the dependent variable measure. If they do not, then it is assumed that they are equated. This equality is supposed to persist over time, so any difference observed during a posttest is attributed to the experimental treatment effect.

Selection-maturation effect
The result of selecting one of two groups in such a way that its subjects develop faster than those in the other group

However, evidence (Campbell and Erlebacher, 1970; Campbell and Boruch, 1975) has revealed that such an assumption may be erroneous because of a statistical regression phenomenon that may occur within the two groups of subjects. This regression phenomenon increases the difference between the two matched groups upon posttesting, apart from any experimental treatment effect. Such a difference could be misinterpreted as being due to a treatment effect or a failure to find a treatment effect, depending on which of the matched groups operated as the experimental group and which operated as the control group.

Assume that we are conducting a study designed to investigate the influence of a Head Start program on children's subsequent school performance. We consider the attitude of the mothers of Head Start and non–Head Start children to be important, so we decide to match on this variable to eliminate its influence. Assume further that the attitude scores obtained from mothers who did and did not have children in the Head Start program are distributed in the manner shown in Table 8.1. From this table, it is readily apparent that most of the Head Start mothers have lower attitude scores than do the non–Head Start mothers. Therefore, matching involves selecting for the experimental group those Head Start mothers with the highest attitude scores and for the control group those non–Head Start mothers with the lowest at-

Table 8.1 *Hypothetical Attitude Scores*

HEAD START SUBJECTS	HEAD START MOTHERS' PRETEST ATTITUDES	MOTHERS' POSTTEST ATTITUDES	NON–HEAD START SUBJECTS	NON–HEAD START MOTHERS' PRETEST ATTITUDES	MOTHERS' POSTTEST ATTITUDES
S_1	5		S_{16}	25	28
S_2	7		S_{17}	27	30
S_3	9		S_{18}	29	32
S_4	11		S_{19}	31	34
S_5	13		S_{20}	33	36
S_6	15		S_{21}	35	
S_7	17		S_{22}	37	
S_8	19		S_{23}	39	
S_9	21		S_{24}	41	
S_{10}	23		S_{25}	43	
S_{11}	25	22	S_{26}	45	
S_{12}	27	24	S_{27}	47	
S_{13}	29	26	S_{28}	49	
S_{14}	31	28	S_{29}	51	
S_{15}	33	30	S_{30}	53	

Matched Subjects

titude scores. In other words, one only includes subjects with extreme scores—the subjects most susceptible to the statistical regression phenomenon. This would not be a serious factor if the distributions of scores of the two groups were the same, but they are not. Statistical regression dictates that the Head Start mothers' scores, upon posttesting, will decline and regress toward the mean of their group and that the control subjects' scores will regress or increase toward their group's mean (also illustrated in Table 8.1). Such a regression phenomenon could indicate that the experimental treatment is detrimental when it actually may not have any effect. If the treatment does have a positive effect, this regression effect might lead one to underestimate it.

Another way of attempting to equate subjects by eliminating the selection-maturation bias artifact is to use a variety of statistical regression techniques, such as analysis of covariance and partial correlation. Campbell and Erlebacher (1970) and Campbell and Boruch (1975) have pointed out the fallacy of such an approach, but it is beyond the scope of this text. Suffice it to say that these researchers as well as others (Lord, 1969; Cronbach and Furby, 1970) have found that such statistical adjustments cannot equate nonequivalent groups unless there is no error in the dependent measures given to these individuals.

A second rival hypothesis existing in the increasing treatment effect I outcome is that of a **local history effect** (Cook and Campbell, 1975). A general history effect, discussed in Chapter 5, is controlled in the nonequivalent control group design by inclusion of a control group. However, the design is still susceptible to a local history effect, which is some event that affects either the experimental or the control group but not both. Such a local history effect could have operated in the Becker et al. study if the subjects in the control group had purchased additional insulation for their homes. The resulting effect would be that the control group would have decreased consumption of electricity not because of the type of payment plan but because of the additional insulation. Such a variable would represent a rival hypothesis for any difference observed between the control and the experimental groups.

Local history effect
The result of an extraneous event's influencing either the experimental or the control group but not both groups

Increasing Treatment and Control Groups.   In the **increasing treatment and control groups outcome,** both the control group and the experimental group show an increment in the dependent variable from pre- to posttesting, as is depicted in Figure 8.5. The difference between the increased growth rates could be the result of an actual treatment effect, but it could also be due to a type of selection-maturation interaction. Figure 8.5 indicates that subjects in both groups are increasing in performance. Note, however, that at the time of pretesting, the treatment group scored higher on the dependent variable. This could mean that the subjects in the experimental treatment group were just naturally increasing faster on the dependent variable than were the control

Increasing treatment and control groups outcome
An outcome in which the experimental and the control groups differ at pretesting and both increase from pre- to posttesting but the experimental group increases at a faster rate

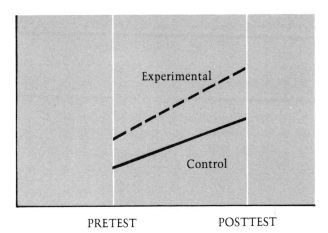

PRETEST   POSTTEST

Figure 8.5 *Increasing treatment and control groups.*
(From Cook, T. D., and Campbell, D. T., "The design and conduct of quasi-experiments and true experiments in field settings," in *Handbook of industrial and organizational psychology* edited by M. D. Dunnette. Copyright © Rand McNally College Publishing Company, 1976.)

subjects. The greater difference between groups of subjects at posttesting may only reflect the fact that the experimental subjects continued to increase faster on the dependent variable than did the control subjects. For example, assume that the dependent variable consisted of a measure of problem-solving ability and the subjects were six years old at the time of pretesting and eight years old at the time of posttesting. Also assume that the experimental subjects were brighter and therefore increasing in problem-solving ability more rapidly than were the control subjects. If this were the case, then one would expect the two groups of subjects to differ somewhat at pretest time. However, subjects would not stop increasing in problem-solving ability at age six, and thus an even greater difference would exist at posttest time, independent of any treatment effect. Where such a differential growth pattern occurs, one may artifactually interpret a greater posttest difference as being the result of a treatment effect when it is really the result of a selection-maturation interaction.

Evidence of the existence of a selection-maturation interaction can be obtained from looking at the variability of the subjects' scores at pretest and posttest time. Random error dictates that the variability of the scores should be the same on both occasions. However, a growth factor dictates that the scores should increase in terms of variability. Therefore, an increase in the variability of the scores for the experimental and control groups from pretest to posttest suggests the possibility of the existence of a selection-maturation interaction.

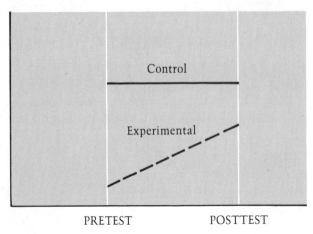

PRETEST   POSTTEST

Figure 8.6 *Increasing treatment effect II.*
(From Cook, T. D., and Campbell, D. T., "The design and conduct of quasi-experiments and true experiments in field settings," in *Handbook of industrial and organizational psychology,* edited by M. D. Dunnette. Copyright © Rand McNally College Publishing Company, 1976.)

Increasing Treatment Effect II.   The **increasing treatment effect II,** depicted in Figure 8.6, is an outcome in which control groups and experimental treatment groups differ rather extensively at pretest time. However, the experimental group improves over time, presumably because of the experimental treatment, so that the posttest difference is decreased. Such an outcome would be desired when the experimental group was a disadvantaged group and the experimental treatment was designed to overcome the disadvantage. For example, Head Start was initiated to overcome the environmental deprivation experienced by many children in the United States and bring the performance of these disadvantaged individuals up to the level of that of nondisadvantaged individuals. If a study were conducted to compare the pretest and posttest performances of a group of control individuals (who had not experienced the environmental handicap) with those of a group of environmentally handicapped individuals who received the Head Start experimental treatment, one would hope to find the type of effect illustrated in Figure 8.6. However, before one can interpret the increase in performance of the experimental treatment group as being the result of the Head Start experience, several rival hypotheses must be ruled out. The first is a local history effect which affects only one of the two groups of subjects. The second and more likely rival hypothesis is a statistical regression effect—a likely source of confounding, since the subjects in the experimental treatment group are typically selected because of their unusually poor performance or low scores. Conse-

Increasing treatment effect II
An outcome in which the control group performs better at pretesting but only the experimental group improves from pre- to posttesting

quently, the regression artifact would predict that the scores of this group should increase during posttesting. Statistical regression could, therefore, produce the outcome depicted in Figure 8.6, which the unwary investigator would interpret as a treatment effect. Therefore, designs that involve administering an experimental treatment to a disadvantaged group should provide a check for the possibility of such a regression artifact.

One indicator of the existence of a regression artifact is the instability of the deprived group's scores in the absence of the experimental treatment. If the deprived group's scores consistently stay low over time, this suggests that the low scores represent the true standing of the individuals. In such cases, a pretest-to-posttest increment would probably represent a true experimental effect or at least one not confounded by the influence of a regression artifact.

Crossover Effect.   Figure 8.7 depicts the **crossover effect,** an experimental outcome in which the treatment group scored significantly lower at pretest time but significantly higher at posttest time. This outcome represents the typical interaction effect. Such an outcome is much more readily interpreted than the others discussed because it renders many of the potential rival hypotheses implausible. Statistical regression can be ruled out because it is highly unlikely that the experimental treatment group's lower pretest scores would regress enough to become significantly higher than those of the control group on posttest-

Crossover effect
An outcome in which the control group performs better at pretesting but at posttesting the experimental group's performance exceeds that of the control group

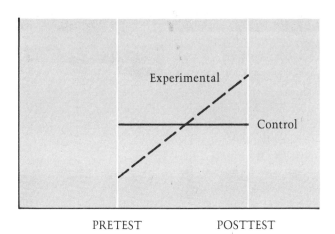

Figure 8.7   *Crossover effect.*
(From Cook, T. D., and Campbell, D. T., "The design and conduct of quasi-experiments and true experiments in field settings," in *Handbook of industrial and organizational psychology* edited by M. D. Dunnette. Copyright © Rand McNally College Publishing Company, 1976.)

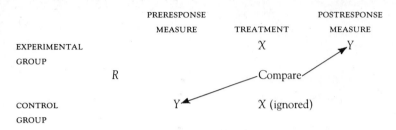

Figure 8.8   *Simulated before-after design. R indicates that the two groups of subjects were randomly selected.*
(Adapted from Campbell, D. T., and Stanley, J. C. *Experimental and quasi-experimental designs for research.* Chicago: Rand McNally and Co., 1963. Copyright 1963, American Educational Research Association, Washington, D.C.)

ing. Second, a selection-maturation effect is improbable because it is typically the higher-scoring pretest subjects who gain faster. The outcome depicted in Figure 8.7 shows that the subjects scoring lower on the pretest increased more rapidly than did the controls scoring higher on that test. This is the opposite of what a selection-maturation outcome would suggest.

Simulated Before-After Design

The **simulated before-after design** is useful in a situation where it is impossible to assign subjects randomly to an experimental condition but it is possible to randomly select two subgroups from the larger population. One of these subgroups serves as the control group and is tested prior to administration of the treatment condition; the other group serves as the experimental group and is tested after the treatment condition is introduced. This design is depicted in Figure 8.8. The pretest scores of the control group are then compared with the posttest scores of the experimental group to assess the influence of the treatment condition.

Simulated before-after design
A quasi-experimental design in which an experimental and a control group are randomly selected and the control group's pretest scores are compared with the experimental group's posttest scores

Star and Hughes (1950) used this design to assess the influence of a six-month experimental campaign program to inform the city of Cincinnati about the United Nations. The campaign was designed to be informational rather than persuasive. To assess the effect of the campaign, Star and Hughes interviewed a representative sample of 745 members of Cincinnati's adult population prior to the start of the campaign. Then, an attempt was made to reach *every* adult resident (1,155,703) within the retail trading zone of Cincinnati with the experimental campaign.

In all, 59,588 pieces of literature were distributed and 2,800 clubs were reached by speakers supplied by a speakers' bureau and by circular, hundreds of documentary films were shown and the slogan, "Peace Begins With the United Nations—The United Nations Begins With You" was exhibited everywhere, in every imaginable form—blotters, matchbooks, streetcar cards, etc.[1] [p. 390]

Following this campaign, a second and different representative sample of 758 adults was interviewed and the results of the interviews for the two groups were compared. The results showed that the campaign had had little effect, since there was very little difference between the responses of the two groups.

This design is not exceptionally strong, but it is much better than the one-group before-after design, as it does eliminate a number of rival hypotheses. Specifically, this scheme controls for such variables as statistical regression and selection biases, but it does not control for history effects. An effect due to history could have occurred during the intervening six-month period of time in which the campaign took place, and this could explain some of the results obtained. Indeed, a real history effect did occur during the Star and Hughes study. At the time of the study, a cold war was taking place with Russia, and this event was a rival hypothesis for some of the results found. Star and Hughes did, in fact, attribute some of their findings to this variable and obtained data to support this interpretation.

Problems such as the history effect can be overcome if the investigator is not restricted to testing only the groups of subjects that *must* receive the treatment effect. If the investigator has the option of testing a comparable though not entirely equivalent group that does not have to receive the treatment effect, then these subjects can serve as a control group. Such a separate-samples simulated before-after design would take the form shown in Figure 8.9. Two randomly selected groups of subjects are used to measure the treatment effect. Following introduction of the treatment condition, one group's pretest scores are subtracted from the other group's posttest scores. This difference is then compared with the difference between one of the control group's pretest scores and the other control group's posttest scores. If a significant difference is obtained, one has added assurance that the difference is the result of the treatment condition—the history rival hypothesis has now been ruled out. This design is much stronger than the simulated before-after type. Star and Hughes wanted to use such a scheme in their study but could not because, they said, no comparable community was available.

[1] From Star, S. A., and Hughes, H. M. Report on an educational campaign: The Cincinnati plan for the United Nations. *American Journal of Sociology*, 1950, 55, 389–400. Composed and printed by the University of Chicago Press, Chicago, Illinois, USA.

		PRERESPONSE MEASURE	TREATMENT	POSTRESPONSE MEASURE	DIFFERENCE	
EXPERIMENTAL	Group I		X	Y	Group I Y	
	R				minus	
	Group II	Y	X (ignored)		Group II Y	Compare
CONTROL	Group I			Y	Group I Y	
	R				minus	
	Group II	Y			Group II Y	

Figure 8.9 *Separate-samples simulated before-after design. R indicates that the two experimental and control groups of subjects were randomly selected.*
(Adapted from Campbell, D. T., and Stanley, J. C. *Experimental and quasi-experimental designs for research.* Chicago: Rand McNally and Co., 1963. Copyright 1963, American Educational Research Association, Washington, D.C.)

Regression-Discontinuity Design

The **regression-discontinuity design** is a plan that can be used in a situation in which a group of individuals is selectively given special attention. For example, some educational systems place students on the dean's list if they acquire a certain level of academic achievement. Similarly, industrial organizations may give a bonus or an award to individuals who demonstrate some exceptional performance. It would be desirable to know if such special attention had any beneficial effect on these individuals' subsequent performance levels. When one seeks to answer such a question, the regression-discontinuity design should be used. This design, depicted in Figure 8.10, involves comparing the scores of the individuals who received the bonus, or special attention, with those of individuals who did not. This is accomplished by examining the pattern of scores before and after the award is administered. If the award did not have any influence on subjects' behavior, one would expect the pattern of the no-treatment scores to continue after the award was administered, as illustrated by the dotted line in Figure 8.10. However, if the award did have some effect, then one would expect a discontinuity to exist between the no-treatment and the treatment scores, as illustrated by the two solid lines. The logic underlying the design is relatively simple. Individuals are classified along some continuum of merit (such as grades). Those who score above a given point are given some special attention, and those scoring below the cutoff point are not. If the special attention has any effect on the individuals' subsequent behavior, one would expect to see a discontinuity of scores between those individuals who did and did not receive the treatment effect.

Regression-discontinuity design
A quasi-experimental design in which the patterns of pre- and posttest scores of individuals who were and were not given an award are compared

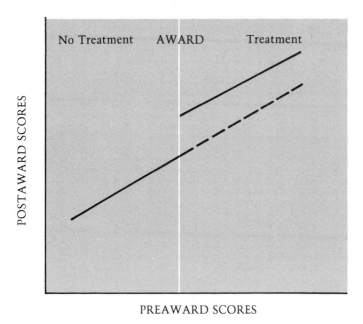

Figure 8.10   *Regression-discontinuity design.*

Cook and Campbell (1975) cite a study by Seaver and Quarton (1973) that used the regression-discontinuity design to examine the influence of being on the dean's list. The investigators examined the grades of 1002 students during two academic quarters. They found that students who made the dean's list during the first quarter in which the study was conducted made better grades during the second quarter of study than would have been predicted. In other words, there was a discontinuity between the pattern of scores of subjects who made the dean's list and those of students who did not, indicating that the dean's list did have a positive influence on subsequent academic performance.

So far, the regression-discontinuity design seems relatively straightforward and easy to interpret. However, there are several difficulties that one may encounter (Cook and Campbell, 1975). For example, assume that an explicit discontinuity did not exist between the treatment and the no-treatment groups. Instead, the slope of the pattern of scores changed as illustrated in Figure 8.11. This could be interpreted as a pretest by treatment interaction effect. People with the higher pretest scores (e.g., grades) are more likely to profit from an award such as being on the dean's list. The slope could also be a result of natural change in the pattern of scores of the more capable individuals. To determine if this is the case, one would need to get indepen-

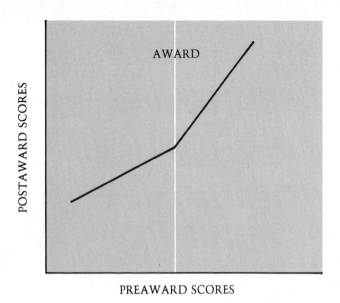

Figure 8.11 *Regression-discontinuity design—change in slope of treatment scores.*

dent evidence by use of some comparable group that did not receive the award.

A second problem with this design is that the treatment tends to be given only to the more gifted or needy individuals. This means that there will be only a narrow range of scores on the treatment side of the cutoff point. For example, if individuals had to have a 3.5 grade point average to be on the dean's list, then the scores on the treatment side of this cutoff point could only range from 3.5 to 4.0. On the no-treatment side, they could range from 0.0 to 3.49. The restricted range of the scores on the treatment side of the cutoff makes it difficult to obtain a good measure of the pattern of these scores. Hence, it may be hard to tell if the treatment scores represent a discontinuity from the no-treatment scores.

A third difficulty is that the cutoff score may not be rigidly adhered to. With the dean's list example, the score is rather explicit. However, assume that you are in charge of distributing a bonus in an industrial organization. You may have an explicit criterion to determine who gets the bonus, but you "bend" it to repay a debt, to avoid disapproval of a friend, or for some other reason. In such cases, the cutoff score is fuzzy (Cook and Campbell, 1975), and it is necessary to identify those individuals for whom it has been altered and remove them from the study.

Cohort Design

The **cohort design** is useful in identifying a treatment effect in a situation where the experimental treatment condition is administered to everyone but there is a regular turnover of individuals receiving the treatment effect. Consider a situation in which a company requires its salespeople to take a sales training class within their first month on the job. All those hired within a 30-day period must take the class, but a new group of individuals is hired every six months. Consequently, a new group takes the training class every six months. If we wanted to identify the effect of this training class, we could not use a true experimental design because the company hiring the sales personnel typically would not permit researchers to randomly assign subjects to control and experimental groups. Similarly, a nonequivalent control group design could not be used because most companies would not hire a matched (though nonequivalent) group of individuals who are not given the sales training just to have a control group. Consequently, one is faced with a situation in which the group of individuals used in the experiment must remain intact and all members of the group must take the treatment condition but there is regular turnover in the group taking the treatment condition.

> *Cohort design*
> A quasi-experimental design in which the posttest scores of two or more cohorts are compared

In this case, about the only plan that can be used is the cohort design. **Cohorts** are groups of individuals that follow one another (for example, one group of newly hired sales personnel represents a cohort of a previously hired group of sales personnel). According to Cook and Campbell (1979), such cohorts can be used for experimental purposes in three ways. First, it is usually possible to identify cohorts that have not received the experimental treatment. In the case of the company requiring all entry-level sales personnel to take a sales training course, there was a time when such a requirement did not exist. Those entry-level sales personnel who were hired when the sales course was not required could represent a control cohort. Second, it is usually reasonable to assume that contiguous cohorts differ in only minor ways. If the company maintained the same criterion for hiring sales personnel, it can be assumed that the previously hired and the newly hired cohorts are similar. Third, it is often possible to use archival records to obtain the independent variable data on cohorts that existed in a company prior to the introduction of a treatment condition. So it is frequently possible to make up an assumption of quasi-comparability between cohorts that have and have not received an experimental treatment, which, in turn, enables us to assess the treatment's effectiveness.

> *Cohort*
> Groups of individuals that follow one another, such as a sixth-grade class in 1981 and a sixth-grade class in 1980

Figure 8.12 presents the basic features of the cohort design. You can see that the design must include a minimum of two cohorts—one

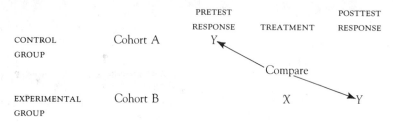

Figure 8.12   *Cohort design.*
(Adapted from Cook, T. D., and Campbell, D. T. *Quasi-experimentation: Design and analysis issues in field settings.* Chicago: Rand McNally and Co., 1979.)

that has been pretested but did not receive the experimental treatment and one that has received the experimental treatment and has been posttested. The pre- and posttests of the two cohorts are then compared to assess the effectiveness of the treatment. In considering the example regarding the sales training program in terms of the cohort design, you might wonder why you must obtain a cohort that did not receive the sales training. In such a situation, you could use the pretest scores obtained on a cohort of individuals prior to their receiving the training and then compare them with the posttest scores of a cohort of individuals who have finished the training.

The design is presented as it is because it is often impossible to get pretest scores prior to the administration of a treatment condition. Consider the controversy over the influence of home computers and video games on children's cognitive skills. Some people believe there is a beneficial effect, whereas others think the effect is detrimental. If you want to test the influence of video games on the mathematical reasoning ability of eight-year-old children, you must identify two equivalent groups of eight-year-old children, one of which has been exposed to video games and one of which has not. Obviously, you could find many eight-year-olds who have been exposed to video games and have taken a mathematical reasoning test. It would be almost impossible, though, to find children of that age who were just beginning to experience video games. About the only recourse you have for finding a control group is to identify a cohort of individuals who were eight years old prior to the advent of video games and who also took a mathematical reasoning test. Note that individuals in this cohort may be twelve years old at the time of the study, but they were eight just before video games inundated the market.

The ability of the cohort design to assess the effect of a treatment condition is almost entirely dependent on the comparability of the cohorts. The comparability of cohorts will never be as great as that of groups formed through random assignment. Consequently, a selection bias always exists as a possible rival hypothesis, as does a history bias. In most cohort designs, the two cohorts are of different ages at the time of data collection, and therefore the life experiences they were subjected to span a different set of years. Since video games appeared on the market in about 1980, members of the experimental cohort in the video experiment would have been born in 1972 or later, whereas members of the control cohort would have to have a birth date earlier than 1972 in order to have reached the age of eight without having been exposed to video games. Since the two cohorts spanned different years, they may have experienced dissimilar events other than the presence or absence of video games that may have caused the difference in the dependent variable.

The cohort design, as it is presented here, is relatively weak with regard to eliminating the selection and history biases. However, there are times when such a design is the only one available for testing a treatment effect. When the cohort design must be used, one must consider the possible existence of rival hypotheses and collect data that would render them implausible.

Time-Series Design

There are research areas in which it is very difficult to find an equivalent group of subjects to serve as a control group. Psychotherapy and education are two such research areas.

Is the one-group before-after design (discussed in Chapter 7) the only available design one can use in such cases? Is there no means of eliminating some of the rival hypotheses that exist in this design? Fortunately, there is a means for eliminating *some* of these hypotheses, but to do so one must think of mechanisms other than the use of a control group. "Control is achieved by a network of complementary control strategies, not solely by control-group designs" (Gottman, McFall, and Barnett, 1969, p. 299). These complementary strategies are illustrated in the following section.

Interrupted Time-Series Design

The **interrupted time-series design** requires the investigator to take a series of measurements both before and after the introduction of some treatment condition, as depicted in Figure 8.13. The result of the treatment condition is indicated by a discontinuity in the recorded series of response measurements. Consider the study conducted by Lawler and Hackman (1969) in which they tried to identify the benefit derived from employee participation in the development and im-

Interrupted time-series design
A quasi-experimental design in which a treatment effect is assessed by comparing the pattern of pre- and posttest scores on one group of subjects

PRERESPONSE MEASURES					TREATMENT	POSTRESPONSE MEASURES				
Y_1	Y_2	Y_3	Y_4	Y_5	X	Y_6	Y_7	Y_8	Y_9	Y_{10}

Figure 8.13 *Interrupted time-series design.*
(Adapted from Campbell, D. T., and Stanley, J. C. *Experimental and quasi-experimental designs for research.* Chicago: Rand McNally and Co., 1963. Copyright 1963, American Educational Research Association, Washington, D.C.)

plementation of an employee incentive plan. Prior research had investigated a variety of payment plans and found that a given plan (e.g., a bonus plan) may be successful in one instance and not in another, indicating that the success of pay incentive plans is a function of factors other than just the plan itself. Lawler and Hackman hypothesized that a particular pay incentive plan would be more effective if the employees participated in its development as opposed to having a plan dictated by management. To assess the validity of this theory, Lawler and Hackman had three work groups meet and develop a bonus incentive plan for reducing absenteeism. Absenteeism rates for these work groups were measured prior to and after the incentive plan was developed. These rates were then converted to a percentage of the number of scheduled hours that the employees actually worked. The average for all subjects of the percentage of scheduled hours actually worked appears in Figure 8.14. From this figure, you can see that there was a rise in this average percentage and that this rise persisted over the 16 weeks during which data were collected. All of this is a visual interpretation, however. Now it is necessary to ask two questions. First, did a significant change occur following the introduction of the treatment condition? Second, can the observed change be attributed to the treatment condition?

The answer to the first question naturally involves tests of significance, since, as Gottman, McFall, and Barnett (1969, p. 301) have stated, "The data resulting from the best of experimental designs is of little value unless subsequent analyses permit the investigator to test the extent to which obtained differences exceed chance fluctuations." However, before presenting the specific tests of significance, I want to follow the orientation set forth by Campbell and Stanley (1963) and Caporaso (1974) and discuss the possible outcome patterns for time series that would reflect a significant change resulting from an experimental alteration. Let us first take a look at the data that would have been obtained from Lawler and Hackman's 1969 study and a study conducted by Vernon, Bedford, and Wyatt (1924) if they had used only a one-group before-after design. The Vernon et al. study was concerned with investigating the influence of introducing a rest period on the productivity of various kinds of factory workers. These data are presented in Figure 8.15. Note that in *both* studies beautiful data seem to

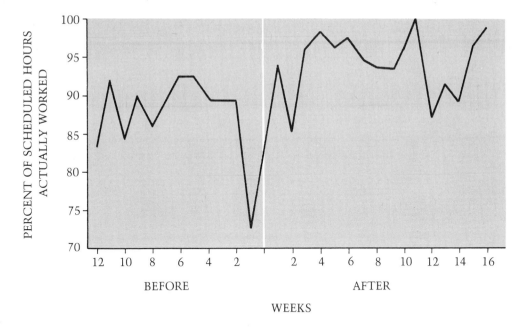

Figure 8.14 *Mean attendance of the participative groups for the 12 weeks before the incentive plan and the 16 weeks after the plan. (Attendance is expressed in terms of the percentage of hours scheduled to be worked that were actually worked.)* (From Lawler, E. E., and Hackman, J. R. (1969). Impact of employee participation in the development of pay incentive plans: A field experiment. *Journal of Applied Psychology, 53,* 467–471. Copyright 1969 by the American Psychological Association. Reprinted by permission of the publisher.)

support the hypothesis that the experimental treatment condition produced a beneficial effect. However, remember that the one-group before-after design does not include a comparison group, so the increase in performance could have been due to many variables other than the experimental treatment condition.

One means of eliminating some of the sources of rival hypotheses is to take a number of pre- and postmeasurements or to conduct an interrupted time-series analysis. When this kind of study is undertaken, we find the data depicted in Figure 8.14 for Lawler and Hackman's study and the data depicted in Figure 8.16 for the Vernon et al. study. The data suggest that the treatment condition investigated by Lawler and Hackman was influential but that the treatment condition investigated by Vernon et al. was not. The pattern of responses obtained by Vernon et al. seems to represent a chance fluctuation rather than a real change in performance. Visual inspection of a pattern of behavior can be very helpful in determining whether or not an experimental treatment had a real effect. Caporaso (1974) has presented a number of

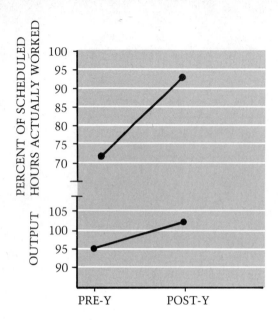

Figure 8.15   *A one-group before-after representation of a portion of the Vernon et al. data.*

additional possible patterns of behavior, shown in Figure 8.17, that could be obtained from time-series data. Note that the first three patterns reveal no treatment effect but merely represent a continuation of a previously established pattern of behavior. Lines D, E, F, and G represent *true* changes (I am assuming that they would be statistically significant) in behavior, although line D represents only a temporary shift.

Now let us return to our original question of whether or not a significant change in behavior followed the introduction of the treatment condition. Such a determination involves tests of significance. The most widely used and, I believe, the most appropriate statistical test is the Bayesian moving average model (Glass, Willson, and Gottman, 1975; Glass, Tiao, and Maguire, 1971; Box and Jenkins, 1970; Box and Tiao, 1965). Basically, this method consists of determining whether the pattern of postresponse measures differs from the pattern of preresponse measures. To make such an assessment using the moving average model does require many data points. Glass, Willson, and Gottman (1975) recommend that at least 50 data points be obtained. If enough data points cannot be collected to achieve the desired level of sensitivity, Cook and Campbell (1975) advocate that one still use the time-series design. The data can be plotted on a graph and visually inspected to determine whether a discontinuity exists between the pre- and postresponse measures. Naturally, this approach should be used only when one cannot use an appropriate statistical test, and one should remember that the number of preresponse data points obtained

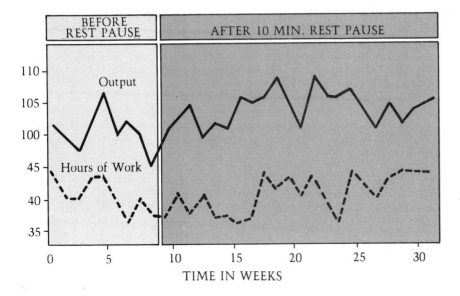

Figure 8.16 *Effect of a 10-minute rest pause on worker productivity.*
(Reprinted from Vernon et al., 1924.)

has to be large enough to identify all the plausible patterns that may exist.

Lawler and Hackman's analysis of their data revealed a significant difference between the patterns of pre- and postresponse measures. This led them to conclude that a nonrandom change occurred following the introduction of the incentive plan. This brings us to the second question—whether or not this significant change can be attributed to the employees' participation in the incentive plan. The primary source of weakness in the interrupted time-series design is its failure to control for the effects of history. Considering Lawler and Hackman's study, assume that at about the same time the treatment condition was introduced, some extraneous event occurred which could also have led to an increase in the number of hours worked. Such an extraneous event serves as a rival hypothesis for the significant nonrandom change. The investigator must consider all the other events taking place at about the same time as the experimental event and determine whether or not they might be rival hypotheses. Actually, Lawler and Hackman included several other control groups in their study to rule out such effects.

The two other potential but unlikely sources of rival hypotheses that could be found in the interrupted time-series design are maturation and instrumentation. The interested reader is referred to Campbell and Stanley (1963, p. 41) for a discussion of the unique situations in which

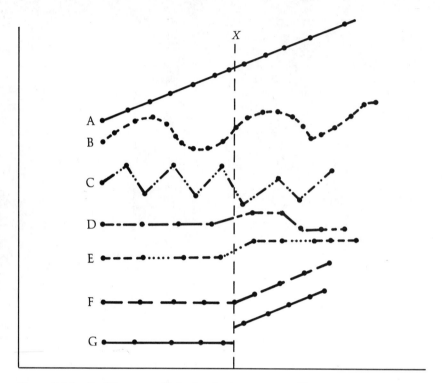

Figure 8.17   *Possible pattern of behavior of a time-series variable.*
(From Caporaso, J. A. Quasi-experimental approaches to social science. In
Quasi-experimental approaches, edited by J. A. Caporaso and L. L. Ross, Jr.
Evanston, Ill.: Northwestern University Press, 1973.)

these biases may crop up. Glass, Willson, and Gottman (1975) also
present a discussion of sources of invalidity in the time-series experiment.

Multiple Time-Series Design

The **multiple time-series design** is basically an extension of the interrupted time-series design. However, it has the advantage of eliminating
the history effect by including an equivalent—or least comparable—
group of subjects that does not receive the treatment condition. As
Figure 8.18 shows, in this design one experimental group receives the
treatment condition and an equivalent or comparable control group
does not. Consequently, the design offers a greater degree of control
over sources of rival hypotheses. The history effects, for example, are
controlled because they would influence the experimental and control
groups equally.

Multiple time-series design
A time-series design in which a
control and an experimental
group are included to rule out a
history rival hypothesis

| | PRERESPONSE | | | | TREATMENT | POSTRESPONSE | | | |
	MEASURE					MEASURE			
EXPERIMENTAL GROUP	Y_1	Y_2	Y_3	Y_4	X	Y_5	Y_6	Y_7	Y_8
CONTROL GROUP	Y_1	Y_2	Y_3	Y_4		Y_5	Y_6	Y_7	Y_8

Figure 8.18 *Multiple time-series design.*
(Adapted from Campbell, D. T., and Stanley, J. C. *Experimental and quasi-experimental designs for research.* Chicago: Rand McNally and Co., 1963. Copyright 1963, American Educational Research Association, Washington, D.C.)

Consider the study conducted by Campbell and Ross (1968) in which they attempted to assess the impact of Connecticut Governor Ribicoff's crackdown on speeding violators in 1955. In one portion of this study, a multiple time-series design was used. The state of Connecticut was naturally used for the experimental group; a number of adjacent states were used for the control group. The number of traffic fatalities was plotted for the years 1951 through 1959, as shown in Figure 8.19. If you look just at the line representing the Connecticut fatality rate, particularly following the year of the crackdown, it seems as though there was a definite decline. If only these data were presented, the design would be of the interrupted time-series type. Remember, however, that history effects may serve as rival hypotheses in such designs. As Campbell and Ross point out, the immediate decline occurring in 1956 could be the result of such effects as less severe winter driving conditions or more safety features on automobiles. These effects may even persist for several years, creating the progressive downward trend indicated.

In order to state conclusively that the downward trend was caused by the crackdown on speeding violators and to eliminate the rival hypothesis of history, it was necessary to use a multiple time-series design that included a comparable control group. As Figure 8.19 illustrates, a comparison group was incorporated into the study. Campbell and Ross used as their comparison group a pool of adjacent states (New York, New Jersey, Rhode Island, and Massachusetts). This group experienced no progressive decline paralleling the one depicted by the Connecticut data. Graphically, it seems as though the crackdown had a slight effect.

However, it is still necessary to statistically analyze the data to determine if this slight decline is significant. Again, the most appropriate approach seems to involve using the moving-average model discussed by Gottman, McFall, and Barnett (1969) and presented in considerable detail in Glass, Willson, and Gottman (1975).

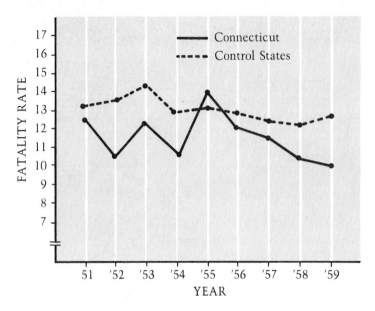

Figure 8.19 *Connecticut and control states' traffic fatalities for the years 1951–1959.*
(From Campbell, D. T., and Ross, H. L. The Connecticut crackdown on speeding: Time series data in quasi-experimental analysis. *The Law and Society Review*, 1968, 3, p. 44. Reprinted by permission from Law and Society Association. *The Law and Society Review* is the official publication of the Law and Society Association.)

Summary

This chapter has deviated considerably from the orientation taken in the previous chapters by presenting a number of quasi-experimental designs, which represent approximations of true experimental designs in the sense that they use the experimental mode of analysis in investigating areas that do not allow for complete control of extraneous variables. Quasi-experimental designs are the best type of design available for use in some field studies in which one wants to make causal inferences. Of the five different quasi-experimental designs presented, two are before-after designs, one is a cohort design, and two are time-series designs.

Of the two before-after types of designs, the nonequivalent control group design is the one most frequently used. It is exactly like the before-after true experimental design except that subjects are not randomly assigned to the experimental and control groups, which means that one does not have the necessary assurance that the two groups of subjects are equated. One could attempt to equate subjects on the important variables using matching techniques. However, this still does not assure one that the subjects are totally equated, and it may produce a statistical regression effect. Nonetheless, the design is useful in that it may control for effects such as history and maturation.

The simulated before-after design can be used when the investigator has the ability to randomly select an experimental and a control group but cannot randomly assign the experimental treatment to one of these groups. In such a case, one group serves as a control group and is tested prior to the administration of the treatment condition and the other group represents the experimental group, which is tested after the administration of the treatment condition. This design controls for the effects of statistical regression and selection bias but does not control for such effects as the history effect. The history effect can, however, be overcome if it is possible to include a comparable group of subjects to form a separate-sample simulated before-after design.

The cohort design can be used in situations characterized by regular turnover (e.g., with educational settings, training programs, and children within a family). In such instances it is sometimes possible to obtain the pretest scores on one cohort, perhaps through the use of archival records. These pretest scores can then be compared with the posttest scores of another cohort that has received some treatment condition. This design allows one to draw causal inferences because the cohorts compared can usually be assumed to differ only in minor ways. However, the cohort design is not without its rival hypotheses; one always has to remember that a selection and/or a history bias can exist. Consequently, use of this design requires that one obtain evidence that would rule out such rival hypotheses.

With the exception of the multiple time-series design, the various time-series designs attempt to eliminate rival hypotheses without the use of a control group. In the interrupted time-series design, a series of measurements is taken on the dependent variable both before and after the introduction of some experimental treatment condition. The effect of that condition is then determined by examining the magnitude of the discontinuity produced by the condition in the series of recorded responses. The primary source of error in this design is the possible history effect. If an equivalent or comparable group of subjects who have not received the experimental treatment condition can be found, the potential history effect can be eliminated by using a multiple time-series design.

Single-Subject
Research Designs

Chapter Overview

Given the material presented in the prior chapters, you may be surprised to discover that there are designs that enable you to conduct research on a single subject. Two of the basic requirements of a true experiment—random assignment and inclusion of a control group—cannot be incorporated, but it is possible to conduct research using only one subject in a manner that rules out most rival hypotheses. In the previous chapters, we have directed our thinking toward the use of control techniques and control groups for ruling out alternative hypotheses. In single-subject designs, we must reorient our thinking; we must ask ourselves how we can use the response of only one subject as a means of ruling out the influence of rival hypotheses. This chapter presents designs that enable us to use only one subject to test the influence of a specific treatment condition. As you read through it, you should answer the following questions:

1. What are the basic single-subject designs, and what is the strategy underlying them?

2. In what situations would each of the designs be used?

3. What methodological issues must be considered in using single-subject designs?

Introduction

Single-subject research designs are designs that use only one subject to investigate the influence of some experimental treatment condition. Encountering these designs for the first time, most people tend to equate them with case studies. This is incorrect; single-subject designs experimentally investigate a treatment effect, whereas case studies provide an in-depth description of an individual. Dukes (1965) found that only 30 percent of all single-subject studies are case studies; the great majority are of the experimental variety. A brief look at the history of experimental psychology reveals that psychological research actually began with the intensive study of a single organism. Wundt's use of the

Single-subject research designs Research designs in which a single subject is used to investigate the influence of a treatment condition

method of introspection required a highly trained single subject. Ebbing-haus (1885) conducted his landmark studies on memory using only one subject—himself. Pavlov's (1928) basic findings were the result of experimentation with a single organism (a dog) but were replicated on other organisms. As you can see, single-subject research was alive and well during the early history of psychology. In 1935, however, Sir Ronald Fisher published a book on experimental design that altered the course of psychological research. In it, Fisher laid the foundation for conducting and analyzing multisubject experiments. Psychologists quickly realized that the designs and statistical procedures elaborated by Fisher were very useful and began to adopt them. With the publication of Fisher's (1935) work, psychologists turned from single-subject studies toward multisubject designs. The one notable exception to this tradition was B. F. Skinner (1953), his students, and his colleagues. They developed a general approach that has been labeled the "experimental analysis of behavior." This method is devoted to experimentation with a single subject (or with only a few subjects) on the premise that the detailed examination of a single organism under rigidly controlled conditions will yield valid conclusions regarding a given experimental treatment condition. Use of this approach led to the development of a variety of single-subject experimental designs, which form the basis of the single-subject research designs.

The single-subject research designs developed by Skinner (1953) and his colleagues and explicated by Sidman (1960) probably would not have experienced the level of acceptability that they currently enjoy without the growth in popularity of behavior therapy (Hersen and Barlow, 1976). In psychotherapy, the case study has been the primary method of investigation (Bolger, 1965). During the 1940s and 1950s (Hersen and Barlow, 1976), researchers grounded in experimental methodology attacked the case study method on methodological grounds. This led some investigators to focus on the percentage of clients that were successfully treated by a given psychotherapy. However, Eysenck (1952) demonstrated the inadequacy of this method by showing that the percentage of success achieved by psychotherapy was no greater than that achieved by a spontaneous remission of symptoms. This disturbing evidence led researchers to focus even more on the multisubject design, and then they found many difficulties in applying this approach (Bergin and Strupp, 1972). More significantly, they found "that these studies did not prove that psychotherapy worked" (Hersen and Barlow, 1976, p. 12). Such evidence left researchers very perplexed, and some wondered if psychotherapy could be evaluated (e.g., Hyman and Berger, 1966). Other researchers lapsed into naturalistic studies of the therapeutic process, and still others engaged in process research, which emphasizes what goes on during therapy and deemphasizes the outcome of therapy. These efforts did little to advance knowledge of psychotherapy. By the 1960s, there was tremendous dissatisfaction with clinical practice and research, prompting the search for other alternatives. Bergin (1966) thought that the multisubject designs were ineffective in demonstrating the effectiveness of therapy because results were averaged. In the studies he reviewed, he noted that some clients improved and some got worse, but when results of these two types of clients were averaged the effects canceled each other out, indicating that therapy had no effect. Given such evidence, and the fact that process research was not beneficial in increasing effectiveness of therapy, some researchers (Bergin and Strupp, 1970) began to advocate turning back to the use of an experimental case study, which employs an experimental analogue. Research was making a change back to single-subject research. However, during the 1960s, an appropriate methodology for experimentally investigating the single subject was not apparent. It took the growing popularity of behavior therapy to provide a vehicle for the use of the appropriate methodology. Since behavior therapy involved the application of many of the principles of learning that had been identified in the laboratory, it was but a small step for these applied researchers to also borrow the procedures used to identify these principles. This methodology, successfully used in applied settings, has become accepted for use in identifying the influence of antecedents on individual behavior.

Single-Subject Designs

When one is planning an experimental study that uses only one subject, it is necessary to use some form of a time-series design. Recall that the time-series design requires that repeated measurements be taken on the dependent variable both *before* and *after* the treatment condition is introduced. This is necessary to enable detection of any effect produced by the treatment condition, because it is not possible to include a control group of subjects. Now consider a single-subject study. There is only one subject, and we want to know whether a given treatment condition has an effect on the subject's behavior. We could administer the treatment condition and measure the subject's response on the dependent variable, but then we would have no basis for determining if the treatment condition produced an effect, because a set of no-treatment responses does not exist. Without such a comparison, it is impossible to infer any effect of the treatment condition.

What can we use as a basis of comparison in a single-subject design? Since only one subject exists in the study, the comparison responses have to be the subject's own pretreatment responses. In other words, the investigator has to record the subject's responses prior to and after administering the independent variable. If we take only one pre- and one postresponse measure, we will have a one-group before-after design, which has many disadvantages. To overcome some of those problems (e.g., maturation), we must obtain multiple pre- and postresponse measures. Now we have a time-series design using one subject, which represents descriptive experimentation because it furnishes a continuous record of the organism's responses during the course of the experiment. It is also experimental because it permits us to interject a planned intervention—a treatment condition—into the program. Consequently, it allows us to evaluate the effect of an independent variable.

Although the basic time-series design can be used in single-subject research, we must remember that it is only a quasi-experimental design. Taking repeated pre- and postintervention measures of the dependent variable does allow us to rule out many potential biasing effects, but it does *not* rule out the possibility of a history effect. Risley and Wolf (1972) have pointed out that the ability to detect a treatment effect with the time-series design hinges on the ability to predict the behavior of the subject if the treatment condition had not been administered. When using the time-series design, we collect both pre- and postintervention measures of the dependent variable. In determining whether or not the treatment or intervention had any effect on behavior, we compare the pre– and post–dependent variable measures to see if there is a change in the level or the slope of the responses. However, in this assessment, the underlying assumption is that the pattern of preresponse measures would have continued if the treatment intervention had not been applied. In other words, the pretreatment responses are used to forecast what the posttreatment responses would have been in the absence of the treatment. If this forecast is inaccurate, then we cannot adequately assess the effects of the treatment intervention, because the pretreatment responses do not serve as a legitimate basis for comparison. The basic time-series design, then, is truly limited in unambiguously identifying the influence of an experimental treatment effect.

A-B-A Design

In order to improve on the basic time-series design in an attempt to generate unambiguous evidence of the causal effect of a treatment condition, a third phase has been added. This third phase, a withdrawal of the experimental treatment conditions, makes the design an

A   B   A   **Figure 9.1**   *A-B-A design.*

Baseline   Treatment   Baseline
Measure   Condition   Measure

A-B-A design. The A-B-A design, depicted in Figure 9.1, represents the most basic of the single-subject research plans. As the name suggests, it has three separate conditions. The A condition is the baseline condition, which is the target behavior as recorded in its freely occurring state. In other words, **baseline** refers to a given behavior as observed prior to presentation of any treatment designed to alter this behavior. The baseline behavior thus gives the researcher a frame of reference for assessing the influence of a treatment condition on this behavior. The B condition is the experimental condition, wherein some treatment is deliberately imposed to try to alter the behavior recorded during baseline. Generally, the treatment condition is continued for an interval equivalent to the original baseline period, or until some substantial and stable change occurs in the behaviors being observed (Leitenberg, 1973).

After the treatment condition has been introduced and the desired behavior generated, the A condition is then reintroduced. There is a return to the baseline conditions—the treatment conditions are withdrawn and whatever conditions existed during baseline are reinstated. This second A condition is reinstituted in order to determine if behavior will revert back to its pretreatment level. It is generally assumed that the effects of the treatment are reversible, but this is not always the case. Reversal of the behavior back to its pretreatment level is considered to be a very crucial element for demonstrating that the experimental treatment condition, and not some other extraneous variable, produced the behavioral change observed during the B phase of the experiment. If the plan had included only two phases (A and B), as in the typical time-series design, rival hypotheses would have existed. However, if the behavior reverts back to the original baseline level when the treatment conditions are withdrawn, rival hypotheses become less plausible.

Consider the study conducted by Walker and Buckley (1968). These researchers investigated the effect of using positive reinforcement to condition attending behavior in a nine-year-old boy named Phillip. A bright, underachieving male, Phillip was referred to the investigator because he exhibited deviant behavior that interfered with classroom performance. Specifically, Phillip demonstrated extreme distractability, which often kept him from completing academic assignments. The investigators first took a baseline measure of the percentage

A-B-A design
A single-subject design in which the response to the treatment condition is compared to baseline responses recorded before and after

Baseline
The target behavior of the subject in its naturally occurring state or prior to presentation of the treatment condition

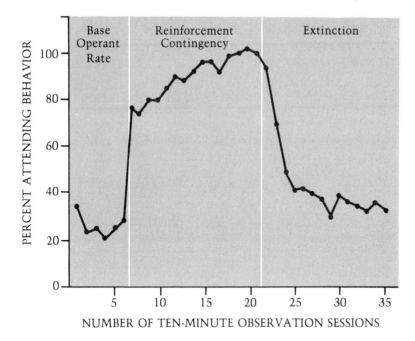

Figure 9.2 *Percentage of attending behavior in successive time samples during the individual conditioning program.*
(From Walker, H. M., and Buckley, N. K. The use of positive reinforcement in conditioning attending behavior. *Journal of Applied Behavior Analysis,* 1968, *1,* p. 136. Copyright 1968 by the Society for the Experimental Analysis of Behavior, Inc.)

of time that Phillip spent on his academic assignment. After the percentage of attending time had stabilized, the treatment condition was introduced, which consisted of enabling Phillip to earn points if no distraction occurred during a given time interval. These points could then be exchanged for a model of his choice. When Phillip had completed three successive ten-minute distraction-free sessions, the reinforcement of being able to earn points was withdrawn. Figure 9.2 depicts the results of this experiment. During the first baseline (A) condition, attending behavior was very low. When the treatment contingency (B) of being able to earn points was associated with attending behavior, percentage of attending behavior increased dramatically. When the contingency was withdrawn and baseline conditions were reinstated (A), attending behavior dropped to its pretreatment level.

In this case, the A-B-A design seems to provide a rather dramatic illustration of the influence of the experimental treatment conditions. However, there are several problems with this design (Hersen and Barlow, 1976). The first of these is that the design ends with the

A	B	A	B
Baseline Measure	Treatment Condition	Baseline Measure	Treatment Condition

Figure 9.3   *A-B-A-B design.*

baseline condition. From the standpoint of a therapist or other individual who desires to have some behavior changed, this is unacceptable because the benefits of the treatment condition are denied. Fortunately, this limitation is easily handled by adding a fourth phase to the A-B-A design in which the treatment condition is reintroduced. We now have an A-B-A-B design, as illustrated in Figure 9.3. The subject thus leaves the experiment with the full benefit of the treatment condition.

Quattrochi-Tubin and Jason (1980) provide a good illustration of the A-B-A-B design. Their study actually used the responses from a single *group* of subjects rather than from a single subject. This design is flexible; it can be used with a single group or with a single subject. Quattrochi-Tubin and Jason investigated a means for getting residents of a nursing home to increase attendance and social interaction in the lounge area instead of remaining in their rooms or passively watching television. (Such increased activity is considered important to the mental and physical well-being of the elderly.) The experiment was divided into four phases, with each phase consisting of four days. The first four days were the baseline phase, during which the experimenters merely recorded, on two different occasions, the number of residents present in the lounge, the number of those present watching television, and the number of those present engaged in social interaction. The second phase was the treatment phase, during which an announcement was made on the public-address system that coffee and cookies were available in the lounge. After four treatment days, the third phase (the baseline conditions) was instituted, which meant that the refreshments were no longer offered. In the fourth phase, refreshments (the treatment condition) were again served. Figure 9.4 depicts the number of elderly residents present in the lounge as well as those engaged in social interaction or watching television during each of the four phases of the experiment. Apparently, attendance and social interaction increased and television watching decreased when refreshments were offered, suggesting that a simple act of incorporating coffee and cookies in a nursing home routine can alter the behavior of its residents.

A second problem of the A-B-A design is not so easily handled. As I have previously stated, one of the basic requirements of the A-B-A design is that a reversal to baseline conditions exist when the experi-

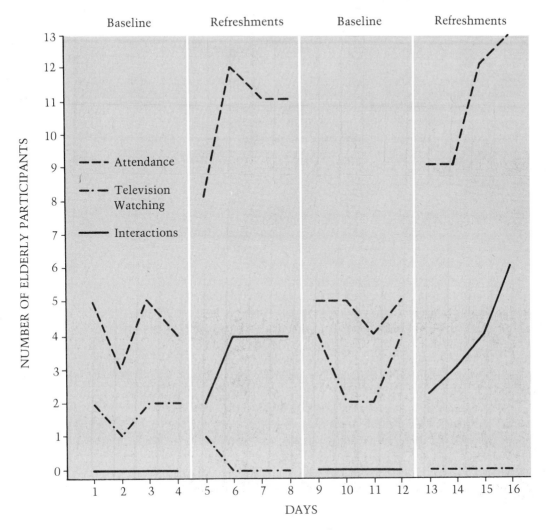

Figure 9.4 *Attendance, television watching, and social interactions during baseline and refreshment phases in the lounge.*
(From Quattrochi-Tubin, S., and Jason, L. A. Enhancing social interactions and activity among the elderly through stimulus control. *Journal of Applied Behavior Analysis*, 1980, *13*, 159–163. Copyright © 1980 by the Society for the Experimental Analysis of Behavior, Inc.)

mental treatment condition is withdrawn. This requirement is neces-sary in order to rule out rival hypotheses such as history, since, if the behavior did not revert to baseline, we would have an A-B, or time-series, design. Quattrochi-Tubin and Jason needed to demonstrate that the attendance, television watching, and social interactions returned to baseline levels once the refreshments were taken away in order to show that the behavior was modified by the experimental treatment. As Gelfand and Hartmann (1968, p. 211) have stated:

> After substantial and apparently reliable behavior modification has taken place, the . . . contingencies should be altered temporarily, for example, reversed, so the problem behavior is once again . . . instated. . . . Correlated changes in the observed response rate provide a convincing demonstration that the target behavior is unmistakably under the therapist's control and not due to adventitious, extratherapeutic factors.

In other words, the reversal is necessary to rule out rival hypotheses such as history.

The problem with the A-B-A design is that a reversal to baseline does not occur with all behavior. Hewett, Taylor, and Artuso (1969) found that removal of a token program increased the target behaviors rather than returning them to baseline. Without the presence of this reversal, the experimenter cannot be sure that the change in behavior following introduction of the treatment condition was not caused by some other extratreatment factor. Failure to reverse may be due to a carry-over effect across phases, whereby the treatment condition was maintained so long that a relatively permanent change in behavior took place. In fact, Bijou et al. (1969) have recommended that short experimental periods be used to facilitate obtaining a reversal effect. This is in line with Leitenberg's (1973, p. 98) statement that "single-case experimental designs are most pertinent to the discovery of short-term effects of therapeutic procedure while they are being carried out." Once the influence of the experimental treatment has been demonstrated, attention can then be placed on its persistence.

While the argument for shortening the experimental treatment to facilitate reversal (thereby demonstrating cause of the change in behavior) is valid, it applies only to behaviors that will in fact reverse. When the investigator is interested in nontransient effects, none of these arguments is valid because a relatively permanent change is instated.

A last issue concerns a distinction between a reversal and a withdrawal A-B-A design. In discussing the A-B-A design, I have described **withdrawal,** in which the treatment condition is removed during the third (second A) phase of the design. Leitenberg (1973) states that the A-B-A withdrawal design should be distinguished from an A-B-A **reversal design.** The distinction occurs in the third phase (second A) of the A-B-A design. In the withdrawal design, the treatment condition is withdrawn; in the reversal design, the treatment condition is applied to an alternative but incompatible behavior. For example, assume that you were interested in using reinforcement to increase the play behavior of a socially withdrawn 4½-year-old girl, as were Allen et al. (1964). If you followed the procedure used by these investigators, you would

Withdrawal
Removal of the treatment condition

Reversal design
A design in which the treatment condition is applied to an alternative but incompatible behavior so that a reversal in behavior is produced

record the percentage of time the girl spent interacting with both children and adults during the baseline phase. During treatment (the B phase), praise would be given whenever the girl interacted with other children, and isolated play and interaction with adults would be ignored. During the third phase of the experiment (the second A phase), the true reversal would take place. Instead of being withdrawn, the contingent praise would be shifted to interactions with adults so that any time the child interacted with adults she would be praised, and interactions with other children would be ignored. This phase was implemented to see if the social behavior would reverse to adults and away from children as the reinforcement contingencies shifted. Although the A-B-A reversal design can reveal rather dramatic results, it is more cumbersome and thus is used much less frequently than the more adaptable withdrawal design. Therefore, most of the single-subject A-B-A designs that you encounter will be of the withdrawal variety.

Interaction Design

A survey of the literature on single-subject designs shows that researchers have not been content to stick to the basic A-B-A design, but instead have extended this basic design in a variety of ways. The most intriguing and valuable extension is used to identify the interactive effect of two or more variables. In discussing multisubject designs, I described interaction as the situation that exists when the influence of one independent variable depends on the specific level of the second independent variable. This definition of interaction was presented because multisubject designs allow one to include several levels of variation for each independent variable being investigated. In a single-subject design, one does not have that degree of flexibility. One of the cardinal rules in single-subject research (Hersen and Barlow, 1976) is that only one variable can be changed from one phase of the research to another. For example, in the A-B-A-B design, one can introduce a specific type or level of reinforcement when changing from the baseline phase to the treatment phase of the experiment. However, only one level of reinforcement can be implemented. Therefore, when I discuss an **interaction effect in single-subject research,** I am referring to the combined influence of two or more specific levels of two or more different independent variables. For example, one could investigate the interaction effect of a concrete reinforcement (giving of tokens) and verbal reinforcement (the experimenter saying "good"). One could not practically investigate the interaction of different forms of material reinforcement (e.g., tokens, points, and candy) with different forms of

Interaction effect in single-subject research
The combined influence of two or more specific levels of two or more treatment conditions

| | SINGLE | | SINGLE | COMBINED | SINGLE | COMBINED |
	BASELINE	TREATMENT	BASELINE	TREATMENT	TREATMENT	TREATMENT	TREATMENT
Sequence 1	A	B	A	B	BC	B	BC
Sequence 2	A	C	A	C	BC	C	BC

Figure 9.5 *Single-subject interaction design.*

praise. Therefore, interaction typically refers to the combined influence of two specific variables.

In order to isolate the interactive effect of two variables from the effect that would be achieved by only one of these variables, it is necessary to analyze the influence of each variable separately and in combination. To complicate the issue further, one must do this by changing only one variable at a time. Thus the sequence in which you test for the influence of each variable separately and in combination must be such that the influence of the combination of variables (interaction effect) can be compared with that of each variable separately. Figure 9.5 illustrates this design. In sequence 1, the effect of treatment B is independently investigated, and then the combined influence of treatments B and C is compared to the influence of treatment B alone. In like manner, sequence 2 enables the investigation of the influence of treatment C independently, and then the combined influence of treatments B and C against treatment C. In this way, it is possible to determine if the combined influence of B and C was greater than that of B or C. If it was, then an interactive effect exists. However, if the combined effect was greater than that of one of the treatment variables (C) but not the other (B), then an interactive effect does not exist because the effect can more parsimoniously be attributed to treatment B.

One of the more adequate illustrations of a test of an interaction effect is found in the combined studies of Leitenberg et al. (1968) and Leitenberg (1973). In the first study, Leitenberg et al. used feedback and praise to overcome a severe knife phobia in a 59-year-old woman. The dependent variable measure was the amount of time the subject could spend looking at an exposed knife. Following the completion of a trial, the subject was given feedback and/or praise regarding the amount of time spent observing the knife. Praise consisted of verbally reinforcing the subject when she would look at the knife for a progressively longer period of time. The specific design of this study is depicted in Figure 9.6. Although it does not correspond exactly to an interaction design, it is close enough to demonstrate the essential components.

The results of this study appear in Figure 9.7. Feedback resulted in an increase in mean viewing time. This increase does not appear to have been altered by the introduction of praise, suggesting that praise

EXPERIMENTAL CONDITION

	B	BC	B	A	B	BC
Leitenberg et al. (1968)	Feedback	Feedback and praise	Feedback	Baseline	Feedback	Feedback and praise
Leitenberg (1973)	Praise	Feedback and praise	Praise	Baseline	Praise	

Figure 9.6 *Design of two studies used to test the interaction of feedback and praise.*

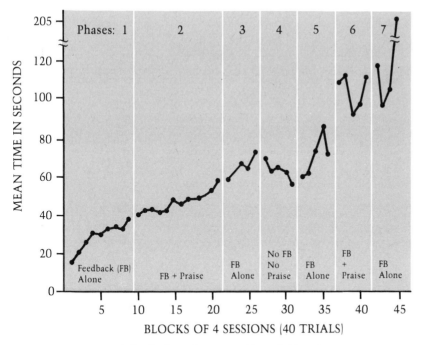

Figure 9.7 *Time in which a knife was kept exposed by a phobic patient as a function of feedback, feedback plus praise, and no feedback or praise conditions.* (From Leitenberg, H., Agras, W. S., Thompson, L. E., and Wright, D. E. Feedback in behavior modification: An experimental analysis in two phobic cases. *Journal of Applied Behavior Analysis*, 1968, *1*, p. 136. Copyright 1968 by the Society for the Experimental Analysis of Behavior, Inc.)

had no effect on the knife phobia. During the third phase of the experiment, when praise was withdrawn, the same increase persisted, lending even more support to the notion that praise was ineffective. Therefore, feedback seems to have been the controlling agent. The second half of the study, where feedback was presented independently and in combination with praise, provides additional support for the notion that feedback is the controlling agent.

Although the apparent conclusion of the Leitenberg et al. (1968) study is that feedback is the sole agent responsible for the reduction in the knife phobia, this is only one of two possible conclusions. As Hersen and Barlow (1976) have pointed out, an alternative interpretation is that praise had an effect but it was masked by the effect of feedback. Feedback may have been so powerful that it enabled the subject to progress at her optimal rate. If such were the case, then there would have been no room for praise to manifest itself, which would lead one to erroneously conclude that praise was ineffective when actually it did have some effect. This is one reason why both of the sequences depicted in Figure 9.5 have to be incorporated in order to isolate an interaction effect.

In accordance with this requirement, Leitenberg (1973) conducted another experiment on a second knife-phobic patient. In this study, praise was presented independently and then in combination with feedback, as illustrated in figure 9.6. Otherwise, the procedure of the study was identical to that of the Leitenberg et al. (1968) study. Figure 9.8 depicts the results of the second study. As you can see, the subject made no progress when only praise was administered. When feedback was combined with praise, progress was made. Interestingly, this progress was maintained even when feedback was subsequently discontinued in the third phase of the study. In the fifth and sixth phases of the study, again no progress was made unless feedback was combined with praise.

Taken together, these two studies reveal that feedback alone was the primary agent in helping the patient overcome the knife phobia, because praise alone had no appreciable effect and adding praise to feedback did not produce a marked increase in progress toward overcoming the phobia. These two studies also show the necessity of testing each variable (e.g., feedback and praise) separately and in combination in order to isolate any interactive effect. Herein lie what may be considered the disadvantages of testing for an interaction effect. First, at least two subjects are typically required since a different subject will have to be tested on each of the two sequences depicted in Figure 9.5. Second, the interaction effect can be demonstrated only under conditions in which each variable alone (e.g., feedback) does *not* produce maximum increment in performance on the part of the subject. As pointed out in the Leitenberg et al. study, it was possible that praise was

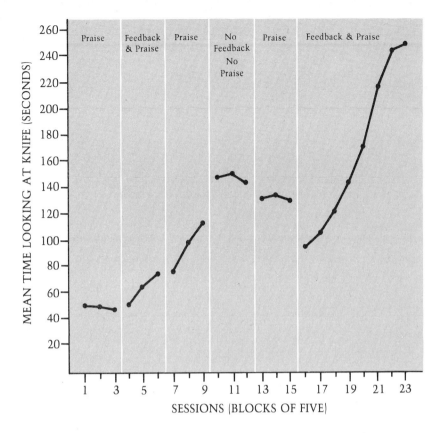

Figure 9.8 *Mean time looking at phobic stimulus as a function of praise and feedback plus praise condition: Subject 1.*
(From Leitenberg, H., Agras, W. S., Allen, R., Butz, R., and Edwards, J. Feedback and therapist praise during treatment of phobia. *Journal of Consulting and Clinical Psychology*, 1975, 43, p. 397. Copyright 1975 by the American Psychological Association. Reprinted by permission.)

effective in overcoming knife phobia, but the feedback variable was so potent that it enabled the subject to respond at the maximum level, thus precluding any possibility of demonstrating an interactive effect. In such cases, the proper conclusion would be that either of the two variables being tested was equally effective, and addition of the second variable was not beneficial. Note that a conclusion could not be drawn regarding the possible interactive effect of the two variables, since this effect could not be tested. In this case, the interaction design is quite effective in demonstrating the continued effects of two or more variables.

Multiple-Baseline Design

One of the primary limiting components of the A-B-A design is its failure to rule out a history effect in situations in which the behavior is such that it does not revert back to baseline level when the treatment condition is withdrawn. When one suspects that such a situation may exist, the multiple-baseline design is a logical alternative because it does not entail withdrawing a treatment condition. Therefore, its effectiveness does not hinge upon a reversal of behavior to baseline level.

In the **multiple-baseline design,** depicted in Figure 9.9, baseline data are collected on several different behaviors for the same individual, on the same behavior for several different individuals, or on the same behavior across several different situations for the same individual. After the baseline data have been collected, the experimental treatment is successively administered to each target behavior. If the behavior exposed to the experimental treatment changes while all others remain at baseline, evidence for the efficacy of the treatment condition is enhanced. This is because it becomes increasingly implausible that rival hypotheses would contemporaneously influence each target behavior at the same time as the treatment was administered.

Sulzer-Azaroff and Consuelo de Santamaria (1980) used the multiple-baseline design in a study that investigated the use of feedback and approval or corrective suggestions in reducing the frequency of occurrence of industrial hazards. Once again, a single group is used in the study as opposed to a single subject. The investigators recorded the frequency, type, and location of hazardous conditions found in each of the six departments in the industrial organization in which the study was conducted. This record of hazardous conditions was kept for a three-week baseline period for Departments 1 and 2, for a six-week period for Departments 4 and 5, and for a nine-week period for Departments 3 and 6. At the conclusion of each department's baseline period, the department supervisor was given feedback as to the number and locations of the hazards observed, and specific suggestions for improvement. This feedback was given twice a week during the treatment phase. The results of the study, as depicted in Figure 9.10, show that

Multiple-baseline design
A single-subject design in which the treatment condition is successively administered to several subjects or to the same subject in several situations after baseline behaviors have been recorded for different periods of time

		T$_1$	T$_2$	T$_3$	T$_4$	T$_5$
BEHAVIORS,	A	Baseline	Treatment			
PEOPLE, OR	B	Baseline	Baseline	Treatment		
SITUATIONS	C	Baseline	Baseline	Baseline	Treatment	
	D	Baseline	Baseline	Baseline	Baseline	Treatment

Figure 9.9 *Multiple-baseline design.*

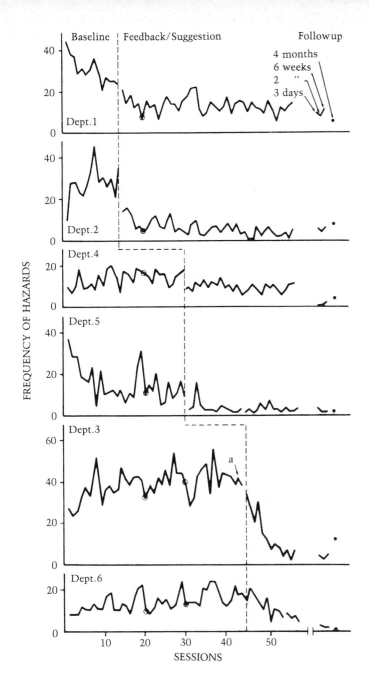

Figure 9.10 *Frequency of hazards across departments as a function of the introduction of the "feedback package." Data for days following unplanned safety meetings are indicated by an open circle. At point "a" there was a change in supervisors.*

(From Sulzer-Azaroff, B., and Consuelo de Santamaria, M. Industrial safety hazard reduction through performance feedback. *Journal of Applied Behavior Analysis,* 1980, *13,* 287–295. Copyright © 1980 by the Society for the Experimental Analysis of Behavior, Inc.)

the frequency of hazardous conditions declined in each department as soon as the feedback-and-suggestions (treatment) phase was initiated. Also note that the frequency of the hazardous conditions did not decline in Departments 4 and 5, even though the treatment condition had already been administered to Departments 1 and 2. Similar conditions existed for Departments 3 and 6. Consequently, a change in behavior did not occur until the treatment condition was administered, providing convincing evidence that the feedback and suggestions were the cause of the reduction in the frequency of occurrence of hazardous conditions.

Although the multiple-baseline design avoids the problem of reversibility, it has another basic difficulty. For this design to be effective in evaluating the efficacy of the treatment condition, the target behaviors must not be highly interrelated. This means that there must not be **interdependence of behaviors** being investigated such that a change in one behavior alters the other behaviors. Figure 9.10 indicates that this requirement was satisfied in the Sulzer-Azaroff and Consuelo de Santamaria study, since the reduction in hazardous conditions occurred only when the experimental treatment was administered. However, such independence is not always found. Kazdin (1973), for example, noted that the classroom behaviors of inappropriate motor behavior, inappropriate verbalizations, and inappropriate tasks are interrelated, and a change in one of these responses can result in a change in one of the other responses. In like manner, Broden et al. (1970), using a multiple-baseline design across individuals, found that contingent reinforcement changed not only the inattentive behavior of the target subject but also that of an adjacent peer.

Interdependence of behaviors
The influence that one behavior has on another

The problem of interdependence of behaviors is real and needs to be considered before the multiple-baseline design is selected, because interdependence will destroy much of the power of this design, resting as it does on its ability to demonstrate change whenever the treatment condition is administered to a given behavior. If administering the experimental treatment to one behavior results in a corresponding change in all other behaviors, then when the experimental treatment is administered to the remaining behaviors, it will have less impact and produce less change because the behavior has previously been altered. When such a case exists, it is not clear what caused the change in behavior. Which behaviors are interrelated is an empirical question. Sometimes data exist on this interdependence, but where none exists the investigator must collect his or her own.

Kazdin and Kopel (1975) provide several recommendations for cases in which independence cannot be achieved. The first is to select behaviors so that they are as independent as possible. Since it may be difficult to predict in advance which behaviors are independent, one should consider using different individuals or situations, as they will probably be more topographically distinct than different behaviors of the same individual.

In attempting to select independent behaviors, investigators often correlate the baseline behaviors. If a low correlation is obtained, they tend to infer that the behaviors are independent. While this could be an indication of independence, it may suggest a level of independence that does not exist. If the baseline behaviors are quite stable or do not change much, a low correlation could result from this limited fluctuation in behavior. Then one might conclude that the behaviors are independent when they really are not. Even if one does have good, valid evidence that baseline behaviors are independent, this does not provide any assurance that they will remain independent after implementation of the treatment condition. For example, implementing a time-out procedure on one child in a classroom for disruptive behavior could affect other children's behavior. Therefore, consideration of independence should take place during the treatment phase as well as during the baseline phase.

A second recommendation made by Kazdin and Kopel for decreasing ambiguity in the multiple-baseline design is to use several baselines to decrease the possibility of dependence across all baselines. Specifically, they recommend using four or more. Even though some baseline behaviors will be dependent, others will be independent. Those that are independent can demonstrate the treatment-effect relationship.

A third recommendation is to implement a reversal on one of the baseline behaviors. If the reversal leads to a generalized reversal effect (reversal on other behaviors), then one has added evidence for the effect of the treatment. One also has evidence for a generalized treatment effect.

Alternating-Treatments Design

The single-subject designs presented in this chapter have all been concerned with the identification of the effectiveness of a given treatment condition or with the interaction of two treatment conditions. There are times when one would like to compare the relative effectiveness of two or more treatment conditions—e.g., the relative effectiveness of drug therapy and psychotherapy in treating depression. Traditionally, such a comparison has been conducted within the framework of a multisubject design; subjects are randomly assigned to two groups, each group of subjects receives a different treatment condition, and then the effects of the conditions are compared using statistical tests. However, there are times when conditions (such as an insufficient number of

BASELINE PHASE			TREATMENT PHASE		
	Stimulus 1	Stimulus 2	Stimulus 1	Stimulus 2
Baseline	Treatment A	Treatment B	Treatment B	Treatment A

Figure 9.11   *Alternating-treatments design.*

subjects) preclude the use of a multisubject design. Then one must resort to a single-subject design, and the appropriate type is the alternating-treatments design.

In the **alternating-treatments design,** several treatment conditions are presented to the subject in alternating sequence following a baseline phase, as depicted in Figure 9.11. The alternation in the treatment conditions is accomplished by counterbalancing the treatment conditions across stimulus conditions (such as different therapists, time periods, settings, or some combination of these). Suppose you want to determine the effect of the extent to which therapist self-disclosure influences client self-disclosure. There are two treatment conditions: presence and absence of therapist self-disclosure. These must be administered across the various stimulus conditions of different therapy sessions. The procedure would be to alternate, in counterbalanced order, the sessions during which the therapist does and does not self-disclose.

Kazdin (1977) used an alternating-treatments design in a study that assessed the effectiveness of two different schedules of administering praise in treating the disruptive and inattentive behavior of an educably retarded child. The two praise-treatment schedules consisted of praising attentive behavior if it was preceded by 20 seconds of inattentive behavior and praising attentive behavior if it was preceded by 20 seconds of attentive behavior. Following an eight-day baseline period in which inattentive behavior was recorded, the two praise schedules were administered by two individuals at two different times. This counterbalancing of treatment conditions across reinforcing agents as well as time of day was designed to eliminate a possible sequencing effect. The results of this study, as illustrated in Figure 9.12, suggest that Schedule 2 (the administering of praise when the attentive behavior is preceded by attentive behavior) resulted in a consistently greater percent of attentive behavior. You can see from Figure 9.12 that Kazdin included a third phase, in which the most effective treatment condition (Schedule-2 praise) was administered across both time periods. This phase demonstrates that Schedule-2 praise was equally effective across both time periods.

The alternating-treatments design has several advantages over the other single-subject designs presented in this chapter: it does not re-

Alternating-treatments design
A single-subject design in which the sequences in which the conditions are presented are alternated in order to compare the relative effectiveness of two or more treatment conditions

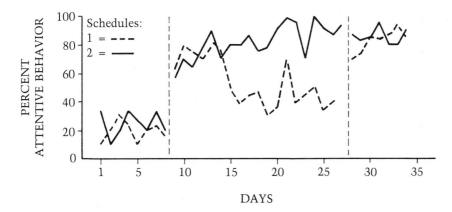

Figure 9.12   *Attentive behavior of Sid across experimental conditions. Baseline—no experimental intervention. Approval 1—implementation of Schedule 1 (approval delivered for attentive behavior preceded by inattentive behavior) and Schedule 2 (approval delivered for attentive behavior preceded by attentive behavior). These schedules were administered each day across different reinforcing agents and time periods. Approval 2—implementation of Schedule 2 across both agents and time periods.*
(From Kazdin, A. E. The influence of behavior preceding a reinforced response on behavior change in the classroom. *Journal of Applied Behavior Analysis*, 1977, *10*, 299–310. Copyright © 1977 by the Society for the Experimental Analysis of Behavior, Inc.)

quire a withdrawal of the treatment condition in order to assess treatment effectiveness, the comparison of treatment effectiveness is accomplished rapidly, and it is possible to proceed without collecting baseline data (Barlow and Hayes, 1979). Although a baseline phase appears in Figure 9.11, it is not a necessary component of the design. The crucial part is the differential response of the subject to the alternating treatments.

The primary disadvantage associated with the alternating-treatments design is that a multiple-treatment interference effect could exist. In other words, there is the possibility that the two treatment conditions will have an effect on each other or that a sequencing effect may exist in the data. Any sequencing effect is assumed to be controlled by the fact that the alternation of the treatment conditions is counterbalanced across the stimulus conditions. However, the extent to which counterbalancing controls the sequencing effects is not known, since carry-over sequencing effects could also exist and counterbalancing does not control such effects when they are nonlinear. Nonetheless, the design can be used to successfully isolate the most effective treatment condition and has the benefit of not requiring a withdrawal of treatment, which could result in a reversal of any therapeutic gain.

A second but less serious problem of the alternating-treatments design is that it is cumbersome to implement. This is because the stimulus conditions must be counterbalanced and the treatment conditions alternated. In spite of these difficulties, it is frequently the design of choice when the effectiveness of treatment conditions must be compared.

Changing-Criterion Design

The **changing-criterion design** is a relative newcomer to the area of single-subject designs. It was described by Sidman in 1960 (pp. 254–256) but not labeled until 1971 (Hall, 1971). More recently it has undergone rather extensive discussion (Hall and Fox, 1977; Hartmann and Hall, 1976). The changing-criterion design, depicted in Figure 9.13, requires an initial baseline measure on a single target behavior. Following this measure, a treatment condition is implemented and continued across a series of intervention phases. During the first intervention or treatment phase, an initial criterion of successful performance is established. If there is successful achievement of this performance level across several trials, or if a stable criterion level is achieved, the criterion level is increased. The experiment moves to the next successive phase, where a new and more difficult criterion level is established while the treatment condition is continued. When behavior reaches this new criterion level and is maintained across trials, the next phase, with its more difficult criterion level, is introduced. In this manner, each successive phase of the experiment requires a step-by-step increase in the criterion measure. "Experimental control is demonstrated through successive replication of change in the target behavior, which changes with each stepwise change in criterion" (Kratochwill, 1978, p. 66).

Hall and Fox (1977) provide a good illustration of the changing-

Changing-criterion design
A single-subject design in which a subject's behavior is gradually shaped by changing the criterion for success during successive treatment periods

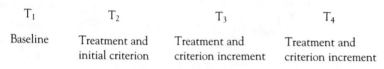

T_1	T_2	T_3	T_4
Baseline	Treatment and initial criterion	Treatment and criterion increment	Treatment and criterion increment

Figure 9.13   *Changing-criterion design. T_1–T_4 refer to four different phases of the experiment.*

DENNIS BASKETBALL CONTINGENT

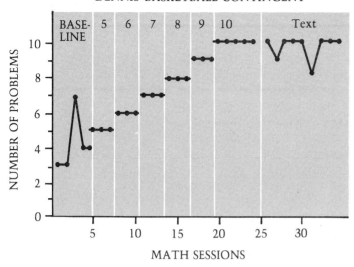

Figure 9.14 *Number of math problems solved in a changing-criterion design.*
(From Hall, R. V., and Fox, R. W. Changing-criterion designs: An alterna-
tive applied behavior analysis procedure. In *New Developments in Behavioral
Research: Theory, Method, and Application.* In honor of Sidney W. Bijou,
edited by C. C. Etzel, G. M. LeBlanc, and D. M. Baer, Hillsdale, N.J.:
Lawrence Erlbaum Associates, 1977.)

criterion design in a study of a child named Dennis who refused to
complete arithmetic problems. To overcome this resistant behavior,
the investigators first obtained a baseline measure of the average number of assigned arithmetic problems (4.25) that he would complete
during a 45-minute session. Then Dennis was told that a specified
number had to be completed correctly during the subsequent session. If
he correctly completed them, he could take recess and play with a
basketball; if he did not, he would have to miss recess and remain in the
room until they were correctly completed. During the first treatment
phase, the criterion number of problems to be solved was set at 5,
which was one more than the mean number completed during the
baseline phase. After successfully achieving the criterion performance
on three consecutive days, Dennis had to finish an additional problem.
The recess and basketball contingencies were maintained. The results
of this experiment, shown in Figure 9.14, reveal that Dennis's performance increased as the criterion level increased. When a change in
behavior parallels the criterion change so closely, it rather convincingly demonstrates the relative effects of the treatment contingency.

Hartmann and Hall (1976) indicate that successful utilization of the changing-criterion design requires attention to three factors: the length of the baseline and treatment phases, the magnitude of change in the criterion, and the number of treatment phases or changes in the criterion. With regard to the length of the treatment and baseline phases, Hartmann and Hall state that the treatment phases should be of different lengths, or, if they are of a constant length, then the baseline phases should be longer than the treatment phases. This is necessary to ensure that the step-by-step changes in the subject's behavior are caused by the experimental treatment and not by some history or maturational variable that occurs simultaneously with the criterion change. Additionally, the baseline data should be stable or changing in a direction opposite to that of the treatment condition so as to establish unambiguously that only the treatment condition produced the observed change. With regard to the actual length of each treatment, the rule of thumb is that each treatment phase must be long enough to allow the behavior to change to its new criterion level and then to stabilize. In other words, the new criterion level must be consistently achieved across trials. If the behavior continues to fluctuate between the new and the old criterion level, stability has not been achieved.

The second consideration is the magnitude of the criterion change. Naturally, it must be large enough so that a detectable change can occur. If the behavior is difficult to change, the criterion change should be small so that it can be achieved, but still large enough to be noticed. If the behavior varies wildly from trial to trial, then the criterion change must be rather large in order to allow the experimenter to detect any change.

Hartmann and Hall (1976) state that two criterion changes may be adequate. This issue is, however, directly dependent on the number of replications that are required to convincingly demonstrate that the behavioral change is the result of the treatment condition. For this reason, Kratochwill (1978) recommends at least four criterion changes. When the subject's behavior is quite variable, Hall and Fox (1977) suggest that one include a reversal in one of the treatment phases. This reversal could consist of reverting back to baseline or to a former criterion level. Such a reversal would provide additional evidence of the influence of the treatment condition.

The changing-criterion design has not been used extensively, and all of its applications and limitations have yet to be identified (Kratochwill, 1978). It seems to be a useful design in studies that require shaping of behavior over a period of time (Hall and Fox, 1977) or where problems in which step-by-step increases in accuracy, frequency, duration, or magnitude are the therapeutic goals (Hartmann and Hall, 1976), as may exist with learning to write or read.

Methodological Considerations in the Use of Single-Subject Designs

The foregoing discussion of single-subject research designs by no means represents an exhaustive survey, but presents the most basic and commonly used designs. Regardless of which design is used, there are several common issues which one must consider when attempting to conduct a single-subject study.

Baseline

Baseline has been defined as the target behaviors in their freely occurring state. Repeatedly, investigators (e.g., Gelfand and Hartmann, 1968) have emphasized the importance of the baseline data in single-subject research. A prime concern is obtaining a **stable baseline,** because the baseline data serve as the standard against which change induced by the experimental treatment condition is assessed. The essential question is "When has a stable baseline been achieved?" There is no final answer. As Sidman (1960, p. 258) states:

Stable baseline
A set of responses that are characterized by the absence of any trend and little variability

> There is, again, no rule to follow for the criterion will depend upon the phenomenon being investigated and upon the level of experimental control that can be maintained. . . . By following behavior over an extended period of time, with no change in the experimental conditions, it is possible to make an estimate of the degree of stability that can eventually be maintained; a criterion can then be selected on the basis of these observations.

The crucial question is "What criteria should be selected?" Kazdin (1978) suggests that a stable baseline is characterized by the absence of trend and only a slight degree of variability in the data. An absence of trend means that the baseline data should not demonstrate an increase or a decrease over time. However, what does a slight degree of variability mean? Kazdin does not clarify this issue, but Sidman (1960) believes that the overall mean response of baseline behavior should be stable within a 5 percent range.

Sometimes it is not possible to eliminate a baseline trend. If the trend occurring during the baseline phase is opposite from that which is expected during the intervention phase when the experimental treatment condition is administered, the experiment demonstrates that the treatment condition is powerful enough not only to produce an effect but also to reverse a previous trend. If the baseline change is in the same direction as is expected from the intervention, it is difficult to draw an unambiguous conclusion regarding the influence of the treatment condition. In such a case, it is best to wait for the baseline to stabilize before introducing the treatment condition. If this cannot be done, one can resort to an alternating-treatments design in which the two treatments are designed to change the trend in opposite directions.

One must also be concerned with excessive variability. Variability will, in most cases, be more of a problem with human subjects than with animals, because a greater degree of control can generally be exercised over the animals. McCullough et al. (1974), for example, found that the frequency with which irrelevant comments were made by high school students during a 50-minute class period ranged from 17 to 104 during an eight-day period. While this may be somewhat atypical, it does illustrate the extent to which baseline data can fluctuate with humans. When extreme fluctuations or unsystematic variations exist in the baseline data, one should check all components of the study and try to identify and control the sources producing the variability. Sometimes the fluctuation can be traced to sources that are important to the validity of the experiment, such as unreliability in scoring subject behavior. When the sources cannot be identified or controlled, one can artificially reduce the variability by averaging data points across consecutive days or sessions. This averaging substantially reduces variability and allows the effect of the treatment condition to be accurately assessed. However, it does distort the day-to-day pattern of performance.

There is one additional problem to be considered when one is obtaining baseline frequencies on humans—the potential reactive effect of the assessment on the behavior under study (Webb et al., 1966). The fact that one is taking baseline data may have an effect on the behavior. This was vividly demonstrated in the classic Hawthorne studies and has also been demonstrated by McFall (1970) and Gottman and McFall (1972), who showed that monitoring of one's own behavior can have a significant influence on that behavior. If one monitors frequency of smoking, one increases the number of cigarettes smoked, whereas if one monitors the frequency of not smoking, one smokes less.

Changing One Variable at a Time

One of the cardinal rules in single-subject research is that only one variable can be changed from one phase of the experiment to the next (Barlow and Hersen, 1973). Only when this rule is adhered to can the variable that produced a change in behavior be isolated. Assume that you want to test the effect of reinforcement on increasing the number of social responses emitted by a chronic schizophrenic. In an attempt to employ an A-B-A design, you first measure baseline performance by recording the number of social responses. Following baseline, you give the schizophrenic a token (which can be redeemed for cigarettes) and say "good" after each social response. At this point you are violating the rule of one variable, because two types of reinforcements are being administered. If the number of social responses increases, you will not know which type of reinforcement is responsible for changing the behavior. In fact, it may not be either reinforcer independently but the combined (interactive) influence that is the catalyst. To isolate the separate and combined influences of the two types of reinforcers an interaction design would be required.

Length of Phases

An issue that must be given consideration when a single-subject study is being designed is the length of each phase of the study. There are few guidelines to follow. Most experimenters advocate continuing each phase until some semblance of stability has been achieved. Johnson (1972) believes that in the study of punishment each phase should be continued until a lack of trend and a constant range of variability are realized. While this is the ideal, in many clinical studies it is not feasible. Additionally, following this suggestion leads to unequal phases, which Barlow and Hersen (1973) consider to be undesirable. According to these investigators, unequal phases (particularly when the treatment phase is extended in time to demonstrate a treatment effect) increase the possibility of a confounding influence of history or maturation. For example, if the baseline phase consisted of recording responses for 7 days and the treatment phase lasted 14 days, one would have to entertain the possibility of a history or maturation variable affecting the data if a behavioral change did not take place until about the seventh day of the treatment phase. Because of such potential confounding influences, Hersen and Barlow (1976) suggest using an equal number of data points for each phase of the study.

There are two other issues that relate directly to the length of phases: carry-over effects and cyclic variations (Hersen and Barlow, 1976). Carry-over effects in single-subject A-B-A-B designs usually appear in the second baseline phase of the study as a failure to reverse to original baseline level. When such effects do occur or are suspected, many single-subject researchers (e.g., Bijou et al., 1969) advocate the use of short treatment condition phases (B-phases). These effects become particularly problematic in a single-subject drug study.

Hersen and Barlow (1976) consider cyclic variations a neglected issue in the applied single-subject literature. It is of paramount concern when subjects are influenced by cyclic factors, such as the menstrual cycle in females. Where the data may be influenced by such cyclical factors, it is advisable to extend the measurement period during each phase to incorporate the cyclic variation in both the baseline and treatment phases of the study. If this is not possible, then one must replicate the results across subjects that are at different stages of the cyclic variation. If identical results are achieved across subjects regardless of the stage of the cyclic variation, then one can still derive meaningful conclusions from the data.

Criteria for Evaluating Change

The single-subject designs discussed in this chapter attempt to rule out the influence of extraneous variables by strategies such as replicating the intervention effect over time, which is quite different from the control techniques employed by multisubject experimental designs. Similarly, single-subject designs use different criteria for evaluating treatment effects than do multisubject designs. The two criteria that are usually used in single-subject research are an experimental criterion and a therapeutic criterion (Kazdin, 1978).

Experimental Criterion

The **experimental criterion** requires a comparison of pre- and postintervention behavior. In making this comparison, most experimenters using a single-subject design do not make use of statistical analyses, which is definitely a source of controversy, as illustrated in Exhibit 9.1. Instead of using statistical analysis, these researchers rely on replicating the treatment effect over time.

    When one can demonstrate that behavior repeatedly changes as the treatment conditions change, the experimental criterion has been fulfilled. In actual practice, the experimental criterion is considered to be met if the behavior of the subject during the intervention phase does not overlap with his or her behavior during the baseline phase or if the trend of the behavior during baseline and intervention phases differs.

Experimental criterion
In single-subject research, repeated demonstration that a behavioral change occurs when the treatment is introduced

Therapeutic Criterion

The **therapeutic criterion** refers to the clinical significance or value of the treatment effect for the subject. Does the treatment effect eliminate some disorder for the subject, or does it enhance the subject's everyday functioning? This criterion is much more difficult to demonstrate than is the experimental criterion. For example, a self-destructive child may demonstrate a 50 percent reduction in self-destructive acts following treatment but still engage in 50 instances of such behavior every hour. Even though the experimental criterion has been satisfied, the child is still far from reaching a normal degree of social interaction.

    In an attempt to resolve this problem, researchers have included a

Therapeutic criterion
Demonstration that the treatment condition has eliminated a disorder or has enhanced everyday functioning

Exhibit 9.1   *Analysis of Data Obtained from Single-Subject Designs*

In the past, when single-subject research designs were conducted predominantly by Skinner, his colleagues, and his students, statistical analysis of single-subject data was shunned. It was deemed to be unnecessary because the studies were conducted on infrahumans and sufficient experimental control of extraneous variables could be established to enable the experimental effect to be determined by visual inspection of the data.

As single-subject designs have become more popular, some people have insisted on the necessity of statistical analysis of the data. However, this point of view is by no means universal.

The arguments against the use of statistical analysis are as follows:

1. Statistical analysis of the data provides evidence of a treatment effect only by demonstrating if the effect is statistically significant. It offers no evidence regarding the treatment's clinical effectiveness. For example, even though a treatment condition that was applied to reduce irrational thought patterns in schizophrenic individuals produces a statistically significant decline in such thought patterns, the patient may not have improved enough to operate effectively outside of an institutional setting.

2. Statistical tests hide the performance of the individual subject because they lump subjects together and focus only on average scores. Consequently, a treatment condition that benefited only a few individuals might not achieve statistical significance and would therefore be considered ineffective when in fact it was beneficial for some individuals.

There are two basic arguments that support the use of statistical analysis:

1. Visual inspection of the data obtained from single-subject designs will not provide an accurate interpretation when a stable baseline cannot be established. When data are not statistically analyzed, investigators must use the trend and the variability of the data to reach a conclusion as to whether the treatment condition produced an effect. If the baseline data and the treatment data have different trends or different levels of performance, then a decision is typically made that the treatment condition produced an effect, particularly if there is a stable baseline. However, if there is a great deal of variability in the data, it is difficult to interpret the data without statistical analysis. Statistical analysis can analyze extremely variable data more objectively than can individuals.

2. Visual inspection of the data leads to unreliable interpretation of the treatment effects. For example, Gottman and Glass (1978) found that the 13 judges given data from a previously published study disagreed on whether the treatment effect was significant. Seven said a treatment effect existed, and six said one did not.

The proponents for and against statistical analysis each have valid points to make. However, doctrinaire positions that unequivocally advocate one strategy to the exclusion of the other would seem to do more harm than good. When a stable baseline and limited variability can be achieved, statistical analysis probably adds little to the interpretation of the data. When they cannot, statistical analysis should be used in addition to visual analysis.

procedure known as social validation in some experiments. **Social validation** of a treatment effect consists of determining if the treatment effect has produced an important change in the way the client can function in everyday life (e.g., after treatment, can a claustrophobic ride in an elevator?). This validation is accomplished by either a social comparison method or a subjective evaluation method.

The **social comparison method** involves comparing the behavior of the client before and after treatment with the behavior of his or her nondeviant peers. If the subject's behavior is no longer distinguishable from the nondeviant peers' behavior, then the therapeutic criterion has been satisfied. The **subjective evaluation method** involves assessing whether the treatment led to qualitative differences in how others view the subject. Individuals who normally interact with the subject and are in a position to assess the subject's behavior may be asked to provide a global evaluation of the client's functioning on an assessment instrument, such as a rating scale or a behavioral checklist. If this evaluation indicates that the client is functioning more effectively, then the therapeutic criterion is considered to have been satisfied. Each of these methods has its own limitations, but both provide additional information regarding the therapeutic effectiveness of the experimental treatment condition.

Social validation
Determination that the treatment condition has significantly changed the subject's functioning

Social comparison method
A social validation method in which the subject is compared with nondeviant peers

Subjective evaluation method
A social validation method in which others' views of the subject are assessed to see if those others perceive a change in behavior

Rival Hypotheses

When discussing and reading literature on single-subject designs (e.g., Leitenberg, 1973), one gets the distinct impression that these designs can effectively identify causal relationships. However, it seems wise to heed Paul's (1969) claim that only multisubject designs are capable of establishing causal relationships:

> This is the case because the important classes of variables for behavior modification research are so closely intertwined that the only way a given variable can be "systematically manipulated" alone somewhere in the design is through the factorial representation of the variables of interest in combination with appropriate controls (p. 51).

Paul *does* admit that the reversal and multiple-baseline designs provide the strongest evidence of causal relationships that can be attained from single-subject designs.

What types of rival hypotheses exist in the single-subject designs presented? The issues of nonreversible changes and interdependence of behavior have already been discussed and therefore will not be repeated. A number of studies (e.g., Packard, 1970) have shown that instructions alone can change behavior. If different instructions are given for the baseline and experimental treatment phases, it is difficult to determine whether the effect was due to the treatment, the instructions, or some combination of the two. The best one can do is to maintain constant instructions across the treatment phases while introducing, withdrawing, and then reintroducing the therapeutic treatment condition (Hersen et al., 1972). Experimenter expectancies are another source of error in single-subject designs. In the majority of studies, the researcher is acutely aware of the time periods devoted to baseline and to the experimental treatment, which may lead to differential reactions on his or her part. These differential reactions may lead the subject's behavior to change in the desired direction. A last possible biasing effect has to do with sequencing (for an extended discussion of such effects in actual research, the reader is referred to Poulton and Freeman, 1966). Since the same subject must perform in all phases of the experiment, order effects and carry-over effects may exist. It is difficult to separate the effects of the particular sequence of conditions from the effect of the treatment condition. If a change in behavior occurs, it could be the result of the sequence effect, the treatment effect, or some combination of these two.

Multisubject or Single-Subject Designs

Since both single-subject and multisubject designs have been presented, one might at this point be wondering which of the two is better or which should be used in a given study. In multisubject research, the basic strategy is to assign a group of subjects randomly to various treatment conditions. The independent variable is then manipulated, and statistical tests are used to determine if there is a significant mean difference in the responses of the subjects in the various treatment groups. In single-subject research, on the other hand, one attempts to assess the effects of a given independent variable by comparing the subject's performance during presentation of the independent variable with performance when the independent variable is not present. Control over a behavior is demonstrated if the behavior can be altered at will by altering the experimental operations.

Traditionally, psychological research has conformed to a multisubject strategy, and most psychologists have accepted this as the research strategy to use. However, as Dukes (1965) has pointed out, single-subject research has always been with us even though its impact, with a few notable exceptions, has not been great. With the publication of Sidman's book in 1960 and the proliferation of behavior therapy research, single-subject experimentation has come into its own. Perhaps the most frequently cited advantage of the single-subject over the multisubject research design is that the former bypasses the variability due to intersubject differences found in multisubject designs. As Kazdin (1973) has noted, this is desirable because intersubject variability is a function of the research design and not a feature of the behavior of the individual subject. Also, group averages often misrepresent individual behavior.

Almost three decades ago, Cronbach (1957) advocated the integration of the experimental and correlational approaches to research in psychology. Experimental multisubject research was dedicated to identifying nomothetic laws of behavior. One of the big obstacles in the path of experimental psychology was individual difference or error variance, which needed to be reduced by any possible device. Cronbach (1957, p. 674) proceeded to identify various ways in which this could be accomplished. One device he advocated was the correlation approach: including the aptitudes of the subjects in an experiment to determine how they interacted with the experimental treatments. In other words, he advocated a science of aptitude by treatment interactions. In a more recent article, Cronbach (1975) reported that this science was flourishing, but at the same time he stated that it was no longer sufficient. In order to reduce the error variance and to explain and predict behavior, dimensions of the situation and the person had to be taken into account.

Another approach that Cronbach (1957) said could be used to eliminate error variance or individual difference was to follow B. F. Skinner's lead and use only one subject. This is the approach advocated strongly by Sidman (1960). There is a definite advantage to studying the individual organism. Variables affecting the behavior of this one organism can be more highly controlled, so the effect of the treatment condition in isolation can be seen. However, the results of the study can be generalized only to another identical organism in the same controlled setting. Cronbach (1975) has documented the fact that behavior is an interactive function of the situation, the subject, and the experimental treatment.

It is impossible to state that either multisubject or single-subject research is the preferred mode. Rather, it seems as though the two techniques should be integrated, just like the correlational and experimental approaches. This is particularly true in light of the fact that the results obtained also seem to be dependent on the research design one uses. For an extended discussion of this issue, see Grice (1966) and D'Amato (1970, pp. 29–30). The question is "How should the two be integrated?" A number of individuals (Paul, 1969; Leitenberg, 1973; Kazdin, 1973; and Shine, 1975), have suggested that the single-subject approach may be the best means for starting an investigation because of its economy in research time and costs. The single-subject approach could be used as an initial probing process to investigate promising experimental treatment conditions and determine if they are functionally related to behavior. However, the single-subject experiment should serve only as a mapping device and not as a final indication of causality because of the possibility of confounding effects from extraneous variables that cannot be controlled. It is important to realize that the fact that a promising hypothesis is not supported with this initial probe does not discredit it. There is often a great deal of variability in the behavior of different individuals, and an experimental treatment condition that does not work on one individual may be effective on another. Therefore, if the hypothesis does not receive support from the one individual on which it was tested, it should be tested on other individuals before it is discarded.

Paul (1969), Kazdin (1973), and Shine (1975) believe that the experimental treatment should then be investigated from a multisubject approach. Switching to the multisubject approach allows one to control for competing rival hypotheses and to examine the degree of generality of the findings ("Is the experimental treatment condition effective when administered to others?"). If a significant effect is found with the multisubject approach, generality is established.

Use of the multisubject approach does, however, bring up the objections voiced by single-subject researchers. Multisubject research focuses on mean differences among groups of subjects, which are not representative of individual performance. Seldom, if ever, does an experimental treatment change the behavior of all subjects in the same way. This individual difference is considered to be error in the system. The single-subject approach should again be used—Shine's (1975) detection and identification function—to attempt to identify what is causing the individual variation in response to the experimental treatment. Each subject's data should be analyzed to determine the magnitude of effect that the experimental treatment had. Once the subjects have been clustered according to the effectiveness of the experimental treatment on their behavior, the experimenter must find what is common to the subjects that are clustered but differs across clusters of subjects. Once the variables have been identified, they must be verified in a multisubject research design.

The process that has just been advocated consists of a continuing interaction between the multi- and single-subject approaches. It seems that this interactive approach will ultimately lead to more accurate prediction and explanation of behavior.

Summary

In conducting an experimental research study that uses only one subject, you must reorient your thinking, because extraneous variables cannot be controlled by using a randomization control technique, nor can they be handled by the inclusion of a control group. To begin to rule out the possible confounding effect of extraneous variables, you must take some form of a time-series approach. This means that multiple pre- and postmeasures on the dependent variable must be made in order to exclude potential rival hypotheses such as maturation. The most commonly used single-subject design is the A-B-A type, which requires the investigator to take baseline measures before and after the experimental treatment effect has been introduced. The experimental treatment effect is demonstrated by a change in behavior when the treatment condition is introduced and a reversal of the behavior to its pretreatment level when the experimental treatment condition is withdrawn. The success of this design depends on the reversal.

Many extensions of the basic A-B-A design have been made; the most valuable one attempts to assess the combined or interactive effect of two or more variables. The influence of each variable is assessed separately and in combination. Additionally, the influence of the combination of variables, or the interaction of the two or more variables, must be compared with that of each variable separately. This means that at least two subjects must be used in the study.

A third type of single-subject design is the multiple-baseline design. This design avoids the necessity for reversibility required in the A-B-A design by calling for successive administration of the experimental treatment condition to different subjects. The influence of the treatment condition is revealed if a change in behavior occurs simultaneously with the introduction of the treatment condition. While the multiple-baseline design avoids the problem of reversibility, it requires that the behaviors under study be independent.

In the alternating-treatments design, the same behavior is subjected to different experimental treatments under different stimulus conditions. The effect of the experimental treatment is demonstrated if the subject's behavior changes as the experimental treatment conditions change.

The changing-criterion design is a relative newcomer to the area of single-subject designs. It is useful in studies that require a shaping of behavior over a period of time. This plan requires that, following baseline, a treatment condition be implemented and continued across a series of intervention phases. Each intervention phase has a progressively more difficult criterion that must be met in order to advance to the next intervention phase. In this way, behavior can gradually be shaped to a given criterion level.

In addition to a basic knowledge of the single-subject designs, you should also have a knowledge of some of the methodological considerations required to appropriately implement the plans. These include the following:

1. *Baseline.* A stable baseline must be obtained, although some variation will always be found in the freely occurring target behaviors.

2. *Changing one variable at a time.* A cardinal rule in single-subject research is that only one variable can be changed from one phase of the experiment to another.

3. *Length of phases.* While there is some disagreement, the rule seems to be that the length of the phases should be kept equal.

4. *Criteria for evaluating change.* An experimental or a therapeutic criterion must be used to evaluate the results from a single-subject design to determine if the experimental treatment condition produced the desired effect.

5. *Rival hypotheses.* Alternative theories must be considered, including the effect of variables such as instructions, experimenter expectancies, and sequencing effects.

Since both single-subject and multisubject designs are available for use, one has to decide which type of design to use in a given study. The best approach seems to be an integration of the two approaches; the single-subject approach is an efficient means of identifying possible causal relations that can be validated by the multisubject approach.

10

Ethics

Chapter Overview

Once you have designed the study and before you begin collecting data in the prescribed manner, you must consider the ethics of the study to be conducted. Psychological research has the potential for endangering the physical and psychological well-being of the research participants. If all scientific investigations consisted of innocuous studies, there would be little need to consider the welfare of the human subject or ethical issues surrounding research conducted on humans. Unfortunately, perusal of the medical and psychological literature reveals that a number of the studies that have been conducted arouse ethical concerns. Consequently, there is a need for a code of ethics to provide guidelines to follow in the conduct of psychological research. In the past, attention has been focused primarily on research conducted with humans. Currently, emphasis is being placed on the ethics of animal research.

This chapter will cover the issues surrounding the ethics of psychological research. Included will be a presentation of the code of ethics adopted by the American Psychological Association (APA) and of the research conducted on the principles contained in this code. As you read this chapter, you should answer the following questions:

1. What are the ethical issues surrounding the conduct of psychological research?

2. What are the principles contained in the APA code of ethics, and what is the meaning of each of them?

3. What does the research say about the principles contained in the APA code of ethics?

Introduction

In their pursuit of knowledge relating to the behavior of organisms, psychologists conduct surveys, manipulate the type of experience that individuals receive, or vary the stimuli presented to individuals and then observe the subjects' reactions to these stimuli. Such manipulations and observations are necessary in order to identify the influence of various experiences or stimuli. At the same time, it is recognized that individuals have the right to privacy and to protest surveillance of their behavior without their consent. Individuals also have the right to know if their behavior is being manipulated and, if so, why. The scientific community is confronted with the problem of trying to satisfy public demand for answers to problems such as cancer, arthritis, alcoholism, child abuse, and penal reform without infringing on people's rights. For a psychologist trained in research techniques, a decision *not* to do research is also considered to be a matter of ethical concern.

In order to advance knowledge and to find answers to questions, it is often necessary to impinge on well-recognized rights of individuals. For example, it is very difficult to investigate topics like child abuse without violating certain rights such as privacy, since it is necessary to obtain information about the child abuser or the child being abused. Such factors create an ethical dilemma—whether to conduct the research and violate certain rights of individuals for the purpose of gaining knowledge or to sacrifice a gain in knowledge for the purpose of preserving human rights. Ethical principles are vital to the research enterprise because they assist the scientist in preventing abuses that may otherwise occur and they delineate the responsibilities of the investigator.

Research Ethics: What Are They?

When most people think of ethics, they think of moralistic sermons and endless philosophical debates. However, **research ethics** should not represent a set of moralistic dictates imposed on the research community by a group of self-righteous busybodies. Rather, they should represent a set of principles that will assist the community of experimenters in deciding which goals are most important in reconciling conflicting values (Diener and Crandall, 1978).

Research ethics
A set of guidelines to assist the experimenter in making difficult research decisions

Within the social and behavioral sciences, ethical concerns can be divided into three different areas (Diener and Crandall, 1978): (1) the relationship between society and science, (2) professional issues, and (3) treatment of subjects.

The ethical issue concerning the relationship between society and science revolves about the extent to which societal concerns and cultural values should direct the course of scientific investigation. Traditionally, science has been conceived of as trying to uncover the laws of nature. It is assumed that the scientist examines the phenomenon being investigated in an objective and unbiased manner. However, the literature dealing with experimenter effects reveals that the scientist can never be totally objective. Similarly, the society surrounding the scientist dictates to a great extent which issues will be investigated.

The federal government spends millions of dollars each year on research, and it sets priorities for how the money is to be spent. To increase the probability of obtaining research funds, investigators orient their research proposals toward these same priorities, which means that the federal government at least partially dictates the type of research conducted. Societal and cultural values also enter into science to the extent that the phenomenon a scientist chooses to investigate is often determined by that scientist's own culturally based interests (e.g., a female psychologist might study sex discrimination in the work force or a black psychologist might study racial attitudes). The scientific enterprise is not value-free; rather, society's values as well as the scientist's own can creep into the research process in subtle and unnoticed ways.

The category of professional issues encompasses the falsifying of research data. It is generally assumed that the scientist is objective, accurate, and honest in reporting research results. However, there are isolated instances in which the investigator has either distorted the evidence obtained from a research study or fabricated the data in order to obtain significant results. Within the field of psychology, one recent disclosure of such a case was in the area of the heritability of intelligence (Evans, 1976). Sir Cyril Burt, a noted British psychologist knighted for his achievements, apparently faked some of the data reported in scientific journals and even made up the names of some of the coauthors of several of his studies. The costs of such fabrication and distortion of data are obviously enormous. Not only is the whole scientific enterprise discredited, but the professional career of the individual is destroyed. In the final analysis, there is no justification for altering or faking scientific data.

The treatment of research subjects is the most fundamental issue confronted by scientists. The conduct of research with humans can potentially create a great deal of physical and psychological harm, as the examples in Exhibit 10.1 illustrate.

Experiments designed to investigate important psychological issues may subject the participants to humiliation, physical pain, and embarrassment. In planning an experiment, the scientist is obligated to consider the ethics of conducting the research. Unfortunately, some studies cannot be designed in such a way that the possibilty of physical and psychological harm is eliminated. Consequently, the researcher is frequently placed in the dilemma of having to determine whether or not the research study should be conducted at all. Since it is so important, we will consider this issue in some detail.

Ethical Dilemmas

The scientific enterprise in which the research psychologist engages creates a special set of dilemmas. On the one hand, the research psy-

---

Exhibit 10.1   *Illustration of Psychological Experiments That Have the Potential for Creating Physical or Psychological Harm*

A number of experiments that have been conducted within psychology have the potential for creating either physical or psychological harm. A sample of such experiments follows.

West, Gunn, and Chernicky (1975) wanted to simulate an entrapment study in which individuals were tempted to participate in a burglary. A private detective contacted criminology students and presented an elaborate plan for burglarizing a specific business establishment. In one treatment condition, subjects were told that they would be paid $2,000 if they would join in the crime. Many of the students contacted agreed to take part. However, the researchers did not carry out the crime. This study was conducted to assess the differences between those who participate and those who observe in how reprehensible a crime is perceived as being.

Berkun et al. (1962) reported on a variety of studies conducted by the military to investigate the impact of stress. In one experiment, army recruits were placed in a DC-3 that apparently became disabled and was preparing to crash-land. Before the impending crash, the recruits were asked to complete a questionnaire that assessed their opinions regarding the disposition of their earthly possessions in case of death, their knowledge of emergency landing procedures, and so forth. After all the questionnaires had been completed, the responses were jettisoned in a metal container so as not to be destroyed, and then the plane landed safely. Only then did the recruits realize that the whole incident was an experiment.

Middlemist, Knowles, and Matter (1976) investigated the impact of an invasion of personal space on arousal. In collecting data on this topic, the authors used hidden periscopes to study the effect of closeness of others on the speed and rate of urination by men in a public lavatory. To manipulate the closeness variable, confederates would rush in and begin to urinate in the urinal next to those subjects assigned to the crowded condition.

---

chologist is trained in the scientific method and feels an obligation to conduct research; on the other hand, doing so may necessitate subjecting research participants to stress, failure, pain, aggression, or deception. Thus there arises the **ethical dilemma** of having to determine if the potential gain in knowledge from the research study is sufficient to outweigh the cost to the subject. In weighing the pros and cons of such a question, primary consideration must be given to the welfare of the subject. Unfortunately, there is no formula or rule that can help investigators. The decision must be based on a subjective judgment, which should not be made entirely by the researcher or his or her colleagues, since such individuals might be too involved in the study and tend to exaggerate its scientific merit and potential contribution. Investigators must seek the recommendations of others such as scientists in related fields, students, or lay individuals. In making the final judgment, however, the investigator must always remember that no amount of advice or counsel can alter the fact that the final ethical responsibility lies with the researcher conducting the study.

Ethical dilemma
The investigator's conflict in weighing the potential cost to the subject against the potential gain to be accrued from the research project

Development of the APA Code of Ethics

Nazi scientists during World War II conducted some grossly inhumane experiments that were universally condemned as being unethical. For example, they immersed people in ice-water to determine how long it would take them to freeze to death. However, these experiments were conducted by individuals living in what is thought to have been a demented society, and it seems to have been assumed that such studies could not be performed in our culture. Prior to the decade of the sixties, comments about the ethics of research were few and far between. Edgar Vinacke's (1954) statement about the ethics of deceiving subjects represents one of the few expressed.

In the mid-1960s ethical issues became a dominant concern, as it grew increasingly clear that science did not invariably operate to benefit others and did not always conduct its experiments in a manner that ensured the safety of participants. In the medical field, Pappworth (1967) cited numerous examples of research conducted on human subjects that violated their ethical rights. One issue of *Daedalus* in 1969 was devoted to the ethics of human experimentation, particularly as it related to medical research. The Tuskegee experiment (Jones, 1981), which appears in Exhibit 10.2, probably epitomizes the type of unethical experimentation that was conducted within the medical field. There was an equal concern about the violation of the rights of human subjects in psychological research. Kelman (1967, 1968, 1972) has by far been the most outspoken on this issue, although others, such as Seeman (1969) and Beckman and Bishop (1970), have also contributed. More recently, entire books have been devoted to this issue (e.g., Klockars and O'Connor, 1979). This widespread concern has led to the development of a code of ethics to be used by the psychologist for guidance in the conduct of research using human subjects.

Before presenting the code of ethics that has been adopted by the American Psychological Association (APA), I want to describe the procedure followed in its development to give you an appreciation of the work and thought that went into it.

Background of the Development of the APA Code of Ethics

The Committee on Ethical Standards in Psychological Research was appointed by the Board of Directors of the American Psychological Association to revise the 1953 code of ethics for research using human

Exhibit 10.2   *The Tuskegee Syphilis Experiment*

In July of 1972, the Associated Press released a story that revealed that the United States Public Health Service (PHS) had for 40 years been conducting a study of the effects of untreated syphilis on black men in Macon County, Alabama. The study consisted of conducting a variety of medical tests (including an examination) on 399 black men who were in the late stages of the disease and on 200 controls. Although a formal description of the experiment could never be found (apparently one never existed), a set of procedures evolved in which physicians employed by the PHS administered a variety of blood tests and routine autopsies to learn more about the serious complications that resulted from the final stages of the disease.

This study had nothing to do with the treatment of syphilis; no drugs or alternative therapies were tested. It was a study aimed strictly at compiling data on the effects of the disease. The various components of the study, and not the attempt to learn more about syphilis, made it an extremely unethical experiment. The subjects in the study were mostly poor and illiterate, and the PHS offered incentives to participate, including free physical examinations, free rides to and from the clinic, hot meals, free treatment for other ailments, and a $50 burial stipend. The participants were not told the purpose of the study or what they were or were not being treated for. Even more damning is the fact that the subjects were followed by a PHS nurse, who informed local physicians that those individuals were taking part in the study and that they were not to be treated for syphilis. Participants who were offered treatment by other physicians were advised that they would be dropped from the study if they took the treatment.

As you can see, the participants were not aware of the purpose of the study or of the danger that it posed to them, and no attempt was ever made to explain the situation to them. In fact, subjects were enticed with a variety of inducements and were followed to ensure that they did not receive treatment from other physicians. This study seems to have included just about every possible violation of our present standard of ethics for research with humans.

(From Jones, 1981.)

---

subjects. This committee patterned its work after that developed by the previous ethics committee, incorporating two distinctive features of the previous committee's method. First, the members of the profession were asked to supply ethical problems to serve as the raw material for the formation of the ethical principles. Two samples of 9000 members of the American Psychological Association, and the entire membership of selected groups such as the Division of Developmental Psychology, were sent a questionnaire requesting a description of research studies that posed ethical problems. From these massive surveys, 5000 research descriptions were obtained that comprised the raw material for the committee. The committee members also interviewed 35 individuals who had either demonstrated a high level of concern for ethical issues or had a great deal of exposure to a variety of research projects.

With this wealth of information in hand, the committee began the process of drafting the proposed principles. Once the initial draft had been completed, the second distinctive feature of the 1953 ethics committee's method was introduced. This involved distributing the proposed principles throughout the profession so that they could be reviewed and criticized by its members. Those attending city, state, regional, and national meetings and conventions, as well as psychology departments and individual psychologists interested in research ethics, discussed these principles. Additionally, the proposed principles appeared in the APA *Monitor,* the monthly newspaper of the association, to ensure that all members had the opportunity to review them. Many reactions were received, as well as reactions to the reactions. The commentaries by Baumrind (1971, 1972), Kerlinger (1972), Pellegrini (1972), Alumbaugh (1972), and May (1972) are all thought-provoking examples of the reactions. The committee then prepared a new draft of the principles and subjected them to the same type of review process that the older draft had undergone. The revised ethical principles received general acceptance from the APA membership. In view of this, the committee recommended adoption of ten principles. These ten principles were adopted by the American Psychological Association and distributed to its membership in 1973.

The committee also recommended a mandatory review of the principles at five-year intervals. Consistent with that recommendation, in 1978 the American Psychological Association established a committee to review and make recommendations regarding the official position of the association on the use of human participants in research. This committee made several changes in the principles, including addition of a more detailed explication of the ethical issues and elaboration of the sections on deception, informed consent, and field research.

The revisions were then submitted to the Board of Scientific Affairs, the Council of Graduate Departments of Psychology, and all members of the first ethics committee. A notice of the availability of the revisions appeared in the APA *Monitor,* and comments were solicited from all those who requested a copy of the revisions. Based on these comments, a second draft was prepared, and its availability was announced in the *Monitor.* It was sent for review to many of the committees, departments, associations, and individuals who had commented on the first draft. Comments about the second draft indicated that this draft was satisfactory or that it represented a better balance of the opinions. Consequently, the committee recommended the approval of the revised set of ethical tenets in August, 1982. It is this set of revised principles that will be presented.

Ethical Principles

Any psychologist conducting research must ensure that the dignity and the welfare of the research participants are maintained and that the investigation is carried out in accordance with federal and state regulations and with the standards set forth by the American Psychological Association. These standards, consisting of ten principles, were published in *Ethical principles in the conduct of research with human participants,* by the American Psychological Association. Each of the ten principles will be presented and then discussed briefly in this section. The discussion is designed to clarify the principle, to focus on potential questions about application of the rule, and to identify the factors that should be given consideration in answering these questions.

Principle A

> In planning a study, the investigator has the responsibility to make a careful evaluation of its ethical acceptability. To the extent that the weighing of scientific and human values suggests a compromise of any principle, the investigator incurs a correspondingly serious obligation to seek ethical advice and to observe stringent safeguards to protect the rights of human participants.[1]

The first principle states that it is the investigator's responsibility to evaluate his or her study in light of each of the following ethical principles. If, in the investigator's opinion, any aspect of the study suggests a compromise of the principles, the investigator incurs the obligation to seek the advice and counsel of others to ensure that the rights and welfare of the research participants are maintained and that the study maximizes the potential knowledge that can be gained. In seeking advice, the investigator can turn to scientific review groups or to colleagues, but such individuals are likely to be more concerned with the scientific merit of the study than with the welfare of the research participants. A better choice would be to turn to groups that were established for the purpose of safeguarding the rights and welfare of research participants, such as departmental ethics committees or institutional review boards. In any case, the investigator should keep in mind that others' decisions are always advisory—responsibility for the ethical acceptability of the study must always reside with the investigator.

Principle B

> Considering whether a participant in a planned study will be a "subject at risk" or "subject at minimal risk," according to recognized standards, is of primary ethical concern to the investigator.

---

[1] Excerpts throughout this chapter are from *Ethical principles in the conduct of research with human participants.* Washington, D.C.: American Psychological Association, 1982. Copyright 1982 by the American Psychological Association. Reprinted by permission of the publisher.

The second principle states that a basic ethical concern of the investigator is to determine the degree of risk imposed by the study. Virtually any research study will impose some demands on the research participant, such as the requirement that the subject devote the length of time it takes to complete the study, and these demands could be perceived as costs to the subject. Usually, such costs are minimal, though, and there is minimal risk to the subject. Exceptions are experiments that use deception, subject the participants to stressful conditions, or require the subjects to take drugs; these certainly pose a threat to the welfare and dignity of the participant. It is the ethical responsibility of the investigator to distinguish between these two conditions and, when the study poses a threat to the subject, to seek the counsel of others to make sure that the subjects are protected.

The decision-making process involves weighing the costs and risks to the participants against the potential benefits that may result from the study. It is not appropriate to conclude that research cannot be conducted if it imposes some risk to the participant. Each study has to be considered separately, and a subjective judgment made about the potential gains and costs. A cost-benefit analysis must be conducted on any study that imposes risk to the participants. If the potential gain exceeds the potential cost, advisory groups typically recommend that the investigator conduct the study. Where the risks are relatively great, the investigator has the obligation to consider alternative approaches that impose smaller risks.

Principle C

> The investigator always retains the responsibility for insuring ethical practice in research. The investigator is also responsible for the ethical treatment of research participants by collaborators, assistants, students, and employees, all of whom, however, incur similar obligations.

In Principle C, it is stated that the final responsibility for the decision to conduct a study falls on the investigator, regardless of the advice received from others, as does the responsibility for maintaining ethical practice throughout the research study. This issue becomes particularly significant when there is more than one person involved in conducting the study. Then, there is the tendency to let the other person take responsibility for ethical conduct. Principle C says that this should never happen. In *no* case does the addition of individuals dilute one's ethical responsibility; instead, it merely multiplies it. Each coprincipal investigator is responsible for the ethical conduct of the study, and where students or assistants are involved, it is the principal investigator's responsibility to train them to be ethically responsible and supervise them to insure that they act in an ethical manner. However, this does not relieve research assistants of all responsibility. They too should be sensitive to the ethical conduct of the study, and if the assistant feels a moral reluctance to conduct the study, then the investigator or supervisor must not pressure the assistant to complete it.

Principle D

Except in minimal-risk research, the investigator establishes a clear and fair agreement with research participants, prior to their participation, that clarifies the obligations and responsibilities of each. The investigator has the obligation to honor all promises and commitments included in that agreement. The investigator informs the participants of all aspects of the research that might reasonably be expected to influence willingness to participate and explains all other aspects of the research about which the participants inquire. Failure to make full disclosure prior to obtaining informed consent requires additional safeguards to protect the welfare and dignity of the research participants. Research with children or with participants who have impairments that would limit understanding and/or communication requires special safeguarding procedures.

Principle D states that, except in minimal-risk situations, the investigator has the ethical responsibility to inform the research participants of their obligations and responsibilities, to inform the participants about all aspects of the research that might influence willingness to participate, and to answer any other questions regarding the project. No one can argue with such a practice, since it tells the participants exactly what is expected of them and of the investigator. With this knowledge, the prospective subjects can evaluate the research and come to a free decision regarding whether or not to participate. The problem is that this ideal cannot always be attained. Some potential subjects (e.g., children) do not have the competence to make the necessary decision and to provide informed consent. In such cases, the legal as well as ethical practice is to obtain the informed consent from a person whose primary interest is the subject's welfare, generally the parent or legal guardian. Even when such consent has been obtained, the subject should also be asked to give permission before participating.

Principle E

Methodological requirements of a study may make the use of concealment or deception necessary. Before conducting such a study, the investigator has a special responsibility to (1) determine whether the use of such techniques is justified by the study's prospective scientific, educational, or applied value; (2) determine whether alternative procedures are available that do not use concealment or deception; and (3) ensure that the participants are provided with sufficient explanation as soon as possible.

Principle E is actually an extension of Principle D, which stated that the investigator should fully inform the participant about all aspects of the study. In many instances, it is not possible to obtain informed consent, either because the information is too technical for the individual to evaluate, the subject is incapable of making a responsible judgment, or, as is most commonly the case, valid data could not be gathered if participants were fully informed about the study. In disguised field experiments, the "people in the street" unknowingly become research participants. In such instances, the ethical issue revolves around the fact that the subjects are not informed about the nature of the experiment or even that they are participating in one. Sometimes participants are misinformed or deceived about the purpose of an experiment or implications of their behavior. Some individuals believe that any research involving concealment or deception is unethical and should not be conducted. Others believe in the necessity of such research, but at the same time acknowledge that it may result in an ethical dilemma for the investigator. Principle E directs the investigator to determine if alternative procedures are available that do not employ deception or concealment. If not, then the researcher must determine if the concealment or deception is justified in terms of the scientific, educational, or applied value of the study. Once the study has been completed, the participant must be given an explanation of the whole research procedure as soon as possible. Principle E provides a guide to be followed when, in the judgment of the investigator, fully informed consent cannot be obtained.

Principle E does not reduce the ethical responsibility of the investigator; rather, it provides criteria for the investigator and his or her advisors to use in making a judgment regarding the ethical dilemma. The American Psychological Association (1982, p. 41) gives four conditions that may make the use of deception more acceptable. These are as follows:

> a. The research objective is of great importance and cannot be achieved without the use of deception;
>
> b. on being fully informed later (Principle E), participants are expected to find the procedures reasonable and to suffer no loss of confidence in the integrity of the investigator or of others involved;
>
> c. research participants are allowed to withdraw from the study at any time (Principle F), and are free to withdraw their data when the concealment or misrepresentation is revealed (Principle H), and
>
> d. investigators take full responsibility for detecting and removing stressful after-effects of the experience (Principle I).

Principle F

The investigator respects the individual's freedom to decline to participate in or to withdraw from the research at any time. The obliga-

tion to protect this freedom requires careful thought and consideration when the investigator is in a position of authority or influence
over the participant. Such positions of authority include, but are not
limited to, situations in which research participation is required as
part of employment or in which the participant is a student, client, or
employee of the investigator.

Principle F asserts that it is ethically unacceptable to coerce a subject to
participate in research. One of our human rights is freedom of choice,
and this extends to participation in psychological research. One runs
into two related problems when attempting to implement this principle. The first difficulty, which Kelman (1972) has eloquently discussed,
is the power relationship that often exists between the researcher and
the subject. Typically, the subject is in a less powerful position, which
places him or her at a perceived disadvantage in feeling free to decline
participation. An investigator, in implementing Principle F, may ask
the group of potential subjects for volunteers to participate in the
research and tell them that they do not have to volunteer. If these
potential subjects are children or the investigator's students or patients,
they may not feel free *not* to volunteer without encountering some
penalty. Investigators must be aware of the power relationship they
hold relative to their subjects and incorporate this when trying to
implement Principle F.

The second difficulty in trying to fulfill Principle F is that the
psychologist has an obligation to conduct research and to advance a
segment of behavioral science. To accomplish this, one needs an available supply of subjects. For those studying humans, there is a need for a
supply of warm bodies, which means that somehow some people need
to be motivated to volunteer for psychological research studies. This
has led many psychology departments to form a subject pool by requiring all introductory psychology students to participate in one or more
psychology experiments. A number of individuals feel that Principle F
is violated by such a requirement. The APA ethics committee (American Psychological Association, 1982, pp. 47–48) has provided a set of
procedures a department can follow in order to maintain Principle F in
spirit while still providing a pool of subjects to serve as research participants. These suggestions are as follows:

> a. Students are informed about the research requirement before
> they enroll in the course, typically by an announcement in an official
> listing of courses. In addition, during the first class meeting, the
> instructor provides a detailed description of the requirement, fre-
> quently in written form, covering the following points: the amount of
> participation required; the available alternatives to actual research
> participation; in a general way, the kinds of studies among which the
> student can choose; the right of the student to drop out of a given
> research project at any time without penalty; any penalties to be
> imposed for failure to complete the requirement or for nonappearance

after agreeing to take part; the benefits to the student to be gained from participation; the obligation of the researcher to provide the student with an explanation of the research; the obligation of the researcher to treat the participant with respect and dignity; the procedures to be followed if the student is mistreated in any way; and an explanation of the scientific purposes of the research carried on in the departmental laboratories.

b. Prior approval of research proposals is required, sometimes by a single faculty member but more often by a departmental committee or an Institutional Review Board, is recommended. The following considerations are appropriate for the review:

Will dangerous or potentially harmful procedures be employed? If so, what precautions have been taken to protect the participants from the possibly damaging effects of the procedure? Will inordinate demands be made upon the participants' time? Will the research involve deception or withholding information? If so, what plans have been developed for subsequently informing the participants? What plans have been made for providing the participants with an explanation of the study? In general, what will the participants gain?

c. Alternative opportunities for research participation are provided. This provision lets students choose the type of research experience and (often of more consequence to students) the time and place where they will participate.

Providing options commensurate in time and effort that do not require service as a research participant is necessary. The student may observe ongoing research and prepare a report based upon this experience or submit a short paper based upon the reading of research reports. Care should be taken to ensure that selecting such options has no punitive consequences.

d. Before beginning participation, the student receives a description of the procedures to be employed and is reminded of the option to drop out later without penalty if so desired. At this point consent is sought, and the student may be asked to document consent in writing. In any event, participation in any teacher's own research project should be optional for all students.

e. Steps are taken to insure that the student is treated with respect and courtesy.

f. Participants receive some kind of reward for their participation. At a minimum this reward involves as full an explanation of the purposes of the research as is possible. In addition, some departments may reward research participation with better grades, although many critics would question the educational propriety of this practice. The assignment of a grade of "incomplete" as a sanction against nonfulfillment is common, although some critics regard this as too coercive. Where this sanction is used, procedures exist for allowing the student to fulfill the requirement later on.

g. There is a mechanism by which students may report any mistreatment. Usually, the mechanism involves reporting questionable conduct on the part of a researcher to the instructor, the departmental ethics committee, or the chair of the department.

h. The recruiting procedure is under constant review. Assessments of student attitudes toward the requirement are obtained at the end of each course having such a requirement each time the course is offered. These data, together with evaluations of the workability of the procedures by the investigators, provide the basis for modifying the procedures in subsequent years.

Principle G

The investigator protects the participant from physical and mental discomfort, harm, and danger that may arise from research procedures. If risks of such consequences exist, the investigator informs the participant of that fact. Research procedures likely to cause serious or lasting harm to a participant are not used unless the failure to use these procedures might expose the participant to risk of greater harm or unless the research has great potential benefit and fully informed and voluntary consent is obtained from each participant. The participant should be informed of procedures for contacting the investigator within a reasonable time period following participation should stress, potential harm, or related questions or concerns arise.

Principle G begins by stating the ideal—that research participants should be protected from any physical or mental discomfort, harm, or danger. Fortunately, most psychological research is relatively innocuous and exposes the participants to little suffering or danger. However, a review of the psychological literature indicates that some studies have indeed subjected research participants to psychological and physical risks. For example, studies have induced physical discomfort and risk through administration of drugs and electric shock. Subjects have also suffered by being exposed to failure, anxiety, frustration, and scenes of extreme human suffering. When exploring such potentially risky issues, a psychologist has the obligation to first investigate alternative means for studying the problem, such as using animals or studying individuals who are in naturally occurring but unavoidable stressful situations (e.g., an individual waiting to undergo an operation). When such alternatives cannot be identified, the investigator is faced with an ethical dilemma. If the investigator determines that the benefits outweigh the costs, he or she has the obligation to inform the participant of the risks. If the research procedure is likely to cause serious or lasting harm, it is not used unless the study has *great* potential benefit or unless failure to use the procedure would expose the participant to even greater risk.

Fully informing the research participant of all risks that may be involved and still attaining valid data is difficult in some studies. If one were investigating failure, for valid data to be generated it would be necessary for the participants to believe that they had actually failed. Where deception can be justified, the investigator incurs an additional responsibility—to insure that the participants experience the least possible psychological damage. In all instances, the participant should be informed of the procedures for contacting the investigator if any stress, harm, or questions arise.

Principle H

> After the data are collected, the investigator provides the participant with information about the nature of the study and attempts to remove any misconceptions that may have arisen. Where scientific or humane values justify delaying or withholding this information, the investigator incurs a special responsibility to monitor the research and to ensure that there are no damaging consequences for the participant.

Several times in this text it has been stated that good research design sometimes necessitates deceiving or withholding information from the research participants. Where such a situation exists, Principle H applies; the investigator has a responsibility to debrief the subject or provide the full details of the study, including why the deception was necessary or why information was withheld. The investigator must also ensure that there are no damaging consequences for the participant.

A number of difficulties can be encountered in trying to satisfy Principle H. The debriefing may anger or disillusion the participants because they learn that they were deceived. Aronson and Carlsmith (1968) discuss this issue at length and propose a debriefing procedure (outlined in Chapter 11) that should minimize this possibility. The fact that the debriefing may not be believed is a particularly difficult problem where the study involves a double deception (two consecutive deception procedures in the same study). The subject has been deceived twice and may think that this is another trick. In cases where children are the research participants, the primary objective of debriefing should be to ensure that they leave with no undesirable side effects because of their limited ability to understand complex explanations.

The timing of the postinterview can also pose a problem in some studies. The investigator may feel that the debriefing should occur en masse after completion of data collection, or, in a multiple-session study, the research design may call for delaying debriefing until the end of the second or third session even though deception occurred in the first session. In such an instance, the investigator must consider the possible detrimental effects that may accrue from allowing the person to leave the laboratory either misinformed or uninformed. In cases where such detrimental effects may exist, the researcher should try to find alternative designs or perhaps abandon the study. At the very least, the investigator should seek the counsel of others regarding the proper procedure to follow.

Principle I

> Where research procedures result in undesirable consequences for the individual participant, the investigator has the responsibility to detect and remove or correct these consequences, including long-term effects.

Although most psychological research is quite innocuous, occasionally stress or some other undesirable consequence is either deliberately or inadvertently imposed on the participants. Principle I states that, regardless of the source of the stress or other undesirable consequence, the investigator is responsible for detecting and removing it. This means that the investigator must be alert to stressful reactions that may occur during the conduct of the experiment and take corrective action immediately. Under some conditions, a long-term follow-up may be necessary to ensure that detrimental effects do not persist over time.

Some studies require the use of a control group to test for the influence of a therapeutic procedure, drug, or educational experience. The typical approach is to withhold the treatment procedure or experience from the control group. In such instances, beneficial alternative procedures should be considered (e.g., giving the control group a different treatment of known benefit).

Principle I also requires the investigator to provide control groups with access to beneficial treatments if these treatments prove to be efficacious. However, if debriefing the research participants about the various components of the study may be detrimental to them, the investigator becomes involved in a special conflict. On the one hand, the researcher is obligated to inform the participants about the study; on the other hand, the investigator must avoid harming the participants. The resolution of this conflict seems to be that the participants should be debriefed only if the harmful information might be uncovered by the subjects at a later date and only if the investigator conducting the debriefing is qualified to handle any resultant distress the participants may experience.

Principle J

> Information obtained about the research participant during the course of an investigation is confidential unless otherwise agreed upon in advance. When the possibility exists that others may obtain access to such information, this possibility, together with plans for protecting confidentiality, is explained to the participant as part of the procedure for obtaining informed consent.

Every person has a right to privacy that cannot be violated without his or her permission. In a research study, the participants provide informed consent that allows the investigator to observe and record their behavior. Consequently, the investigator has a great deal of personal information that could be passed on to others. Principle J asserts that any data obtained about a research participant must be kept confidential. There are a number of situations in which the experimenter may be pressured to release information. Parents, friends, a teacher, a therapist, a school, a clinic, or an industrial organization may request information. The investigator is ethically bound to maintain the confidentiality of the information, however, unless consent is given by the research participant to release the information.

Some other situations pose an even greater threat to Principle J. The law does not provide protection for the confidentiality of research data, so the courts can demand that the investigator release the data. Also, there is the case in which the experimenter uncovers information that suggests that the participants might harm themselves or others. Then the investigator also has the obligation to disclose this information to others. Loss of confidentiality can occur when the data obtained from the participants are published or placed in a data bank. According to Principle J, the investigator has a responsibility to inform the research participants of the possibility that the data may not remain confidential and also of the steps that are taken to ensure confidentiality. For example, the investigator could promise to store and code the information in a way that makes identification impossible.

Possible Consequences of Adopting the APA Code of Ethics

The above represents a summary of the final product produced by the APA ethics committee (American Psychological Association, 1982). The ten principles developed by the committee have been adopted by the association as its official position and, therefore, are to be used by psychologists conducting human research. The question that must be asked is "What are the potential consequences of adopting this particular ethical posture?" West and Gunn (1978) have found that research proposals have received increased scrutiny since the adoption of the original code of ethics. In some cases, independent variable manipulations that previously would have been used and considered appropriate are having to be altered. For example, anger manipulations traditionally used in aggression research are being changed so that a less severe anger manipulation is used (Baron, 1976). The ethical guidelines have created a shift toward the use of milder and less deceptive manipulations. The implications of this, according to West and Gunn (1978), are twofold. First, the number of subjects used in a given experiment will have to be increased in order to detect a difference between treatment conditions. Second, there will be an accelerated trend toward nonmotivational theories because the experimental manipulations generated by psychologists will be so mild that it is unlikely they will arouse motives that will support a motivational interpretation.

Gergen (1973, p. 912) has summarized his position as follows:

> I have argued that from a research standpoint, there is little to merit the promulgation of the proposed ethical principles. Not only have we failed to demonstrate that our present procedures are detrimental to human subjects, but there is good reason to suspect that the principles would be detrimental to the profession and to the enhancement of knowledge should they be adopted. It has further been maintained that great danger lies behind our attempts at moralizing. What is needed is factual advice about the possible harmful consequences of various research strategies. Such advice could be embodied in a series of advisory statements for researchers. While these statements would primarily be conjectural at this point in time, we should ultimately be able to replace conjecture with fact.

Gergen's position, is that we should determine the effects of each principle before incorporating it into a set of ethical standards for everyone to use. As Gergen (1973, p. 907) states:

> If subjects remain unaffected by variations along these dimensions, then the establishment of the principles becomes highly questionable. If subjects are generally unconcerned about what is to happen to them, if they find experimental deceptions rather intriguing, if they do not generally care abut the rationale of the research, and if their attitudes about life and themselves remain untouched regardless of whether the ethical principles are experimentally realized, then establishing and reinforcing the principles simply pose unnecessary hardships for the scientist. The life of the research psychologist is difficult enough without harnessing him with research restrictions that have little real-world consequence.

When the original ethical principles (American Psychological Association, 1973) were adopted, little research had been conducted on their influence. A decade later, we find ourselves in a slightly different position. Results of a number of studies seem to have been incorporated into the current revision of the ethical principles (American Psychological Association, 1982). For example, while the initial set of principles said that participants must be informed of all features of the study that might affect their willingness to participate (Principle C), the current edition recognizes that concealment or deception within a study may be necessary (Principle E). This alteration may have been prompted by research such as that conducted by Resnick and Schwartz (1973). These investigators attempted to determine the impact of following the informed consent principle to its logical extreme in a simple but widely used verbal conditioning task developed by Taffel (1955).

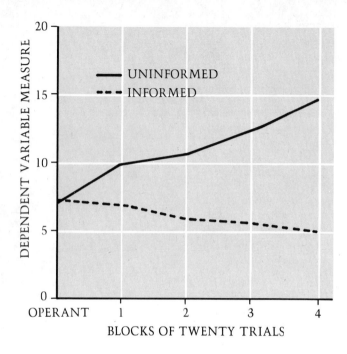

Figure 10.1   *Verbal conditioning data obtained by Resnick and Schwartz.* (Adapted from Resnick, J. H., and Schwartz, T. Ethical standards as an independent variable in psychological research. *American Psychologist,* 1973, *28*, p. 136. Copyright 1973 by the American Psychological Association. Reprinted by permission of the author.)

The control, or noninformed, group was given typical instructions, which gave them a rationale for the study and informed them of the task that they were to complete. The experimental, or informed, group received *complete* instructions regarding the true reason for conducting the experiment and the *exact* nature of the Taffel procedure. Figure 10.1 depicts the results of the data obtained from the 14 subjects in each treatment condition. The uninformed subjects performed in the expected manner, demonstrating verbal conditioning. However, the informed group revealed a reversal in the conditioning rate. Such data show that maintaining maximum ethical conditions alters the knowledge that we accumulate. This altered information might represent inaccurate information, which would create a *lack* of external validity.

In addition to finding a drastic difference in response on the part of the informed subjects, Resnick and Schwartz also found that informing subjects of the entire experiment apparently destroys any incentive to participate in the experiment. Uninformed subjects were enthusiastic and appeared at the scheduled time, but informed subjects were generally uncooperative and "often haughty, insisting that they had only one time slot to spare which we could either take or leave" (p. 137). It actually took Resnick and Schwartz *five weeks* to collect the data on the 14 informed subjects for such reasons. These researchers suggested that completely informing subjects makes some subjects very suspicious and may cause them to stay away. However, for most participants, fully disclosing the research to the subjects causes them to lose interest, which "suggests that people enjoy an element of risk and nondisclosure and become bored rapidly with the prospect of participating in something of which they already have full knowledge" (Resnick and Schwartz, 1973, p. 137). This view is supported by a survey of student opinion conducted by Epstein, Suedfeld, and Silverstein (1973). They found that more than 70 percent of the college students they surveyed did *not* expect to be told the purpose of the experiment and that deception, though not desirable, was not an inappropriate feature of the research setting.

Let us now look at the three issues raised by the code of ethics that are generating some research: deception, the participants' freedom to decline to participate in or withdraw from the study at any time, and the possibility of coercion (Principles E and F).

Deception

A number of investigators have attempted to determine the extent to which deception is used in psychological studies. Table 10.1 summarizes the results of such surveys. It is obvious from these surveys that deception has been steadily increasing since 1948 and that this increase resides primarily within the personality and social areas.

Given that deception is here to stay and that alternatives to deception—e.g., role playing (Kelman, 1967)—are inadequate substitutes (Miller, 1972), we need to take a look at two questions.

The first question is "Is it possible to incorporate a compromise between the need for deception and the ethical principle of informed consent?" This compromise could take the form of informing all potential subjects in, say, the departmental subject pool that some of the experiments they are to engage in will include some form of deception. Campbell (1969a, p. 370) suggests the following as a possible procedure:

> Announce to all members of the subject pool at the beginning of the term, "In about half of the experiments you will be participating in this semester, it will be necessary for the validity of the experiment for the experimenter to deceive you in whole or in part as to his exact purpose. Nor will we be able to inform you as to which experiments these were or as to what their real purpose was, until after all the data for the experiment have been collected. We give you our guarantee

Table 10.1   *Use of Deception in Psychological Research*

AUTHOR(S)	JOURNALS	YEAR	PERCENTAGE OF DECEPTION STUDIES
Seeman (1969)	*Journal of Abnormal and Social Psychology*	1948	14.3
Seeman (1969)	*Journal of Personality*	1948	23.8
Seeman (1969)	*Journal of Consulting Psychology*	1948	2.9
Seeman (1969)	*Journal of Experimental Psychology*	1948	14.6
Menges (1973)	*Journal of Abnormal and Social Psychology*	1961	16.3
Seeman (1969)	*Journal of Abnormal and Social Psychology*	1963	36.8
Seeman (1969)	*Journal of Personality*	1963	43.9
Seeman (1969)	*Journal of Consulting Psychology*	1963	9.3
Seeman (1969)	*Journal of Experimental Psychology*	1963	10.8
Menges (1973)	*Journal of Personality and Social Psychology*	1971	47.2
Menges (1973)	*Journal of Abnormal and Social Psychology*	1971	21.5
Menges (1973)	*Journal of Educational Psychology*	1971	8.3
Menges (1973)	*Journal of Consulting Psychology*	1971	6.3
Menges (1973)	*Journal of Experimental Psychology*	1971	3.1
Carlson (1971)	*Journal of Personality and Journal of Personality and Social Psychology*	1968	57.0
Levenson, Gray, and Ingram (1976)	*Journal of Personality*	1973	42.0
Levenson, Gray, and Ingram (1976)	*Journal of Personality and Social Psychology*	1973	62.0

that no possible danger or invasion of privacy will be involved, and that your responses will be held in complete anonymity and privacy. We ask you at this time to sign the required permission form, agreeing to participate in experiments under these conditions." This would merely be making explicit what is now generally understood, and probably would not worsen the problem of awareness and suspicion that now exists.[2]

Again, we must ask if this procedure is a legitimate alternative that would still enable us to obtain unbiased data. Holmes and Bennett

[2] From Campbell, D. Prospective: Artifact and control. In *Artifact in behavioral research*, edited by R. Rosenthal and R. L. Rosnow. New York: Academic Press, 1969. Used with permission of the author and publisher.

Table 10.2 *Potential Harms or Ethical Objections to Kinds of Deception in Research*

	POTENTIAL HARM OR ETHICAL OBJECTION					
KIND OF DECEPTION	INVADES PRIVACY	NO CONSENT	NO SELF-DETERMINATION	NO DEBRIEFING	LIES	RESEARCHER CONCEALS
Deception not by the researcher						
Self-deception	4	3	3	3	2	3
Third-person deception	4	4	4	3	2	4
Deception by researcher						
Informed consent	1	1	1	1	1	4
Consent to deception	3	1	1	1	4	4
Waives informing	3	4	1	2	4	4
False informing	4	4	4	2	4	4
No informing	4	4	4	3	4	4

Key: 4 = accompanies, 3 = likely to accompany, 2 = unlikely to accompany, 1 = does not accompany.

From Sieber, J. E. Deception in social research I: Kinds of deception and the wrongs they may involve. IRB: *A Review of Human Subjects Research*, 1982, 4(No. 9), 1–5. Reprinted by permission of The Hastings Center. © Institute of Society, Ethics, and the Life Sciences, 360 Broadway, Hastings-on-Hudson, N.Y. 10706.

(1974) provided data on this question. One of their groups of subjects, the informed group, was told that deception was involved in some psychological experiments. The researchers found that giving this group of subjects such information in no way affected their performance; they performed in the same manner as did the deceived subjects. Consequently, it seems that informing subjects that they may be deceived but not of the exact nature of the deception does not alter results.

The second question is "What effect may deception have on the subject?" The generally accepted view is that deception has a significant potential for wronging and harming subjects. Sieber's (1982) stance perhaps epitomizes this view. She identified seven types of deception as well as the types of potential harm or ethical objections that accompany each. According to Sieber, Table 10.2, which illustrates these types of deceptions and the potential objections, indicates that at least one objection exists to each type of deception and at least six ethical objections or sources of potential harm can be generated by deception. For example, a study that deceived subjects and did not obtain their informed consent would involve an invasion of privacy, denial of self-determination, concealment, and lying. Based on such a position, Sieber (1983a) proceeded to provide a taxonomy of factors to be used in assessing the risk/benefit ratio of deception research. Expositions such as those presented by Sieber give the impression that deception is not only ethically objectionable but potentially harmful. However, these writings seem to be based on the authors' opinions, which may or may not conform to reality. The only way to determine if such expositions represent moral philosophizing or actual ethical objections is to investigate the perceptions of participants who have been subjected to deception.

There are three relatively recent experiments that have studied the potential harm inflicted on the research participant by deception. Pihl, Zacchia, and Zeichner (1981) conducted a follow-up investigation of subjects who had participated in a series of studies that included deception and potential physical and mental stress. Subjects who had been in a study of the effects of alcohol on aggression were telephoned by a caller who asked them to recall all components of the experiment and then asked if they would complete a questionnaire that would be mailed to them. This questionnaire asked if anything about the experiment bothered them (and, if so, to what degree and for how long), if they felt free to discontinue the experiment at any time, and if they would be willing to participate in a similar study in the future. Results showed that, of the subjects contacted, only 19 percent reported being bothered by any aspect of the experiment, and four percent said they were bothered by the deception. Most of the factors that bothered the subjects dealt with issues other than deception or the fact that the experiment required them to deliver shocks. The components that upset the subjects were mostly rather trivial (one subject felt that using a cloth holder for the drinking glass was unsanitary). The greatest distress surrounded the type of alcohol consumed, the dose, and the speed with which it had to be consumed. One subject reported being bothered for several days because "laboratory and not commercial alcohol was consumed" (Pihl et al., 1981, p. 930). Interestingly, this subject was in a placebo group that did not even consume alcohol. It is also interesting to note that the length of distress was shorter for the deception and averse stimuli variables than it was for other seemingly trivial variables such as boredom. As is illustrated in Figure 10.2, the duration of distress over the deception or shock was only an hour or less, whereas the dissatisfaction with the alcohol lasted an average of 20 hours.

Smith and Richardson (1983) have produced results that apparently confirm the findings of Pihl et al. Smith and Richardson questioned 215 male students and 249 female students at the end of the academic quarter, following the students' participation in the minimum number of required psychology experiments. The subjects were questioned on a variety of issues, including the potential harmful effects that deception may have on research participants. The results of this study, contrary to statements made by Sieber (1982), revealed that the subjects who had participated in deception experiments reported enjoying the experiment more, felt that they had received more educational benefit from the experiment, and perceived their participation in the

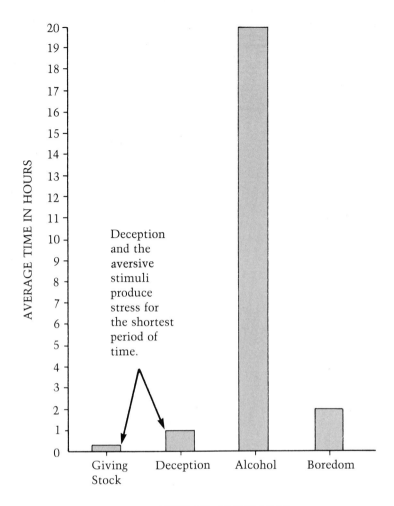

Deception
and the
aversive
stimuli
produce
stress for
the shortest
period of
time.

Figure 10.2 *Average length of distress for four categories of complaints.*
(Based on data from Pihl, R. O., Zacchia, C., and Zeichner, A. Follow-up
analysis of the use of deception and aversive contingencies in psychological
experiments. *Psychological Reports*, 1981, 48, 927–930.)

research as being more satisfactory than did other subjects. Not only
did Smith and Richardson not find support for the notion that deception is harmful—they provided data suggesting that deception may be
advantageous.

The results obtained by Pihl et al. and Smith and Richardson are
contrary to nearly all the assumptions made about deception in psycho-

logical research. However, a case could be made for the fact that the detrimental effects of deception depend on the type of study being conducted, and the study conducted by Smith and Richardson averaged the responses of subjects who had participated in many different types of studies. Such an argument might be valid if Pihl et al. had also averaged across many deception studies, but they did not. Also, Gerdes (1979) had subjects participate in several different experiments in which the type and the degree of deception were varied. This study did not show any differences in subjects' reactions to the deception, but it did indicate that subjects did not mind being misled and were not annoyed by having details of the experiment withheld. Thus the evidence shows that deception is not necessarily the harmful component many individuals assume it to be. This does not mean that the potential harmful effects of deception can be forgotten, though. One of the primary modes used to eliminate any harmful effects of deception is debriefing, or a postexperimental interview with the subject, in which the components of the experiment are explained. All of the studies that investigated the impact of deception incorporated a debriefing procedure, and if such a procedure does in fact eliminate any harmful effects of deception, this may explain the positive findings of these experiments.

In his reply to Baumrind's (1964) criticism of his earlier (Milgram, 1963) study, which investigated the extent to which subjects would obey instructions to inflict extreme pain on confederates, Milgram (1964) reported that, upon extensive debriefing, only 1.3 percent of his subjects reported any negative feelings about their experiences within the experiment. Such evidence would indicate that the debriefing was probably effective in eliminating the extreme anguish that these subjects apparently experienced.

Ring, Wallston, and Corey (1970) lent considerable support to Milgram's 1964 findings. In their quasi-replication of Milgram's 1963 experiment, they found that only 4 percent of the subjects who had been debriefed indicated they regretted having participated in the experiment, and only 4 percent indicated that the experiment should not be permitted to continue. On the other hand, about 50 percent of the subjects who had not been debriefed responded in this manner. Berscheid et al. (1973) found similar ameliorative effects of debriefing on consent-related responses. Holmes (1973) and Holmes and Bennett (1974) took an even more convincing approach and demonstrated that debriefing reduced the arousal produced in a stress-producing experiment (expected electric shock) to the prearousal level, as assessed by both physiological and self-report measures.

Smith and Richardson (1983) asserted that their deceived subjects received better debriefings than did their nondeceived subjects and that this more effective debriefing may have been the factor that caused the deceived subjects to have more positive responses than the non-deceived subjects.

This suggests that debriefing is quite effective in eliminating the stress produced by the experimental treatment condition. However, Holmes (1976a,b) has appropriately pointed out that there are two goals of debriefing and both must be met for debriefing to be maximally effective. These two goals are dehoaxing and desensitizing. **Dehoaxing** refers to debriefing the subjects about any deception that may have been used by the experimenter. In the dehoaxing process, the problem is one of convincing the subject that the fradulent information given was, in fact, fraudulent. **Desensitizing** refers to debriefing the subjects about their behavior. If the experiment has made subjects aware that they have some undesirable features (e.g., that they could and would inflict harm on others), then the debriefing procedure should attempt to help the subjects deal with this new information. This is typically done by suggesting that the undesirable behavior was caused by some situational variable rather than by some dispositional characteristic of the subject. Another tactic used by experimenters is to point out that the subjects' behavior was not abnormal or extreme. The big question is whether or not such tactics are effective in desensitizing or dehoaxing the subjects. In Holmes's (1976a,b) review of the literature relating to these two techniques, he concluded that they were effective. However, this only means that effective debriefing is *possible*. These results hold *only* if the debriefing is carried out properly. A sloppy or improperly prepared debriefing session may very well have a different effect.

Dehoaxing
Debriefing the participants about any deception that was used in the experiment

Desensitizing
Eliminating any undesirable influence that the experiment may have had on the subject

There is one more point that needs to be made regarding debriefing. Perhaps debriefing should not be universally applied in all experiments. Aronson and Carlsmith (1968) and Campbell (1969) have discussed the potentially painful effects that debriefing can have if the subject learns of his or her own gullibility, cruelty, or bias. It is for this reason that Campbell (1969a) suggested that debriefing be eliminated when the experimental treatment condition falls within the subject's range of ordinary experiences. This recommendation has also been supported by survey data collected by Rugg (1975).

The results of the studies presented so far have indicated that deception seems to have a more negative effect on researchers than it does on the participants. Sullivan and Deiker (1973), Rugg (1975), and Collins, Kuhn, and King (1979) have all investigated this question and found that, of the individuals surveyed, the participants were much more lenient in their perceptions of the ethical issues of human research than were the researchers. Rugg (1975) extended this survey to include additional significant groups, such as ethics committee members and law professors, and found these individuals without exception to be much stricter in their interpretation of the ethics of human research than were the participants (college students). It appears that individuals conducting human research constitute a strict self-regulating force that is sensitive to the rights and welfare of their research participants. Wilson and Donnerstein (1976) do, however, make the point that the participants' attitudes toward a given research procedure should be considered, since they found that some procedures did elicit a negative reaction from a substantial minority of the individuals surveyed.

Coercion and Freedom to Decline Participation

Principle F of the code of ethics is quite explicit in ensuring freedom from coercion to participate in psychological experiments. There is rather widespread use of "subject pools" consisting of all students enrolled in certain courses (e.g., an introductory psychology course). Concern over the coercive nature of this influence led the American Psychological Association (1982) to issue its set of eight guidelines to follow in the use of subject pools. However, given the evidence regarding the apparent positive influence of deception experiments, one must wonder whether the research participants who are exposed to the potentially coercive measures really perceive the measures to be that negative and whether this coercion harms the participants in any way. Leak (1981) investigated subjects' reactions to their research experience after being induced to participate in research by the offer of extra credit points. Leak found that the students were divided on their perception of the coercive nature of the means used for attaining participation. About half of the students thought the means were coercive, and half did not; however, all students overwhelmingly viewed the research participation as positive. Overall, the subjects viewed the research experience as being worthwhile, as contributing to their knowledge and interest in psychology, and as having scientific merit. Also, somewhat surprisingly, the students did not resent or object to being offered the extra credit for participation, even though about 50 percent of them considered it to be coercive. Leak's results, then, indicate that most students do not view the subject pool negatively. Britton (1979) reached the same conclusion. He found that students evaluated their experience as a research participant very favorably and that only 4 percent acknowledged experiencing any discomfort from the experience. Such evidence should not be taken to suggest that concern for the coercive influence surrounding the subject pool should be diminished but rather should be used as evidence that the current procedures must be operating effectively.

In addition to the issue of coercion, Principle F discusses the necessity of ensuring that individuals always feel free to decline to participate in or withdraw from the research at any time. This principle seems

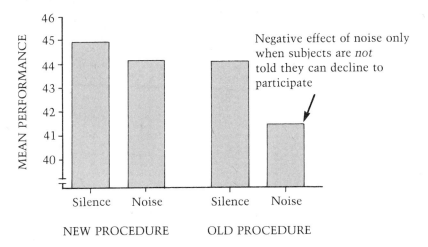

Figure 10.3 *Accuracy of performance of subjects during silence or environmental noise conditions after being instructed or not instructed that they can decline to participate.*
(Based on data from Gardner, G. T. Effects of federal human subjects regulations on data obtained in environmental stressor research. *Journal of Personality and Social Psychology*, 1978, 36, 628–634.)

quite reasonable and relatively innocuous. However, Gardner (1978) has asserted that such a perception, even though ethically required, can influence the outcome of some studies. The subtle influence of telling subjects that they were free to discontinue participation was discovered quite accidentally. Gardner had been experimenting on the detrimental impact of environmental noise. Prior to the incorporation of a statement informing potential subjects that they could decline to participate without penalty, he always found that environmental noise produced a negative after-effect. However, after he incorporated this statement, he could not produce the effect. In order to verify that a statement regarding freedom to withdraw was the factor causing the elimination of the negative after-effect of environmental noise, Gardner replicated the experiment, telling subjects in one group that they could decline to participate at any time without penalty and not giving such instructions to those in another group. As Figure 10.3 illustrates, the environmental noise caused a decline in performance under the old procedures, but not under the new procedures. This study indicates the very subtle effects that ethical principles can have and suggests that such effects should be considered when prior results are not replicated and the only difference in procedure is the incorporation of the ethical principles.

Ethics of Animal Research

Considerable attention has been focused on the ethics of human research. It is not infrequent that a project is judged to be too dangerous
to conduct on humans for one reason or another. Where does this leave
the investigator? In such cases, rather than scrapping the research
project, the investigator redesigns the study to use infrahumans as
research subjects. This does not imply that there are no ethics involved
in the use of infrahumans as subjects; rather, it means that some types
of research that are not permissible with humans are permissible with
infrahumans.

The ethical issues surrounding the use of infrahumans are primarily
concerned with the proper care and treatment of the animals. Various
groups such as the People for the Ethical Treatment of Animals, the
Animal Rights Coalition, and the Society Against Vivisection are currently protesting the use of animals in research. The main thrust of
their argument is that animals have rights and do not belong in labs.
They assume that animal research says little about human behavior.
Regardless of the validity of their position, the proponents of animal
rights are definitely organized and will have an impact on the ethics of
animal research. The American Psychological Association has issued
the following set of principles for the care and use of animals:

1. The acquisition, care, use, and disposal of all animals shall be
in compliance with current federal, state or provincial, and local laws
and regulations.

2. A scientist trained in research methods and experienced in
the care of laboratory animals shall closely supervise all procedures
involving animals and be responsible for insuring appropriate consideration of their comfort, health, and humane treatment.

3. Scientists shall insure that all individuals using animals under
their supervision have received explicit instruction in experimental
methods and in the care, maintenance, and handling of the species
being used. Responsibilities and activities of individuals shall be consistent with their respective competencies.

4. Scientists shall make every effort to minimize discomfort,
illness, and pain to the animals. A procedure subjecting animals to
pain, stress, or privation shall be used only when an alternative
procedure is unavailable and the goal is justified by its prospective
scientific, educational, or applied value. Surgical procedures shall be
performed under appropriate anesthesia; techniques to avoid infec-
tion and minimize pain must be followed during and after surgery.
Euthanasia shall be prompt and humane.

5. Investigators are strongly urged to consult with the Committee on Animal Research and Experimentation at any stage preparatory to or during a research project for advice about the appropri-

ateness of research procedures or ethical issues related to experiments involving animals. Concerned individuals with any questions concerning adherence to the Principles should consult with the committee.

6. Apparent violations of these Principles shall be reported immediately to the facility supervisor whose signature appears below:

Name: _____

Position: _____   Phone: _____

If a satisfactory resolution is not achieved, a report should be made to the responsible institution authority designated below:

Name: _____

Position: _____   Phone: _____

Unresolved allegations of serious or repeated violations should be referred to the APA Committee on Animal Research and Experimentation.

7. These Principles shall be posted in every Laboratory, teaching facility, and applied setting where animals are being used. All persons in each laboratory, classroom, or applied facility shall indicate by signature and date on the attached sheet that they have read these Principles.

By signing and dating this sheet, I signify that I have read the Principles for the care and use of animals of the American Psychological Association and affirm that my use of animals in research, teaching, and practical applications will conform with them.

Name	Date	Name	Date
_____	____	_____	____
_____	____	_____	____
_____	____	_____	____
_____	____	_____	____

Summary

A great deal of psychological research requires the use of humans as subjects. These individuals have certain rights, such as the right to privacy, that must be violated if we are to attempt to attain answers to many significant questions. This naturally imposes a dilemma on the researcher as to whether to conduct the research and violate the rights of the research participant or abandon the research project. Increased attention to ethical concerns has resulted in the development of a set of ethical principles published by the American Psychological Association. This code of ethics consists of ten principles to be followed by research psychologists in the conduct of their research.

A great deal of time, effort, and thought went into the APA code of ethics. Since the adoption of the 1973 set of principles, some studies have been conducted to assess the impact these principles may have. The 1982 revised ethical principles seem to have incorporated the results of these studies. However, there are still issues that need to be discussed, including the effects of deception, the coercion placed on students to participate, and the freedom to withdraw.

A number of individuals have suggested alternatives to deception, such as role playing. Research studies, however, have shown that such alternatives are poor substitutes; therefore, deception will remain a part of numerous psychological studies and its potential effects must be considered. It is generally assumed that deception creates stress and that this stress or invasion of privacy is ethically objectionable and perhaps harmful to the subjects. Yet research indicates that participants do not view deception as detrimental and that those who have been involved in deception studies view their research experience as more valuable than do those who have not. This phenomenon may be due to the increased attention given in deception studies to debriefing, which seems to be effective in eliminating the negative components of deception as well as any stress that may have occurred.

Investigators also are quite concerned about coercing students to become research participants. Experiments investigating the perceptions of research participants drawn from a subject pool reveal that they generally view their research experience quite positively.

While there does not seem to be a negative effect resulting from deception or from the use of subject pools, it has been demonstrated that informing subjects that they are free to withdraw at any time without penalty can influence the outcome of some experiments.

11

Data Collection and Hypotheses Testing

Chapter Overview

Once the researcher has specified the concrete operations that will represent the independent and dependent variables, the variables to be controlled, and the control techniques to be used and has given due consideration to the ethics of the study, there are still many decisions that must be made prior to beginning actual data collection. And, once data collection has been completed, there are various steps that must be taken in order to reach a decision regarding the outcome of the study. These decisions and steps will be discussed in this chapter. As you read

through it, you should answer the following questions:

1. What decisions must be made after the research study has been designed but before data collection begins?

2. Why is it necessary to conduct a pilot study prior to data collection?

3. What procedure must be initiated immediately following data collection?

4. What type of errors can be made when one is making a decision regarding the outcome of the research study?

Introduction

Once a study has been designed, the researcher may feel as though most of the decisions required for completion of the experiment have been made. However, when the study is implemented as designed, it immediately becomes apparent that a great deal of decision making lies ahead. For example, the researcher must determine what types of subjects are to be used in the study, where they are to be obtained, and how many should be used. The researcher must decide if human subjects are to be used and, if they are, what instructions should be given. As you can see, the design only provides the framework of the study. Once established, this outline must be implemented. This chapter is oriented toward answering the questions that may arise when one is implementing a research design. These questions will, of necessity, be answered in a general way, since each study has its own unique characteristics, but this discussion should provide a basic framework that will assist you in conducting your own research study.

Subjects

Psychologists investigate the behavior of organisms, and there are a wealth of organisms that can potentially serve as subjects. What determines which organism will be used in a given study? In some cases, the question asked dictates the type of organism used. If, for example, a study is to investigate imprinting ability, then one must select a species, such as ducks, that demonstrates this ability. However, the primary determining factor in most studies is precedent; most investigators use subjects that have been used in previous studies. As Sidowski and Lockard (1966, pp. 7–8) state:

> Most of the common laboratory animals are mammals; man, several species of monkey, numerous rodents, a few carnivores, and one cetacean, the porpoise. Other than mammals, teleost fishes and one species of bird, the pigeon, have mainly represented the other classes of chordates; amphibians and reptiles have been rare. The 21 phyla below the chordates have been underrepresented. . . .[1]

Other than man, precedent has established the albino variant of the brown rat as the standard laboratory research animal. The concentrated use of the albino rate in infrahuman research has not gone without criticism. Beach (1950) and Lockard (1968) have eloquently criticized the fact that psychologists have focused too much attention on the use of the albino rat as a research animal. As Lockard has argued, rather than using precedent as the primary guide for selecting a particular organism as a subject, one should look at the research problem and select the type of animal that is best for its study.

Once a decision has been made regarding the type of organism to be used, the next questions are where to get the subjects and how many subjects to use. Researchers who use rats typically select from one of three strains: the Long-Evans hooded, the Sprague-Dawley albino, and the Wistar albino. The researcher must decide on the strain, sex, age, and supplier of the albino rats, since each of these variables can influence the results of the study (see Sidowski and Lockard, 1966).

---

[1] From *Experimental methods and instrumentation in psychology*, by Sidowski and Lockard. Copyright © 1966 by McGraw-Hill, Inc. Used with permission of McGraw-Hill Book Co.

Once the albino rats have been selected, ordered, and received, they must be maintained in the animal laboratory, often by the experimenter. Few beginning researchers have the knowledge required to maintain the animals properly. For this reason, a number of publications are available through several sources to acquaint the researcher with the appropriate guidelines. The Institute of Laboratory Animal Resources, National Academy of Sciences–National Research Council, 2101 Constitution Avenue, N.W., Washington, D.C., publishes several manuals on the care of laboratory animals. The U.S. Department of Health, Education, and Welfare, Public Health Service, National Institutes of Health has a manual titled *Care and use of laboratory animals,* which is available from the U.S. Government Printing Office, Washington, D.C., 20402. Either of these sources will provide the necessary information on maintenance.

Researchers selecting humans as their subjects experience varying degrees of ease in finding participants. In most university settings, the psychology department has a subject pool consisting of introductory psychology students (see Chapter 10). These students are motivated to participate in a research study because it is a requirement of the course, or they are offered an improved grade, or they are offered this activity as an alternative to some other requirement such as writing a term paper. Disregarding the ethical issue of such coerced participation and the possible biasing factors that it may produce (e.g., Cox and Sipprelle, 1971), subject pools provide a readily available supply of subjects for the researcher. However, for many types of research studies, introductory psychology students are not appropriate. A child psychologist wishing to study kindergarten children usually will try to solicit the cooperation of a local kindergarten. In a similar manner, to investigate incarcerated criminals, one must seek the cooperation of prison officials as well as the criminals.

When one has to seek subjects from sources other than a departmental subject pool, a new set of problems arises because many individuals other than the subject become involved. Assume that a researcher is going to conduct a study using kindergarten children. The first task is to find a kindergarten that will allow her or him to collect the data needed for the study. In soliciting the cooperation of the individual in charge, the researcher has to be as tactful and diplomatic as possible because many people are not receptive to psychological research. If the person in charge agrees to allow the researcher to collect that data, the next task is to obtain the parents' permission to allow their children to participate. This frequently involves having parents sign permission slips that explain the nature of the research and the tasks required of their children. Where an agency is involved, such as an institution for mentally retarded persons, one might be required to submit a research proposal for their research committee to review.

After identifying the subject population, the researcher must select individual subjects from that group. Ideally, this should be done randomly. In a study investigating kindergarten children, a sample should be randomly selected from the population of kindergarten children. However, this is often impractical—not only in terms of cost and time but also in terms of the availability of the subjects. Not all kindergartens or parents will allow their children to participate in a psychological study. Therefore, human subjects are generally selected on the basis of convenience and availability. The kindergarten children used in a study are those who live closest to the university and who cooperate with the investigator.

Because of this restriction in subject selection, the researcher may have a built-in bias in the data. For example, the children whose parents allow them to participate may perform differently than would children whose parents restrict their participation. Rosenthal and Rosnow (1975) have summarized research exposing the differences in the responses of volunteer and nonvolunteer subjects. The next best solution if random selection is not possible is to assign subjects randomly to treatment conditions. In this way, the investigator is at least assured that no systematic bias exists among the various groups of available subjects. Because of the inability to select subjects randomly, the investigator *must* report the nature of subject selection and assignment, in addition to the characteristics of the subjects, to enable other investigators to replicate the experiment and assess the comparability of the results.

It is similarly inappropriate to assume that any sample of albino rats is representative of the population of all rats. As Sidowski and Lockard (1966, pp. 8–9) point out,

> Freshly received animals are not uniform products from an automatic production line, nor are they a random sample from the world's population of rats. Animal suppliers differ greatly in such environmental practices as the ambient temperature, light-dark cycle, type of food, cage size and animal density, and the physical arrangements of food and water devices. . . . To further complicate the picture, two shipments from the same firm may not be equivalent. Most companies use tiers of cages, with some high and some almost on the floor. The high animals may be in as much as ten times the illumination as the low ones because of ceiling and light fixtures. Vertical gradients of temperature are also common, with the high animal's warmer. . . . Since shipments of animals tend to be drawn by the supplier from the same cage, a given shipment is not a random sample but rather an overly homogeneous subset not representative of the range of conditions within the colony.[2]

[2] From *Experimental methods and instrumentation in psychology*, by Sidowski and Lockard. Copyright © 1966 by McGraw-Hill, Inc. Used with permission of McGraw-Hill Book Co.

Sample Size

After you have decided which type of organisms will be used in the research study and have obtained access to a sample of such subjects, you must determine how many subjects are needed to adequately test the hypothesis. This decision must be based on a variety of issues, such as the design of the study and the variability of the data. The relationship between the design of the study and sample size can be seen rather clearly by contrasting a single-subject and a multisubject design. Obviously, a single-subject design requires a sample size of one, so sample size is not an issue. However, the sample size is important in multisubject designs because the number of subjects used can theoretically vary from two to infinity. We usually want more than two subjects, but it is impractical and unnecessary to use too many subjects. Unfortunately, there are few guidelines to use in deciding how large the sample size must be. The primary guide used by most researchers is precedent, which may be just as inappropriate in sample size selection as in subject selection (Beach, 1950; Lockard, 1968). The issue surrounding sample size in multisubject designs really boils down to the number of subjects needed in order to detect an effect caused by the independent variable, if such an effect really exists. As the number of subjects within a study increases, the ability of our statistical tests to detect a difference increases: i.e., the power of the statistical test increases. This is why some investigators, when asked how many subjects should be used, state that the larger the sample size the better the study.

There are only two sources I am aware of that provide some specific indication of the number of subjects needed in a multisubject research study. The National Education Association (NEA) Research Division (Small sample techniques, 1960) has developed a formula that allows one to determine the sample size needed for a sample to be representative of a given population. Based on this formula, Krejcie and Morgan (1970) have computed the sample size required for populations of up to 1,000,000 when the .05 confidence level is desired. The results of these calculations appear in Figure 11.1. Several difficulties arise, however, when one attempts to use these results when conducting an experimental study. The most serious is that it is seldom possible or practical to select subjects randomly from a given population. While this is a procedural difficulty and not one inherent in the formula, it still leaves us with the problem of determining sample size for a study that cannot randomly select from the population.

Cowles (1974) is rather definitive in his suggestion as to the required number of subjects. Based on such considerations as the power of the statistical test, the significance level (.05), and the strength of the relationship between the independent and dependent variables, Cowles suggests that 35 subjects should be used for most preliminary

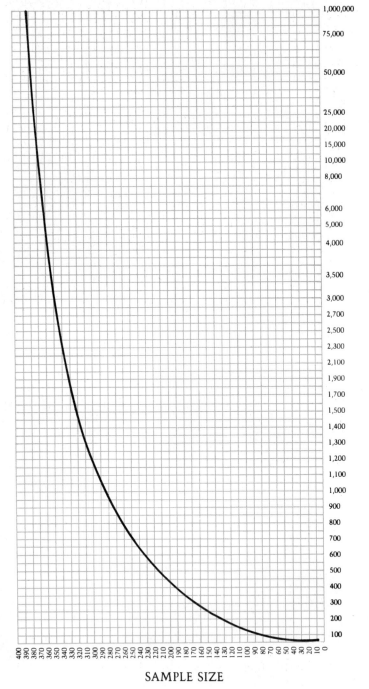

Figure 11.1 *Relationship between sample size and total population.* (From Krejcie, R. V., and Morgan, D. W. Determining sample size for research activities. *Educational and Psychological Measurement,* 1970, 30, p. 609.

Copyright 1970 by Frederick Kuder. Reprinted by permission.)

studies. If one is using an analysis of variance design with several levels of the independent variable, then 15 subjects per cell is recommended. This is just one approach, however. Others such as Cox (1958) have suggested statistical procedures for identifying the number of subjects needed for a given experiment.

Apparatus

In addition to securing subjects, the investigator must select the apparatus to be used for the presentation of the independent variable and/or for the measurement of the dependent variable. As McGuigan (1983) states, apparatus facilitates the administration of the independent variable and assists in recording the dependent variable. For example, if the independent variable consists of presenting words on a screen for different periods of time, the experimenter could try to manually control how long the words were presented. However, it is virtually impossible for a human to consistently present words for a very specific duration of time; thus we use a tachistoscope. Similarly, if the dependent variable is the recorded heart rate, we could use a stethoscope and count the number of times per minute a subject's heart beats. It is much more accurate and far simpler, however, to use an electronic means for measuring this kind of dependent variable.

Exhibit 11.1 illustrates that an apparatus can also serve as a source of restraint that enables the investigator to systematically present the independent variable and to measure the dependent variable.

Since the apparatus for a given study can serve a variety of purposes, the investigator must consider the particular study being conducted and determine the type of apparatus that is most appropriate. There is a journal, *Behavioral Research Methods and Instrumentation*, devoted specifically to apparatus and instrumentation. If you have difficulty in identifying an instrument that will perform a certain function, a review of the contents of this journal and of prior research conducted in the area of your investigation will probably be of assistance.

Instructions

The investigator conducting an experiment using human subjects must prepare a set of instructions. This brings up such questions as "What should be included in the instructions?" and "How should they be presented?" Sidowski and Lockard (1966) state that instructions serve

Exhibit 11.1 *Apparatus Used for Restraining Cats in Aversive Conditioning Studies*

Wolfe and Soltysik (1981) have described a method of restraining cats that allows leg flexion, walking, and running; maintains the animal in its natural position; and enables the investigator to record physiological responses. This restraint apparatus, depicted in the accompanying photograph, consists of a metal frame with a movable canvas treadmill floor, and a head restraint mechanism. The cat's head is placed in the head restraint, which is held in position by means of two rods. The body of the cat is supported and positioned in the center of the frame by means of a canvas harness. Thus the apparatus restrains a cat and at the same time allows for considerable freedom of movement and recording of neurophysiological, physiological, and behavioral data.

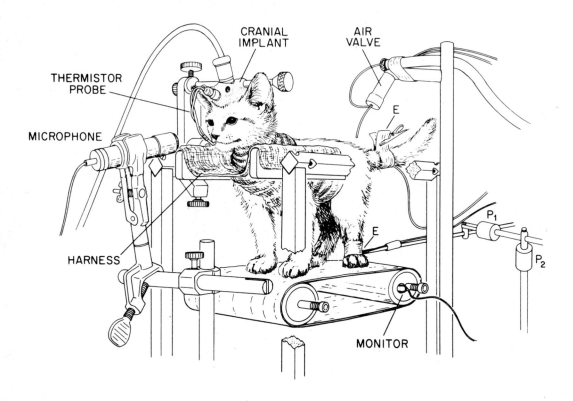

(From Soltysik, S. S.; Wolfe, G. E.; Nicholas, T.; Wilson, W. J.; and Garcia-Sanchez, J. L. Blocking of inhibitory conditioning within a serial conditioned stimulus-conditioned inhibitor compound: Maintenance of acquired behavior without an unconditioned stimulus. *Learning and Motivation*, 1983, *14*, 1-29.)

the purposes of defining the task, directing attention, developing a set, and perhaps motivating the subject. Instructions are quite important, and considerable care must be exercised in their formulation. They must include a clear description of the purpose, or disguised purpose, and the task that the subjects are to perform. Certain types of instructions may be ineffectual in producing the desired outcome. Instructions requesting that the subjects "pay attention," "relax," or "ignore distractions" are probably ineffective because subjects are constrained by other factors that limit their ability to adhere to the commands. Instructions sometimes request that the subjects perform several operations at the same time. If this is not possible, then they will choose one of the possible operations to perform and the experimenter will not know which choice was made. For example, if the subjects receive the instruction to work quickly and accurately, they may concentrate on accuracy at the expense of speed, since both speed and accuracy cannot be accomplished simultaneously. This means that the experimenter will not know which component of the instructions contributed most to the dependent variable measure. Similarly, vague instructions (e.g., instructions telling the subjects to imagine, guess, or visualize something) allow the subjects to place their own interpretations on the task. It is best to avoid such instructions whenever possible.

As you can see, instructions should be clear, unambiguous, and specific, but at the same time they should not be too complex because of the possibility of a memory overload (Sutcliffe, 1972). Beginning researchers often think that directions should be extremely terse and succinct. While this style is good for writing the research report, in writing instructions one runs the risk of the subjects' not grasping important points. Instructions should be very simple, down to earth, and at times even redundant. This will provide added assurance that the subjects understand all of the instructions.

Scheduling of Subjects

Scheduling of subjects' participation in the experiment involves consideration not only of when the researcher has time available but also of the type of subjects being used. With rats, for example, there is the problem of the lighting cycle. As Sidowski and Lockard (1966, p. 10) have noted:

> Rats and other nocturnal animals are most active in the dark phase of the lighting cycle and do most of their eating and drinking then. From the animal's point of view, the light portion of the day is for sleeping and inactivity but may be interrupted by an experimenter who requires him to run or bar-press for food. It is unfortunate that

the amount of lighting and the timing of the cycle are usually arranged for the benefit of the caretaker and not the animals or the experimenter.[3]

This problem is most commonly handled by leaving the light on in the animal laboratory 24 hours a day. In this way, the animals will not form a schedule based on the light/dark phase of the lighting cycle, and thus the lighting cycle should not represent a source of confounding.

When one is scheduling human subjects, there is a whole different set of issues to consider. First, one has to schedule the experiment at a time when the experimenter and the subjects are all available. Some subjects will undoubtedly fail to show up at that time, so it is often advisable to allow for limited rescheduling. Some subjects who do not show up at the designated time will not want to be rescheduled, which creates a problem with the randomization control technique. In such instances, the researcher may want to use replacement subjects, in which case more subjects must be selected than the experiment calls for and then replacement subjects must be scheduled to substitute for those who drop out.

Procedure

After the scheduling of subjects has been completed, you must specify the procedure to be used in data collection. The events to take place in the experiment must be arranged so that they flow smoothly. Awareness of what is to take place is not sufficient; the investigator must carefully think through the whole experiment and specify the sequence in which each activity is to take place, laying down the exact procedure to be followed during data collection. For animal research, this means not only specifying the conditions of the laboratory environment and how the animals are going to be handled in the laboratory, but also specifying how they are to be maintained in their maintenance quarters and how they are to be transferred to the laboratory. These are very important considerations, since such variables can influence the subjects' behavior in the laboratory. For an extended discussion of transient and environmental factors that can influence animals' behavior, see Sidowski and Lockard (1966, pp. 10–14).

With human subjects, the researcher must specify what the subjects are to do, how they are to be greeted, and the type of nonverbal behavior (e.g., looking at the subject, smiling, tone of voice in reading instructions, etc.) as well as verbal behavior in which the experimenter is to engage. Friedman (1967) has shown the wide variety of ways in

[3] From *Experimental methods and instrumentation in psychology,* by Sidowski and Lockard. Copyright © 1966 by McGraw-Hill, Inc. Used with permission of McGraw-Hill Book Co.

which the same experimenter may react to different subjects, both verbally and nonverbally. Every attempt should be made to eliminate these variations.

Once each of the above phases has been specified, the investigator must then conduct a pilot study. A **pilot study** represents a run-through of the experiment with a small number of subjects. It is actually a pretest of the experiment and should be conducted as conscientiously as if data were actually being collected. The pilot study can provide a great deal of information. If the instructions are not clear, this will show up either in the debriefing session or by virtue of the fact that the subjects do not know what to do after the instructions have been read.

Pilot study
An experiment that is conducted on a few subjects prior to the actual collection of data

The pilot study can also indicate whether or not the independent variable manipulation produced the intended effect. Debriefing can help to determine if fear, surprise, or some other state was actually generated. If none of the pilot subjects report the particular emotion under study, then their help can be solicited in assessing why it was not generated, after which changes can be made until the intended state is induced. In a similar manner, the sensitivity of the dependent variable can be checked. Pretesting may suggest that the dependent variable is too crude to reflect the effect of the manipulation and that a change in a certain direction would make it more appropriate.

The pilot study also gives the researcher experience with the procedure. The first time the experimenter runs a subject, he or she is not yet wholly familiar with the sequence and therefore probably does not make a smooth transition from one part of the study to another. With practice, one develops a fluency in carrying out these steps, which is necessary if constancy is to be maintained in the study. Also, when running pilot subjects, the experimenter tests the procedure. Too much time may be allowed for certain parts and not enough for others, the deception (if used) may be inadequate, etc. If so, the experimenter identifies problems *before* any data are collected, and the procedure can be altered at this time.

There are many subtle factors that can influence the experiment, and the pilot phase is the time to identify them. Pilot testing involves checking all parts of the experiment to determine if they are working appropriately. If a malfunction is isolated, it can be corrected without any damage resulting. If a malfunction is not spotted until after the data have been collected, it *may* have had an influence on the results of the study.

Data Collection

Once you have laid out the procedure, tested the various phases of the experimental procedure with the pilot study, and eliminated the bugs, you are ready to run subjects and collect data. The primary rule to follow in this phase of the experiment is to adhere as closely as possible to the procedure that has been laid out. A great deal of work has gone into developing this procedure, and if it is not followed exactly, you run the risk of introducing contaminants into the experiment. If this should happen, you will not have the well-controlled study you worked so hard to develop, and you may not attain an answer to your research question.

Debriefing, or Postexperimental Interview

Once the data have been collected, there is the tendency to think that the job has been completed and the only remaining requirement (other than data analysis) is to thank the subjects for their participation and send them on their way. However, the experiment does not—or should not—end with the completion of data collection. In most studies, following data collection, there should be a **postexperimental interview** with the subjects which allows them to comment freely on any part of the experiment. This interview is very important for several reasons. In general, the interview can provide information regarding the subjects' thinking or strategies used during the experiment, which can help explain their behavior. Orne (1962) used this interview to assess why subjects would persist at a boring, repetitive task for hours. Martin, in the course of conducting learning studies with extremely bright subjects, found that these subjects could learn a list of nonsense syllables in one trial.[4] Upon seeing such a performance, he essentially asked them, "How did you do that?" They relayed a specific strategy for having accomplished this task, which led to another study (Martin, Boersma, and Cox, 1965) investigating strategies of learning.

Tesch (1977) has identified three specific functions of debriefing. First, debriefings have an ethical function. In many studies, research participants are deceived about the true purpose of an experiment. Ethics dictate that one must undo such deceptions, and the debriefing session is the place to accomplish this. Other experiments generate some negative affect in the subjects or in some other way create physical (e.g., electric shock) or emotional (e.g., lowered self-esteem) stress. The researcher must attempt to return the subjects to their preexperimental state by eliminating any stress that the experiment has generated. Second, debriefings have an educational function. The typical rationale used to justify requiring participation of introductory psy-

Postexperimental interview
An interview with the subject following completion of the experiment in which all aspects of the experiment are explained and the subject is allowed to comment on the study

---

[4]C. J. Martin, 1975: personal communication.

chology students in experiments is that they learn something about psychology and about psychological research. The third function of debriefing is methodological. Debriefings are frequently used to provide evidence regarding the effectiveness of the independent variable manipulation or of the deception. They are also used to probe the extent and accuracy of subjects' suspicions as well as to give the experimenter an opportunity to convince the subjects not to reveal the experiment to others.

Sieber (1983) has added a fourth function. She states that subjects should, from their participation in the study, receive a sense of satisfaction from the knowledge that they have contributed to science and to society. This perceived satisfaction is to be derived from the debriefing procedure.

Given these functions of debriefing, how does one proceed? Two approaches have been used. Some investigators have used a questionnaire approach, in which subjects are handed a postexperimental survey form to complete. Others have used a face-to-face interview, which seems to be the best approach because it is not as restrictive as the questionnaire.

If you want to probe for any suspicions that the subjects may have had about the experiment, this is the first order of business. Aronson and Carlsmith (1968) believe that one should begin by asking the subjects if they have any questions. If so, the questions should be answered as completely and truthfully as possible. If not, the experimenter should ask the subjects if all phases of the experiment—both the procedure and the purpose—were clear. Next, depending on the study being conducted, it may be appropriate to ask a subject to "comment on how the experiment struck him, why he responded as he did, how he felt at the time, etc. Then he should be asked specifically whether there was any aspect of the procedure that he found odd, confusing, or disturbing" (p. 71).[5]

If the experiment contained a deception and the subjects suspected that it did, they are almost certain to have revealed this fact by this time. If no suspicions have been revealed, the researcher can ask the subjects if they thought there was more to the experiment than was immediately apparent. Such a question cues the subjects that there must have been. Most subjects will therefore say "yes," so this should be followed with a question about what the subjects thought was involved and how this may have affected their behavior. Such questioning will give the investigator additional insight into whether or not the subjects had the experiment figured out and also will provide a

---

[5] Reprinted by special permission from Aronson and Carlsmith, "Experimentation in Social Psychology," *The handbook of social psychology,* Second Edition, Volume Two, 1968, edited by Lindzey and Aronson, Addison-Wesley, Reading, Mass., p. 71.

perfect point for the experimenter to lead into an explanation of the purpose of the study. The experimenter could continue "the debriefing process by saying something like this: 'You are on the right track, we *were* interested in some problems that we didn't discuss with you in advance. One of our major concerns in this study is . . .' " (Aronson and Carlsmith, 1968, p. 71).[6] The debriefing should then be continued in the manner suggested by Mills (1976). If the study involved deception, the reasons for the necessity of deception should be included. The purpose of the study should then be explained in detail, as well as the specific procedures for investigating the research question. This means explaining the independent and dependent variables and how they were manipulated and measured. As you can see, the debriefing requires explaining the total experiment to the subjects.

The last part of the debriefing session should be geared to convincing the subjects not to discuss any components of the experiment with others, for obvious reasons. This can be accomplished by asking the subjects not to describe the experiment to others until after the date of completion of the data collection, pointing out that communicating the results to others may invalidate the study. If the study were revealed prematurely, the experimenter would not know that the results were invalid and the subjects would probably not tell (Altemeyer, 1971), so the experimenter would be reporting inaccurate data to the scientific community. Aronson (1966) has found that we can have reasonable confidence in the fact that the subjects will not tell others, but Altemeyer (1971) has shown that if subjects do find out they will probably not tell the experimenter.

At this point you might wonder whether or not the preceding debriefing procedure accomplishes the functions it is supposed to accomplish. As you saw in Chapter 10, the ethical function seems to be accomplished quite well if these procedures are followed. Utility and completeness are lacking in the educational function. Most investigators seem to think, or rationalize, that the educational function is served if the subjects participate in the experiment and are told of its purpose and procedures during debriefing. Tesch (1977) believes that this function would be served better if the researcher also required the subject to write a laboratory experience report, which would relate the experimental experience to course material. However, data indicate that subjects perceive psychological experiments to be most deficient in the area of educational value, although they view debriefing in general to be quite effective (Smith and Richardson, 1983). It is possible that our psychological experiments are not as educational as might be

---

[6] Reprinted by special permission from Aronson and Carlsmith, "Experimentation in Social Psychology," *The handbook of social psychology,* Second Edition, Volume Two, 1968, edited by Lindzey and Aronson, Addison-Wesley, Reading, Mass., p. 71.

hoped, and even a good debriefing procedure cannot adequately enhance their educational value. The methodological function seems to be served quite well, since the validity of the experiment is often dependent on it. The investigator sometimes does extensive pilot study work to ensure such things as that the manipulation checks actually verify the manipulations.

Hypotheses Testing

Once you have collected the data, you are ready to analyze it statistically to obtain an answer to the research question and to determine if the stated hypothesis has been supported. You will recall from Chapter 2 that the scientific hypothesis is the predicted relationship among the variables being investigated, and the null hypothesis is a statement of no relationship among the variables being tested. Any statistical test represents a test of the null hypothesis. In order to obtain evidence for the existence of the scientific hypothesis one must reject the null hypothesis, for if you can reject the null hypothesis (that there is no relationship among the variables being investigated) then a relationship must exist among the variables. Thus support for the scientific hypothesis is obtained indirectly by rejecting the null hypothesis.

In order to determine if the data enable you to reject the null hypothesis, it is necessary to analyze the data statistically in the manner suggested by the study design. It may not be readily apparent why statistical analysis needs to be conducted. If you asked a naive person how you could determine if the experimental treatment condition had an effect on the subjects' performance, he or she would probably tell you to compare the performance of the experimental and the control groups. In other words, compute the mean performance score for each group and see if the experimental group's score was greater than (or less than) the control group's score. This would be sufficient to describe the performance of the two groups. But remember that you want to determine if the experimental treatment condition produced a real effect. It is possible that the difference between the two groups' mean scores could have occurred by chance. This is because no two subjects are alike, which means that the different subjects in the two groups would respond differently. It would be a rare occurrence to find two groups of subjects with the same mean performance score.

Knowing that there is variability in behavior and that some difference between the groups' performance is to be expected on this basis, how can you assess whether the observed difference in the experimental and control groups is real or just a chance difference due to the variability in subject performance? At this point, the beginning researcher may say that the necessary information could be attained by repeating the experiment with different subjects and seeing if the same results occurred again. This would give evidence of the reliability of the obtained findings. The more often the study was repeated with identical results, the more faith we would have in the fact that the experimental treatment produced the results and a real difference existed, because if the difference were chance, it should average out to zero over many replications of the experiment. Sometimes the experimental group's scores would be greater than the control group's scores; but, by the same token, sometimes the control group's scores would be greater than those of the experimental group. Therefore, a reliable finding would not exist, suggesting that a given control- versus treatment-group difference was the result of chance.

While it is possible to determine if the obtained difference between the experimental and control groups' scores is real or chance by repeating the study many times on different groups of subjects, this is not a very economical approach. Statistical tests enable us to accomplish the same thing by allowing us to estimate or infer what would have happened if we had followed the repetition procedure. Statistical procedures estimate the amount of difference that could be expected between the groups' scores by chance, and then they pit this against what was actually found. If the difference actually found is much greater than that which would be expected by chance, we say that the difference found is a real difference.

Is there a guideline that determines how large a difference must be to be considered real? This is a good question because only rarely can we be *absolutely* sure that the obtained difference is not due to chance. Even very large differences could occur by chance, though the probability of this happening would be very low. Figure 11.2 illustrates the distribution of mean differences that would be expected to occur by chance. Note that the tails of the distribution approach the baseline but never touch it. Therefore, a very large difference *could* occur by chance, which means, except in rare cases with a restricted and finite population, that we can never be completely sure that a difference is real and not due to chance. We can, however, determine the probability that a given difference is the result of chance. Between the dashed lines of Figure 11.2, we would find 95 percent of all chance difference scores; between the solid lines in Figure 11.2, we would find 99 percent of all chance difference scores. If the difference that we find in our experiment is so large that it falls on one of the two dashed lines, it could have occurred only 5 times in 100 by chance. In like manner, if our obtained difference is so large that it falls on one of the two solid lines, it could have occurred only 1 time in 100 by chance.

How certain do we have to be before we will say that the obtained difference between groups is real? The most common practice is to state

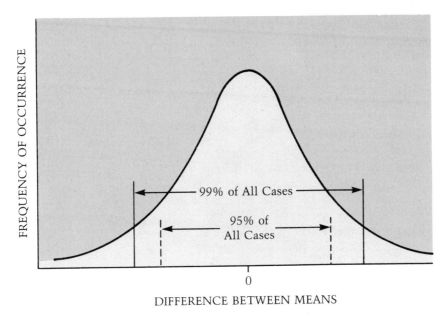

Figure 11.2 *Sample distribution of mean difference scores.*

a significance level that has to be reached. A **significance level** is a statement of the probability that an observed difference is a chance difference. The most often used significance levels are .05 and .01. If you decide, prior to calculating your statistical tests, that the .05 significance level is to be used, this means that you will accept as a real difference only one that is so large that it could have occurred by chance only 5 times in 100. If the .01 significance level is selected, than the difference can be expected to occur only 1 time in 100 by chance.

The above should give some appreciation of the necessity of performing statistical tests on the data. If the statistical tests reveal that a significant difference (one that has reached the specified significance level) exists between the scores of the various groups, then the scientific hypothesis is accepted as real. If the obtained difference does not reach the specified significance level, then the experimenter *fails* to reject the null hypothesis. The expression "fails to reject" is used because it is very difficult to obtain evidence supportive of a null or no-difference conclusion. At first glance, it seems that if the null hypothesis cannot be rejected, it should logically be accepted. To see why the null hypothesis cannot be accepted if the significance level is not attained, consider the following experiment. Nation et al. (1983) studied the effects of chronic cobalt exposure on the behavior of adult rats. The experimental group of rats was fed laboratory chow laced with

Significance level
The probability that the difference between the mean scores of the experimental and control groups is due to chance

cobalt chloride, and their lever-pressing speed was compared with that of a control group of rats who were fed standard laboratory chow. The results of one component of this study revealed that there was not a significant difference between lever-pressing responses of the control and experimental groups at the .05 significance level. Consequently, the null hypothesis could not be rejected. However, while the experimental and control groups did not differ in lever-pressing response rates at the .05 level, a difference in response rate did exist. In order to accept the null hypothesis, we have to be able to state that the observed variance represents a chance difference, and to assume that any observed difference is entirely chance is very hazardous. In the Nation et al. experiment, it is possible that the cobalt did have an effect but that the effect was too weak to be detected at the .05 significance level. In such a situation, some of the observed difference in response would be due to the treatment condition, which means that it would be inappropriate to accept a no-difference or null conclusion. Thus the expression "fails to reject" is used in place of "accept."

While it is logically impossible to accept the null hypothesis of no-difference, "practical concerns demand that we sometimes have to provisionally act as though the null hypothesis were true" (Cook et al., 1979). As Greenwald (1975) has pointed out, there is a pervasive anti-null-hypothesis prejudice, which can lead to a variety of behavioral symptoms, such as "continuing research on a problem when results have been close to rejection of the null hypothesis ('near significant'), while abandoning the problem if rejection of the null hypothesis is not close" (Greenwald, 1975, p. 3). Such undesirable behavioral manifestations have led Greenwald to conclude that we should do research in which any outcome, including a null hypothesis outcome, is possible. This does, however, mean that the research has to be conducted in such a manner as to allow for the tentative acceptance of the null hypothesis. Explication of such a procedure is beyond the scope of this text. However, Greenwald (1975) and Cook et al. (1979) present guidelines that one should follow when conducting research that may lead to support for the tentative acceptance of the null hypothesis.

Potential Errors in the Statistical Decision-Making Process

In the preceding section, primary concern was given to determining when one should accept a difference as being significant. The commonly accepted significance levels of .05 and .01 mean that a wrong decision would occur only 5 times or 1 time in 100, respectively. In setting this stringent level, we are being very conservative, making sure that the odds of being correct are definitely in our favor. It is somewhat like going to the horse races with the intention of maximizing the possibility of winning—you increase your chances of winning if you bet on a horse that has only a 5 percent chance of losing rather than one that has a 50 percent chance of losing. In like manner, scientists have set the odds so that they are quite sure of making the correct decision. Note, however, that even with this stringent significance level, scientists will be wrong a given percentage of the time; 5 percent of the time if they operate at the .05 significance level, and 1 percent of the time if they operate at the .01 significance level. In other words, if we conduct the same experiment 100 times, we can expect that 5 of these times we will, by chance alone, obtain a mean difference large enough to allow us to reject the null hypothesis at the .05 significance level. This means that we could be wrong when we reject the null hypothesis, whether we are operating at the .05 or the .01 significance level.

When we falsely reject the null hypothesis, we commit a Type I error. A **Type I error** refers to accepting the scientific hypothesis as true when it is in fact false, or falsely rejecting the null hypothesis. Type I error is controlled by the significance level that is set. If the .05 significance level is set, the probability of being wrong and committing a Type I error is 5 times in 100. It may appear that there is an easy solution to this type of problem: simply set a more stringent significance level, such as .0001. There are two difficulties with this approach. First, it is not possible to eliminate Type I error, since, by definition, there will always be some possibility of obtaining a chance finding as large as the observed difference. Second, and more important, another type of error *tends* to be inversely related to Type I error. As the probability of accepting the scientific hypothesis when it is false (Type I error) decreases, the probability of rejecting the scientific hypothesis when it is true **(Type II error)** tends to increase. Although there is not a direct relationship between Type I and Type II errors, the risk of committing a Type I error generally increases as the risk of committing a Type II error decreases, and the risk of committing a Type II error generally increases as the risk of committing a Type I error decreases. Therefore, we are placed in somewhat of a dilemma. We must make a decision based on the results of our experiment, but we always run the risk of making an error.

As scientists, we must weigh the hazards of committing each of the two types of errors and determine which mistake would be more detrimental. In most instances, it is assumed that a Type I error is worse, which is why the rather stringent .05 or .01 significance level is used as the decision point for rejection of the null hypothesis. However, there are times when committing a Type II error would be very detrimental. For example, if a drug were needed to combat a deadly epidemic, it would be important to make sure that an effective drug was identified.

Type I error
Falsely rejecting the null hypothesis

Type II error
Rejecting the scientific hypothesis when it is true

Avoiding a type II error in such an instance would be considered more important, so the significance level would be raised to, say, the .15 level, to maximize the chances of identifying a drug that would combat the disease.

There are two steps that the experimenter can take to minimize Type II errors—increase the probability of rejecting the null hypothesis when it is in fact false—while at the same time maintaining a stringent significance level that controls for the effect of Type I errors. First, the experimenter can use more powerful statistical tests (parametric tests) when analyzing the data. Second, the experimenter can increase the sample size. As the sample size becomes larger, the probability of detecting a real difference between the groups increases. This is why some people state that the larger the sample size, the better.

Summary

Following the completion of the study design, the investigator must make a number of additional decisions before beginning to collect data. The investigator must first decide on the type of organism to be used in the study. While precedent has been the primary determining factor guiding the selection of a particular organism, the research problem should be the main determinant. The organism that is best for investigating the research problem should be used when possible.

Once the question of type of organism has been resolved, one needs to determine where these organisms can be attained. Infrahumans, particularly rats, are available from a number of commercial sources. Most human subjects used in psychological experimentation come from the departmental subject pools, which usually consist of introductory psychology students. If the study calls for subjects other than those represented in the subject pools, the investigator must locate an available source and make the necessary arrangements.

In addition to identifying the source subjects, one needs to determine how many subjects should be used. For studies in which one has the ability to randomly select from the population, the NEA Research Division has published a formula that can be used for this purpose. However, most experimental studies do not have this capability. Based on a variety of statistical issues, one recommendation is that at least 15 subjects per cell be used.

Instructions must also be prepared for studies using human subjects. The instructions should include a clear description of the purpose (or disguised purpose) of the task required of the subject.

Next, the investigator must specify the procedure to be used in data collection—the exact sequence in which all phases of the experiment are to be carried out, from the moment the investigator comes in contact with the subjects until that contact terminates. It is helpful to conduct a pilot study to iron out unforeseen difficulties. Once the procedure has been specified, it is time to collect data according to this procedure.

Immediately following data collection, the experimenter must conduct a postexperimental interview, or debriefing session, with the subjects. During this interview, the experimenter attempts to detect any suspicions that the subjects may have had. Additionally, the experimenter explains to the subjects the reasons for any deceptions that may have been used as well as the total experimental procedure and purpose.

The data then must be statistically analyzed to determine if the hypothesis has been validated. While it is not possible to determine *absolutely* if the hypothesis is validated, it is possible to determine the probability that the hypothesis is true. The most common practice is to say that the hypothesis has been validated if there is only a 5 percent or a 1 percent chance that the hypothesis is not true. These levels are rather stringent, indicating the conservative nature of science. Note, however, that there will still be an error either 1 percent or 5 percent of the time. This is referred to as a Type I error—the probability of accepting a hypothesis that is false. The Type I error could be decreased by setting a more stringent level for acceptance of the hypothesis, but then the probability of rejecting the hypothesis when in fact it is true (Type II error) tends to increase. There needs to be a balance between these two types of error, and the typical balance is obtained by using the .05 and .01 significance levels.

Internal validity
— if the effects
obtained in the
experiment are
due to only the
experimental
conditions manipulated,
the experiment has
internal validity.

12

External Validity

Chapter Overview

While there are times when we are interested only in the response of the subjects participating in a certain experiment (Mook, 1983), usually we would like to be able to state that the results of our study generalize to individuals responding in different settings at different times. However, a number of characteristics of an experiment may limit a researcher's ability to generalize the results. This chapter is devoted to discussing these limiting characteristics. As you read it, you should try to answer the following questions:

1. What is external validity?

2. In an experiment, what are the characteristics that may threaten external validity?

3. What cautions should be exercised in assessing the external validity of an experiment?

4. What is the relationship between external and internal validity?

Introduction

The immediate purpose of any well-conducted experiment is to assess the relationship between the independent and the dependent variables, but the long-range goal is to understand the basic underlying laws of behavior. In Chapter 1, it was stated that one of the basic assumptions of any science is that there are uniformities in nature. Science attempts to isolate these uniformities in order to explain the world in which we live. Psychology is the branch of science that endeavors to understand the behavior of organisms by isolating the lawful relationships that exist in nature. This purpose of psychology transcends the question of internal validity and addresses the question of **external validity**—the extent to which the results of an experiment can be generalized to and across different persons, settings, and times. Assessment of external validity is an inferential process because it involves making broad statements based only on limited information. For example, stating that a study

External validity
The extent to which the results of an experiment can be applied to and across different persons, settings, and times

296

conducted in a psychology laboratory using 20 college students is externally valid implies that the results obtained from this experiment would also be true for all college students responding in any of a variety of settings and at different times. Such inference is a necessary component of the scientific process, since all members of a defined population can seldom be studied in all settings at all times. In order to generalize the results of a study, we must identify a target population of people, settings, and times and then randomly select individuals from these populations so that the sample will be representative of the defined population. For a variety of reasons (e.g., cost, time, and accessibility), most studies do not randomly sample the specified population. Failure to randomly sample the population means that a study may contain characteristics that threaten its external validity. Such threats fall into the three broad categories of lack of population validity, ecological validity, and time validity (Bracht and Glass, 1968; Wilson, 1981). Becoming aware of some of the factors in these three categories that limit the generalizability of the results of a study will help you to design studies that circumvent these difficulties.

Population Validity

Population validity refers to the ability to generalize from the sample on which the study was conducted to the larger population of individuals in which one is interested. Bracht and Glass (1968) have reiterated Kempthorne's (1961) distinction between the target population and the experimentally accessible population. The **target population** is the larger population (e.g., all college students) to whom the experimental results are generalized, and the **experimentally accessible population** is the one that is available to the researcher (e.g., the college students at the university at which the investigator is employed). Two inferential steps are involved in generalizing from the results of the study to the larger population, as illustrated in Figure 12.1. First, one has to generalize from the sample to the experimentally accessible population. This step can be easily accomplished if the investigator *randomly* selects the sample from the experimentally accessible population. If the sample is randomly selected, it should be representative, which means that the characteristics of the experimentally accessible population can be inferred from the sample. If you conduct an experiment on a sample of 50 subjects randomly selected from a given university, you can say that the obtained results are characteristic of students at that university.

The second step in the generalization process requires moving from the experimentally accessible population to the target population. This ultimate generalization seldom can be made with any degree of

Population validity
The extent to which the results of a study can be generalized to the larger population

Target population
The larger population to which the results are to be generalized

Experimentally accessible population
The population of subjects available to the investigator

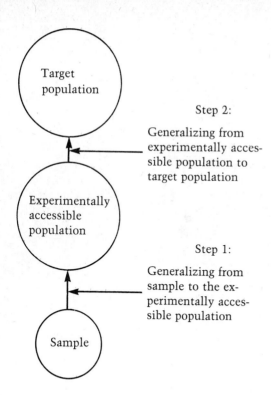

Figure 12.1 *Two-step inferential process involved in generalizing from the sample to the target population.*

Target population

Step 2:

Generalizing from experimentally accessible population to target population

Experimentally accessible population

Step 1:

Generalizing from sample to the experimentally accessible population

Sample

confidence, because only rarely is the experimentally accessible population representative of the target population. For example, assume that you are conducting a study using college students as the target population. You would want to be able to say that the results of the study will hold for all college students. To be able to make such a statement, you would have to select randomly from the target population, which is rarely possible. Therefore, you probably will have to settle for randomly selecting from the nonrepresentative experimentally accessible population.

It is difficult to select randomly even from the experimentally accessible population. This is why experimenters select subjects based on availability or precedent. The two categories of organisms that have most often been used in psychological studies are the albino rat and the college sophomore taking an introductory psychology course. A number of individuals have attacked the use of these two categories of organisms. Beach (1950, 1960), Boice (1973), Ehrlich (1974), Eysenck (1967), Kavanau (1964, 1967), Richter (1959), and Smith (1969) have all questioned the degree to which the research results produced from laboratory rats can be generalized to other animals. Also, as Sidowski and Lockard (1966) point out, the ones that are used in a given study are definitely not a random sample of the experimentally accessible population.

Even more attention has been directed toward the research conducted on human subjects, much of which has been directed toward identifying laws governing human behavior. Implicit in this objective is the notion that the results from the sample of subjects on which the research was conducted will generalize to all humans, the target population. There is increasing suspicion among behavioral researchers that the subjects in research studies are not representative of humans in general. As far back as 1946, McNemar (1946, p. 333) issued a warning regarding the biased nature of the human subject research pool. He stated that "the existing science of human behavior is largely the science of the behavior of sophomores." Table 12.1 summarizes the results of surveys that have computed the percentage of studies using college students. You can see from this table that, at least for the journals surveyed, the percentage of psychological studies using college students increased from 1949 to 1964 and then stabilized at about 75 percent

Table 12.1   *Percentage of Studies Using College Students as Subjects*

AUTHOR	SOURCE	YEAR(S)	PERCENTAGE USING COLLEGE STUDENTS
Christie (1965)	*Journal of Abnormal and Social Psychology*	1949	20
Christie (1965)	*Journal of Abnormal and Social Psychology*	1959	49
Smart (1966)	*Journal of Abnormal and Social Psychology*	1962–1964	73
Smart (1966)	*Journal of Experimental Psychology*	1963–1964	86
Schultz (1969)	*Journal of Personality and Social Psychology*	1966–1967	70
Schultz (1969)	*Journal of Experimental Psychology*	1966–1967	84
Carlson (1971)	*Journal of Personality and Social Psychology and Journal of Personality*	1968	66
Higbee and Wells (1972)	*Journal of Personality and Social Psychology*	1969	76
Levenson, Gray, and Ingram (1976)	*Journal of Personality and Social Psychology*	1973	72
Levenson, Gray, and Ingram (1976)	*Journal of Personality*	1973	74

through 1973. There is no indication that this situation has changed since then.

The potential lack of generalizability when college students are used as the predominant source of subjects in psychological experiments is illustrated by Oakes (1972). He showed that he could not replicate, using a non–college student population, a reinforcement effect that had reliably been demonstrated on college students. He did, however, make an interesting point in defense of research using the college student. Oakes (1972) stated:

> The point I am suggesting is that research with college students is just as valid as research drawing on any other subject population. A behavioral phenomenon reliably exhibited is a genuine phenomenon, no matter what population is sampled in the research in which it is demonstrated. For any behavioral phenomenon, it may well be that members of another population that one could sample might have certain behavioral characteristics that would preclude the phenomenon being demonstrated with that population. Such a finding would suggest a restriction of the generality of the phenomenon, but it would not make it any less genuine. No matter what population a researcher samples, whether it be psychology students, real-people volunteers, public school students, or whatever, there are probably some behavioral phenomena that would be manifested differently in that population due to an interaction effect of the particular characteristics of that subject population.
>
> This suggests, then, that the generalizability of the results of behavioral research is not a function of the population sampled, but rather that the external validity of the research depends on the interaction of subject characteristics and the particular behavioral phenomenon with which one is concerned. For some behavioral phenomena, probably those closer to the reflex level of response, there may be no interaction with subject characteristics. Thus, it might make no difference what population one sampled in a study of critical flicker fusion frequency. For other behavioral phenomena, however, especially those beyond the reflex level, one might well expect interactions with subject characteristics.
>
> Thus, I would suggest that our "science of the behavior of sophomores," to the extent that it has discovered reliable behavioral phenomena, is just as valid as a science of behavior based on the sampling of any other population one could tap. The generalizability of any particular finding, however, may be limited by interaction with behavioral characteristics peculiar to any population to which one is attempting to generalize. But this would be true no matter what population one sampled in the original research.[1]

---

[1]Oakes, W. External validity of the use of real people as subjects, *American Psychologist*, 1972, 27, 961–962. Copyright 1972 by the American Psychological Association. Reprinted by permission of the author and publisher.

Bracht and Glass (1968) and Cook and Campbell (1979) reached essentially the same conclusion. The important issue in external validity is the extent to which the experimental results can generalize across different persons, settings, and times; hence, the problem boils down to a test of interactions. Since population validity refers to the ability to generalize across persons, it is threatened by a selection by treatment interaction. If a selection by treatment interaction (Campbell and Stanley, 1963) exists, the experiment is externally invalid or cannot be generalized to the target population. This means that the particular sample of subjects that are selected for use in a study may respond differently to the experimental treatment condition than would another sample of subjects with different characteristics. Rosenthal and Rosnow (1975) have summarized the wealth of literature showing that volunteer and nonvolunteer subjects respond differently to many experimental treatment conditions. Kendler and Kendler (1959) found that kindergarten children did not achieve results consistent with those obtained from college students. They suggest that perhaps a maturational variable exists, causing subjects at different maturational levels to respond differently to selected tasks. Such research indicates that a selection by treatment interaction limits the extent to which the results of a study can be generalized beyond the groups used to establish the initial relationship.

Ecological Validity

Ecological validity refers to the ability to generalize the results of the study across settings or from one set of environmental conditions to another. For example, the environmental setting of an experiment may require a specific arrangement of the equipment, a particular location, or a certain type of experimenter. If the results of a laboratory experiment that requires such a setting can be generalized to other settings (e.g., a therapy setting or a labor relations setting), then the experiment possesses ecological validity. Consequently, ecological validity exists to the extent that the treatment effect is independent of the experimental setting. The following discussion will focus on some of the characteristics of experimental settings that can threaten ecological validity.

Ecological validity
The extent to which the results of a study can be generalized across settings or environmental conditions

Multiple-Treatment Interference

The **multiple-treatment interference** phenomenon refers to the effect that participation in one treatment condition has on participation in a second treatment condition. The multiple-treatment interference phenomenon represents a sequencing effect and, therefore, impedes direct

Multiple-treatment interference
The sequencing effect that can occur when subjects participate in more than one treatment condition

generalization of the results of the study in addition to threatening internal validity, because it is difficult to separate the effect of the particular order of conditions from the effect of the treatment conditions. Any generalization that is made regarding the results of the study is restricted to the particular sequence of conditions that was administered.

There are at least two situations in which the multiple-treatment interference phenomenon may occur. Multiple-treatment interference may occur in an experiment in which the subject or subjects are required to participate in more than one treatment condition. Fox (1963) found such an effect in his investigation of reading speed as related to typeface. In an incomplete counterbalanced design, one group of subjects first read material typed in Standard Elite and then read material typed in Gothic Elite, whereas the second group of subjects took the reverse order. When the data from the reading of the Standard Elite and Gothic Elite were combined across groups, no reliable difference related to typeface was found. However, when the two typefaces were compared for the first reading, it was found that the Standard Elite typeface was read significantly faster than was the Gothic Elite. When the two groups switched to material typed in the other typeface, they continued to read at the average speed previously established. Thus, the reading rate subjects established when reading the first typeface transferred over to the second treatment effect and thus affected the reading rate for the second typeface. Consequently, the order of presentation of the typeface determined reading speed.

Multiple-treatment interference may also occur between experiments. The effect of participation in a previous experiment may affect the subject's response to the treatment condition in a current experiment. Underwood (1957), for example, has demonstrated that recall of serially presented adjective lists is to a great extent a function of the number of previous lists that have been learned. If a subject had previously been required to recall serial adjective lists, the current one would be more difficult to recall. Holmes (1967) and Holmes and Applebaum (1970) found that prior participation in psychological experiments affects performance in verbal conditioning experiments. However, Cook et al. (1970) found no such effect in one of their studies. It may be that a subject's history of experimental participation affects performance only in certain types of studies. Such preliminary indicators need to be pursued to determine what types of data are affected by a subject's prior experimental history and how they are affected, so that such effects can be taken into consideration in attempts to generalize experimental data.

Investigators using albino rats in their studies also must think about the potential effects of using the same rats in more than one study. The generally accepted procedure is to use the rats in *only* one study. When another study is to be conducted, a new sample of albino rats must be purchased. In this way, the investigator ensures that the rats are naive in the sense of not having previously participated in a psychological study.

The Hawthorne Effect

The **Hawthorne effect** refers to the fact that one's performance in an experiment is affected by knowledge that one is in an experiment. It is similar to the effect of being on television: once you know the camera is on you, you shift to your "television" behavior.

Hawthorne effect
The influence produced by knowing that one is participating in an experiment

Bracht and Glass (1968) suggest several reasons why subjects may respond differently when they know that they are participating in an experiment. Subjects may, for example, display a high degree of compliance and diligence in performing the experimental task because they are motivated by a high regard for the aims of science and experimentation. Consequently, subjects who know they are in an experiment may agree to perform a task that they otherwise would refuse to do. For example, if you walked up to a person and asked her to do 10 pushups, she might tell you where to go. However, if you added that you were conducting an experiment on physical fitness, you would probably find that many people would comply. To the extent that such effects alter the subject's performance, the experimental results cannot be accounted for by just the treatment effect.

A phenomenon similar to the Hawthorne effect is a **novelty or disruption effect.** If the experimental treatment condition involves something new or unusual, a treatment effect may result by virtue of this fact. When the novelty or disruption diminishes, the treatment effect may disappear. Van Buskirk (1932) found that placing a red (novel) nonsense syllable in the most difficult position in a serial list of black-on-white nonsense syllables greatly facilitated its original learning and later recall. Brownell (1966) also provided an example of a novelty treatment effect. He set out to compare two different instructional programs in England and Scotland. However, results of the study from the two countries conflicted. This conflict was attributed to the novelty effect that existed in Scotland but not in England. Teachers and pupils in England were accustomed to innovation and new programs, whereas those in Scotland were not. Consequently, the new program was enthusiastically inaugurated in Scotland, whereas it was seen as just a continuation of an established pattern in England. Conditions such as novelty and the Hawthorne effect limit one's ability to generalize the results of a given study to populations where such an effect does not exist.

Novelty or disruption effect
A treatment effect that occurs when the treatment condition involves something new or different

The Experimenter Effect

Chapter 5 covers in detail the potential biasing effects that the experimenter can have on the results of the experiment. Experimenter effects are a limiting factor in generalization of results to the extent that experimenter bias is not controlled and the results of the experiment interact with the attributes or expectancies of the experimenter. In other words, if the results of the experiment are partially dependent on the experimenter's particular attributes or expectancies, the results are generalizable only to other similar situations.

The Pretesting Effect

The **pretesting effect** refers to the influence that administering a pretest may have on the experimental treatment effect. Administering a pretest may sensitize the subject in such a way that he or she approaches the experimental treatment differently than does the subject who did not receive the pretest and thus influence external validity in addition to internal validity. If it is true that pretested subjects respond differently to the dependent variable than do unpretested subjects, the results of a study that pretests subjects can be generalized only to a pretested population. However, Lana (1969) concluded that pretesting did not have the sensitizing effect that others had previously postulated. Rosenthal and Rosnow (1975) have suggested, based on the research of Rosnow and Suls (1970), that the failure to find a pretest sensitization effect was due to the failure to distinguish between the motivational sets of volunteer and nonvolunteer subjects—volunteers being the willing and eager subjects, and nonvolunteers being the unwilling subjects. Rosnow and Suls found a pretest sensitization effect operating among volunteers and an opposite dampening effect operating among nonvolunteers. This indicates that the pretest sensitization variable may be specific to the type of subject that is used in the study (a selection by treatment interaction). However, it seems that these results should be replicated before a firm conclusion is drawn regarding the volunteer status by pretest sensitization interaction.

Pretesting effect
The effect that pretesting has on the influence of the treatment condition

---

Time Validity

Time validity refers to the extent to which the results of an experiment can be generalized across time. Most psychological studies are conducted during one time period. Carlson (1971), for example, found that 78 percent of the studies published in the *Journal of Personality and Social Psychology* and the *Journal of Personality* were based on only a

Time validity
The extent to which the results of an experiment can be generalized across time

single session. Five years later, Levenson, Gray, and Ingram (1976) found that 89 percent of the articles published in the same two journals were based on a single session. If these two periodicals are representative of most of the work being conducted in psychology, we are not taking the time variable into consideration. Experimenters seem to be assuming that the time during which the experiment is conducted has little influence on its outcome. However, it has been demonstrated that changing the point in time at which an experiment is conducted can lead to differential effects. For example, Hunsicker and Mellgren (1977) placed rats in a white compartment and then pretrained them to drink a sugared milk solution in an adjacent black compartment. Then, 0.25, 3, 6, 9, 12, 15, 18, or 24 hours after this pretraining, rats were administered a five-second shock when they entered the black compartment. The rats were once again placed in the white compartment 24 hours after receiving the shock and allowed to enter the black compartment to get the milk solution. Figure 12.2 illustrates that the length of time required to enter the black compartment (exit latency) varied in a cyclical fashion with the length of time that had transpired between pretraining and shock administration. It seems that the ability of the organism to retain an event such as shock depends on the point in time at which it is administered. Thus failure to consider the time variable can threaten the external validity of experiments. Following are some of the specific time variations identified by Willson (1981) that can threaten external validity.

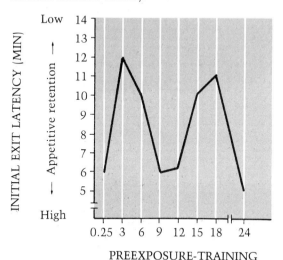

Figure 12.2   *Mean initial exit latencies for the eight preexposure training interval treatments collapsed across the two preexposure periods.*

(From Hunsicker, J. P., and Mellgren, R. J. Multiple deficits in the retention of an appetitively motivated behavior across a 24-hr. period in rats. *Animal Learning and Motivation*, 1977, 5, 14–16. Used with permission.)

Time variations:

Seasonal Variation

A **seasonal variation** is a variation that appears regularly over time in parts of the population. If the automobile accident rate were plotted over time, we might find that it increased during the winter months in states such as South Dakota (Willson, 1980). This increase would naturally be due to adverse weather conditions.

There are actually two forms of seasonal variation: fixed time and variable time. A **fixed-time variation** refers to a change that occurs at specific, predictable points in time, such as on holidays or weekends. For example, it is well known that traffic accidents increase during holidays and that airline traffic increases over the summer months and over holidays. In contrast, the timing of a **variable-time variation** cannot be predicted except in terms of a specific event, the timing of whose occurrence is not known. For example, exactly when a loved one will die is not known; all we know is that when it happens, a predictable psychological reaction will follow.

Seasonal variation
A variation in results that occurs at regular time intervals

Fixed-time variation
A seasonal variation that occurs at specific points in time

Variable-time variation
A seasonal variation that occurs after specific events

Cyclical Variation

A **cyclical variation** is actually a form of seasonal variation. But whereas a seasonal variation appears regularly across units of the population or across people, the cyclical variation occurs within people or other organisms. Hunsicker and Mellgren (1977) demonstrated that rats apparently operate on a 12-hour cycle and at certain points during this cycle retention is maximized. Similarly, within humans there are cyclical variations that can interact with experimental treatment conditions. For example, pulse rate, temperature, endocrine function, and kidney function operate on a circadian (about 24-hour) rhythm (Conroy and Mills, 1970). The many cyclical variations that exist within the organisms on which we conduct our experiments can potentially alter the influence of the experimental treatment or interact with the experimental treatment. If such an interaction takes place, the results of the experiment are generalizable only to the specific point in the cycle during which the experiment was conducted.

Cyclical variation
A regular variation that occurs within people or other organisms

Personological Variation

Personological variation refers to variation in the characteristics of individuals over time. While it is generally assumed that the characteristics within a person are relatively stable across time, this may not be true for all traits. For example, an individual's evaluation of self and others and his or her political leanings are to a great extent dependent on the environmental stimuli to which the individual is exposed. Gergen (1973) has noted that the variables that predicted political

Personological variation
A variation that occurs in the characteristics of an individual as a function of time

activism during the early years of the Vietnam war differed from those that successfully predicted political activism during later periods. This means that the factors motivating activism changed over time, much as our preference for clothing varies over the course of years. If the characteristics being investigated are subject to change, the outcome of the study will be valid only for the period during which the study is conducted and will not be generalizable across time.

Relationship Between Internal and External Validity

Given knowledge of the three general classes of variables that threaten external validity, it would seem logical to design experiments using a diverse sample of subjects and settings across several different time periods in order to increase external validity. The problem with such a strategy is that there tends to be an inverse relationship between internal and external validity. When external validity is increased, internal validity tends to be sacrificed; when internal validity is increased, external validity tends to suffer (Kazdin, 1980).

To gain insight into this relationship between internal and external validity, consider the following characteristics of a well-designed study. From the previous chapters, you know that a well-designed study attempts to control for the effects of all extraneous variables. The researcher selects as subjects a specific subsample of the population, such as females or sixth-grade children, in order to control for variation in different subsamples of individuals, or to create a more homogeneous sample so as to maximize the possibility of detecting a treatment effect. The experimenter conducts the experiment within the confines of a controlled laboratory setting in order to present a specific amount of the treatment condition and to eliminate the influence of extraneous variables, such as the presence of noise or weather conditions. While in the laboratory setting, the subjects receive a set of standardized instructions delivered by one experimenter or maybe by some automated device, and the study is conducted at one specific point in time. But these same features that maximize the possibility of attaining internal validity—using a restricted sample of subjects and testing them in the artificial setting of a laboratory at one specific time—limit the external validity (Kazdin, 1980) by excluding different persons, settings, and times. However, if an experimenter tried to maximize external validity by conducting the experiment on diverse groups of individuals in many settings and at different points in time, the experiment's internal validity would tend to decrease. As the number of settings or the number of types of subjects is increased, control of the extraneous variables that may influence the independent variable decreases, decreasing the likelihood that the study will identify the influence produced by the independent variable. This does not mean that external validity should be disregarded. Rather, it suggests that the first and foremost objective should be the identification of the influence of a treatment effect. Once an effect has been verified by means of well-controlled, internally valid studies, external validity can be investigated.

Cautions in Evaluating the External Validity of Experiments

The external validity of an experiment has been defined as the extent to which the experimental results will generalize to and across different persons, settings, and times. The present chapter has considered a number of the specific threats to the external validity of an experiment. Given such a listing of possible threats, one is tempted to compare the list to the characteristics of a given study and conclude that the study does not possess external validity if a number of the threats legitimately apply. However, such a procedure is not always valid. Let us consider the study conducted by Berkowitz and LePage (1967). These researchers investigated the influence of the mere presence of weapons on aggression as measured by the number of shocks subjects delivered to an accomplice of the experimenter. A hundred college students were randomly assigned to one of three experimental treatment conditions. Subjects were seated at a table that had on it a telegraph key either alone, with neutral objects (e.g., a badminton racket), or with a shotgun and a revolver. The telegraph key was connected to a shock machine. The subject's partner, in one condition, was told to come up with ideas to boost the image and the record sales of a popular singer. If the subject did not like the partner's ideas, the subject was to deliver several shocks to the partner by pressing the telegraph key. Berkowitz and LePage found that subjects delivered more shocks to their partners in the condition that had the weapons on the table even though the subjects were told that these weapons were not part of the experiment but had been left by the previous researcher. The experiment suggests that the mere presence of weapons can enhance aggression. However, does this experiment have external validity—can the results be applied to the world at large?

If we look at the threats to external validity, we can see that many of them apply to the Berkowitz and LePage study. The experiment did not contain a random sample of subjects or even a diverse sample of college students. The study was conducted at only one time in a college laboratory in which subjects were told that the experiment was measuring their physiological reactions to stress. The task the students were performing was one of brainstorming ideas to improve the image and record sales of a popular singer. The study would seem to be a total failure with regard to external validity, since it did not sample across people, settings, or times. However, there are several cautions one should be aware of in assessing the external validity of experiments such as this.

Mook (1983) has appropriately pointed out that experiments are conducted for a variety of purposes and that some of them do not attempt to relate to real-life behavior. The issue of external validity is moot for such experiments. For example, we may conduct an experiment in order to determine if something *can* happen and not necessarily if it really does happen. Person-perception studies have revealed that people wearing glasses are judged as more intelligent when seen for only 15 seconds. However, if these same people are viewed for five minutes, the glasses make no difference. The temporary effect of the glasses seems to have no meaning in real life. If the experiment had not been conducted, though, this temporary effect would not have been identified. Although it says little about real-life behavior, it does say something about humans as judges, so the experimental results are important.

A second significant point made by Mook (1983) is that the component of an experiment that is to be generalized is often the theoretical process that is being tested or the understanding that accrues from the experiment. For example, consider the difference between a study investigating the influence of a new teaching technique and a study investigating the influence of the presence of weapons. Researchers investigating a new technique for teaching basic arithmetic to seven-year-old children would like to have their results generalize to all seven-year-olds. They would like to be able to state that this specific technique or procedure could be used for all seven-year-old children. Contrast their situation with that of Berkowitz and LePage, who found that if a weapon was present on the table a subject delivered more shocks as an indication of not liking a partner's ideas. In no way would they want to generalize the specific procedure of this experiment to other people, settings, or times. A person in a setting other than the laboratory might indeed give more shocks to a partner if a weapon were placed on the table. However, such a situation or procedure would seldom exist in real life, and it was not Berkowitz and LePage's intention to generalize the specific experimental procedure. Rather, it is the understanding of the impact of the presence of weapons that is to be extracted from the study and generalized, not the specific procedure.

One must also exercise caution in placing too much emphasis on the setting in which the experiment is conducted. Laboratory research has been criticized because of the artificiality of the setting, and this artificiality can impose a severe restraint on the external validity of the experiment. Because of the intuitive logic that is inherent in this criticism, a number of investigators have advocated that psychologists move out of the laboratory and into a real-world setting, such as a mental health clinic. The assumption seems to be that if we change the experimental setting, we will enhance external validity. For example, some people believe that if industrial psychologists conducted their research in an organizational setting, both the setting and the subjects would be more representative of the real-world population. Dipboye and Flanagan (1979) have demonstrated that such an assumption is not valid. They showed that the field research conducted in industrial organizational psychology has been performed on male, professional, technical, and managerial personnel in productive economic organizations through use of self-report inventories. Thus in at least this one area of psychology the assumption of greater external validity of field research has not been supported, since the field research has used a limited sample of individuals, in limited field settings, over one time period.

A last caution has to do with the assessment of the interaction between the treatment effect and any of the traits that threaten external validity. Earlier in this chapter, it was stated that assessing external validity boils down to determining whether or not an interaction exists between the experimental treatment and one of the characteristics that threaten external validity. If the experimental treatment effect does not interact with persons, settings, or times, then the treatment effect can be generalized. Within the field of psychology, however, most of the phenomena we investigate do interact with one of these types of characteristics. Does this mean that none of our experimental results have external validity? Such a conclusion would obviously be rash and false. When interactions do exist, it is important to distinguish between ordinal and disordinal interactions (Lindquist, 1953; Lubin, 1961). An **ordinal interaction** is one in which the rank order of the treatment effects remains the same across persons, settings, and times. Figure 12.3 illustrates an ordinal treatment by persons' interactions. Note that the rank order of the treatments remains the same for both categories of persons, with treatment C producing the highest dependent variable scores and treatment A producing the lowest dependent variable scores.

A **disordinal interaction,** on the other hand, is one in which the rank order of the treatments changes across persons, settings, or times, as illustrated in Figure 12.4. Here, treatment A is most effective for low-ability persons, treatment C is most effective for high-ability persons, and treatment B is equally effective for both types. Consequently, the effectiveness of the condition depends on the type of person receiving the treatment.

Ordinal interaction
An interaction in which the rank order of the treatment effects remains the same across persons, settings, and times

Disordinal interaction
An interaction in which the rank order of the treatment effects changes as a function of persons, settings, and times

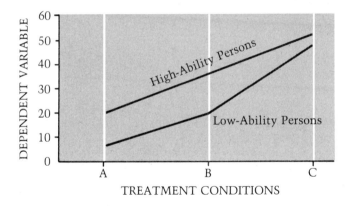

Figure 12.3   *Ordinal interaction.*

What do these two types of interactions say about generalizations? Ordinal interactions do not limit generalizability of the results, whereas disordinal interactions do. For ordinal interactions, the one best treatment condition can be prescribed for all individuals. As Figure 12.3 illustrates, treatment condition C is superior for both types of individuals. The ordinal interaction reveals the differential effectiveness of the three treatments and so lends support to the meaningfulness of interpreting the data; however, it does not limit the ability to generalize the data. Therefore, if the lines of the graph do not cross, generalization of the data is not limited, in spite of the fact that a significant interaction exists.

If there is a statistically significant interaction and the lines of the graph cross as illustrated in Figure 12.4, a disordinal interaction exists

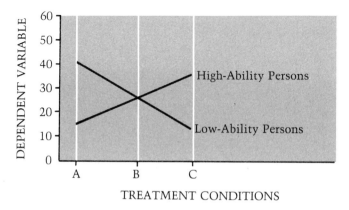

Figure 12.4   *Disordinal interaction.*

and generalizability of the data is limited. From this figure, it is readily apparent that one of the three treatment conditions is not superior for both types of individuals; the *most* effective treatment depends on the type of person (high or low ability) being considered. Note that the differences between groups, settings, or times *must* be statistically significant. For example, the scores of the high- and low-ability persons must be significantly different for treatments A and C for there to be a disordinal interaction. This is because the lines of a graph may cross as a function of random variation in response, whereas a true disordinal interaction represents a real difference suggested by statistical tests.

e: lines can but there may not be a problem.

Summary
— not yet read

Superimposed on the researcher's concern for conducting an internally valid experiment is a concern for understanding behavior. In addition to wanting our experiments to be internally valid, we want to produce results that will have implications for the larger population of individuals behaving in diverse settings and at different points in time. When the results of an experiment can be generalized across persons, settings, and times, the experiment is externally valid. Threats to external validity fall into three broad categories: lack of population, ecological, and time validity.

Population validity refers to the ability to generalize from the experimental sample of subjects to the larger population from which the sample was drawn. For population validity to exist, the experimental subjects must be randomly selected from the larger population. Seldom, however, does this happen. Most animal research has been performed on a nonrandom sample of albino rats, and most human research has been conducted on college sophomores taking an introductory psychology course. The behavioral phenomena manifested in these nonrandom samples are still real; whether the results will generalize depends on whether there is an interaction between these behavioral phenomena and subjects with characteristics different from those of subjects who participated in the study. Assessing generalizability boils down to determining if there is a subject, setting, or time characteristic by treatment interaction.

Ecological validity refers to the ability to generalize the results of the study across settings or environmental conditions. Every experiment is conducted within a specific setting. If the results of the experiment cannot be generalized to other settings, then the treatment effect is limited to the setting in which it was demonstrated. There are a number of experimental environmental conditions that can limit one's ability to generalize the results to other situations. The multiple-treatment interference phenomenon is a sequencing effect. If the experimental effect occurs only when a particular order of conditions exists, then generalization is limited to this order of conditions. The Hawthorne effect refers to the alteration that occurs in the subject's behavior when the subject knows he or she is in an experiment. If the experimental effect is a function of this fact, then generalization is limited to similar environments. Other limiting factors include the potential influence of the experimenter, of pretesting, and of having conducted the study over only a single session. To the extent that these variables affect the results, the results can be generalized only to other environments that include these factors.

Time validity refers to the influence of time on the results of experiments. If an experimental result changes over time, the influence of the treatment condition is limited to the point in time at which the experiment was conducted. The primary time variables seem to be seasonal variations and cyclical variations, but characteristics of individuals may also change over time and produce a personological variation.

While it is desirable to conduct an externally valid experiment, the first requirement is to conduct an internally valid experiment. Unfortunately, the factors a researcher must include in order to conduct an internally valid experiment tend to preclude the attainment of external validity. Thus the concern for external validity should arise only after an effect has been verified with an internally valid study.

Appendix
The Research Report

Throughout this book, I have presented the various steps involved in the research process and discussed in detail the intricacies of each. A thorough presentation was made to enable you to conduct a sound scientific study. However, as a scientist, you have a responsibility not only to conduct a well-designed and well-executed study, but also to communicate the results of the study to the rest of the scientific community. Your study may have answered a very significant research question, but the results are of no value unless they are made public. The primary mechanism for communicating results is through professional journals. Within the field of psychology, the American Psychological Association publishes 18 journals. As Table A illustrates, these pe-

Table A *Journals Published by the American Psychological Association*

NAME OF JOURNAL	AREA COVERED
American Psychologist	Contains the American Psychological Association's archival documents as well as articles relating to problems and issues facing psychology, trends within the field, the relation between psychology and society, and the current status and applications of psychological knowledge.
Behavioral Neuroscience	Contains research papers, reviews, and theoretical papers on the biological basis of behavior.
Contemporary Psychology	Reviews material relevant to psychology, such as books, films, and tapes
Developmental Psychology	Publishes articles relating to human development across the life span.
Journal of Abnormal Psychology	Publishes articles relating to the determinants, theories, and correlates of abnormal behavior.

Table A   (continued)

NAME OF JOURNAL	AREA COVERED
Journal of Applied Psychology	Publishes articles that contribute to our understanding of any applied area of psychology except clinical psychology.
Journal of Comparative Psychology	Contains behavioral studies that relate to evolution, development, ecology, control, and functional significance of various species.
Journal of Consulting and Clinical Psychology	Contains research investigations pertaining to development, validity, and use of various techniques for diagnosing and treating disturbed behavior in all populations.
Journal of Counseling Psychology	Contains articles pertaining to evaluation, application, and theoretical issues surrounding counseling.
Journal of Educational Psychology	Publishes studies and theoretical papers concerned with learning and cognition.
Journal of Experimental Psychology: Animal Behavior	Publishes studies relating to nonhuman learning, memory, perception, motivation, and performance.
Journal of Experimental Psychology: General	Publishes integrative articles of interest to all experimental psychologists.
Journal of Experimenal Psychology: Human Perception and Performance	Focuses on perception, verbal and motor performance.
Journal of Experimental Psychology: Learning, Memory, and Cognition	Contains original studies and theory on encoding, transfer, memory, and cognitive processes in human memory.
Journal of Personality and Social Psychology	Contains articles on all areas of personality and social psychology.
Professional Psychology: Research and Practice	Focuses on the application of psychology.
Psychological Bulletin	Publishes evaluative and integrative reviews of both methodological and substantive issues.
Psychological Review	Publishes articles that make a theoretical contribution to psychology.

riodicals cover a wide variety of areas and provide an outlet for studies conducted within just about any field of interest. There are other journals affiliated with the APA that also publish the results of psychological studies. In order to facilitate clear communication of research results, the APA has published a manual (American Psychological Association, 1983) that gives a standardized format for authors to follow when preparing research reports. Since many periodicals instruct their authors to prepare their manuscripts according to the style specified in the APA manual, this is the format I will present for writing a research report.

Prior to preparing a report of a study that you have completed, you must ask yourself if the study is important enough to justify publication. Would others be interested in it, and, more importantly, would it influence their work? If you think the study is significant, you must ask yourself if it is free from flaws that would preclude drawing any causal relation between the independent and the dependent variables. For example, you must ask yourself if you have built in the controls needed to eliminate the influence of rival hypotheses. If you can satisfy yourself with regard to these two questions, then you are justified in proceeding with the preparation of the research report.

The APA Format

The structure of the research report is very simple and tends to follow the steps one takes in conducting a research study. In order to present the format of the research report, a portion of an article that I have prepared and submitted for publication has been reproduced on the following pages. Adjacent to each section of the actual research report is an explanation of the material that should be included in that section. The adjacent explanation may include some recommendations that are not incorporated in the research report, since each study does not include all of the elements listed in the publication manual (American Psychological Association, 1983).

When reading through each of the sections of the research report, and then when writing your own report, you should keep its purpose in mind. The primary goal is to report as precisely as possible what you did, including a statement of the problem investigated, the methods used to investigate the problem, the results of your investigation, and any conclusions you may have reached. Is there any criterion you can use to determine whether or not you have clearly and explicitly reported your study? The criterion of replication is possibly the most important. If another investigator could read your research report and precisely replicate your study, then you have, in all probability, made a clear and complete report.

The following sample research report was prepared according to the guidelines specified in the APA publication manual. This type of research report could be submitted to journals such as *Journal of Consulting and Clinical Psychology, Behavior Therapy*, or *Nutrition and Behavior.*

Dietary Change
1

The Impact of a Dietary Change on Symptom Remediation
Larry B. Christensen, Beth White, and Kelly Kreitsch
Texas A&M University

Running head: DIETARY CHANGE ON SYMPTOMS

Page number and short title
The page number as well as a shortened title should appear in the upper right-hand corner of all manuscript pages except those containing figures. The shortened title should consist of the first two or three words of the running head, which will allow for identification of the pages of the manuscript if they are separated during the actual review process. All pages should be numbered consecutively, beginning with the title page.

Title
The title should be centered on the first page of the manuscript and typed in upper- and lowercase letters. It should inform the readers about the study by concisely stating the relationship between the independent and the dependent variables. A typical title length in 12 to 15 words.

Name and affiliation of author(s)
The names of any authors who have made a substantial contribution to the study should appear immediately below the title and should be typed in upper- and lowercase letters and centered on the page. The preferred form is to list first name, middle initial, and last name, with titles and degrees omitted. The affiliation usually identifies the institution where the investigation was conducted. Departmental affiliation is included only if the author is not associated with a psychology department.

Running head
The running head is centered at the bottom of the first (title) page and is typed in all uppercase letters. It is an abbreviated title of not more than 50 characters in length, counting letters, punctuation, and spaces between words.

Dietary Change

2

Abstract

The impact of a dietary change on symptom remediation was investigated in a female graduate student, in an ABAB single-subject design. This individual was instructed to record daily the frequency of symptoms she was experiencing while consuming her typical diet (baseline condition) and while consuming a high protein–low carbohydrate diet void of refined carbohydrates, alcohol, and caffeine (treatment condition). Results of the study revealed that there was a significant change ($p < 0.01$) in the slope and level of the subject's self-report of symptoms. A progressive decline in the subject's self-report of symptoms occurred during the treatment phase and recurred when baseline conditions were reinstituted. The findings suggest that a dietary intervention may be beneficial in the remediation of symptoms of some individuals.

Abstract

The abstract is a comprehensive summary of the contents of the research report, 100 to 150 words in length. It is typed on a separate page, with the word "Abstract" centered at the top of the page in upper- and lower-case letters, without paragraph indentation. It should include a brief statement of the problem, a summary of the method used (including a description of the subjects, instruments, or apparatus), the procedure, the results (including statistical significance levels), and any conclusions and implications.

Dietary Change

3

The Impact of a Dietary Change on Symptom Remediation

For the past several decades, a number of individuals—e.g., Feingold (1972)—have suggested that the food consumed by the American public can have a detrimental impact on behavior. Specifically, Feingold has advocated that a relationship exists between hyperactivity and dietary elements such as food colors and preservatives. While such connections have not been substantiated by subsequent investigators (Conners, 1980), more evidence has appeared in the professional literature that seems to support a possible dietary-behavior connection. Kwok (1968) has described the adverse behavioral effects (e.g., headache and nausea) that can occur from the ingestion of monosodium L-glutamate. Green (1969), Powers (1973), and Von Hilsheimer (1974) have reported case studies of children whose behavioral disturbances, irritability, hyperactivity, and short attention spans improved following a dietary change consisting of a reduction or elimination of refined carbohydrates. Mikkelsen (1978), Greden (1974), and others have reported that paranoid delusions, headaches, anxiety symptoms, depression, and insomnia have disappeared or been dramatically reduced following the elimination or limitation of caffeine intake.

These case studies suggesting that various dietary substances can influence behavior are supported by a number of correlational studies. Prinz, Roberts, and Hantmann (1980) found a significant relationship between the consumption of carbohydrates and the destructive-aggressive and restless behaviors of hyperactive children. Lester, Thatcher, and Monroe-Lord (1982) revealed that refined carbohydrate intake was negatively correlated with academic achievement. Winstead (1976) and Greden, Fontaine, Lubetsky, and Chamberlain (1978) found that caffeine consumption was related to anxiety and depression in adult psychiatric patients. There are also a few experimental studies that suggest that various foods can create psychological disturbances. King (1981), for example, randomly selected 30 patients from a private allergy clinic. Using a double-blind design, he administered either a food extract or a placebo to these subjects and then recorded their self-reports of any symptoms experienced. This study showed that significantly more cognitive-emotional, somatic, and mixed (headache, fatigue, and other aches and pains) symptoms were reported by the subjects given the food extracts.

Introduction

The research report begins with the introduction, which is not labeled because of its position in the paper. The introduction is funnel-shaped in the sense that it is broad at the beginning and narrow at the end. It should begin with a very general introduction to the problem area and then start to narrow by citing the results of prior works that have been conducted in the area and that bear on the specific issue that you are investigating, leading into a statement of the variables to be investigated. In citing prior research, do not attempt to make an exhaustive review of the literature. Cite only those studies that are directly pertinent, and avoid tangential references. This pertinent literature should lead directly into your study and thereby show the continuity between what you are investigating and prior research. You should then state, preferably in question form, the purpose of your study. The introduction should give the reader the rationale for the given investigation, explaining how it fits in with, and is a logical extension of, prior research.

This summary of the literature on the nutrition-behavior connection seems to indicate that the food ingested by the public can indeed produce a variety of maladaptive behaviors and symptoms in some individuals. Currently, however, most of the evidence supporting the nutrition-behavior connection, as is evident from the above review, consists of uncontrolled case studies and a few correlational studies. Except in the area of hyperactivity, few experimental studies have been conducted to investigate the behavioral-emotional alteration that can accompany a dietary change.

In order to more convincingly demonstrate the influence of diet on behavior, two important elements must be identified: first, the offending dietary substances, and second, the individuals who are susceptible to them. The literature has implicated refined carbohydrates and caffeine as offending substances and has extolled the benefits of a high protein–low carbohydrate diet for a subsample of the population. This diet appears to be a logical candidate for manipulation in a dietary change experiment. However, the literature gives few if any guidelines regarding the individuals who may be susceptible to such substances.

In an attempt to develop a means for identifying individuals who may profit from a dietary change, a literature search was conducted to identify those symptoms and behaviors reported as being remediated by a dietary change. These symptoms were compiled and served as a basis for the construction of a symptom checklist. This checklist was then administered to introductory psychology students, and those reporting many of the symptoms were selected for further study. The selected students were asked to restrict themselves for two weeks to a high protein–low carbohydrate diet that totally excluded refined sugar, caffeine, and alcohol. Subjects were instructed to record the symptoms they experienced during the day for this two-week period. Those subjects who demonstrated a progressive decrease in symptoms and reported a beneficial impact of the dietary change were subjected to a rather intensive interview regarding the exact nature of their symptoms. Approximately 20 such individuals were interviewed over the course of two years. These interviews and the experience gained from working with these participants led to the development of the Behavioral Index of Metabolic Imbalance. This pilot work has strongly suggested

Dietary Change
5

that there is a subsample of individuals whose emotional and/or behavioral disorders are due to dietary factors.

The purpose of this study was to investigate the impact of a dietary manipulation on the emotional and/or behavioral symptoms experienced by an individual selected by means of the Behavioral Index of Metabolic Imbalance (BIMI). It was hypothesized that a dietary change consisting of a high protein–low carbohydrate diet totally void of refined carbohydrates, caffeine, and alcohol would remediate the emotional and behavioral symptoms of the selected individual and that a return to a "typical" diet that included such foods would result in a recurrence of these symptoms. In order to support the hypothesis that the beneficial effect was due to the diet alone, it had to be determined that the selected subject was not suffering from the disorder of hypoglycemia. Not only do hypoglycemic individuals experience some of the same symptoms as those portrayed on the BIMI, but this condition is controlled by a high protein–low carbohydrate diet. If the selected individual were hypoglycemic, then the emotional disturbance being experienced would have to be attributed to this physical disorder and not to diet.

Method

Subject

M.W. was a 24-year-old female graduate student who approached the senior author regarding her symptoms following his presentation of a departmental seminar. She was administered the Behavioral Index of Metabolic Imbalance and then interviewed regarding each of the items she had endorsed on this instrument. This subsequent interview has been shown, through pilot studies, to be necessary for maximizing the probability of selecting individuals who will profit from a dietary change. The interview is oriented toward ensuring that the items endorsed on the BIMI are answered appropriately. For example, the third item, which asks subjects if they become depressed for no apparent reason, often receives an affirmative response. However, probing on this issue not infrequently reveals that there is a specific reason for the

Method
The primary purpose of the method section is to tell the reader exactly how the study was conducted. This is the part of the research report that must directly satisfy the criterion of replication. If another investigator could read the method section and replicate the study you conducted, then you have adequately described it. Stating exactly how you conducted the study is necessary so that the reader can evaluate the adequacy of the research.

In order to facilitate communication, the method section is typically divided into subsections: subjects; apparatus, materials, or instruments; and procedure. Deviation from this format may be necessary if the experiment is complex or a detailed description of the stimuli is called for. In such instances, additional subsections may be required to help readers find specific information.

Subject
The subject subsection should tell the reader who the research participants were, how many there were, their characteristics (age, sex), and how they were selected. Any other pertinent information regarding the subjects should also be included, such as how they were assigned to the experimental condition, the number of subjects that were selected for the study but did not complete it (and why), and any inducements that were given to encourage participation.

depression, such as a problem with a roommate, school, or parents. Consequently, at the present time the interview appears to be a necessary ingredient of the selection process. Based on the score received on the BIMI and the subsequent interview, M.W. was selected for the experiment.

Materials

The Behavioral Index of Metabolic Imbalance[1] is a 72-item inventory specifically devised to select individuals who may profit from a dietary change. This instrument was developed through interviews with individuals reporting beneficial effects of a dietary change. The items on this scale assess components of the individual's cognitive (e.g., mental confusion and depression), behavioral (e.g., moodiness and aggression), and somatic (e.g., unexpected sweating and indigestion) status. Respondents are required to evaluate the frequency of occurrence of each symptom on a five-point rating scale, with 1 representing "not at all" and 5 representing "every day." The severity of the occurrence of each symptom is rated on a four-point scale ranging from very mild to extremely severe. In order to be selected by the BIMI, a potential subject must score 170 or more on the frequency scale and 100 or more on the severity scale. This set of cutoff scores was selected because pilot studies indicated that individuals attaining lower scores typically do not report a beneficial impact of a dietary intervention.

A symptom checklist scale was constructed to assess the subject's self-report of symptoms experienced each day. This scale consisted of a listing of the symptoms assessed by the BIMI.

Design and Procedure

A five-hour oral glucose tolerance test was administered to M.W. following a three-day consumption of 200 to 300 grams of carbohydrates to test for the existence of hypoglycemia. Consumption of the high carbohydrate diet prior to taking the oral glucose tolerance test is necessary to preclude a diabetic-type glucose response or a spuriously low glucose nadir (Conn, 1940; Permutt, Delmez, and Stenson, 1976).

An ABAB single-subject design was used to assess the impact of a dietary change on frequency of the symptoms M.W. reported experiencing each day. Baseline conditions for this design consisted of having M.W. consume her typical diet, and the treatment condition consisted of

If animals were used, their genus, species, strain number, and supplier should be specified, in addition to their sex, age, weight, and physiological condition.

Apparatus, materials, measures, and instruments
In this subsection, the reader can learn what apparatus or materials were used. Sufficient detail should be used to enable the reader to obtain comparable equipment. Additionally, the reader should be told why the equipment was used. Any mention of commercially marketed equipment should be accompanied by the firm's name and the model number or, in the case of a measuring instrument such as an anxiety scale, a reference that will enable the reader to obtain the same scale. Custom-made equipment should be described; in the case of complex equipment, a diagram or photograph may need to be included.

Design and procedure
In the procedure subsection, the reader is told exactly how the study was executed, from the moment the subject and the experimenter came into contact, to the moment their contact was terminated. Consequently, this subsection represents a step-by-step account of what both the experimenter and the subject did during the study. This section should include any instructions or stimulus conditions

Dietary Change

7

having M.W. consume a high protein–low carbohydrate diet that was void of refined carbohydrates, caffeine, and alcohol. M.W. was also instructed to eat a snack between meals and at bedtime during the treatment phase of the study. During both the baseline and treatment conditions, each evening just prior to retiring M.W. recorded the symptoms she had experienced during the day on the symptom checklist.

Results

Table 1 shows the results of the oral glucose tolerance test. Since the diagnostic criteria used for identification of hypoglycemia consist of a history of symptoms and a serum or plasma glucose nadir of less than 50 milligrams per deciliter (mg/dl) occurring simultaneously with a re-production of symptoms (Leichtner, 1979), M.W. was not classified as hypoglycemic. As can be seen from Table 1, at no time did the serum glucose level even reach a nadir of 50 mg/dl.

Insert Table 1 about here

Figure 1 depicts the frequency of daily symptoms reported by M.W. during baseline and dietary intervention. It can readily be seen from this figure that many ($M = 16.32$) symptoms were reported each day of the initial baseline phase. However, following dietary intervention the frequency of reported symptoms gradually declined to zero. Reintroduction of baseline conditions produced an immediate return of the symptoms, which gradually increased in frequency. The occurrence of these symptoms again declined to zero upon return to the treatment conditions. A time-series analysis was conducted to supplement this visually based interpretation. The analysis showed that a significant change in the level, $F(3, 51) = 12.54$, $p < 0.01$, as well as in the slope, $F(3, 51) = 7.93$, $p < 0.01$, of response had been produced. Therefore, the time-series analysis supports the visual interpretation of the effects of the dietary intervention.

Insert Figure 1 about here

presented to the subjects and the responses that were required of them, as well as any control techniques used (such as randomization or counterbalancing). In other words, you are to tell the reader exactly what both you and the subjects did and how you did it.

Results
The purpose of the results section is to tell the reader exactly what data were collected, how they were analyzed, and what the outcome of the data analysis was. This section should tell what statistical tests were used. Significant values of any inferential tests (e.g., *t* tests, *F* tests, and chi-square measures) should be accompanied by the magnitude of the obtained value of the test, along with the accompanying degrees of freedom, probability level, and direction of the effect. In reporting and illustrating the direction of a significant effect (nonsignificant effects are not elaborated on for obvious reasons), you need to decide on the medium that will most clearly and economically serve your purpose. If a main effect consisting of three groups is significant, your best approach is probably to incorporate the mean scores for each of these groups into the text of the report. If the significant effect is a complex interaction, the best approach is to summarize your data by means of a figure or a table. If you do use a figure or table (a decision that you must make), be sure to tell the reader, in the text of the report,

Discussion

The results obtained from this study reveal that the frequency of re-ported symptoms can be altered quite dramatically with the introduc-tion of a high protein—low carbohydrate diet. Such evidence would seem to suggest that the emotional and behavioral symptoms experi-enced by some individuals may be due to dietary factors. The results of the five-hour oral glucose tolerance test indicate that M.W. was not hypoglycemic, so this physical disorder cannot be advocated as an explanation for the dramatic effects produced by the dietary change.

It is possible that the change was due to an expectancy effect. Be-cause of the impossibility of disguising the administration of the treat-ment effect or the dietary change, M.W. may have expected the dietary change to remediate her symptoms, particularly since she recorded her own symptoms. The power of a placebo or expectancy effect has long been recognized in psychopharmacology, clinical psychology, and psychiatry (O'Leary and Borkovec, 1978). Consequently, such effects must be controlled in order to draw any conclusions regarding the influence of a dietary intervention. Unfortunately, an expectancy effect functions as a possible rival hypothesis explaining the results attained from the present study. There is a series of studies currently underway, however, in which expectancy effects are controlled. So far, the data from these studies are confirming that the results attained from studies such as this one are due to the dietary change and not a placebo effect.

what data it depicts. Then give a sufficient explanation of the presented data to make sure that the reader interprets them correctly.

In writing the results section, there are several things you should not include. Individual data are not included unless a single-subject study is con-ducted. Statistical formulas are not included unless the statisti-cal test is new, unique, or in some other way not standard or commonly used. The time-series analysis was not actually con-ducted because of the clarity of the results. Fictitious statistical analyses are included to illus-trate the manner in which sta-tistical tests are to be incorpo-rated in the research report.

Discussion

The purpose of the discussion section of the research report is to interpret and evaluate the re-sults obtained, giving primary emphasis to the relationships between the results and the hy-potheses of the study. It is rec-ommended that you begin the discussion by stating whether the hypothesis of the study was or was not supported. Following this statement, you should inter-pret the results, telling the

reader what you think they mean. In doing so, you should attempt to integrate your re-search findings with the results of prior research. Note that this is the only place in the research report where you are given any latitude for stating your own opinion, and even then you are limited to stating your interpre-tation of the results and what you think the major shortcom-ings of the study are. When dis-

cussing the shortcomings, you should mention only the flaws that may have had a significant influence on the results ob-tained. You should accept a negative finding as such rather than attempting to explain it as being due to some methodolog-ical flaw (unless, as may occa-sionally occur, there is a very good and documented reason why a flaw did cause the nega-tive finding).

Dietary Change
9

References

Conn, J. W. (1940). Interpretation of the glucose tolerance test: The necessity of a standard preparatory diet. American Journal of Medical Science, 199, 555–564.

Connors, C. K. (1980). Food additives and hyperactive children. New York: Plenum Press.

Feingold, B. F. (1972). Why is your child hyperactive? New York: Random House.

Greden, J. F. (1974). Anxiety or caffeinism: A diagnostic dilemma. American Journal of Psychiatry, 331, 1089–1092.

Greden, J. F., Fontaine, P., Lubetsky, M., and Chamberlain, K. (1978). Anxiety and depression associated with caffeinism among psychiatric inpatients. American Journal of Psychiatry, 135, 936–966.

Green, R. G. (1969). Reading disability. Canadian Medical Association Journal, 100, 586.

King, D. S. (1981). Can allergic exposure provoke psychological symptoms? A double-blind test. Biological Psychiatry, 16, 3–19.

Kwok, R. H. M. (1968). Chinese restaurant syndrome. New England Journal of Medicine, 278, 270.

Leichtner, S. B. (1979). Alimentary hypoglycemia: A new appraisal. American Journal of Clinical Nutrition, 32, 2104–2114.

Lester, M. L., Thatcher, R. W., and Monroe-Lord, L. (1982). Refined carbohydrate intake, hair cadmium levels, and level of cognitive functioning in children. Nutrition and Behavior, 1, 3–13.

Mikkelsen, E. J. (1978). Caffeine and schizophrenia. The Journal of Clinical Psychiatry, 39, 732–736.

O'Leary, K. D., and Borkovec, T. D. (1978). Conceptual, methodological, and ethical problems of placebo groups in psychotherapy research. American Psychologist, 33, 821–830.

Permutt, M. A., Delmez, J., and Stenson, W. (1976). Affects of carbohydrate restriction on the hypoglycemic phase of the glucose tolerance test. Journal of Clinical Endocrinology and Metabolism, 43, 1088–1093.

Powers, H. W. S. (1973). Dietary measures to improve behavior and achievement. Academic Therapy, 9, 203–214.

References
The purpose of the reference section, as you might expect, is to provide an accurate and complete list of all the references cited in the text of the report. All of the listed references must be cited in the text.

Prinz, R. J., Roberts, W. A., and Hantmann, E. (1980). Dietary correlates of hyperactive behavior in children. Journal of Consulting and Clinical Psychology, 48, 760–769.

Von Hilsheimer, G. (1974). Allergy, toxins and the learning disabled children. San Rafael, California: Academic Therapy Publications.

Winstead, G. K. (1976). Coffee consumption among psychiatric inpatients. American Journal of Psychiatry, 133, 1447–1450.

Dietary Change
11

Author Notes

Requests for reprints of the complete manuscript should be sent to Larry Christensen, Department of Psychology, Texas A&M University, College Station, Texas, 77843.

Author notes

Author identification notes appear with each printed article and are for the purpose of acknowledging the basis of a study (such as a grant or a dissertation), acknowledging assistance in the conduct of the study or preparation of the manuscript, specifying a change in the institutional affiliation of the author, and designating the address of the author to whom reprint requests should be sent. These notes are typed on a separate page, with the words "Author Notes" centered at the top of the page in upper- and lower-case letters. Each note should start with a paragraph indentation. The order is acknowledgments first, then any change in affiliation of the author, and finally the author's address. These notes are not numbered or cited in the text and appear on the title page if the report is to be blind-reviewed, or reviewed in the absence of any information that would identify the author.

Dietary Change

12

Footnotes

¹This scale is currently being validated, and sample copies can be attained from the senior author upon completion of the validation studies.

Footnotes

Footnotes are numbered consecutively, with a superscript arabic numeral, in the order in which they appear in the text of the report. Most footnotes are content footnotes, containing material needed to supplement the information provided in the text. Such footnotes are typed on a separate page, with the word "Footnotes" centered in upper- and lowercase letters. The first line of each footnote is indented five spaces, and the superscript numeral of the footnote should appear in the space just preceding the beginning of the footnote. Footnotes are typed in the order in which they are mentioned in the text.

Table 1

Oral Glucose Tolerance Test Results

	Serum Glucose Concentrations					
Fasting	1/2 hr	1 hr	2 hr	3 hr	4 hr	5 hr
86 mg/dl	69 mg/dl	88 mg/dl	83 mg/dl	84 mg/dl	73 mg/dl	81 mg/dl

Figure Caption

<u>Figure 1</u>.   Reported symptom frequency during baseline and dietary intervention.

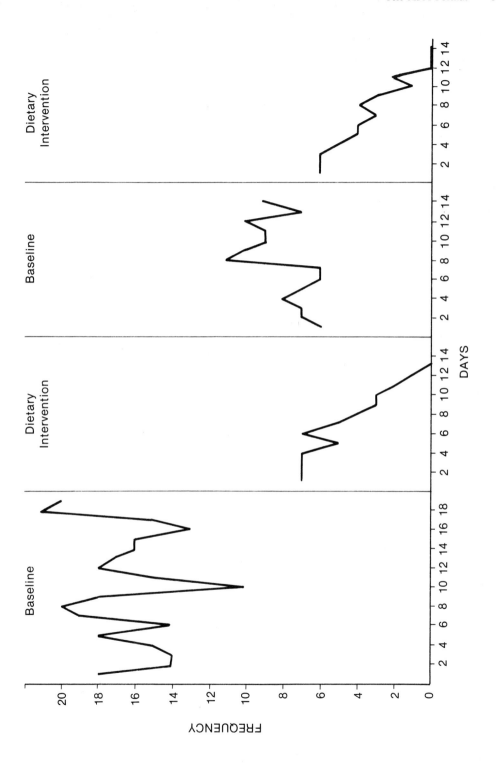

Preparation of the Research Report

In the preceding section, you saw an example of the way a research report must be prepared in order to be submitted for possible publication in a psychological journal. While the essence of the report was discussed in the marginal notes, there are still many style rules that must be considered. In order to maintain consistency across articles and ensure that articles are clear, journal editors want research reports prepared in accordance with the following principles.

Language

The language used to communicate the results of a research study should be nonsexist: that is, it should be free from bias. Sexism in journal writing usually boils down to problems of designation and evaluation. Problems of designation occur when the writer makes reference to one or more people. Perhaps the most common example is referring to people in general as "man" or "mankind." Such designations may imply that women are of secondary importance and therefore should be avoided. Problems of evaluation occur from the habitual use of familiar expressions such as "man and wife" as opposed to "man and woman." The former may imply a difference in the freedom and activities of each individual, whereas the latter implies parallel status. The American Psychological Association (1977) has published a set of guidelines that can be used by authors to help them avoid the use of sexist language; however, the procedure is rather lengthy and time consuming. Bass (1979) has identified a set of rules that will more efficiently enable you to avoid the use of sexist language in most instances:

1. Rather than using men, man, or mankind to refer to people in general, use the words people, individuals, or persons.
2. Switch from the active to the passive voice.
3. Eliminate the singular since words as they, their, and them are genderless. For example, rather than stating "The manager and his subordinates" you could state "The managers and their subordinates."

When writing a research report, you also have to decide whether to use a first- or third-person writing style. Some individuals prefer a first-person writing style, while others believe the research report should be impersonal and written in the third person. Polyson, Levinson, and Miller (1982) found that journal editors do not agree on which type of writing style should be used. Similarly, the publication manual does not take a specific position on this issue. Rather, the emphasis is on clarity and precision in word choice. In the final analysis, it seems as though the writing style that should be used is the one that will facilitate communication of the research study.

Abbreviations

Abbreviations are to be used sparingly. Generally speaking, abbreviate only when the abbreviations are conventional and likely to be familiar to the reader (such as IQ), or only when it is necessary to abbreviate to save space and avoid cumbersome repetition. In all instances, the Latin abbreviations cf (compare), e.g. (for example), etc. (and so forth), i.e. (that is), viz. (namely), and vs. (versus, against) are to be used only in parenthetical material. The only exception to this rule is the Latin abbreviation et al., which can be used in the text of the manuscript. The unit of time "second" is abbreviated s rather than sec. Periods are omitted with nonmetric measurements such as ft and lb. The only exception is inch, which is abbreviated in. with the period. Units of time such as day, week, month, and year are never abbreviated.

Headings

Headings serve to outline the manuscript and to indicate the importance of each topic. There are five different levels of headings that can be used in an article. These are rank ordered as follows: centered main heading in uppercase letters, centered main heading in uppercase and lowercase letters, centered main heading in underlined upper- and lowercase letters, flush side heading in underlined upper- and lowercase letters, and indented paragraph heading in underlined lowercase letters and ending with a period.

Since all articles do not require all five types of headings, you should decide how many levels are required for your article and then order them appropriately. The following illustrates the way in which you would place the headings if your article contained two, three, four, or five headings.

1. Example of the use of two headings.

Method

<u>Subjects</u>

2. Example of the use of three headings.

Method

Instruments

    MMPI.

3. Example of the use of four headings.

Experiment 1
Method

Instruments

    MMPI.

4. Five headings. Use all of the headings in the order listed above.

Numbers

The general rule about expressing numbers in the text is to use words to express any number that begins a sentence as well as any number below 10. Use figures to express all other numbers. There are several exceptions to this rule, and the APA publication manual should be consulted for these exceptions. A second rule to follow in stating numbers is to use arabic and not roman numerals.

Physical Measurements

All physical measurements are to be stated in metric units. If a measurement is expressed in nonmetric units, it must be accompanied, in parentheses, by its metric equivalent.

Presentation of Statistical Results

When presenting the results of statistical tests in the text, give the symbol of the statistical test, its degrees of freedom, the value obtained from the test, and its probability value, as follows:

$$t(36) = 4.52, p < .01$$
$$F(3,52) = 17.36, p < .01$$

When reporting a chi-square value, you should report the degrees of freedom and the sample size in parentheses as follows:

$$\chi^2 (6, N = 68) = 12.64, p < .05$$

Such common statistical tests are not referenced, and the formulas are not included in the text. Referencing and formulas are included only when the statistical test is new, rare, or essential to the manuscript, as when the article concerns a given statistical test.

After the results of a statistical test are reported, descriptive statistical data such as means and standard deviations must be included to clarify the meaning of a significant effect.

Tables

Tables are expensive to publish and therefore should be reserved for use only when they can convey and summarize data more economically and clearly than can a lengthy discussion. If you decide to use tables, you should number them consecutively with arabic numerals. Although a table is prepared on a separate page in the manuscript submitted for publication, it appears in the body of the published article. Therefore, you should indicate the approximate position of the table by an obvious break in the text, with instructions indicated as follows:

Insert Table 1 about here

In preparing the table, you can use the table presented in the sample article as a guide. Each table should have a brief title that clearly explains the data it contains. This title and the word "Table" and its number are typed flush with the left margin and at the top of the table. Each column and row of data within the table should be given a label that identifies, as briefly as possible, the data contained in that row or column. Columns within the table should be at least three spaces apart. The publication manual (American Psychological Association, 1983) lists the various types of headings that can be used in tables. When placing data in the rows and columns, carry each data point out to the same number of decimal places, and place a dash to indicate an absence of data.

When writing the manuscript, you should refer to the table somewhere in the text. This reference should tell what data are presented in the table and briefly discuss the data. When referring to a table, identify it by name, as in "the data in Table 3." Do not use a reference such as "the above table" or "the table on page 12."

Figures

Figures are also very time consuming and expensive to produce and so should be used only when they complement the text or eliminate a lengthy discussion of the data. Figures may consist of charts, graphs, photographs, drawings, or other similar means of representing data or pictorial concepts. In preparing a figure, you should usually use a professional drafting service because most individuals do not have the technical skill to produce an acceptable product. Computer-generated figures are generally unacceptable because they cannot be reproduced satisfactorily. If you do not use a professional drafting service, you should consult the publication manual (American Psychological Association, 1983) for guidelines for the production of an acceptable figure. The publication manual also presents information on the type of figure to use in presenting certain types of data.

Once the figures have been prepared, you should number them consecutively with arabic numerals in the order in which they are used in the manuscript. On the back and also near the edge of the figure, write the number of the figure and a short title in pencil. Also write the word "top" on the back to designate the top of the figure. The figure's location in the body of the manuscript should be indicated by a break in the text, as follows:

Insert Figure 6 about here

Figure Captions

Each figure has a caption that not only provides a brief description of the contents but also serves as a title. However, these captions are not placed on the figure but are typed on a separate page with the words "Figure Captions" centered and typed in upper- and lowercase letters at the top of the page. Flush with the left margin of the page, each caption should begin with the word "Figure" and the number of the figure, both of which are underlined, followed by a period. The caption is typed on the remainder of the line. If more than one line is needed, each subsequent line also begins flush left.

Reference Citations

In the text of the research report, particularly in the introductory section, you must reference other works you have cited. The APA format is to use the author-data citation method, which involves inserting the author's surname and the publication data at the appropriate point, as follows:

> Doe (1975) investigated the . . .
>   or
> It has been demonstrated (Doe, 1975) . . .

With this information, the reader can turn to the reference list and locate complete information regarding the source. Multiple citations involving the same author are arranged in chronological order:

> Doe (1970, 1971, 1972, 1973)

Multiple citations involving different authors are arranged alphabetically, as follows:

> Several studies (Doe, 1970; Kelly, 1965; Mills, 1975) have revealed . . .

If a citation includes more than two but fewer than six authors, all authors should be cited the first time the reference is used. Subsequent citations include only the name of the first author, followed by the words "et al." and the year the article was published. If six or more authors are associated with a citation, only the surname of the first author followed by "et al." is used for all citations.

Reference List

All citations in the text of the research report must be accurately and completely cited in the reference list so that it is possible for readers to locate the works. This means that each entry should include the name of the author, year of publication, title, publishing data, and any other information necessary to identify the reference. All references are to appear in alphabetical order. Rather than elaborate on the specific style of presentation, I refer you to the reference list in the sample article, which gives many examples. However, you should be aware of one type of reference that is not illustrated. If you have cited an article that has been accepted for publication but has not as yet been published, you should reference this citation by including the author's name, followed by the words "in press" in parantheses where the date of publication would otherwise appear. This is followed by the title and the journal in which the article is to be published.

All references are to be typed on a separate page, with the word "References" centered at the top of the page in uppercase and lowercase letters.

Typing

In typing the manscript, double-space all material. The rule is to set the typewriter on double-spacing and leave it there. There should be 1½ in. margins at the top, bottom, right, and left of every page. Words should not be divided at the end of the page, and each page should contain no more than 25 lines of text.

Ordering of Manuscript Pages

The pages of the manuscript should be arranged as follows:

1. *Title page.* This is a separate page (numbered page 1) and includes the title, author's name and institutional affiliation, and running head.
2. *Abstract.* This is a separate page, numbered page 2.
3. *Text of the manuscript.* The text begins on page 3 and continues on consecutive pages until the completion of the discussion section.
4. *References.* References begin on a separate page.
5. *Author identification notes.* These notes begin on a new page.
6. *Footnotes.* Footnotes also begin on a new page.
7. *Tables.* Each table should be placed on a separate page.
8. *Figure captions.* Captions should be listed on a separate page.
9. *Figures.* Each figure should be placed on a separate page.

Writing Style

Many people have difficulty communicating by means of the written word. A clear, concise writing style is something that must be acquired. Unfortunately, many individuals conducting research have not yet mastered this skill; this becomes painfully apparent when they attempt to write the research report. Teaching the art of writing is beyond the scope of this text. However, for the student who has difficulty in writing, I recommend an excellent book by W. Strunk, Jr., and E. B. White, *The Elements of Style,* 2nd ed. (New York: Macmillan, 1972). This book is a classic and has the virtue of being short.

In conclusion, I suggest that you read the very humorous remarks that H. F. Harlow made in the article "Fundamental Principles for Preparing Psychology Journal Articles," *Journal of Comparative and Physiological Psychology,* 1976, 55, 893–896, regarding the content and style of a research report.

Bibliography

Abelson, R. P., and Miller, J. C. Negative persuasion via personal insult. *Journal of Experimental Social Psychology*, 1967, *3*, 321–333.

Adair, J. G. *The human subject.* Boston: Little, Brown, 1973.

Adair, J. G. Open peer commentary. *Behavioral and Brain Sciences*, 1978, *3*, 386–387.

Adair, J. G., and Spinner, B. Subjects' access to cognitive processes: Demand characteristics and verbal report. *Journal for the Theory of Social Behavior*, 1981, *11*, 31–52.

Altemeyer, R. A. Subject pool pollution and the postexperimental interview. *Journal of Experimental Research in Personality*, 1971, *5*, 79–84.

Alumbaugh, R. V. Another "Malleus Maleficarum." *American Psychologist*, 1972, *27*, 897–899.

American Psychological Association, ad hoc Committee on Ethical Standards in Psychological Research. *Ethical principles in the conduct of research with human participants.* Washington, D.C., 1973.

American Psychological Association Publication Task Force. Guidelines for nonsexist language in APA journals. *American Psychologist*, 1977, *32*, 487–494.

American Psychological Association. *Ethical principles in the conduct of research with human participants.* Washington, D.C., 1982.

American Psychological Association. *Publication manual of the American Psychological Association.* 3rd ed. Washington, D.C., 1983.

Aronson, E. The effect of effort on the attractiveness of rewarded and unrewarded stimuli. *Journal of Abnormal and Social Psychology*, 1961, *63*, 375–380.

Aronson, E. Avoidance of inter-subject communication. *Psychological Reports*, 1966, *19*, 238.

Aronson, E., and Carlsmith, J. M. Performance expectancy as a determinant of actual performance. *Journal of Abnormal and Social Psychology*, 1963, *66*, 584–588.

Aronson, E., and Carlsmith, J. M. Experimentation in social psychology. In *The handbook of social psychology*, edited by G. Lindzey and E. Aronson. 2nd ed. Reading, Mass.: Addison-Wesley, 1968.

Aronson E., and Cope, V. My enemy's enemy is my friend. *Journal of Personality and Social Psychology*, 1968, *8*, 8–12.

Aronson, E., and Linder, D. Gain and loss of esteem as determinants of interpersonal attractiveness. *Journal of Experimental Social Psychology*, 1965, *1*, 156–171.

Aronson, E., and Mills, J. The effect of severity of initiation on liking for a group. *Journal of Abnormal and Social Psychology*, 1959, *59*, 177–181.

Asch, S. E. Studies of independence and conformity: A minority of one against a unanimous majority. *Psychological Monographs*, 1956, *70*, No. 9 (Whole No. 416).

Atkeson, B. M., Calhoun, K. S., Resick, P. A., and Ellis, E. M. Victims of rape: Repeated assessment of depressive symptoms. *Journal of Consulting and Clinical Psychology*, 1982, *50*, 96–102.

Baltes, P. B., Reese, H. W., and Nesselroade, J. R. *Life-span developmental psychology: Introduction to research.* Monterey, Calif.: Wadsworth Publishing Co., 1977.

Bannister, D. Psychology as an exercise in paradox. *Bulletin of British Psychological Society,* 1966, *19,* 21–26.

Barber, T. X. *Pitfalls in human research: Ten pivotal points.* New York: Pergamon Press, 1976.

Barber, T. X., and Silver, M. J. Fact, fiction, and the experimenter bias effect. *Psychological Bulletin Monograph,* 1968, *70,* 1–29.

Barlow, D. H., and Hayes, S. C. Alternating treatments design: One strategy for comparing the effects of two treatments in a single subject. *Journal of Applied Behavior Analysis,* 1979, *12,* 199–210.

Barlow, D. H., Sakheim, D. K., and Beck, J. G. Anxiety increases sexual arousal. *Journal of Abnormal Psychology,* 1983, *92,* 49–54.

Baron, R. A. Threatened retaliation from the victim as an inhibitor of physical aggression. *Journal of Research in Personality,* 1973, *7,* 103–115.

Baron, R. A. Effects of victim's pain cues, victim's race, and level of prior instigation upon physical aggression. Unpublished manuscript, Purdue University, 1976.

Bass, B. M. Confessions of a former male chauvinist. *American Psychologist,* 1979, *34,* 194–195.

Baumrind, D. Some thoughts on ethics of research: After reading Milgram's "Behavioral study of obedience." *American Psychologist,* 1964, *19,* 421–431.

Baumrind, D. Principles of ethical conduct in the treatment of subjects: Reaction to the draft report of the committee on ethical standards in psychological research. *American Psychologist,* 1971, *26,* 887–896.

Baumrind, D. Reactions to the May 1972 draft report of the ad hoc committee on ethical standards in psychological research. *American Psychologist,* 1972, *27,* 1083–1086.

Beach, F. A. The snark was a boojum. *American Psychologist,* 1950, *5,* 115–124.

Beach, F. A. Experimental investigations of species specific behavior. *American Psychologist,* 1960, *15,* 1–8.

Becker, L. J., Rabinowitz, V. C., and Seligman, C. Evaluating the impact of utility company billing plans on residential energy consumption. *Evaluation and Program Planning,* 1980, *3,* 159–164.

Beckman, L., and Bishop, B. R. Deception in psychological research: A reply to Seeman. *American Psychologist,* 1970, *25,* 878–880.

Beecher, H. K. Pain: One mystery solved. *Science,* 1966, *151,* 840–841.

Bergin, A. E. Some implications of psychotherapy research for therapeutic practice. *Journal of Abnormal Psychology,* 1966, *71,* 235–246.

Bergin, A. E., and Strupp, H. H. New directions in psychotherapy research. *Journal of Abnormal Psychology,* 1970, *76,* 13–26.

Bergin, A. E., and Strupp, H. H. *Changing frontiers in the science of psychotherapy.* New York: Aldine-Atherton, 1972.

Berkowitz, L., and LePage, A. Weapons or aggression-eliciting stimuli. *Journal of Personality and Social Psychology,* 1967, *7,* 202–207.

Berkun, M., Bialek, H. M., Kern, P. R., and Yagi, K. Experimental studies of psychological stress in man. *Psychological Monographs: General and Applied,* 1962, *76*(15), 1–39.

Berscheid, E., Baron, R. S., Dermer, M., and Libman, M. Anticipating informed consent: An empirical approach. *American Psychologist,* 1973, *28,* 913–925.

Bijou, S. W., Peterson, R. F., Harris, F. R., Allen, K. E., and Johnston, M. S. Methodology for experimental studies of young children in natural settings. *Psychological Record,* 1969, *19,* 177–210.

Billewicz, W. Z. The efficiency of matched samples: An empirical investigation. *Biometrics,* 1965, *21,* 623–644.

Boice, R. Domestication. *Psychological Bulletin,* 1973, *80,* 215–230.

Bolger, H. The case study method. In *Handbook of Clinical Psychology,* edited by B. B. Wolman, pp. 28–39. New York: McGraw-Hill, 1965.

Boring, E. G. The nature and history of experimental control. *American Journal of Psychology,* 1954, *67,* 573–589.

Box, G. E. P., and Jenkins, G. M. *Time-series analysis: Forecasting and control.* San Francisco: Holden-Day, 1970.

Box, G. E. P., and Tiao, G. L. A change in level of a non-stationary time series. *Biometrics,* 1965, *52,* 181–192.

Bracht, G. H., and Glass, G. V. The external validity of experiments. *American Educational Research Journal*, 1968, 5, 437–474.

Bradley, A. W. Self-serving bias in the attribution process: A reexamination of the fact or fiction question. *Journal of Personality and Social Psychology*, 1978, 36, 56–71.

Brady, J. V. Ulcers in "executive monkeys." *Scientific American*, 1958, 199, 95–100.

Brand, M. *The nature of causation*. Urbana, Ill.: University of Illinois Press, 1976.

Bridgman, P. W. *The logic of modern physics*. New York: Macmillan, 1927.

Britton, B. K. Ethical and educational aspects of participation as a subject in psychology experiments. *Teaching of Psychology*, 1979, 6, 195–198.

Broden, M., Bruce, M., Mitchell, M., Carter, V., and Hall, R. V. Effects of teacher attention on attending behavior of two boys at adjacent desks. *Journal of Applied Behavior Analysis*, 1970, 3, 199–203.

Brown, R., Cayden, C. B., and Bellugi-Klima, U. The child grammar from I to III. In *Minnesota symposia on child psychology*, edited by J. P. Hill. Minneapolis: The University of Minnesota Press, 1969, 2, 28–73.

Brown, W. F., Wehe, N. O., Zunker, V. G., and Haslam, W. L. Effectiveness of student-to-student counseling on the academic adjustment of potential dropouts. *Journal of Educational Psychology*, 1971, 62, 285–289.

Brownell, W. A. The evaluation of learning under dissimilar systems of instruction. In *Introduction to research and evaluation*, edited by J. D. Finn. Buffalo: State University of New York at Buffalo, 1966.

Campbell, D. Factors relative to the validity of experiments in social settings. *Psychological Bulletin*, 1957, 54, 297–312.

Campbell, D. T. Quasi-experimental design. In *International Encyclopedia of the Social Sciences*, 5, edited by D. L. Gills. New York: Macmillan and Free Press, 1968.

Campbell, D. T. Prospective: Artifact and control. In *Artifact in behavioral research*, edited by R. Rosenthal and R. L. Rosnow. New York: Academic Press, 1969. (a)

Campbell, D. T. Reforms as experiments. *American Psychologist*, 1969, 24, 409–429. (b)

Campbell, D. T., and Boruch, R. F. Making the case for randomized assignments to treatments by considering the alternatives: Six ways in which quasi-experimental evaluations in compensatory education tend to underestimate effects. In *Evaluation and experiment: Some critical issues in assessing social programs*, edited by C. A. Bennett and A. A. Lumsdaine. New York: Academic Press, 1975.

Campbell, D. T., and Erlebacher, A. How regression artifacts in quasi-experimental evaluations can mistakenly make compensatory education look harmful. In *Compensatory education: A national debate, Vol. 3, Disadvantaged Child*, edited by J. Hellmuth. New York: Brunner, Mazel, 1970.

Campbell, D. T., and Ross, H. L. The Connecticut crackdown on speeding: Time series data in quasi-experimental analysis. *Law and Society Review*, 1968, 3 (1), 33–53.

Campbell, D. T., and Stanley, J. C. *Experimental and quasi-experimental designs for research*. Chicago: Rand McNally, 1963.

Campbell, K. E., and Jackson, T. T. The role of and need for replication research in social psychology. *Replications in Social Psychology*, 1979, 1, 3–14.

Caporaso, J. A. *The structure and function of European integration*. Pacific Palisades, Calif.: Goodyear Publishing Co., 1974.

Carlopia, J., Adair, J. G., Lindsay, R. C. L., and Spinner, B. Avoiding artifact in the search for bias: The importance of assessing subjects' perceptions of the experiment. *Journal of Personality and Social Psychology*, 1983, 44, 693–701.

Carlsmith, J. M., Collins, B. E., and Helmreich, R. L. Studies in forced compliance I: The effect of pressure for compliance on attitude change produced by face-to-face role playing and anonymous essay writing. *Journal of Personality and Social Psychology*, 1966, 4, 1–3.

Carlston, D. E., and Cohen, J. L. A closer examination of subject roles. *Journal of Personality and Social Psychology*, 1980, 38, 857–870.

Christensen, L. Intrarater reliability. *The Southern Journal of Educational Research*, 1968, 2, 175–182.

Christensen, L. The negative subject: Myth, reality or a prior experimental experience effect. *Journal of*

Personality and Social Psychology, 1977, *35,* 392–400.

Christensen, L. Positive self-presentation: A parsimonious explanation of subject motives. *The Psychological Record,* 1981, *31,* 553–571.

Christensen, L. A critique of Carlston and Cohen's examination of subject roles. *Personality and Social Psychology Bulletin,* 1982, *8,* 579–582.

Church, R. M. Systematic effect of random errors in the yoked control design. *Psychological Bulletin,* 1964, *62,* 122–131.

Cochran, W. G., and Cox, G. M. *Experimental designs.* New York: Wiley, 1957.

Collins, F. L., Jr., Kuhn, I. F., Jr., and King, G. D. Variables affecting subjects' ethical ratings of proposed experiments. *Psychological Reports,* 1979, *44,* 155–164.

Conrad, H. S., and Jones, H. E. A second study of familial resemblances in intelligence. *39th Yearbook of the National Society for the Study of Education.* Chicago: University of Chicago Press, 1940 (II), 97–141.

Conroy, R. T., and Mills, J. N. *Human circadian rhythms.* London: J. & A. Church, 1970.

Cook, T. D., Bean, J. R., Calder, B.J., Frey, R., Krovetz, M. L., and Reisman, S. R. Demand characteristics and three conceptions of the frequently deceived subject. *Journal of Personality and Social Psychology,* 1970, *14,* 185–194.

Cook, T. D., and Campbell, D. T. Experiments in field settings. In *Handbook of industrial and organizational research,* edited by M. D. Dunnette. Chicago: Rand McNally, 1975.

Cook, T. D., and Campbell, D. T. Quasi-experimentation. *Design and analysis issues for field settings.* Chicago: Rand McNally, 1979.

Cook, T. D., Gruder, C. L., Hennigan, K. M., and Flay, B. R. The history of the sleeper effect: Some logical pitfalls in accepting the null hypothesis. *Psychological Bulletin,* 1979, *86,* 662–679.

Cowles, M. F. N = 35: A rule of thumb for psychological researchers. *Perceptual and Motor Skills,* 1974, *38,* 1135–1138.

Cox, D. E., and Sipprelle, C. N. Coercion in participation as a research subject. *American Psychologist,* 1971, *26,* 726–728.

Cox, D. R. *Planning of experiments.* New York: Wiley, 1958.

Cronbach, L. The two disciplines of scientific psychology. *American Psychologist,* 1957, *12,* 671–684.

Cronbach, L. Beyond two disciplines of scientific psychology. *American Psychologist,* 1975, *30,* 116–127.

Cronbach, L., and Furby, L. "How should we measure change"—or should we? *Psychological Bulletin,* 1970, *74,* 68–80.

D'Amato, M. R. *Experimental psychology methodology: Psychophysics and learning.* New York: McGraw-Hill, 1970.

Davis, H., and Memmott, J. Autocontingencies. Rats count to three to predict safety from shock. *Animal Learning and Behavior,* 1983, *11,* 95–100.

Deese, J. *Psychology as science and art.* New York: Harcourt Brace Jovanovich, Inc., 1972.

Diener, E., and Crandall, R. *Ethics in social and behavioral research.* Chicago: University of Chicago Press, 1978.

Dipboye, R. L., and Flanagan, M. F. Research settings in industrial and organizational psychology. Are findings in the field more generalizable than in the laboratory? *American Psychologist,* 1979, *34,* 141–150.

Dukes, W. F. N = 1. *Psychological Bulletin,* 1965, *64,* 74–79.

Ebbinghaus, H. *Memory, a contribution to experimental psychology.* 1885. Translated by Ruger and Bussenius. New York: Teachers College, Columbia University, 1913.

Ehrlich, A. The age of the rat. *Human Behavior,* 1974, *3,* 25–28.

Ellsworth, P. C. From abstract ideas to concrete instances: Some guidelines for choosing natural research settings. *American Psychologist,* 1977, *33,* 604–615.

Ellsworth, P. C. Open peer commentary. *The Behavioral and Brain Sciences,* 1978, *3,* 386–387.

Ellsworth, P. C., Carlsmith, J. A., and Henson, A. The stare as a stimulus to flight in human subjects. *Journal of Personality and Social Psychology,* 1972, *21,* 302–311.

Epstein, S. The stability of behavior: I. On predicting most of the people much of the time. *Journal of*

Personality and Social Psychology, 1979, *37,* 1097–1126.

Epstein, S. The stability of behavior: II. Implications for psychological research. *American Psychologist,* 1981, *35,* 790–806.

Epstein, T. M., Suedfeld, P., and Silverstein, S. J. The experimental contact: Subject's expectations of and reactions to some behavior of experimenters. *American Psychologist,* 1973, *28,* 212–221.

Ericsson, K. A., and Simon, H. A. Verbal reports as data. *Psychological Review,* 1980, *87,* 215–251.

Evans, P. The Biert affair . . . Sleuthing in science. *APA Monitor,* 1976, *7,* 1–4.

Eysenck, H. J. The effects of psychotherapy: An evaluation. *Journal of Consulting Psychology,* 1952, *16,* 319–324.

Eysenck, H. J. *The biological basis of personality.* Springfield, Ill.: Charles C Thomas, 1967.

Ferguson, G. A. *Statistical analysis in psychology and education.* New York: McGraw-Hill, 1966.

Ferster, C. B., and Skinner, B. F. *Schedules of reinforcement.* New York: Appleton-Century-Crofts, 1957.

Festinger, G. L., and Carlsmith, J. M. Cognitive consequences of forced compliance. *Journal of Abnormal and Social Psychology,* 1959, *58,* 203–211.

Festinger, L. *A theory of cognitive dissonance.* Evanston, Ill.: Row, Peterson, 1957.

Fillenbaum, S. Prior deception and subsequent experimental performance: The faithful subject, *Journal of Personality and Social Psychology,* 1966, *4,* 532–537.

Fisher, R. A. *The design of experiments.* 1st ed. London: Oliver and Boyd, 1935.

Flaherty, C. F., and Checke, S. Anticipation of incentive gain. *Animal Learning and Behavior,* 1982, *10,* 177–182.

Fouts, R. S. Acquisition and testing of gestural signs in four young chimpanzees. *Science,* June 1, 1973.

Fox, J. G. A comparison of Gothic Elite and Standard Elite type faces. *Ergonomics,* 1963, *6,* 193–198.

Freedman, J. L., and Fraser, S. C. Compliance without pressure: The foot-in-the-door technique. *Journal of Personality and Social Psychology,* 1966, *4,* 195–202.

Friedman, N. *The social nature of psychological research.* New York: Basic Books, 1967.

Gadlin, H., and Ingle, G. Through the one-way mirror: The limits of experimental self-reflection. *American Psychologist,* 1975, *30,* 1003–1009.

Gagné, R. M., and Baker, K. E. Stimulus pre-differentiation as a factor in transfer of training. *Journal of Experimental Psychology,* 1950, *40,* 439–451.

Gaito, J. Statistical dangers involved in counterbalancing. *Psychological Report,* 1958, *4,* 463–468.

Gaito, J. Repeated measurements designs and counterbalancing. *Psychological Bulletin,* 1961, *58,* 46–54.

The Gallup opinion index: Political, social and economic trends. January 1980, Report No. 174, p. 29.

Gardner, G. T. Effects of federal human subjects regulations on data obtained in environmental stressor research. *Journal of Personality and Social Psychology,* 1978, *36,* 628–634.

Gelfand, D., and Hartmann, D. Behavior therapy with children: A review and evaluation of research methodology. *Psychological Bulletin,* 1968, *69,* 204–215.

Gerdes, E. P. College students' reactions to social psychological experiments involving deception. *Journal of Social Psychology,* 1979, *107,* 99–110.

Gergen, K. J. Social psychology as history. *Journal of Personality and Social Psychology,* 1973, *26,* 309–320. (a)

Gergen, K. J. The codification of research ethics: Views of a doubting Thomas. *American Psychologist,* 1973, *28,* 907–912. (b)

Glass, G. V., Tiao, G. C., and Maguire, T. O. The 1900 revision of German divorce laws. *Law and Society Review,* 1971, *5,* 539–562.

Glass, G. V., Willson, V. L., and Gottman, J. M. *Design and analysis of time series.* Boulder, Colo.: Laboratory of Educational Research Press, 1975.

Gottman, J. M., and Glass, G. V. Analysis of interrupted time-series experiments. In *Single subject research. Strategies for evaluating change,* edited by T. R. Kratochwill. New York: Academic Press, 1978.

Gottman, J. M., and McFall, R. M. Self-monitoring effects in a program for potential high school dropouts: A time-series analysis. *Journal of Consulting and Clinical Psychology*, 1972, *39*, 273–281.

Gottman, J. M., McFall, R. M., and Barnett, J. T. Design and analysis of research using time series. *Psychological Bulletin*, 1969, *72*, 299–306.

Greenwald, A. G. Consequences of prejudice against the null hypothesis. *Psychological Bulletin*, 1975, *82*, 1–20.

Grice, G. R. Dependence of empirical laws upon the source of experimental variation. *Psychological Bulletin*, 1966, 66, 488–498.

Hackett, G. Survey research methods. *The Personnel and Guidance Journal*, 1981, 599–604.

Hall, J. F., and Kobrick, J. L. The relationships among three measures of response strength. *Journal of Comparative and Physiological Psychology*, 1952, *45*, 280–282.

Hall, R. V., ed. *Behavior management series: Part II, Basic principles.* Lawrence, Kans.: H. and H. Enterprises, 1971.

Hall, R. V., and Fox, R. W. Changing-criterion designs: An alternative applied behavior analysis procedure. In *New developments in behavioral research: Theory, method, and application,* In honor of Sidney W. Bijou, edited by C. C. Etzel, G. M. LeBlanc, and D. M. Baer. Hillsdale, N.J.: Lawrence Erlbaum Associates, 1977.

Hartmann, D. P., and Hall, R. V. A discussion of the changing criterion design. *Journal of Applied Behavior Analysis*, 1976, *9*, 527–532.

Hashtroudi, S., Parker, E. S., DeLisi, L. E., and Wyatt, R. J. On elaboration and alcohol. *Journal of Verbal Learning and Verbal Behavior*, 1983, *22*, 164–173.

Haslerud, G., and Meyers, S. The transfer value of given and individually derived principles. *Journal of Educational Psychology*, 1958, *49*, 293–298.

Hauri, P., and Ohmstead, E. What is the moment of sleep onset for insomniacs? *Sleep*, 1983, *6*, 10–15.

Hayes, S. C., and Cone, J. D. Reduction of residential consumption of electricity through simple monthly feedback. *Journal of Applied Behavior Analysis*, 1981, *14*, 81–88.

Helmstadter, G. C. *Research concepts in human behavior.* New York: Appleton-Century-Crofts, 1970.

Hersen, M., and Barlow, D. H. *Single case experimental designs: Strategies for studying behavioral change.* New York: Pergamon Press, 1976.

Hersen, M., Gullick, E. L., Matherne, P. M., and Harbert, T. L. Instructions and reinforcement in the modification of a conversion reaction. *Psychological Reports*, 1972, *31*, 719–722.

Hewett, F. M., Taylor, F. D., and Artuso, A. A. The Santa Monica project: Evaluation of an engineered classroom design with emotionally disturbed children. *Exceptional Children*, 1969, *35*, 523–529.

Holmes, D. S. Amount of experience in experiments as a determinant of performance in later experiments. *Journal of Personality and Social Psychology*, 1967, *7*, 403–407.

Holmes, D. S. Effectiveness of debriefing after a stress-producing deception. *Journal of Research in Personality*, 1973, *7*, 127–138.

Holmes, D. S. Debriefing after psychological experiments: I. Effectiveness of postdeception dehoaxing. *American Psychologist*, 1976, *31*, 858–867. (a)

Holmes, D. S. Debriefing after psychological experiments: II. Effectiveness of postexperimental desensitizing. *American Psychologist*, 1976, *31*, 868–875. (b)

Holmes, D. S., and Applebaum, A. S. Nature of prior experimental experience as a determinant of performance in a subsequent experiment. *Journal of Personality and Social Psychology*, 1970, *14*, 195–202.

Holmes, D. S., and Bennett, D. H. Experiments to answer questions raised by the use of deception in psychological research: I. Role playing as an alternative to deception; II. Effectiveness of debriefing after a deception; III. Effect of informed consent on deception. *Journal of Personality and Social Psychology*, 1974, *29*, 358–367.

Hunsicker, J. P., and Mellgren, R. L. Multiple deficits in the retention of an appetitively motivated behavior across a 24-hr period in rats. *Animal Learning and Behavior*, 1977, *5*, 14–16.

Hyman, R., and Berger, L. Discussion. In *The effects of psychotherapy,* edited by H. J. Eysenck, pp. 81–86. New York: International Science Press, 1966.

Johnson, J. M. Punishment of human behavior. *American Psychologist*, 1972, *27*, 1033–1054.

Johnson, R. F. Q. The experimenter attributes effect: A methodological analysis. *Psychological Record*, 1976, 26, 67–78.

Johnson, R. W., and Adair, J. G. Experimenter expectancy vs. systematic recording errors under automated and nonautomated stimulus presentation. *Journal of Experimental Research in Personality*, 1972, 6, 88–94.

Jones, J. H. *Bad blood: The Tuskegee syphilis experiment*. New York: Free Press, 1981.

Jung, J. *The experimenter's dilemma*. New York: Harper, 1971.

Karhan, J. R. A behavioral and written measure of the effects of guilt and anticipated guilt on compliance for Machiavellians. Unpublished thesis, Texas A&M University, May 1973.

Kavanau, J. L. Behavior: Confinement, adaptation, and compulsory regimes in laboratory studies. *Science*, 1964, 143, 490.

Kavanau, J. L. Behavior of captive whitefooted mice. *Science*, 1967, 155, 1623–1639.

Kazdin, A. E. The role of instructions and reinforcement in behavior changes in token reinforcement programs. *Journal of Educational Psychology*, 1973, 64, 63–71.

Kazdin, A. E. Assessing the clinical or applied importance of behavior change through social validation. *Behavior Modification*, 1977, 1, 427–449.

Kazdin, A. E. Methodological and interpretive problems of single-case experimental designs. *Journal of Consulting and Clinical Psychology*, 1978, 46, 629–642.

Kazdin, A. E. *Research design in clinical psychology*. New York: Harper & Row, 1980.

Kazdin, A. E., and Kopel, S. A. On resolving ambiguities of the multiple-baseline design: Problems and recommendations. *Behavior Therapy*, 1975, 6, 601–608.

Kelman, H. C. Human use of human subjects. *Psychological Bulletin*, 1967, 67, 1–11.

Kelman, H. C. *A time to speak*. San Francisco: Jossey Bass, 1968.

Kelman, H. C. The rights of the subject in social research: An analysis in terms of relative power and legitimacy. *American Psychologist*, 1972, 27, 989–1016.

Kempthorne, O. The design and analysis of experiments with some reference to educational research. In *Research design and analysis: Second annual Phi Delta Kappa symposium on educational research*, edited by R. O. Collier, Jr., and S. M. Elam. Bloomington, Ind.: Phi Delta Kappa, 1961, 97–126.

Kendler, T. S., and Kendler, H. H. Reversal and nonreversal shifts in kindergarten children. *Journal of Experimental Psychology*, 1959, 58, 56–60.

Kendler, T. S., Kendler, H. H., and Learnard, B. Mediated responses to size and brightness as a function of age. *American Journal of Psychology*, 1962, 75, 571–586.

Kennedy, J. L., and Uphoff, H. F. Experiments on the nature of extrasensory perception: III. The recording error criticism of extra-chance scores. *Journal of Parapsychology*, 1939, 3, 226–245.

Kerlinger, F. Draft report of the APA committee on ethical standards in psychological research: A critical reaction. *American Psychologist*, 1972, 27, 894–896.

Kerlinger, F. N. *Foundations of behavioral research*. New York: Holt, 1973.

Kerlinger, F. N., and Pedhazur, E. J. *Multiple regression in behavioral research*. New York: Holt Rinehart and Winston, 1973.

Klockars, C. B., and O'Connor, F. W. (eds.) *Deviance and decency: The ethics of research with human subjects*. London: Sage Publications, 1979.

Kratochwill, T. R. Foundations of time-series research. In *Single subject research: Strategies for evaluating change*, edited by T. R. Kratochwill. New York: Academic Press, 1978.

Krejcie, R. V., and Morgan, D. W. Determining sample size for research activities. *Educational and Psychological Measurement*, 1970, 30, 607–610.

Kruglanski, A. W. On the paradigmatic objections to experimental psychology: A reply to Gadlin and Ingle. *American Psychologist*, 1976, 31, 655–663.

Kusche, C. A., and Greenberg, M. T. Evaluative understanding and role-taking ability: A comparison of deaf and hearing children. *Child Development*, 1983, 54, 141–147.

Lana, R. Pretest-treatment interaction effects in longitudinal studies. *Psychological Bulletin*, 1959, 56, 293–300.

Lana, R. E. Pretest sensitization. In *Artifact in behav-*

ioral research, edited by R. Rosenthal and R. L. Rosnow. New York: Academic Press, 1969.

Lawler, E. E., III, and Hackman, J. R. Impact of employee participation in the development of pay incentive plans: A field experiment. *Journal of Applied Psychology*, 1969, 53, 467–471.

Leak, G. K. Student perception of coercion and value from participation in psychological research. *Teaching of Psychology*, 1981, 8, 147–149.

Lefkowitz, M., Blake, R. R., and Mouton, J. S. Status factors in pedestrian violation of traffic signals. *Journal of Abnormal and Social Psychology*, 1955, 51, 704–705.

Leitenberg, H. The use of single-case methodology in psychotherapy research. *Journal of Abnormal Psychology*, 1973, 82, 87–101.

Leitenberg, H., Agras, W. S., Thompson, L., and Wright, D. E. Feedback in behavior modification: An experimental analysis in two phobic cases. *Journal of Applied Behavior Analysis*, 1968, 1, 131–137.

LeUnes, A., Christensen, L., and Wilkerson, D. Institutional tour effects on attitudes related to mental retardation. *American Journal of Mental Deficiency*, 1975, 79, 732–735.

Levenson, H., Gray, M., and Ingram, A. Current research methods in personality: Five years after Carlson's survey. *Personality and Social Psychology Bulletin*, 1976, 2, 158–161.

Liddle, G., and Long, D. Experimental room for slow learners. *Elementary School Journal*, 1958, 59, 143–149.

Liebert, R. M., Odem, R. D., Hill, J., and Huff, R. Effects of age and rule familiarity on the production of modeled language constructions. *Developmental Psychology*, 1969, 1, 108–112.

Lindquist, E. F. *Design and analysis of experiments in psychology and education.* New York: Houghton Mifflin, 1953.

Lockard, R. B. The albino rat: A defensible choice or a bad habit? *American Psychologist*, 1968, 23, 734–742.

Lord, F. M. Statistical adjustments when comparing preexisting groups. *Psychological Bulletin*, 1969, 72, 336–337.

Lubin, A. The interpretation of significant interaction. *Educational and Psychological Measurement*, 1961, 21, 807–817.

Lyons, J. On the psychology of the psychological experiment. In *Cognition-theory, research, promise*, edited by C. Schurer. New York: Harper, 1964.

Maier, N. R. F. *Frustration: The study of behavior without a goal.* New York: McGraw-Hill, 1949.

Marks-Kaufman, R., and Lipeles, B. J. Patterns of nutrient selection in rats orally self-administering morphine. *Nutrition and Behavior*, 1982, 1, 33–46.

Martin, C. J., Boersma, F. J., and Cox, D. L. A classification of associative strategies in paired-associate learning. *Psychonomic Science*, 1965, 3, 455–456.

Marx, M. H. *Theories in contemporary psychology.* New York: Macmillan, 1963.

Marx, M. H., and Hillix, W. A. *Systems and theories in psychology.* New York: McGraw-Hill, 1973.

Masling, J. Role-related behavior of the subject and psychologist and its effects upon psychological data. *Nebraska Symposium on Motivation*. Lincoln: University of Nebraska Press, 1966, 14, 67–103.

May, W. W. On Baumrind's four commandments. *American Psychologist*, 1972, 27, 899–902.

McCullough, J. P., Cornell, J. E., McDaniel, and Mueller, R. K. Utilization of the simultaneous treatment design to improve student behavior in a first-grade classroom. *Journal of Consulting and Clinical Psychology*, 1974, 42, 288–292.

McFall, R. M. Effects of self-monitoring on normal smoking behavior. *Journal of Consulting and Clinical Psychology*, 1970, 35, 135–142.

McGraw, D. L., and Watson, G. L. *Political science inquiry.* New York: Wiley, 1976.

McGuigan, F. J. The experimenter: A neglected stimulus object. *Psychological Bulletin*, 1963, 60, 421–428.

McGuigan, F. J. *Experimental psychology: Methods of research.* New Jersey: Prentice-Hall, 1983.

McNemar, Q. Opinion-attitude methodology. *Psychological Bulletin*, 1946, 43, 289–374.

Mellgren, R. L., Nation, J. R., and Wrather, D. M. Magnitude of negative reinforcement and resistance to extinction. *Learning and Motivation*, 1975, 6, 253–263.

Mellgren, R. L., Seybert, J. A., and Dyck, D. G. The order of continuous, partial and nonreward trials and resistance to extinction. *Learning and Motivation*, 1978, 9, 359–371.

Middlemist, R. D., Knowles, E. S., and Matter, C.

F. Personal space invasions in the lavatory: Suggestive evidence for arousal. *Journal of Personality and Social Psychology*, 1976, *33*, 541–546.

Milgram, S. Behavioral study of obedience. *Journal of Abnormal and Social Psychology*, 1963, *67*, 371–378.

Milgram, S. Group pressure and action against a person. *Journal of Personality and Social Psychology*, 1964, *69*, 137–143. (a)

Milgram, S. Issues in the study of obedience: A reply to Baumrind. *American Psychologist*, 1964, *19*, 848–852. (b)

Mill, J. S. *A system of logic*. New York: Harper, 1874.

Miller, A. G. Role playing: An alternative to deception? A review of the evidence. *American Psychologist*, 1972, *27*, 623–636.

Miller, N. E. Objective techniques for studying motivational effects of drugs on animals. In *Psychotropic drugs*, edited by S. Garettini and V. Ghetti. Amsterdam: Elsevier, 1957.

Mills, J. A procedure for explaining experiments involving deception. *Personality and Social Psychology Bulletin*, 1976, *2*, 3–13.

Mook, D. G. In defense of external invalidity. *American Psychologist*, 1983, *38*, 379–387.

Morison, R. S. "Gradualness, gradualness, gradualness" (I. P. Pavlov). *American Psychologist*, 1960, *15*, 187–198.

Nation, J. R., Bourgeois, A. E., Clark, D. E., and Hare, M. F. The effects of chronic cobalt exposure on behaviors and metallothionein levels in the adult rat. *Neurobehavioral Toxicology and Teratology*, 1983, *9*, 9–15.

Neale, J. M., and Liebert, R. M. *Science and behavior: An introduction to methods of research*. New Jersey: Prentice-Hall, 1973.

Nicewander, W. A., and Price, J. M. Dependent variable reliability and the power of significance tests. *Psychological Bulletin*, 1978, *85*, 405–409.

Oakes, W. External validity and the use of real people as subjects. *American Psychologist*, 1972, *27*, 959–962.

Oliver, R. L., and Berger, P. K. Advisability of pretest designs in psychological research. *Perceptual and Motor Skills*, 1980, *51*, 463–471.

Orne, M. T. On the social psychology of the psychological experiment: With particular reference to demand characteristics and their implications. *American Psychologist*, 1962, *17*, 776–783.

Orne, M. Communication by the total experimental situations: Why is it important, how is it evaluated, and its significance for the ecological validity of findings. In *Communication and affect*, edited by P. Pliner, L. Kramer, and T. Alloway. New York: Academic Press, 1973.

Ossip-Klein, D. J., Epstein, L. H., Winter, M. K., Stiller, R., Russell, P., and Dickson, B. Does switching to low tar/nicotine/carbon monoxide–yield cigarettes decrease alveolar carbon monoxide measures? A randomized trial. *Journal of Consulting and Clinical Psychology*, 1983, *51*, 234–241.

Packard, R. G. The control of "classroom attention": A group contingency for complex behaviors. *Journal of Applied Behavior Analysis*, 1970, *3*, 13–28.

Page, M. M. Modification of figure-ground perception as a function of awareness of demand characteristics. *Journal of Personality and Social Psychology*, 1968, *9*, 59–66.

Page, M. M. Social psychology of a classical conditioning of attitudes experiment. *Journal of Personality and Social Psychology*, 1969, *11*, 177–186.

Page, M. M., and Kahle, L. R. Demand characteristics in the satiation-deprivation effect on attitude conditioning. *Journal of Personality and Social Psychology*, 1971, *20*, 304–318.

Page, M. M., and Scheidt, R. J. The elusive weapons effect: Demand awareness, evaluation apprehension, and slightly sophisticated subjects. *Journal of Personality and Social Psychology*, 1976, *33*, 553–562.

Page, S., and Yates, E. Attitudes of psychologists toward experimenter controls in research. *The Canadian Psychologist*, 1973, *14*, 202–207.

Pappworth, M. H. *Human guinea pigs: Experimentation on man*. Boston: Beacon Press, 1967.

Paul, G. L. Behavior modification research: Design and tactics. In *Behavior therapy appraisal and status*, edited by C. M. Franks. New York: McGraw-Hill, 1969.

Pavlov, I. P. *Lecture on conditioned reflexes*. Translated by W. H. Gantt. New York: International, 1928.

Pellegrini, R. J. Ethics and identity: A note on the call to conscience. *American Psychologist, 1972, 27,* 896–897.

Pfungst, O. *Clever Hans (the horse of Mr. Von Osten): A contribution to experimental, animal, and human psychology.* Translated by C. L. Rahn. New York: Holt, Rinehart and Winston, 1911. (Republished, 1965.)

Pihl, R. D., Zacchia, C., Zeichner, A. Follow-up analysis of the use of deception and aversive contingencies in psychological experiments. *Psychological Reports, 1981, 48,* 927–930.

Plutchik, R. *Foundations of experimental research.* New York: Harper, 1974.

Polyson, J., Levinson, M., and Miller, H. Writing styles: A survey of psychology journal editors. *American Psychologist, 1982, 37,* 335–338.

Popper, K. R. *The logic of scientific discovery.* London: Hutchinson and Co., 1968.

Poulton, E. C., and Freeman, P. R. Unwanted asymmetrical transfer effects with balanced experimental designs. *Psychological Bulletin, 1966, 66,* 1–8.

Pribram, K. H. *Languages of the brain: Experimental paradoxes and principles in neuropsychology.* Englewood Cliffs, N.J.: Prentice-Hall, 1971.

Quattrochi-Tubin, S., and Jason, L. A. Enhancing social interactions and activity among the elderly through stimulus control. *Journal of Applied Behavior Analysis, 1980, 13,* 159–163.

Resnick, J. H., and Schwartz, T. Ethical standards as an independent variable in psychological research. *American Psychologist, 1973, 28,* 134–139.

Richter, C. P. Rats, man, and the welfare state. *American Psychologist, 1959, 14,* 18–28.

Ring, K., Wallston, K., and Corey, M. Mode of debriefing as a factor affecting reaction to a Milgram-type obedience experiment: An ethical inquiry. *Representative Research in Social Psychology, 1970, 1,* 67–88.

Risley, T. R., and Wolf, M. M. Strategies for analyzing behavioral change over time. In *Life-span de-velopmental psychology: Methodological issues,* edited by J. R. Nesselroade and H. W. Reese. New York: Academic Press, 1972.

Ritchie, E., and Phares, E. J. Attitude change as a function of internal-external control and communicator status. *Journal of Personality, 1969, 37,* 429–443.

Robinson, J., and Cohen, L. Individual bias in psychological reports. *Journal of Clinical Psychology, 1954, 10,* 333–336.

Rosenberg, M. J. The conditions and consequences of evaluation apprehension. In *Artifact in behavioral research,* edited by R. Rosenthal and R. L. Rosnow. New York: Academic Press, 1969.

Rosenberg, M. J. Experimenter expectancy, evaluation apprehension, and the diffusion of methodological angst. *The Behavioral and Brain Sciences, 1980, 3,* 472–474.

Rosenthal, R. *Experimenter effects in behavioral research.* New York: Appleton-Century-Crofts, 1966.

Rosenthal, R. Interpersonal expectations: Effects of the experimenter's hypothesis. In *Artifact in Behavioral Research,* edited by R. Rosenthal and R. L. Rosnow. New York: Academic Press, 1969.

Rosenthal, R. *Experimenter effects in behavioral research.* 2nd ed. New York: Irvington, 1976.

Rosenthal, R. How often are our numbers wrong? *American Psychologist, 1978, 33,* 1005–1007.

Rosenthal, R. Replicability and experimenter influence: Experimenter effects in behavioral research. *Parapsychology Review, 1980, 11,* 5–11.

Rosenthal, R. Pavlov's mice, Pfungst's horse, and pygmalion's PON's: Some models for the study of interpersonal expectancy effects. In *The Clever Hans phenomenon: Communication with horses, whales, apes, and people,* edited by T. A. Sebeak and R. Rosenthal. Annals of the New York Academy of Sciences, 1981, 364, 182–198.

Rosenthal, R., and Fode, K. L. Three experiments in experimenter bias. *Psychological Reports, 1963, 12,* 491–511. (a)

Rosenthal, R., and Fode, K. L. The effect of experimenter bias on the performance of the albino rat. *Behavioral Science, 1963, 8,* 183–189. (b)

Rosenthal, R., Persinger, G. W., Vikan-Kline, L., and Mulry, R. C. The role of the research assistant in the mediation of experimenter bias. *Journal of Personality, 1963, 31,* 313–335.

Rosenthal, R., and Rosnow, R. L. *The volunteer subject.* New York: Wiley, 1975.

Rosenthal, R., and Rubin, D. B. Interpersonal expectancy effects: The first 345 studies. *The Behavioral and Brain Sciences,* 1978, *3,* 377–415.

Rosnow, R. L., and Suls, J. M. Reactive effects of pretesting in attitude research. *Journal of Personality and Social Psychology,* 1970, *15,* 338–343.

Rugg, E. A. Ethical judgments of social research involving experimental deception. Unpublished doctoral dissertation, George Peabody College for Teachers, Nashville, Tenn., May 1975.

Rumenik, D. K., Capasso, D. R., and Hendrick, C. Experimenter sex effects in behavioral research. *Psychological Bulletin,* 1977, *84,* 852–877.

Ryan, J. P., and Isaacson, R. L. Intraaccumbens injections of ACTH induce excessive grooming in rats. *Physiological Psychology,* 1983, *11,* 54–58.

Sanders, G. S., and Simmons, W. L. Use of hypnosis to enhance eyewitness accuracy: Does it work? *Journal of Applied Psychology,* 1983, *68,* 70–77.

Schachter, S., and Singer, J. E. Cognitive, social and physiological determinants of emotional state. *Psychological Review,* 1962, *69,* 379–399.

Schafer, R., and Murphy, G. The role of autism in visual figure-ground relationship. *Journal of Experimental Psychology,* 1943, *32,* 335–343.

Scholtz, J. A. Defense styles in suicide attempters. *Journal of Consulting and Clinical Psychology,* 1973, *41,* 70–73.

Seaver, W. B., and Quarton, R. J. Social reinforcement of excellence: Dean's list and academic achievement. Paper presented at the 44th annual meeting of the Eastern Psychological Association, Washington, D.C., May 1973.

Seeman, J. Deception in psychological research. *American Psychologist,* 1969, *24,* 1025–1028.

Selltiz, C., Jahoda, M., Deutsch, M., and Cook, S. W. *Research methods in social relations.* New York: Holt, 1959.

Shine, L. C., II. Five research steps designed to integrate the single-subject and multi-subject approaches to experimental research. *Canadian Psychological Review,* 1975, *16,* 179–183.

Shuell, T. J. Distribution of practice and retroactive inhibition in free-recall learning. *Psychological Record,* 1981, *31,* 589–598.

Sidman, M. *Tactics of scientific research.* New York: Basic Books, 1960.

Sidowski, J. B., and Lockard, R. B. Some preliminary considerations in research. In *Experimental methods and instrumentation in psychology,* edited by J. B. Sidowski. New York: McGraw-Hill, 1966.

Sieber, J. E. Deception in social research I: Kinds of deception and the wrongs they may involve. *IRB: A Review of Human Subjects Research,* 1982, *4*(9), 1–5.

Sieber, J. E. Deception in social research II: Evaluating the potential for wrong. *IRB: A Review of Human Subjects,* 1983, *5*(1), 1–5. (a)

Sieber, J. E. Deception in social research III: The nature and limits of debriefing. *IRB: A Review of Human Subjects,* 1983, *5*(3), 1–4. (b)

Sigall, H., Aronson, E., and Van Hoose, T. The cooperative subject: Myth or reality. *Journal of Experimental Social Psychology,* 1970, *6,* 1–10.

Silverman, I. The experimenter: A (still) neglected stimulus object. *The Canadian Psychologist,* 1974, *15,* 258–270.

Skinner, B. F. *Walden two.* New York: Macmillan, 1948.

Skinner, B. F. *Science and human behavior.* New York: Macmillan, 1953.

Skinner, B. F. *Beyond freedom and dignity.* New York: Knopf, 1971.

Skinner, B. F. A case history in scientific method. In *Cumulative record,* p. 112. New York: Appleton-Century-Crofts, 1972.

Small-sample techniques. *The NEA Research Bulletin,* 1960, *36,* 99–104.

Smith, R. E. The other side of the coin. *Contemporary Psychology,* 1969, *14,* 628–630.

Smith, S. S., and Richardson, D. Amelioration of deception and harm in psychological research: The important role of debriefing. *Journal of Personality and Social Psychology,* 1983, *44,* 1075–1082.

Solomon, R. An extension of control group design. *Psychological Bulletin,* 1949, *44,* 137–150.

Star, S. A., and Hughes, H. M. Report on an educational campaign: The Cincinnati plan for the United Nations. *American Journal of Sociology,* 1950, *55,* 389–400.

Stevens, S. S. Psychology and the science of science. *Psychological Bulletin,* 1939, *36,* 221–263.

Sullivan, D. S., and Deiker, T. E. Subject-experimenter perception of ethical issues in human research. *American Psychologist*, 1973, *28*, 587–591.

Sulzer-Azaroff, B., and Conseulo De Santamaria, M. Industrial safety hazard reduction through performance feedback. *Journal of Applied Behavior Analysis*, 1980, *13*, 287–295.

Sutcliffe, J. P. On the role of "instructions to the subject" in psychological experiments. *American Psychologist*, 1972, *27*, 755–758.

Taffel, C. Anxiety and the conditioning of verbal behavior. *Journal of Abnormal and Social Psychology*, 1955, *51*, 496–501.

Tedeschi, J. T., Schlenker, B. R., and Bonoma, T. V. Cognitive dissonance: Private ratiocination or public spectacle. *American Psychologist*, 1971, *26*, 685–695.

Tesch, F. E. Debriefing research participants: Though this be method there is madness to it. *Journal of Personality and Social Psychology*, 1977, *35*, 217–224.

Tunnell, G. B. Three dimensions of naturalness: An expanded definition of field research. *Psychological Bulletin*, 1977, *84*, 426–437.

Turner, L. H., and Solomon, R. L. Human traumatic avoidance learning: Theory and experiments on the operant-respondent distinction of failures to learn. *Psychological Monographs*, 1962, *76*(Whole No. 559), 1–32.

Underwood, B. J. Interference and forgetting. *Psychological Review*, 1957, *64*, 49–60.

Underwood, B. J. Verbal learning in the educative process. *Harvard Educational Review*, 1959, *29*, 107–117.

Van Buskirk, W. L. An experimental study of vividness in learning and retention. *Journal of Experimental Psychology*, 1932, *15*, 563–573.

Vernon, H. M., Bedford, T., and Wyatt, S. *Two studies of rest pauses in industry.* Medical Research Council, Industrial Fatigue Research Board Report No. 25. London: His Majesty's Stationary Office, 1924.

Videbeck, R., and Bates, H. D. Verbal conditioning by a simulated experimenter. *Psychological Record*, 1966, *16*, 145–152.

Vinacke, E. Deceiving experimental subjects. *American Psychologist*, 1954, *9*, 155.

Wade, E. A., and Blier, M. J. Learning and retention of verbal lists: Serial anticipation and serial discrimination. *Journal of Experimental Psychology*, 1974, *103*, 732–739.

Walker, H. M., and Buckley, N. K. The use of positive reinforcement in conditioning attending behavior. *Journal of Applied Behavior Analysis*, 1968, *1*, 245–250.

Watts, W. A. Relative persistence of opinion change induced by active compared to passive participation. *Journal of Personality and Social Psychology*, 1967, *5*, 4–15.

Webb, E. J., Campbell, D. T., Schwartz, R. D., and Sechrest, L. *Unobstructive measures: Nonreactive research in the social sciences.* Chicago: Rand McNally, 1966.

Wellman, P. J., Malpas, P. B., and Witkler, K. C. Conditioned taste aversion of unconditioned suppression of water intake induced by phenylpropanolamine in rats. *Physiological Psychology*, 1981, *9*, 203–207.

West, S. G., and Gunn, S. P. Some issues of ethics and social psychology. *American Psychologist*, 1978, *33*, 30–38.

West, S. G., Gunn, S. P., and Chernicky, P. Ubiquitous Watergate: An attributional analysis. *Journal of Personality and Social Psychology*, 1975, *32*, 55–65.

Wilson, D., and Donnerstein, E. Legal and ethical aspects of nonreactive social psychological research: An excursion into the public mind. *American Psychologist*, 1976, *31*, 765–773.

Willson, V. L. Estimating changes in accident statistics due to reporting requirement changes. *Journal of Safety Research*, 1980, *12*, 36–42.

Willson, V. L. Time and the external validity of experiments. *Evaluation and Program Planning*, 1981, *4*, 229–238.

Wolfe, G. E., and Soltysik, S. S. An apparatus for behavioral and physiological study of aversive conditioning in cats and kittens. *Behavioral Research Methods and Instrumentation*, 1981, *13*, 637–642.

Wyer, R. S., Jr., Dion, K. L., and Ellsworth, P. C. An editorial. *Journal of Experimental Social Psychology*, 1978, *14*, 141–147.

Yoburn, B. C., Cohen, P. S., and Campagnoni, F. R. The role of intermittent food in the induction of attack in pigeons. *Journal of the Experimental Analysis of Behavior*, 1981, *36*, 101–117.

Zimney, G. H. *Method in experimental psychology*. New York: Ronald Press, 1961.

Index